MAY 2 9 2006

REFERENCE

WAYNE PUBLIC LIBRARY
MAIN LIBRARY
461 Valley Road
Wayne, NJ 07470

D1170836

First Edition

biography for beginners

Inventors

Laurie Lanzen Harris,
Editor

Favorable Impressions

P.O. Box 69018 • Pleasant Ridge, MI 48069

Laurie Lanzen Harris, *Editor*

Frank R. Abate, PhD; Kevin P. Decker; Claire A. Rewold, PhD,
Contributing Editors

Dan R. Harris, *Senior Vice President, Sales and Marketing*

John C. Thomson, *Science Advisor*

Library of Congress Cataloging-in-Publication Data

Biography for beginners : inventors.
    p. cm.
   Includes bibliographical references and index.
   ISBN 1-931360-27-8 (alk. paper)
   1. Inventors–Biography–Juvenile literature. 2. Scientists—Biography—
Juvenile literature. I. Harris, Laurie Lanzen.
  T39.B496 2006
  609.2′2—dc22
  [B]

                         2006010476

Copyright © 2006 by Laurie Lanzen Harris

ISBN 1-931360-27-8

The information in this publication was compiled from the sources cited and from other sources considered reliable. While every possible effort has been made to ensure reliability, the publisher will not assume liability for damages caused by inaccuracies in the data, and makes no warranty, express or implied, on the accuracy of the information contained herein.

This book is printed on acid-free paper meeting the ANSI Z39.48 Standard. The infinity symbol that appears above indicate that the paper in this book meets that standard.

Printed in the United States

Contents

Preface ix

Introduction xiii

Inventors

Archimedes (c. 287 B.C. - c. 212 B.C.) 1
Greek Mathematician and Inventor of the Archimedean Screw

Leo Baekeland (1863 - 1944) 6
Belgian-Born American Chemist and Inventor of the First Synthetic Plastic

Benjamin Banneker (1731 - 1806) 12
American Astronomer and Inventor, Considered the First Black American Scientist

Frederick Banting (1891 - 1941) 16
Canadian Scientist and Doctor, Co-Discoverer of Insulin, the Medicine that Treats
Diabetes

Alexander Graham Bell (1847 - 1922) 22
Scottish-born American Scientist and Inventor of the Telephone

Karl Benz (1844 - 1929) 34
German Engineer and Industrialist, Inventor of the First Three-Wheeled
Gasoline-Powered Automobile

Tim Berners-Lee (1955 -) 42
British Computer Scientist and Inventor of the World Wide Web

Henry Bessemer (1813 - 1898) 49
English Engineer and Inventor of the Steel Converter

Clarence Birdseye (1886 - 1956) 53
American Businessman and Inventor, "The Father of Frozen Food"

Katharine Blodgett (1898 - 1979) 61
American Scientist and Inventor of Non-Reflective Glass

Louis Braille (1809 - 1852) 66
French Educator and Inventor of the Braille System of Printing and
Writing for the Blind

Rachel Fuller Brown (1898 - 1980) **73**
American Scientist and Co-Creator of the First Anti-Fungal Antibiotic

William Seward Burroughs (1855 - 1898) **78**
American Manufacturer and Inventor of the First Adding Machine

Wallace Carothers (1896 - 1937) **82**
American Chemist and Inventor of Nylon, the First Synthetic Fiber

Willis Carrier (1876 - 1950) **88**
American Engineer and Inventor, "The Father of Air Conditioning"

George Washington Carver (1864? - 1943) **94**
American Inventor, Farmer, Educator and Food Scientist, Created more than 300
Products Using Peanuts

Jacques Cousteau (1910 - 1997) **108**
French Ocean Explorer, Film Producer, and Inventor of SCUBA Diving Equipment

Seymour Cray (1925 - 1996) **113**
American Computer Designer and Inventor of the First "Supercomputer"

Gottlieb Daimler (1834 - 1900) **121**
German Engineer and Industrialist, Inventor of the First Four-Wheeled
Automobile, First Motorcycle and First Gasoline Engine

Raymond Damadian (1936 -) **129**
American Businessman and Inventor of the Magnetic Resonance Imaging (MRI)
Scanner

Leonardo Da Vinci (1452 - 1519) **133**
Italian Artist, Inventor, Scientist, and Engineer

John Deere (1804 - 1886) **139**
American Blacksmith and Inventor of the Steel Plow

Georges de Mestral (1907 - 1990) **145**
Swiss Inventor of Velcro

Rudolf Diesel (1858 - 1913) **148**
German Engineer and Industrialist, Inventor of the Diesel Engine

Herbert Henry Dow (1866 - 1930) **153**
American Chemist and Inventor, Founder of the Dow Chemical Company

George Eastman (1854 - 1932) **159**
American Inventor of Rolled Photographic Film and the Hand-Held Camera,
Founder of Kodak

Thomas Edison (1847 - 1931)................................166
American Inventor of More Than 1,184 Items, Including the Incandescent Electric
Lamp (Light Bulb), Phonograph and the Motion Picture Projector

Gertrude Elion (1918 - 1999)................................184
American Scientist and Inventor of Life-Saving Drugs to Treat Leukemia and Other
Diseases, Winner of the Nobel Prize

Daniel Gabriel Fahrenheit (1686 - 1736)................................192
Dutch Instrument Maker and Inventor of the Mercury Thermometer

Philo Farnsworth (1906 - 1971)................................196
American Scientist and Inventor of Electronic Television

Alexander Fleming (1881 - 1955)................................203
Scottish Doctor and Scientist Who Discovered Penicillin, the First Successful
Antibiotic, Winner of the Nobel Prize

Henry Ford (1863 - 1947)................................210
American Industrialist, Inventor, and Philanthropist, Developed Mass Production

Benjamin Franklin (1706 - 1790)................................222
American Statesman, Printer, and Inventor of the Lightning Rod, the Franklin Stove,
and Bifocals

Robert Fulton (1765 - 1815)................................232
American Inventor of the First Successful Commercial Steamboat

Galileo Galilei (1564 - 1642)................................237
Italian Mathematician, Physicist, and Astronomer, Inventor of the Thermometer
and the First Practical Telescope and "Father of the Scientific Method"

Bill Gates (1955 -)................................243
American Computer Software Pioneer and Co-Founder of Microsoft

King Gillette (1855 - 1932)................................253
American Businessman and Inventor of the Safety Razor

Robert Hutchings Goddard (1882 - 1945)................................257
American Physicist and Pioneer of Modern Rocketry, Inventor of the Liquid Fueled
Rocket

Charles Goodyear (1800 - 1860)................................265
American Inventor of the Vulcanized Rubber Process

Gordon Gould (1920 - 2005)................................271
American Scientist and Inventor of the Laser

Temple Grandin (1947 -) **278**
American Animal Scientist and Inventor of Equipment for Humane Treatment of
Livestock

Wilson Greatbatch (1919 -) **286**
American Engineer and Inventor of the Implantable Cardiac Pacemaker

Johannes Gutenberg (1400? - 1468) **291**
German Printer and Inventor of the Movable-Type Printing Press

Elizabeth Lee Hazen (1885 - 1975) **297**
American Scientist and Co-Creator of the First Anti-Fungal Antibiotic

Elias Howe (1819 - 1867) **302**
American Inventor of the First Practical Sewing Machine

Edward Jenner (1749 - 1823) **306**
English Physician and Creator of Vaccination, "The Father of Immunology"

Steven Jobs (1955 -) **312**
American Computer Pioneer, Co-Founder of Apple Computer, and Head of Apple
and Pixar

Dean Kamen (1951 -) **322**
American Inventor, Physicist, and Engineer, Inventor of the iBot and Segway

W. K. Kellogg (1860 - 1951) **328**
American Businessman and Cereal Manufacturer, Inventor of Corn Flakes

Willem Kolff (1911 -) **336**
Dutch-Born American Doctor and Inventor of the Kidney Dialysis Machine

Stephanie Kwolek (1923 -) **341**
American Chemist and Inventor of Kevlar

Rene Laennec (1781 - 1826) **347**
French Doctor and Inventor of the Stethoscope

Edwin Land (1909 - 1991) **352**
American Physicist, Businessman and Inventor of Instant Photography

Jerome Lemelson (1923 - 1997) **360**
American Inventor of More than 500 Items

Joseph Lister (1827 - 1912) **366**
English Surgeon Who Created the Antiseptic Technique, Making Surgery Safe

Guglielmo Marconi (1874 - 1937) **371**
Italian Scientist and Inventor of Successful Long-Distance Transmission of Radio

Cyrus McCormick (1809 - 1884) **381**
American Businessman and Inventor of the Mechanical Reaper

Elijah McCoy (1844? - 1929) **389**
Canadian-Born American Inventor of the Automatic Lubricating Cup,
"The Real McCoy"

Joseph-Michael Montgolfier (1740 - 1810)
Jacques-Etienne Montgolfier (1745 - 1799) **395**
French Inventors of the First Practical Balloon, Making Possible the
First Human Flight

Garrett Morgan (1877 - 1963) **400**
American Inventor of the Traffic Signal and the Gas Mask

Samuel F.B. Morse (1791 - 1872) **406**
American Inventor of Morse Code and the First Practical Electric Telegraph

Isaac Newton (1642 - 1727) **415**
English Physicist, Mathematician, and Inventor, Who Formulated Key Laws of
Motion and Invented the Reflecting Telescope

Alfred Nobel (1833 - 1896) **421**
Swedish Scientist, Businessman, and Inventor of Dynamite, Creator of the Nobel
Prizes

Ellen Ochoa (1958 -) **427**
American Astronaut and Inventor of Optic Systems Used in Space Flight

Louis Pasteur (1822 - 1895) **434**
French Chemist, Biologist, and Educator; the Father of Microbiology and
Immunology, and Inventor of the "Pasteurization" Process

Roy J. Plunkett (1910 - 1994) **445**
American Chemist and Inventor of Teflon

Wilhelm Roentgen (1845 - 1923) **449**
German Physicist and Inventor of the X-Ray

Jonas Salk (1914 - 1995) **454**
American Physician and Scientist Who Developed the First Polio Vaccine

Patsy Sherman (1930 -) **464**
American Chemist and Co-Inventor of Scotchgard Fabric Protector

Christopher Sholes (1819 - 1890) **469**
American Inventor of the First Practical Typewriter and the "QWERTY" Keyboard

Igor Sikorsky (1889 - 1972) **473**
Russian-Born American Engineer and Inventor of the Helicopter and the First
Multimotor Airplane

Percy Spencer (1894 - 1970) **479**
American Scientist and Inventor of the Microwave Oven

George Stephenson (1781 - 1848) **485**
English Engineer and Inventor, Pioneer of the First Successful Steam-Powered
Locomotive

Levi Strauss (1829 - 1902) **491**
German-Born American Inventor of Blue Jeans

Nikola Tesla (1856 - 1943) **496**
Croatian-Born American Inventor, Electrical Engineer, Physicist, Researcher, and
Pioneer in Electricity; Inventor of the AC Electric Motor, and the Tesla Coil

Alessandro Volta (1745 - 1827) **502**
Italian Physicist and Inventor of the First Battery

James Watt (1736 - 1819) **506**
Scottish Inventor of an Improved Steam Engine

George Westinghouse (1846 - 1914) **512**
American Industrialist and Inventor of the Railroad Air Brake, Developed an
Alternating Current System for Electrical Transmission

Eli Whitney (1765 - 1825) **520**
American Inventor of the First Practical Cotton Gin

Frank Whittle (1907 - 1996) **526**
British Inventor of the Jet Engine

Steve Wozniak (1950 -) **532**
American Computer Designer and Engineer, Co-Founder of Apple Computer and
Inventor of the Apple II

Wilbur Wright (1867 - 1912) **542**
Orville Wright 1871 - 1948
American Inventors of the First Aircraft Capable of Powered, Sustained, and
Controlled Flight

Vladimir Zworykin (1889 - 1982) **561**
Russian-Born American Scientist and Inventor, Pioneer in the field of Electronic
Television

Photo and Illustration Credits **567**

Timeline of Invention **569**

Subject Index **583**

Preface

Welcome to *Biography for Beginners: Inventors*. Since beginning the *Biography for Beginners* series in 1995, we've published three monographs in areas of high interest for young readers, including U.S. Presidents, world explorers, and authors. Two years ago we surveyed librarians for additional areas of interest for young readers, and they suggested a volume on Inventors.

The Plan of the Work

Like *Biography for Beginners: Presidents of the United States* and *World Explorers*, *Inventors* is written for early readers, ages 7 to 10. The volume is especially created for young students in a format they can read, understand, and use for assignments. The 83 entries are arranged alphabetically. Each entry begins with a heading listing the inventor's name, birth and death dates, nationality, and a brief description of the individual's importance to the history of invention. Boldfaced headings lead readers to information on birth, youth, growing up, education, marriage and family, and the nature of the individual's invention. Every effort has been made to use only solid historical data in composing the biographical profiles. Whenever there is not definitive historical data, or if the information available is largely derived from legend or lore, that is clearly stated in the text.

Entries end with a list of World Wide Web sites. These sites have been reviewed for accuracy and suitability for use by young students. They were last accessed in April 2006. A bibliography of works used in the compilation of the entries is at the end of the Preface.

The entries also include portraits of the inventors, as well as paintings, photos, and other illustrations to enhance the reader's understanding of the individuals.

Audience

This book is intended for young readers in grades two through five who are studying inventors for the first time. Most children will use this book to study one inventor at a time, usually as part of a class assignment. For this reason, information relevant to major categories of invention, such as automobile engines and computers, are repeated in several entries. Within the entries, the names of other inventors who appear in the volume are bold-faced, as a cross-reference. Because the topic of patents is common to almost all the entries, the word is bold-faced in the entries, to lead students to a special section in the Introduction outlining the history of patents.

We had at first planned a two-volume set on the Inventors, covering 200 people. But we later rethought the two-volume idea, and, with the help of our Advisory Board, cut the book back to one volume. In this volume, we have profiled 85 of the most important and relevant inventors in the fields of: cloth and clothing, communication, computers, electricity, food and agriculture, industrial materials, medicine and medical devices, scientific devices, and transportation. As we began to research the entries in these areas, we decided to delete inventors of toys, games, and candy. But we haven't abandoned these often fascinating stories. We plan to do a "supplement" devoted to the creators of the best-known, best-loved toys and games, to satisfy the curiosity of young researchers.

Appendix

The Appendix contains a Timeline of Invention, to give historical context to the biographical profiles.

Index

An Index covering names, inventions, and key words concludes the volume. The Index has been created with the young reader in mind, and therefore contains a limited number of terms that have been simplified for ease of research.

Our Advisors

Biography for Beginners: Inventors was reviewed by an Advisory Board that included school librarians and public librarians. The thoughtful comments and suggestions of all the Board members have been invaluable in developing this publication. Any errors, however, are mine alone. I would like to list the members of the Advisory Board and to thank them again for their efforts.

Linda Carpino	Detroit Public Library Detroit, MI
Nina Levine	Blue Mountain Middle School Cortlandt Manor, NY
Nancy Margolin	McDougle Elementary School Chapel Hill, NC
Laurie Scott	Farmington Hills Community Library Farmington Hills, MI
Joyce Siler	Westridge Elementary School Kansas City, MO

Your Comments Are Welcome

Our goal is to provide accurate, accessible biographical information for early readers. Please write or call me with your comments.

Acknowledgments

I would like to thank the staffs of the many companies and organizations who provided photos and illustrations for the volume, as well as the Library of Congress, whose archives are truly a national treasure. Thank you to Sans Serif for outstanding design and layout.

Bibliography

This is a listing of works used in the compilation of the biographical profiles. Most of the works cited here are written at the middle school or high school reading level and are generally beyond the reading level of early elementary students. However, many librarians consider these reliable, objective points of departure for further research.

Columbia Encyclopedia, 2001 - 2005 edition.
Compton's Encyclopedia, 2005 edition.
Encyclopedia Britannica, 2005 edition.
Flatow, Ira. *They All Laughed*, 1992.
Macaulay, David. *The New Way Things Work*, 1998.

Laurie Harris, Editor and Publisher

Introduction

Why does someone become an inventor? And what does it mean to invent? The 85 people profiled here come from many different backgrounds, and their inventions cover many different fields. Yet in certain ways they are similar. Like the earliest "inventors," ancient peoples whose tools for hunting, farming, building, and transportation were truly the first "inventions," they were motivated to create something—a device, a process, or a product—that would help people live better lives. **Johannes Gutenberg**'s printing press, **Edward Jenner**'s smallpox vaccine, **Alexander Graham Bell**'s telephone, **Thomas Edison**'s lightbulb, the **Wright brothers'** airplane, and **Steve Job**'s and **Steve Wozniak**'s personal computer are just a few of the inventions described in this volume that have truly changed people's lives. And, as different as they are, there are certain traits that unite these inventors, including curiosity, perseverance, and a fascination with the newest technologies of their time.

As children, these people were a curious bunch. Time and again, history records their relentless desire to understand how things worked, to take things apart, and put them back together. At Christmas **Henry Ford**'s brothers and sisters would surround their toys and say, "Don't let Henry have them. He just takes them apart." Another unifying theme in their young lives is the love and inspiration of nature. **Leonardo Da Vinci** and **Wilbur and Orville Wright** all studied birds' wings in designing their flying machines. Da Vinci said, "Human subtlety will never devise an invention more beautiful, more simple, or more direct than does Nature, because in her inventions, nothing is lacking and nothing is superfluous."

As individuals, they are also a tenacious group. When confronted with failure—of an experiment, an early version of a device, or even a business—they persevered. When **James Watt**'s first steam engine business went broke, he made his living surveying, all the while planning to return to building engines. When the **Wright brothers'** planes were destroyed by wind, they learned from their mistakes and built a better plane. After months of research trying to find the right filament for his light bulb, **Thomas Edison** claimed, "If I find 10,000 ways something won't work, I haven't failed. I am not discouraged, because every wrong attempt discarded is often a step forward."

Many of the inventors in this book came upon their greatest discoveries through mistakes. **Charles Goodyear**'s discovery of vulcanized rubber, **Percy Spencer**'s invention of the microwave, **Roy Plunkett**'s discovery of Teflon, **Patsy Sherman**'s invention of Scotchgard—all came about by accident, usually from an experiment that didn't turn out as planned. The difference is the inventor's vision—the possibilities he or she sees in the "mistake" that turns it into an invention.

They were also fascinated by the "newest" technology of their day, particularly in the fields of communication. Electricity fired the imaginations of inventors for generations, beginning with **Benjamin Franklin** and **Alessandro Volta** in the 18th century. Understanding electricity, and seeing its implications for communication, emerged in the 19th century. Insights into electricity led **Samuel F.B. Morse** to invent the telegraph, which inspired many 19th century inventors, including **Alexander Graham Bell**. Along with Morse's telegraph, Bell's invention of the telephone led to the era of instant communication.

Morse's invention came about at the same time as the railroads were being built. The telegraph lines ran along the rail lines. With new technologies in communication and transportation came the need for accurate time-keeping. The time zones used nationwide to this day are one of the many innovations that arose from Morse's invention.

Young **Thomas Edison** worked as a telegrapher, leading him to a lifelong fascination with the potential of electricity. He was especially dedicated to the practical application of electricity, which led him to such inventions as the carbon filament light bulb, the electrical lighting of homes, the phonograph, and motion pictures.

It is striking how many of the inventors in this book were drawn to electricity as children. **Edwin Land** helped wire his summer camp at the age of 12. **Philo Farnsworth** made his mother an electric washing machine at the age of 13. This early inspiration led Land to invent instant photography, and Farnsworth to invent the first electronic television.

In the 20th century, the computer became the newest technology to captivate a generation of inventors. **Tim Berners-Lee** built a computer out of cardboard as a child. In college he found himself kicked off the university computers, so built one of his own, out of an old television. **Steve Wozniak** had built a simple computer by the fifth grade that could play "Tic-Tac-Toe." This fascination continued into early adulthood, when he and **Steven Jobs** built the first PC. The revolution brought about by their invention has changed nearly all aspects of our modern lives.

Other inventions discussed in the volume also brought about profound changes in society. **James Watt**'s invention of the steam engine, and **Henry Bessemer**'s invention of the steel converter are two of these. Watt's steam engine powered factories that ran machines made of Bessemer's steel. These two innovations helped bring about the Industrial Revolution of the 19th century. As the Industrial Revolution swept through England, Europe, and the U.S., people left farms to find jobs in the new factories in urban centers. The switch from farm to factory-based work led to great economic and social changes we still see around us in our country and throughout the developing world.

Who Was First?

It's important to note that many of the people profiled here are not the original inventors of the devices linked to their names. **Eli Whitney** didn't invent the first cotton gin, **Elias Howe** didn't invent the first sewing machine, **Samuel Morse** didn't invent the first telegraph, **James Watt** didn't invent the first steam engine, **Thomas Edison** didn't invent the first light bulb. What each of these inventors *did* do was create the first practical device derived from someone else's idea. Some, like Henry Ford, were innovators. That is, they took someone else's invention and created the *process* that made an invention, like the car, an affordable product for many people.

Patents

Any discussion of inventions must also include information about **patents** and the patent process. A patent is a right granted by a government to an inventor that provides the individual with exclusive rights to *make, use, import, sell, and offer for sale* the invention for a specific number of years. Patent laws have existed for centuries. The laws vary from country to country, but they basically grant rights for a number of years, thereby giving the inventor a term to profit from the invention.

Sadly, as long as there have been patents, there has been "patent infringement." That is the unauthorized, and illegal, use of someone else's patented idea. Many of the inventors in this volume were involved in lawsuits related to their inventions. They were forced to spend time and money away from their inventions, to defend their rights. Sometimes the toll taken by their legal battles ruined their health. **Wilbur Wright** died at 45, worn out after years of patent battles. **Philo Farnsworth** spent almost 10 years defending his invention in court, against the resources of a huge corporation. He finally won, but at great personal and financial loss. Even **Thomas Edison** spent the equivalent of $20 million, in today's dollars, over the years defending his patents.

It is also interesting to note the individuals in this volume who chose *not* to patent their inventions. **Benjamin Franklin, Frederick Banting, Jonas Salk,** and **Tim Berners-Lee** all believed that their inventions belonged to the world, and refused to make a profit from them. Similarly, **Elizabeth Hazen** and **Rachel Fuller Brown** never personally received money from their patent for the first antifungal antibiotic. Instead, they invested all the funds in a nonprofit foundation that still provides funding for medical research.

Capitalization, Distribution, and Marketing of Inventions

Capitalization, distribution, and marketing are concepts many people—students and adults—find rather boring. But they are crucial to an understanding of the invention process. A good idea for a product is just that—only a good idea—if the product can't be built, sold, and distributed to the public. The history of invention outlined in this volume is full of financial failure. Again and again, the profiles here recount the story of the inventor trying to find funding to manufacture and sell a product. Sometimes they succeeded; often they didn't.

Johannes Gutenberg, inventor of movable-type printing, created a process that made books—and through them education and knowledge—affordable and available to common people. Yet because of financial problems, Gutenberg lost control of his invention. He'd built a printing plant and financed the printing of his famous Bible with money borrowed from a man named Johannes Fust. Fust sued Gutenberg over misusing the borrowed funds, and they went to court. Gutenberg lost. He had to hand over the printing workshop and half the Bibles to Fust.

Charles Goodyear never made a profit from his invention of vulcanized rubber. Instead, he was unable to find a continuing source of money to develop his invention, to sell products, and to profit from them. He died at 60, leaving his family with $200,000 in debt.

James Watt's first steam engine company went broke. His second partner, a wealthy financier, had enough money—capital—to develop the second company created to make and market his steam engine. The success of that company made him a very wealthy man.

Even those inventors who made fortunes, like **Thomas Edison** and **Henry Ford,** also lost millions over the years, trying to develop other products. Luckily for them, they had the money to continue in business.

Edison is a pivotal figure in the history of invention for many reasons. He represents the "tinkerer," the individual without much education, who learned by doing. He also created the first "invention factory," at Menlo Park, devoted to research and development of ideas. In the 20th century, this became the basis for such facilities as Bell Labs. Many of the inventions of the past 100 years have come from organizations like Bell Labs, as well as separate research departments of major corporations like DuPont and Microsoft. These have become "invention factories" themselves, funding, developing, marketing, and selling products to the public.

The history of invention is outlined, in brief, in this volume. What does the future hold? Devices, medicines, and theories that we can't even imagine will be brought to life by men and women of vision. That vision will both define the future and challenge present assumptions about who we are and how we live. And they will be brought to us by people of curiosity, tenacity, and fascination with the next, new thing.

Inventors

This Italian stamp shows an image of Archimedes on the right and the Archimedean Screw on the left.

Archimedes
c. 287 B.C. - c. 212 B.C.
Greek Mathematician and Inventor
Inventor of the Archimedean Screw

ARCHIMEDES WAS BORN around the year 287 B.C. He was born in Syracuse, which was then a Greek colony on Sicily. At that time, people didn't have first and last names. So he is known to us simply as "Archimedes." His name is pronounced "ahr-kah-MEED-ees." His father, Phidias (FID-ee-as), was an astronomer. No information is available about his mother. No one knows if Archimedes ever married or had children.

ARCHIMEDES WENT TO SCHOOL in Alexandria, in Egypt. There, he studied mathematics with a scholar named Conon. Conon had studied under the famous mathematician Euclid. After his schooling, Archimedes returned to Syracuse. Most historians think he remained there for the rest of his life.

A MATH GENIUS: Archimedes is considered one of the most important mathematicians of all time. In fact, he didn't think much of his inventions. He thought of them as "toys."

In math, Archimedes proposed theories that were thousands of years ahead of his time. He came up with the mathematical formula known as "pi." Pi is a "ratio." A ratio shows the relationship between one part of a shape and another. Pi shows the relationship between the diameter of a circle (the distance across) and the circumference (the distance around).

Archimedes also developed a formula for measuring a curve. These theories are very similar to the area of math known as calculus. But calculus wasn't created until the time of **Isaac Newton,** nearly 2,000 years after Archimedes lived.

EUREKA: Archimedes didn't just like to think up theories. He liked to see how those theories worked in real life. One of the most famous stories about Archimedes involved King Hieron of Syracuse. The King ordered a crown made of gold for himself. But when the crown arrived, he thought the maker had cheated him. He thought the goldsmith had made the crown of silver, which is cheaper, and covered it in gold.

The King asked Archimedes to figure out the truth. Archimedes was thinking about the problem one day while taking a bath. All at once, he knew the answer. He figured out that the water spilled *out* of the tub in proportion to how much of his body was placed *in* it.

Legend has it that Archimedes leapt from his bath and ran down the street shouting "Eureka!" (That means "I have found it.") Archimedes used his new theory to prove that the crown was indeed made of silver, coated in gold. In developing his formula, he came up with the theory of "relative density." He proved it by placing first, the crown, then equal amounts of gold and silver, into water. The amount of water displaced by the element showed its density.

INVENTING THE ARCHIMEDEAN SCREW: Archimedes's most famous invention was the "Archimedean Screw." It was a simple, yet incredibly useful device. It was able to raise and move water, and became the idea behind irrigation.

HOW IT WORKED: The Archimedean screw is basically a corkscrew in a cylinder, wound by a hand crank. One end of the device is placed in water, at one level. Winding the crank moves the water up, in a spiral, following the grooves of the screw. The device pushes the water out the other end, at a higher level. It was a water pump that could easily be used to provide water for homes or farming. In some parts of the world, it is still used for irrigating crops.

The Archimedean screw was also the basis for many other tools developed over thousands of years. Modern drills and combine harvesters are based on it.

OTHER INVENTIONS: Archimedes also invented weapons to protect Syracuse from warring armies. He invented catapults used to bombard invaders with large stones. He also worked with ropes and pulleys. Using them, he created what look like modern-day cranes. One of these was supposedly used to upend a boat full of Roman invaders.

Another famous legend tells of how Archimedes used a giant mirror to concentrate the sun's energy to set fire to an invader's ship. No one knows if the legend is true or not. But students at the Massachusetts Institute of Technology recently tried to recreate the results of this famous tale. And it worked.

Archimedes also invented what is considered the first planetarium. He created spheres representing the Earth, sun, moon, and the known planets and constellations of his time. Then, using pulleys, he showed how the planets and stars moved. It was so accurate that it could predict eclipses. Sadly, there are no known copies of Archimedes's planetarium. We only know of it because of what was written during his lifetime.

THE DEATH OF ARCHIMEDES: When Archimedes was in his 70s, Sicily was invaded by Roman soldiers. Archimedes died during the invasion. A legend has grown about his death. It relates that Archimedes was working on a math diagram when a Roman soldier came upon him. The soldier told him to stop what he was doing and follow him. Archimedes refused, and the soldier killed him.

While it's only a legend, it is a tribute to this great man of science. He devoted his life to trying to understand the way things work, developing and testing theories in his endless pursuit of knowledge.

HIS INVENTIONS: Today, Archimedes is known for his groundbreaking math theories and his invention of the Archimedean screw. It is still the basis of simple water irrigation systems in use throughout the world. For his logical, practical methods, leading to mathematical theories as well as important inventions, Archimedes is called "the father of experimental science."

WORLD WIDE WEB SITES:

http://www.mcs.drexel.edu/~crorres/Archimedes/contents.html
http://www-groups.dcs.st-and.ac.uk/~history/Mathematicians/
    Archimedes.html

Baekeland and his family, in the early 1900s.

Leo Baekeland
1863 - 1944
Belgian-Born American Inventor and Chemist
Inventor of the First Synthetic Plastic

LEO BAEKELAND WAS BORN on November 14, 1863, near Ghent, Belgium. His parents were Karel and Rosalia Baekeland. Karel was a shoemaker and Rosalia had been a maid before she married. Neither could read or write. Leo had one sister, who was 13 years younger.

LEO BAEKELAND GREW UP in a very poor family. His father wanted Leo to become a shoemaker, like him. In fact, Leo became his father's apprentice at 13. But Leo's mother had bigger plans for her son. She knew he was bright and capable of more. She encouraged him to do well in school.

Leo was smart and ambitious. He had read the *Autobiography* of **Benjamin Franklin.** He was impressed, and influenced, by Franklin's ideas. Like Franklin, Baekeland thought that through hard work, he could make money and a better life.

LEO BAEKELAND WENT TO SCHOOL at a local government school. He was an excellent student. While in high school, he also took chemistry and physics classes at a technical college. And he tutored other students.

Leo won a scholarship to study at the University of Ghent. He was so bright that he finished his bachelor's degree in just two years (it usually takes four). And two years later, in 1884, he finished his PhD in science at the age of 21.

FIRST JOBS: After graduating, Baekeland took a job teaching chemistry at Ghent. While there, he met his future wife, Celine, whose father had been his professor.

In 1887, Baekeland entered a contest and won a scholarship for foreign study. He traveled to England, Scotland, Germany, and America.

COMING TO AMERICA: Baekeland and his wife moved to New York in 1889. Shortly after their arrival, Celine found out she was going

"The Bakelizer."

to have a baby. She moved back to Belgium to be with her family, and Baekeland began his life in America.

INVENTING VELOX: Baekeland worked for a chemical company. He also worked on an invention that would change the way photographs are made.

At that time, the paper used to develop photos could only use natural sunlight. Baekeland's breakthrough was the invention of a new photographic paper, Velox. Velox used *artificial* light to develop photos. **Thomas Edison** had recently developed electric lighting, so artificial light was widely available.

Also, in 1888 easy to use and inexpensive box cameras and roll film became available. They had been invented by **George Eastman.** Baekeland's invention became a huge success, based on innovation, and perfect timing. In 1893, he founded a company to produce Velox. In 1899, Eastman's company, Kodak, bought Baekeland's company for almost $1 million. Baekeland became a rich man.

He bought a big house in Yonkers, New York. There, he had a laboratory, where he continued to invent. He also started to teach at Columbia University.

Baekeland's next big project would make him one of the most famous inventors of all time. While trying to create artificial shellac, he invented the first synthetic plastic.

INVENTING PLASTIC: At that time, shellac was a natural product that came from Asian beetles. It had been used for years to coat wood. In the early 1900s, demand for shellac exploded. It was used as insulation on electrical wires, and as the need for electricity increased, so did the need for shellac. But beetles can only produce so much. Chemists everywhere focused on developing artificial shellac.

Baekeland began to work on the problem. For three years, he experimented with different compounds. Finally, in 1907, he came up with the right chemical mixture. He mixed formaldehyde with carbolic acid. Next, he heated the mixture in a container he called a "Bakelizer."

The result wasn't just an artificial shellac. Baekeland had invented something new. It was a clear substance that resisted heat, water, and other chemicals. It also wouldn't conduct electricity, so it was a perfect insulator. It could be molded into all kinds of shapes and sizes. He called it "Baekelite." We know it as plastic.

Plastic revolutionized the world. Products of all kinds were made from it, from toys to buttons to parts for other manufactured items. Baekeland presented his new invention at a scientific meeting in 1909. His fellow scientists gave him a standing ovation. He started a new company, the General Bakelite Company, to manufacture and license his new invention.

Baekeland received a **patent** for his invention. He spent many years protecting his patent. Finally, he bought up his competitors and created the Bakelite Corporation.

Baekeland was a rich and famous man. Radios made of Bakelite became enormously popular. Consumer items of all sorts—from toothbrushes to billiard balls to furniture—were made of the new plastic.

Baekeland ran his company, and was also active in scientific societies. He received many honors and awards over the years, too. In 1936, he entered the National Academy of Sciences. That's one of the most prestigious organizations in science.

LATER LIFE: Baekeland was a private man who never enjoyed being famous. He decided to sell his company in 1939. He retired to

Florida, and lived a quiet life until his death in 1944. He was 81 years old.

LEO BAEKELAND'S HOME AND FAMILY: Baekeland met his wife, Celine, when he was a student in Belgium. They married in 1889. They had three children, Jenny, George, and Nina. Jenny died at the age of five. George grew up and entered the family business. But he and his father didn't get along very well. He left the family business when his father sold it in 1939.

HIS INVENTION: Baekeland's invention of plastic is one of the most important in history. He created a substance useful in manufacturing thousands of products. By the end of the 20th century, 50 million tons of plastic were manufactured worldwide each year. He was named one of "The Most Important People of the Century" by *Time* magazine. He was also inducted into the Inventor's Hall of Fame in 1978.

WORLD WIDE WEB SITES:

http://web.mit.edu/invent/iow/baekeland.html
http://www.chemheritage.org/classroom/chemach/plastics/
    baekeland.html
http://www.invent.org/hall_of_fame/7html

Benjamin Banneker
1731 - 1806
American Astronomer, Mathematician, and Inventor
Considered the First Black American Scientist

BENJAMIN BANNEKER WAS BORN on November 9, 1731, in Ellicott's Lower Mills, Maryland. His parents were Robert and Mary Banneker. Robert was born in West Africa. He had been enslaved and brought to Maryland. After years as a slave, he bought his freedom. Mary's father was a former slave from Africa. Her mother was an indentured servant from England. Both of them had won their freedom. Benjamin was born a free black, in an era when that was extremely rare.

MARYLAND IN THE 18TH CENTURY: Banneker was born before there was a United States. At the time of his birth, Maryland was one of several colonies ruled by Great Britain. He was also born when most black people in the colonies were slaves. Benjamin was one of only 200 free black people in a county where there were 4,000 slaves.

Robert and Mary Banneker were farmers. They worked land inherited from Mary's family. Benjamin was the oldest of three children. He had two younger sisters, Minta and Molly.

BENJAMIN BANNEKER GREW UP on the family farm. He was bright and curious, and loved learning everything about farming and tools. He was taught to read and write by his grandmother. He loved numbers, and enjoyed making up math games.

BENJAMIN BANNEKER WENT TO SCHOOL at a local Quaker school. The Quakers were a Christian group who believed in racial equality. The teacher encouraged Benjamin, and he was an excellent student. No one is sure how many years he went to school. He probably left in his teens.

CLOCK MAKER: Around 1753, Banneker saw a watch for the first time. He was fascinated. He took the watch apart, and studied how it worked. Then, he built his own clock, entirely out of wood. It is

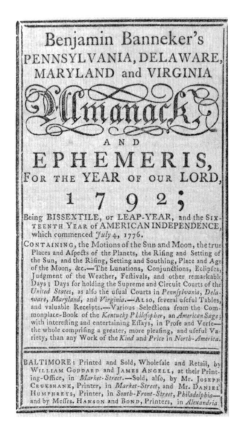

considered the first wooden clock built in the New World. It kept time for 40 years.

ALMANAC: Banneker inherited the family farm when his father died in 1757. He learned all he could about farming techniques. That included studying rain and weather patterns. He also examined the movement of the stars. A neighbor, George Ellicott, lent Banneker books on astronomy and math. From this research, he developed an "Almanac."

An almanac is a collection of data that includes information about weather, seasons, tides, sunrises and sunsets, and other natural happenings. In Banneker's time, they were used by farmers, sailors, and others for planning harvesting, shipping, and fishing. Banneker's almanac also included bits of history, literature, poems, and proverbs.

Banneker published his almanac from 1792 to 1797. They were a great success. He sent a copy to Thomas Jefferson, who was then Secretary of State for President George Washington. Banneker included a letter to Jefferson challenging his racist views. Jefferson believed that black people were inferior to white people. Jefferson responded to Banneker, thanking him for the almanac. He also acknowledged that Banneker had changed his thinking.

SURVEYOR: In 1791, the new capital of the new United States was being built in Washington, DC. The architect hired to plan the city was Pierre-Charles L'Enfant. Banneker was hired to be part of the six-man team to survey the new city. They were in charge of planning out the streets, buildings, and general outline of the city.

L'Enfant quit suddenly, taking the plans with him. The team was in trouble. But Banneker saved the day. He reconstructed L'Enfant's plan, completely from memory.

BENJAMIN BANNEKER'S HOME AND FAMILY: Banneker never married. He lived on his farm with his sisters until his death. Over the years his health failed, and he had to sell off most of the land. Tragically, when he died on October 9, 1806, his house burned down. All his books, and his clock, perished in the fire.

HIS INVENTIONS: Banneker is considered the first black scientist in the U.S. His clock is considered the first working wooden clock built in the New World.

WORLD WIDE WEB SITES:

http://www.benjaminbanneker.org
http://www.pbs.org/wgbh/aia/part2/2p84.html
http://www.web.mit.edu/invent/iow/Banneker.html

Frederick Banting
1891 - 1941
Canadian Scientist and Doctor
Co-Discoverer of Insulin, for
Treating Diabetes
Winner of the Nobel Prize

FREDERICK BANTING WAS BORN on November 14, 1891, in Alliston, Ontario, Canada. His parents were William and Margaret Banting. William was a farmer and Margaret was a homemaker. Frederick was the youngest of five children. He had three brothers, Nelson, Thompson, and Kenneth, and one sister, Essie.

FREDERICK BANTING GREW UP on the family farm. All the children worked on the farm. Frederick and his brothers took care of the farm animals. When an animal died, their father had the children look into the cause. That sparked Frederick's interest in science, and later, in medicine.

Another experience from his childhood drove his interest in medicine. When he was in grade school, a friend developed diabetes. At that time, there was no treatment. Banting's friend died.

FREDERICK BANTING WENT TO SCHOOL at the local public schools. He was a good student, and enjoyed sports, too. After high school, Banting went on to college at the University of Toronto. He originally planned to be a minister, but then changed his major to science.

Banting received his bachelor's in medicine and planned to go on to medical school. But his studies were interrupted by World War I (1914 - 1918). Banting joined the Canadian Army Medical Corps in 1916 and served in Europe. He became an assistant to one of the best surgeons of the time. Banting served as a military surgeon until 1918. That year, he was seriously wounded while treating soldiers on a battlefield in France. He recovered, and, when the war ended, returned to Toronto. Banting returned to medical school, finishing his degree in 1922.

MEDICAL CAREER: While finishing his degree, Banting worked at a children's hospital in Toronto. Then, he set up a small medical practice in London, Ontario. But he didn't have many patients. He decided to take a part-time teaching job at the University of Western Ontario. While preparing for a lecture one day, he was

Banting at his college graduation, 1916.

struck by an idea on how diabetes might be treated.

DIABETES AND INSULIN: Diabetes is an ancient disease. Mummies from the early Egyptian era indicate that it dates back thousands of years. Diabetes occurs when the body can't make an important chemical called "insulin." Insulin is a hormone. Its job is to help the body break down sugar in foods and convert it into energy. Without insulin, sugar builds up in the blood. The body can't handle high levels of blood sugar. The patient develops diabetes.

Before Banting's discovery, people who developed diabetes usually died within a few years. Researchers like Banting knew that diabetics suffered from a problem relating to their blood sugar levels. But there was no clear understanding of just what was involved. There was neither cure nor treatment.

Scientists knew that diabetes was caused by a lack of insulin. They also knew that insulin was created by an organ called the pancreas. Banting's breakthrough happened when he decided to focus on *how* the pancreas worked.

Banting in his lab, c.1922.

Banting concentrated on the section of the pancreas that created insulin. That part is called "the islands of Langerhans." Banting decided to target that same part of the pancreas in dogs. Using dogs as laboratory subjects, he would test his theory. Now he needed a lab.

THE DISCOVERY OF INSULIN: Banting talked to diabetes expert J. J. R. Macleod. Macleod was head of a lab at the University of Toronto. He told Banting he could use his lab, and introduced him to research student Charles Best. Banting and Best began their experiments in 1921.

Banting and Best first located the insulin in the dogs' pancreases. Then, they extracted the insulin. Another researcher, James Collip, helped them use the hormone to develop a sample that could be injected into human diabetics.

On January 23, 1922, a 14-year-old diabetic named Leonard Thompson received the first dose of insulin. Thompson was just 65 pounds at the time. He was very sick. Leonard didn't respond to the first dose. The researchers refined the insulin and gave him another injection. This time it worked. Soon Leonard was gaining weight and strength.

People around the world learned of Banting's incredible discovery. The researchers turned their research over to the University of Toronto. Soon, insulin was mass-produced, and diabetics were able to live long and healthy lives.

THE NOBEL PRIZE: In 1923, Banting and Macleod were awarded the Nobel Prize for their discovery. That is one of most important prizes in the world. Banting was angry at first, because Best had not been acknowledged. Also, Macleod had not contributed to the research and work. Banting split the prize money with Best. Macleod, too, split his portion of the award money, with researcher Collip. Banting was the first Canadian ever to receive the prize.

It is important to note that Banting and his co-workers received no money for their discovery. They felt that insulin belonged to the people. They "sold" the rights to the **patent** for $1 to the University of Toronto. They wanted to make sure that insulin could be manufactured inexpensively. That way, people all over the world could afford it.

In 1923 Banting became head of the Banting and Best Department of Medical Research at the University of Toronto. He continued to research other diseases, including cancer. He also became chairman of the Canadian Aviation Medical Research society.

In that role, he helped pilots understand, and avoid, the problems of high speed air travel.

FREDERICK BANTING'S HOME AND FAMILY: Banting married Marion Robinson in 1924. They had one son, William. They divorced in 1932. Banting married again in 1937. His second wife was Henrietta Ball. In his spare time, Banting loved to paint. He once took a trip to the Arctic to paint landscapes.

When Canada entered World War II in 1939, Banting again became an army doctor. He was killed in an airplane crash over Newfoundland on February 21, 1941. He was 49 years old.

HIS INVENTION: Banting's work discovering insulin, as well as the methods to produce it as a medicine, have saved the lives of millions of people. He is one of the most important medical researchers in history.

WORLD WIDE WEB SITES:

http://nobelprize.org/medicine/laureates/1923/banting-bio.html
http://www.cbc.ca/greatest/top_ten/nominee/banting-frederick.html
http://www.discoveryof insulin.com/Banting.htm
http://www.invent.org/hall_of_fame/220.html
http://www.pbs.org/wgbh/aso/databank/entries/bmbant.html

Alexander Graham Bell
1847 - 1922
Scottish-born American Scientist and Inventor
Inventor of the Telephone

ALEXANDER GRAHAM BELL WAS BORN on March 3, 1847, in Edinburgh, Scotland. His name at birth was Alexander Bell. He added the middle name of Graham later.

Alexander was the son of Alexander Melville Bell and Eliza Symonds. His father was a teacher and speech specialist and his mother was a homemaker. She was also deaf. Alexander was one of three boys. Melville was two years older and Edward was one year younger.

ALEXANDER GRAHAM BELL GREW UP in a family fascinated by communications. Alexander's father had developed an idea called "Visible Speech." Visible Speech was a kind of alphabet. It used symbols that represented all the sounds of the human voice. Bell promoted the use of Visible Speech as a way of teaching deaf mutes. Deaf mutes are people who cannot hear, and because of their disability, cannot speak.

Bell's method was a way of teaching deaf mutes to speak. He also explained how deaf mutes could use "lip reading." That is, to understand what people are saying by the way they move their lips to form words.

Alexander learned to read and write at a very young age. He also loved music, and his mother was a talented pianist. He formed a close bond with his mother. He communicated with her by speaking in low tones close to her forehead. Alexander believed that his mother could "hear" him through the vibrations his voice made. This idea was the beginning of his understanding of sound waves. That concept would later help him with his work on the telephone.

When Alexander was 11 years old, he decided to add the name "Graham" as his middle name. It was in honor of a close family friend he greatly admired named Alexander Graham. From then on, he was known as Alexander Graham Bell.

ALEXANDER GRAHAM BELL WENT TO SCHOOL at the Royal High School of Edinburgh until he was 13. When he was 16, he became a

The Bell Family, late 1880s.

student and a teacher of elocution and music at the Weston House Academy in Elgin, Scotland. "Elocution" is the art of public speaking. Alexander later attended the University of Edinburgh and the University of London. He also studied with his grandfather, who was a noted speech teacher.

Alexander's main interests were speech and sound. He devoted his career to educating the deaf and inventing devices to help them speak and hear better. Much of his work centered on his wish to "cure" the deafness of his mother.

ALEXANDER THE INVENTOR: At the age of 14, Alexander created his first invention. It was a machine designed to remove the husks from wheat. It was made of a nail brush and a paddle that turned like a wheel.

He attempted other early inventions, too. Fascinated by a "speaking machine" they had seen in London while visiting their grandfather, Alexander and his brother Melville tried to create one of their own. This invention was made of an imitation mouth, throat, nose, moving tongue, and lungs. When it was finished, it actually produced sounds like a human voice.

TUBERCULOSIS: All three Bell brothers developed tuberculosis (TB) in the late 1860s. TB is a disease that destroys the lungs. Today, its victims are treated with antibiotics. But in Bell's time, antibiotics hadn't yet been invented. Instead, many people died of the disease. Tragically, Edward died of the disease in 1867 and Melville in 1870.

MOVING TO CANADA: After their deaths, the Bell family moved to Brantford, Ontario. Alexander's parents were hopeful that the climate would improve the health of their only living son. It was here that Alexander made his first sketches of the telephone.

BELL IN BOSTON: Moving to the United States in 1871, Alexander continued to follow his interests in deafness and sound. He began teaching at the Boston School for Deaf Mutes. One of his students, Mabel Hubbard, had become deaf at the age of four from scarlet fever. They fell in love, and married in 1877.

While in Boston, Bell lectured to teachers of the deaf and taught classes in speech and "vocal physiology" at Boston University. "Vocal physiology" is the study of the human organs involved in speech. In 1882, Bell became a U.S. citizen.

THE TELEPHONE: After all his years of study and research, Bell was beginning to understand the science of human speech. He had already discovered that vowels (a, e, i, o, and u) each vibrated at a different rate when spoken. He used a tuning fork to learn this. He also read about experiments done by Hermann von Helmholtz in Germany that used electricity to send vowel sounds through a wire. If vowel sounds could travel through wire, Bell thought, then consonants could, too.

By the 1870s, the telegraph of **Samuel Morse** had revolutionized communication. The telegraph used wires to electronically send messages. It was a huge improvement in the speed of communications. But in 1872, the telegraph could carry only one message at a time, and it was very expensive. Bell knew the challenge was to invent a way to send more than one message at a time.

Bell continued to teach during the day and invent at night. He studied the possibilities of sending multiple messages through a single wire at different pitches. The Massachusetts Institute of Technology (MIT) loaned him a laboratory in which to work and test his ideas.

In 1874, Bell spent the summer back in Brantford, Ontario. By this time, he understood that sound was made up of a series of waves. He believed that each sound would create a distinct electric current that would rise and fall according to the vibration of the

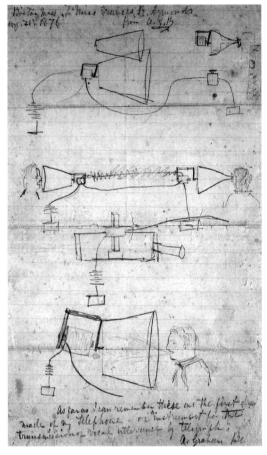

Bell's drawings for the telephone, 1876.

sound. He also believed that a current could be changed back into sound at the receiving end.

Bell saw similarities between multiple messages and notes in a musical chord. He called his idea a "harmonic telegraph." As a musical chord is a "message" made up of multiple notes, so a vocal "message" is made up of multiple sounds. Although he hadn't discovered any new scientific principles, Bell put existing ideas together in a new way. What he had discovered described the fundamental principle of the telephone.

Now Bell needed help. He needed supplies, money, and an experienced electrician to try out his idea. Because of his dedication to deaf children, the fathers of two of his students were willing to help. They agreed to pay for materials and an assistant.

Thomas Watson, a young electrician, became Bell's assistant. Together, these two men worked on Bell's telephone design ideas. Bell and Watson knew that they were competing against other inventors. They worked long hours creating and testing their new device.

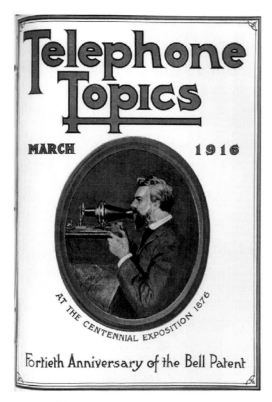

Magazine cover showing Bell demonstrating the first telephone, 1876.

On June 2, 1875, Bell and Watson were working in their lab using the instruments they had invented. They used two identical instruments: one for sending (or transmitting) the sound and one for receiving it. Thin metal strips (called reeds) were built into both instruments and were connected to each other by wires. The design was based on Bell's theory that sound could be sent through wire and that each sound made would produce a unique current.

At one point during their experiments, with the electric current turned off, Watson plucked a reed on his receiver. It produced a "twang" sound. In the other room, Bell heard the sound coming from the transmitter. The "twang" had the quality of human voice. He knew instantly that a single metal strip could create enough current to send sounds from one room to another. At that moment, Bell became the first person to understand how and why a telephone could work.

In February 1876, Bell filed an application for a **patent** at the United States Patent Office. On March 7, 1876, United States Patent Number 174,465 was officially given to Bell's telephone.

On March 10, 1876, Bell and Watson were again at work in their lab. Bell knocked over the liquid they were testing as a sound transmitter. It was battery acid, and as it spilled, Bell shouted, "Mr. Watson, come here. I want you!" Watson, who was working in another room, heard the words through the wire. This was the first telephone call.

IMPACT OF THE TELEPHONE: The first public demonstration of the telephone was given at the American Academy of Arts and Sciences in Boston on May 10, 1876. The telephone was introduced to the world at the Centennial Exhibition in Philadelphia later that year. It was a sensation. People wanted the instant communication offered by the telephone.

It is interesting to note that two other men also claimed that they had invented the telephone—Elisha Gray and Antonia Meucci. But because Bell was the first to file his patent, he was the only one allowed to produce telephones in the United States for a period of 19 years.

The Bell Telephone Company was founded on July 9, 1877, with Bell as its head. The invention spread throughout the country. By 1917, telephone service was available in most of the United States.

Alexander Graham Bell had changed communication. He became a rich and famous person. But his company was involved in lawsuits defending his invention. Over the years, the Bell Company fought more than 600 patent battles in court.

OTHER INVENTIONS AND ACCOMPLISHMENTS: The invention of the telephone made Bell rich enough to never need to work again. He had little interest in running a company. Instead, he wanted to study and learn new things. He also wanted to continue inventing.

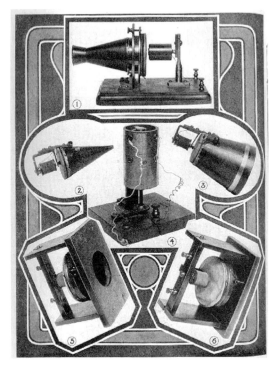

A group of early telephone devices.

In 1880, Bell and his partner Charles Sumner Tainter invented a "photophone" which allowed sound to be carried on a beam of light. After they successfully sent a message from one building to another, Bell declared: "This is the greatest invention I have ever made—greater than the telephone!"

For his inventions, Bell was awarded the Volta Prize for scientific achievement in electricity. (The prize is named for **Alessandro Volta**, who invented the battery.) With the prize money, Bell set up a scientific laboratory in Washington, D. C. It became a permanent place for scientists to experiment and invent.

In 1881, at the Volta Laboratory, Bell, his cousin Chichester Bell, and Tainter developed a way to make wax records for use on **Thomas Edison**'s phonograph. That same year, Bell invented an electric metal detector to try to locate the bullet lodged inside President Garfield after he was assassinated. Sadly, Bell's invention didn't save Garfield's life.

Bell's son Edward had died as an infant from breathing difficulties. Bell invented a machine to help patients with breathing disorders that was the forerunner to the iron lung.

Bell with a radio, c. 1922

In 1883, Bell started a school for deaf children in Washington, D.C. That same year, he was elected to the National Academy for the Sciences. He also helped start the magazine *Science*. It is still an important scientific journal today.

In 1887, Bell met six-year-old Helen Keller, who was blind and deaf. Because he knew so much about deafness and its treatment, he was able to help her family find a private teacher for her.

In 1888, Bell was one of the founding members of the National Geographic Society. With the help of his future son-in-law, Gilbert Grosvenor, he established the *National Geographic Magazine*. Like *Science*, it is still being published today. From 1898 to 1903, Bell was the President of the National Geographic Society.

THE SILVER DART: Bell was also interested in aircraft. At the suggestion of his wife, he formed the Aerial Experiment Association in Baddeck, Nova Scotia. Here he experimented with propellers and kites. With four young engineers (Glenn Curtiss, William "Casey" Baldwin, Thomas Selfridge and J.A.D. McCurdy), Bell worked on early aircraft. All together, the group made four aircraft, and in 1909, six years after the **Wright Brothers** flew at Kitty Hawk, Bell's *Silver Dart* made the first controlled powered flight in Canada.

THE HYDROFOIL: In keeping with his fascination with motion, Bell began to sketch ideas for what we now call a hydrofoil boat. He conducted experiments to see how airplanes could take off from water. In 1919, a water craft developed by Bell and Casey Baldwin, called the HD-4, set a world record when it traveled at 70.86 miles per hour. Their record was not broken for 44 years.

HONORS AND DISTINCTIONS: Today, Bell is known for his inventions and his part in creating scientific journals and organizations. His life was spent discovering and testing ideas. As a result of his curiosity and intelligence, Alexander Graham Bell was named one of the top ten Greatest Canadians, Greatest Britons, and "American Greats".

ALEXANDER GRAHAM BELL'S HOME AND FAMILY: Bell met his wife, Mabel, when she was his student in Boston. They married in 1877. The couple had four children, Elsie May, Marian, Edward, and Robert. Edward and Robert died as infants.

Alexander Graham Bell died on August 2, 1922, and was buried in Nova Scotia. He was 75 years old. In tribute to the man whose passion for communication had made them possible, all telephones in the United States did not ring for an entire minute on that day.

HIS INVENTIONS: Bell is one of the greatest inventors who ever lived. The telephone is a communication device found in nearly every home, business, and organization in the world. It changed the speed and ability of people to communicate. Bell's devotion to communication, seen in both the telephone and in his work on behalf of the deaf, have made him one of the most important figures in history.

WORLD WIDE WEB SITES:

http://bell.uccb.ns.ca/
http://memory.loc.gov/ammem/bellhtml/bellhome.html
http://sln.fi.edu/franklin/inventor/bell.html
http://www.alexandergrahambell.org
http://www.pbs.org/wgbh/amex/telephone/peopleevents/
    mabell.html

Karl Benz
1844 - 1929
German Engineer and Industrialist
Inventor of the First Three-Wheeled
Gasoline-Powered Automobile

KARL BENZ WAS BORN on November 25, 1844, in Karlsruhe, Germany. His father was an early railroad engineer. His mother was a homemaker.

KARL BENZ GREW UP in a poor family. His father died when he was two years old. As soon as he was old enough, he had to work to help support his family. Karl was always fascinated by machines. He became a skilled mechanic and earned money by fixing clocks and watches. He also loved photography. He built a darkroom, and sold photographs to visiting tourists.

KARL BENZ WENT TO SCHOOL in Karlsruhe. After graduating from high school, he enrolled in the Karlsruhe Polytechnic School to learn engineering.

FIRST JOBS: After he finished his studies at the Polytechnic School, Karl went to work at an engine factory in Karlsruhe. There he became interested in the possibilities of the internal combustion engine. He began to think about building a "horseless carriage"—an automobile.

In 1871, Benz opened a machine shop in Mannheim with August Ritter, a mechanic. His partner proved unreliable, so Benz took full control of the company with financial help from his wife, Bertha Ringer. During this time, he started to work on building an internal combustion engine. He succeeded in building a working engine in 1879.

In 1882, Benz started the Gasmotoren-Fabrik Mannheim (Mannheim Gas Engine Factory), where he built stationary gas engines. He also started to work on his idea for a "horseless carriage." This led to disagreements with his business partners. They didn't want him spending time on his invention. Benz decided to resign and start a new company. It left him free to study and improve his internal combustion engine.

THE INTERNAL COMBUSTION ENGINE: All engines require heat in order to work. Heat causes the gas in the cylinder to expand, which provides the force to move the piston. The steam engines created by **James Watt** and others are examples of "external combustion" engines. That means that the heat is produced away from the piston. In a steam engine the heat (or combustion) is applied to a

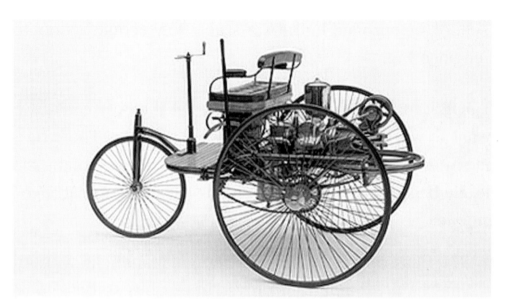

1886 Benz Patent Motor Car.

boiler, to make steam. The steam then goes to the cylinder, where the pressure moves the piston.

In an "internal combustion" engine, the heat (or combustion) takes place inside the cylinder. The first internal combustion engine used a gunpowder charge to move the piston. This wasn't practical. In 1860 the Belgian inventor Etienne Lenoir (1822 - 1900) developed the first practical internal combustion engine. It used illuminating gas as the fuel. Illuminating gas, also called coal gas, is a mixture of hydrogen, methane, and ethylene.

The next major advance came in 1876, when Nikolaus Otto (1832 - 1891) built the first four-stroke engine. The Otto engine operates in four separate steps, or strokes:

Intake stroke: The air-fuel mixture moves into the cylinder as the piston slides down.

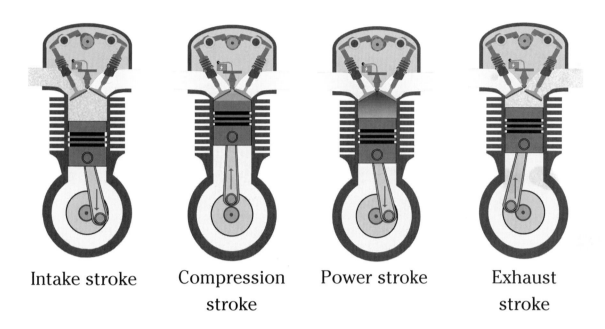

Intake stroke   Compression   Power stroke   Exhaust
                    stroke   stroke

Compression stroke: The piston slides up, compressing the
    mixture.

Power stroke: The mixture is ignited, and the pressure from the
    burning mixture pushes the piston back down.

Exhaust stroke: The exhaust fumes from the burnt mixture is
    pushed out of the cylinder as the piston slides back up.

This is basically the way most internal combustion engines
work today. Otto's first engines still used illuminating gas. In 1882,
Gottlieb Daimler and Wilhelm Maybach developed the carburetor,
which made it possible for the engine to use liquid fuel (gasoline).
They also developed an improved method for ignition. These refinements finally made it possible to build a lightweight and portable
engine.

INVENTING THE AUTOMOBILE: In 1883 Benz founded Benz & Co.
with a new group of investors. They agreed to let him work on his
horseless carriage. As the engine business grew, Benz continued to

Painting depicting Bertha Benz and sons and their 1888 ride.

work on his invention. He finished his first automobile in 1885. It had three wheels, and used a small gasoline-powered engine, placed behind the seat. He was awarded a **patent** in 1886 for his "vehicle powered by a gas engine".

Even though Benz's invention created a sensation, people were not interested in buying his new automobile. They thought it was an interesting novelty. But they didn't think it was a practical means of transportation.

BERTHA BENZ AND THE FIRST LONG-DISTANCE TRIP IN AN AUTOMOBILE: One morning in August 1888, Karl's wife, Bertha, decided to prove the value of her husband's automobile. While Karl was still in bed, she and two of their sons, Eugen and Richard, took one of his three-wheeled automobiles for a ride. They drove from Mannheim to her parents' home in Pforzheim, a distance of about

35 miles. When they reached Pforzheim that night, Bertha sent a telegraph to Karl and told him their trip was a success. This was the first long-distance trip in an automobile. Bertha became the first woman motorist. She had accomplished what she had set out to do. Critics of the automobile were silenced. Soon everyone was talking about the Benz Patent Motor Car.

Benz & Co. prospered as his automobile gained public acceptance. He continued to refine and improve his cars. In 1890, he began building four-wheeled automobiles, due in part to the popularity of **Gottlieb Daimler**'s successful models.

In 1894, Benz introduced the Velo, a lower-priced, lightweight car. He built 1200 Velos between 1894 and 1901. It is considered the first car to be built as part of a series. Before the Velo, cars were built to order, one at a time.

By the end of the 19th century, Benz & Co. was the largest automobile manufacturer in the world. But compared to the later success of **Henry Ford** in the U.S., Benz's output was small. In 1899 his company built a total of 572 vehicles. Growing competition from the Daimler Mercedes car caused Benz's partners to push for major design changes. Benz disagreed with his partners, and resigned from Benz & Co. in 1903.

In 1906 he started a new company, Karl Benz & Sons. His partners were Eugen and Richard, the sons who took the first automobile trip with their mother. Together, they continued to build cars until the company closed in 1923. Karl Benz died on April 4, 1929, at his home in Ladenburg, Germany.

1894 Benz "Velo"—The first series car.

KARL BENZ'S HOME AND FAMILY: Benz married Bertha Ringer on July 20, 1872. Bertha believed in her husband's vision of building the automobile. She gave him much support throughout their marriage. She used her own money to help finance his first business. Her "first automobile trip" captured the public's interest in Karl's new vehicles. Benz wrote in his memoirs, "Only one person remained with me in the small ship of life when it seemed destined to sink. That was my wife. Bravely and resolutely she set the new sails of hope." Karl and Bertha had five children. Bertha Benz died on May 5, 1944, two days after her 95th birthday.

MERCEDES-BENZ: Karl Benz and Gottlieb Daimler developed their vehicles within months of each other, and were rivals in the early automobile business. Although they were aware of each other's efforts, they never met. Gottlieb Daimler died in 1900 just as the automotive industry was beginning to grow. Germany faced an economic depression after World War I (1914 - 1918). In 1926, Benz

& Co. merged with Daimler-Mercedes in order to increase their chances of survival. The new company was called Mercedes-Benz. Karl Benz served on the board of directors until his death in 1929.

HIS INVENTION: Karl Benz was an innovator who made many improvements to the internal combustion engine. His three-wheeled vehicle was patented as the first automobile. He also developed Velo, which was the first series automobile. It is interesting to note that Daimler's and Benz's automobiles had less of an impact on European society than **Henry Ford**'s Model-T did on American life. That is because their cars were more expensive and weren't mass-produced. So they didn't become a common purchase for most people at the time of their invention. It wasn't until after World War II that Europeans began to buy cars in similar numbers to Americans.

WORLD WIDE WEB SITES:

http://www.autonews.com/files/euroauto/inductees/benz.htm
http://www.mercedes-benz.com/content/mbcom/international/
http://www.3wheelers.com/benz.html

Tim Berners-Lee
1955 -
British Computer Scientist
Inventor of the World Wide Web

TIM BERNERS-LEE WAS BORN on June 8, 1955, in London, England.
His parents are Conway and Mary Berners-Lee. They are both
computer scientists. They met while working on the first commercial computer. Tim has one brother, Peter.

TIM BERNERS-LEE GREW UP in a family that encouraged his talent for math. He and his brother used to play math games with imaginary numbers.

Tim loved computers. He built a cardboard model of the one his parents had created. He also loved trains, and had a model set. Fascinated by the way the trains worked, he created some electronic gadgets to run his set.

Tim also loved to read science fiction books. One particular favorite was a story called "Dial F for Frankenstein." It featured computers linked together that come "alive," acting and thinking on their own.

Tim also remembers a conversation he had with his dad when he was young. His dad said that computers would be so much more useful if, like the human brain, they could connect random pieces of information.

TIM BERNERS-LEE WENT TO SCHOOL at a private boys' school called Emmanuel. He was an excellent student. He went on to Queen's College, which is part of Oxford University. In college, he studied physics. "I thought science might turn out to be more practical than math," he says. He calls physics "halfway between math and electronics." And, for him, physics "turned out to be very special all of itself, and fascinating."

While in college, he couldn't use the university's computers. He'd broken the rules for student use of computers. So he bought an old TV set and made a computer out of it. "I soldered by hand every wire in it," he recalls. The machine was all his own. "Knowing it would do anything I had the imagination to program was a great feeling."

FIRST JOBS: After graduating from college in 1976, Berners-Lee got a job with a telecommunications company. He developed software. Software programs tell computers what to do. After two years, he moved on to another company, where he created typesetting software.

In 1980, Berners-Lee spent six months working as a software specialist for CERN. CERN is the world's major research institute for particle physics. Scientists from all over the world come to CERN, in Geneva, Switzerland, to work. While Berners-Lee was there, he developed a program, called "Enquire." It was an early attempt to link pieces of information.

INVENTING THE WORLD WIDE WEB: Berners-Lee began to work for CERN full time in 1984. He set out to solve a huge problem that kept the CERN scientists from being able to share information. "There was different information on different computers," he recalled. 'But you had to log on to different computers to get at it." There was no universal computer language that the computers could share. So, there was no way for them to share information.

"I actually wrote some programs to take information from one system and convert it," he recalls. That got him to thinking of a solution to the problem. He asked himself, "Can't we convert every information system so that it looks like part of some imaginary information system which everyone can read? And that became the WWW," he explains.

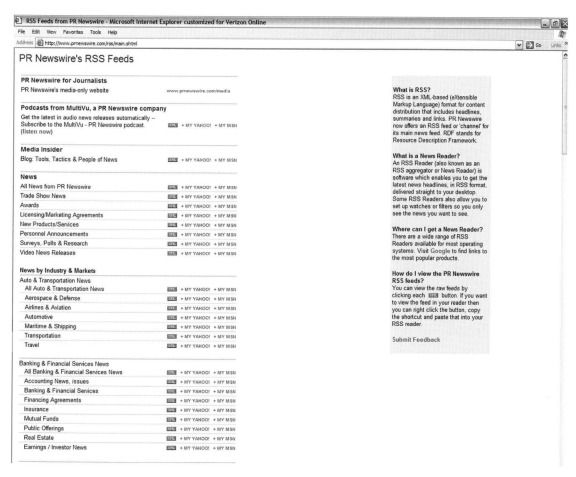

A page from the World Wide Web, created using HTTP protocol and HTML language, both created by Berners-Lee.

THE INTERNET: The Internet and the World Wide Web are not the same thing. The Internet is a "network of networks." It was created in the 1970s by the U.S. military as a way to link computers around the world. It became popular in universities, too, as a means to transfer information. It was a global network, but the data it contained couldn't be searched and used easily.

Berners-Lee defined the challenge. He wanted to find a way to assign a *code* to documents. He needed to develop a system of rules that would *link* the documents. He needed to create a way to

45

identify each document, in a universal language. His goal was to create a "single, global information space." In that space, "anything could be linked to anything." That "space" became the World Wide Web.

HTML, HTTP and URL: In 1990, Berners-Lee developed the *coding* system. He called it HyperText Markup Language (HTML). It is used to code text, pictures, and sound. This is the "language" people use to create hypertext Web pages. It is the language that's used for the hypertext "links" you click on to transfer between Web pages.

Next, Berners-Lee created HTTP. HTTP stands for HyperText Transfer Protocol. It's the communication standard that allows pages to be linked across the web. It also provides a standardized format, so the information on Web pages can be displayed and read.

Berners-Lee's next created URLs. URL stands for Universal Resource Locator. It is the unique Web "address" for every Web page.

Berners-Lee named his project the "World Wide Web." He called it that to describe his vision of a web of information spanning the globe. It's the "www" you see in front of every Web address.

In 1991, Berners-Lee shared the program with the scientists at CERN. In the summer of 1991, he posted the software on the Internet. It became available to anyone who wanted it, for free.

Berners-Lee had created a browser, to allow searching, but it didn't utilize the "point and click" function (using a computer mouse) to activate hyperlinks. Marc Andreessen, founder of Netscape, developed a browser that could do that. Andreessen sold the software for the browser, becoming a millionaire in the process. The Web became easy to navigate, even for beginners. Millions of people began to use their computers to connect to the Web. It was an explosion in information sharing, even greater than Berners-Lee had imagined. Today there are billions of Web pages, and millions of users, worldwide.

It's important to note that Berners-Lee never made money, or tried to **patent**, any of the technology that went into creating the World Wide Web. Instead, he thought it should be free to be shared by people everywhere. He knew that making money off his invention would create competitive products that would use different and incompatible systems. That would be the opposite of the universal source of communication he envisioned.

Berners-Lee has never wanted to be rich, or famous. "What is maddening is the terrible notion that a person's value depends on how important and financially successful they are," he says.

WORLD WIDE WEB CONSORTIUM: Today, Berners-Lee is head of the World Wide Web Consortium, or W3C. That is the group that coordinates the development of the Web. He works out of an office at the Massachusetts Institute of Technology (MIT), in Cambridge, Massachusetts.

Now, Berners-Lee is at work on a "semantic Web." That will allow documents on the Web to make sense to machines, not just people. He's creating a system to label information on Web pages that says what it is. This would allow information to be searched in a broader way. Right now, it's being used by science researchers to organize information from different fields.

TIM BERNERS-LEE'S HOME AND FAMILY: Berners-Lee is married to Nancy Carlson. They met while they were both working for CERN. They have two sons and live in the Boston area. He likes to keep his private life private, and asks people to respect that.

HIS INVENTION: The World Wide Web has been a truly revolutionary force in modern life. It has changed the way people relate to one another and their world. Information, and the transmission of information, has always been a transforming force in society. The World Wide Web has allowed the free distribution of information in a way never before possible. And, as Berners-Lee says, it is still changing.

Berners-Lee hopes that the Web will be used for positive things. "Any really powerful thing can be used for good or evil. So what is made of the Web is up to us. You, me, everyone else. Here is my hope. The Web is a tool for communicating. The Web can help people understand each other. Let's use the web to create neat, new, exciting things. Let's use the Web to help people understand each other."

WORLD WIDE WEB SITES:

http://www.time.com/time/time100/scientist/profile/bernerslee.html
http://www.W3org/People/Berners-Lee/Kids

Henry Bessemer
1813 - 1898
English Engineer and Inventor of the Steel Converter

HENRY BESSEMER WAS BORN on January 19, 1813, in Charlton, England. His father was an engineer and metalsmith. His mother was a homemaker. Henry had one sister.

HENRY BESSEMER GREW UP a lively and creative boy. His father had set up a metal working foundry on the family property. There, Henry learned about metal working. It fascinated him.

HENRY BESSEMER WENT TO SCHOOL for a brief period. He was more interested in inventing and learning from his father. He left school after a few years and studied metal working with his father.

EARLY INVENTIONS: Henry started to invent when he was still a young boy. One of his first inventions was a brick-making machine. He was so fascinated with this kind of work that he set to work developing different kinds of molds. He'd make something out of clay, then mold and cast it in metal at his father's foundry.

When he was 17, Henry moved with his family to London. Soon, he'd invented a machine that made a stamp used on important government documents. The government's stamps then in use were easy to "forge," or copy. Bessemer's machine pressed the stamp onto the document. That made the stamp harder to forge. The government was delighted with Bessemer's invention, and bought the machine for its use.

Another important early invention had to do with decorative writing. Bessemer's sister had collected her paintings in a book. She wanted Henry to create a title page, with gold lettering. Gold powder was very expensive. Henry invented a way of making a brass powder that looked like gold. It could be used for lettering, and all kinds of artistic design. It was very successful, and made him a lot of money.

Bessemer had learned much about metalworking from his father. He had also learned about "alloys." Those are materials made of blending different metals. It was his work in that area that made him famous.

INVENTING THE STEEL CONVERTER: In the 1850s, England was fighting the Crimean War. The cannon used by the British Army wasn't strong enough. Bessemer set out to create a stronger metal for use in British weapons.

At that time, iron was the main metal used in building and manufacturing. There were two types of iron: cast iron and wrought iron. Cast iron was made by heating iron ore and coal. Wrought iron was made by heating cast iron in a furnace and removing the impurities.

There was a material known as "steel" at the time. It was made from a mixture of carbon and wrought iron. But it was costly and time-consuming. Bessemer began to experiment with making the process cheaper and faster.

Bessemer started with iron, which he heated in a converter he'd invented. The converter was an egg-shaped device. He filled the converter with molten iron. Next, he blasted cold air into the mixture. This removed the carbon and other impurities from the iron. The result was steel that could be molded into many shapes and sizes. It was also very strong.

Bessemer's process could also make 30 tons of steel in just 30 minutes. The previous steel-making process could only make 50 pounds of steel at a time.

THE INDUSTRIAL REVOLUTION: As happens so often in the history of invention, Bessemer had invented a process for a product that was in huge demand. The Industrial Revolution was sweeping through England, Europe, and the U.S. People were leaving farms and finding jobs in the new factories in urban centers. It was a time of great economic and social change.

Plants needed tons of steel to make machinery. Manufacturers needed tons of steel to make products. And the railways needed steel for tracks and railroad cars. Steel produced using Bessemer's process fed the demand.

Bessemer **patented** his invention in 1856. He started his own steel manufacturing company, Henry Bessemer and Company. He was able to make steel cheaply and quickly. Soon he began licensing his steel making process to others in the industry. All this made him very rich.

LATER LIFE: Bessemer continued to invent in his later years. He created a solar furnace, a telescope, and machines for processing diamonds.

HENRY BESSEMER'S HOME AND FAMILY: Bessemer married when he was 21. He and his wife had three children. He died in London on March 15, 1898, at the age of 85.

Bessemer received many honors and awards. He was made a knight by Queen Victoria. He also was made a member of the Royal Society.

HIS INVENTION: Bessemer's invention of the steel converter made mass production of steel possible. The Industrial Revolution would have been impossible without the inexpensive manufacture of steel. It was used to build factories, products, railroads, and even skyscrapers. Bessemer's converter was so successful that the process was used worldwide until the mid-1950s.

WORLD WIDE WEB SITES:

http://web.mit.edu/invent/iow/bessemer.html
http://www.invent.org/hall_of_fame/183.html

Clarence Birdseye
1886 - 1956
American Businessman and Inventor
"The Father of Frozen Food"

CLARENCE BIRDSEYE WAS BORN on December 9, 1886, in Brooklyn, New York. He was one of eight children. His parents were Frank and Ada Birdseye. Frank was a lawyer and Ada was a homemaker.

Their unusual last name—Birdseye—has an interesting story behind it. Family legend said that an ancestor had saved the life of an English queen. As a hawk swooped down to attack her, the relative shot the hawk in the center of its eye. That earned him the nickname of "Bird's Eye."

CLARENCE BIRDSEYE GREW UP spending summers in the country. The family had a large farm on Long Island. As a young boy, he was interested in nature and the land. He spent most of his time outdoors at the beach or in the fields.

CLARENCE BIRDSEYE WENT TO SCHOOL in Brooklyn until high school. When he was a teenager, his family moved to Montclair, New Jersey. In school, Clarence was interested in food preparation and took a cooking class.

Outside of school, Clarence continued to study nature. One of his first jobs was catching muskrats. He sold them to a wealthy man who wanted them for their fur.

Birdseye graduated from high school in June of 1908. He worked that summer as an office boy for a business on Wall Street in New York City.

In the fall of 1908, he entered Amherst College in Massachusetts. He studied biology. Birdseye had to work to help pay for college. Once again his interest in nature helped him make money. As he walked around the fields of Amherst, he noticed a water spring that was filled with tiny frogs. Birdseye wrote a letter to the Bronx Zoo in New York City asking if they needed live frogs to feed to their snakes. They said that they did. They paid Birdseye $115 for the hundreds of frogs he caught and shipped to them in burlap bags.

After two years, Birdseye ran out of money. He had to leave college and go to work. His first job was with the United States Department of Agriculture's Biological Survey. He moved West to collect examples of animals and birds in Arizona and New Mexico. During this time, Birdseye discovered that he was able to eat very unusual foods. He tried rattlesnake and ate soups that he made from mice, chipmunks, gophers and packrats.

For two years Birdseye worked for the Biological Survey in the summers. He went back to New York for the winters. He also bought bobcat and coyote skins from fur trappers in the West. He sold them at a good profit in New York to companies that made fur coats.

LIVING IN LABRADOR: In 1911 Birdseye quit his job with the government. He went on a six-week cruise off the coast of Labrador, in northeast Canada. When he arrived, he learned that men were making big profits trapping foxes and selling their furs.

For the next five years, Birdseye traveled all over Canada by dog sled collecting furs. In 1915 he married Eleanor Gannett. Soon they had a son. They lived in Labrador in a three-room cabin, 250 miles away from the nearest doctor.

Still an adventurous eater, Birdseye tried starlings, blackbirds, whale, porpoise, lynx, alligator, and other large lizards. As he himself said, "I ate about everything—beaver tail, polar bear and lion tenderloin. And I'll tell you another thing—the front half of a skunk is excellent!"

LEARNING FROM ESKIMOS: Birdseye noticed that food could be preserved easily in the cold climate of the arctic. He watched the

Birdseye in Labrador, c. 1915.

Eskimos fishing. He saw that when the fish were pulled out of the water they froze almost instantly in the cold arctic air. When the fish were thawed and cooked weeks later they tasted almost as good as when they were first caught.

Birdseye watched the Eskimos freeze fresh meat and fish in barrels of salty sea water. He noted that food quickly frozen in the extreme cold tasted better when thawed than food frozen in the warmer temperatures of spring or fall.

Birdseye experimented with freezing cabbage for his own family. He placed it in barrels of salt water, then left them outside in the cold. He also tried this method with caribou meat.

QUICK FREEZING: The process that Birdseye learned by watching the Eskimos came to be known as "quick freezing." He discovered that when food is frozen quickly, only small ice crystals form. The small crystals do not damage the cells of the food. So flavor, color, and texture do not change very much. When the food is thawed, it looks and tastes almost the same as before it was frozen.

BACK IN THE UNITED STATES: In 1917 the Birdseye family returned to the United States. Birdseye worked for the United States Fisheries Association. In 1922 he started his own fish processing business. He used what he had learned from the Eskimos to quick freeze fish. He became determined to figure out how to develop a way to quick freeze food on a large scale. He wanted to make frozen food available to people who shopped in markets.

In 1923, Birdseye spent $7.00 to buy an electric fan, buckets to fill with brine (water and salt), and large cakes of ice. With this equipment, he experimented in his kitchen. At last, he developed a system of packing food into waxed cardboard packages and freezing it rapidly. Because he was working at home some of his experiments affected his family. One time his wife complained about having live fish in the bathtub.

One year later, he and three partners founded the General Seafoods company in Massachusetts. They sold frozen fish. It was the first company to use Birdseye's method of quick freezing food in small packages and selling it directly to shoppers. He invented what he called a "quick freeze machine" which froze food very quickly between two metal plates that had been refrigerated.

The first machine weighed 20 tons. Birdseye knew that he had to make it lighter, and easier to ship. He worked on the design until he had developed a machine that could be sold and delivered anywhere in the world.

Now Birdseye needed money to be able to produce his new frozen food machines. How he got it is a fascinating story.

Marjorie Merriweather Post, heiress to the Postum Cereal fortune, was vacationing on her yacht in Gloucester, Massachusetts. One night she was served goose for dinner. She said it was the best she'd ever eaten. When she asked where her cook had found fresh goose, he told her that it had been purchased frozen. It was one of Birdseye's products.

Post had inherited her father's company. She was interested in expanding Postum's food offerings. She decided she wanted to buy Birdseye's company. In 1929 Birdseye received 22 million dollars for his frozen food company. It became part of the Postum empire.

Postum then changed its name to the General Foods Corporation. Birdseye was made the head of the laboratory in Gloucester. One of his first innovations was using a new packaging material—coated cellophane—to help preserve frozen food.

BIRDS EYE FROZEN FOODS: In March 1930, Clarence Birdseye's frozen foods first appeared in 18 grocery stores in Springfield, Massachusetts. This was the "test market" used to see if people would buy frozen food.

The name on the packages was Birdseye, in honor of the man who had invented the process. But the name was divided into two words—Birds Eye. This did not bother Birdseye, however. It reminded him of the family legend about his ancestor and the queen.

In 1934, 27 frozen food items (vegetables, fruits, fish, and meats) became available in stores in Syracuse and Rochester, New York. They were a great success. After this, Birds Eye frozen foods were delivered and sold all over the country.

EARLY TROUBLES: Birdseye encountered some problems early on. Many store owners couldn't afford the large freezers needed to keep and display the new foods. And there weren't enough refrigerator railroad cars to get the food to market without thawing.

To solve these problems, Birdseye made an affordable freezer case to lease to store owners. He also leased refrigerated railroad cars.

At first, people weren't eager to buy Birdseye's product. Previous brands of frozen food hadn't been successful, because the food didn't taste very good. So it took a while before people were willing to try Birdseye's brand. When they did, they found that it did, in fact, taste almost as good as fresh. Over the years, it became a staple in refrigerators all over the country. In fact, refrigerator manufacturers began to increase the size of the freezer portion of the appliance to make room for more frozen foods.

OTHER INVENTIONS: Birdseye **patented** more than 300 products. His interest in science and his curious nature kept him experimenting and inventing into old age. Some of his other inventions included a one-man harpoon gun, an infrared heat lamp, a spotlight for store window displays, an electric fishing reel, and paper pulp made from sugar cane.

CLARENCE BIRDSEYE'S HOME AND FAMILY: Birdseye married Eleanor Gannett in 1915. They had four children: Kelog, Henry, Ruth, and Eleanor. Birdseye continued to work for General Foods, give lectures, and write articles until the end of his life. He died in New York City on October 7, 1956, of a heart attack. He was 69 years old.

HIS INVENTION: Birdseye wasn't the first person to freeze food. But his invention of the "quick freezing" process produced food with the flavor, texture, and most of the nutrition of fresh food. He created and leased freezers and railroad cars that made it possible

One of Birdseye's frozen food display cases.

for frozen food to be shipped all over the world. His inventions helped improve people's diet, providing nutritious foods that could be preserved for a long time. For these reasons, he is known as "The Father of Frozen Food." Birdseye was named to the National Inventors Hall of Fame in 2005.

WORLD WIDE WEB SITES:

http://www.birdseyefoods.com
http://www.invent.org/hall_of_fame/232/html

Blodgett, center, talks with visitors to the G.E. labs.

Katharine Blodgett
1898 - 1979
American Scientist
Inventor of Non-Reflective Glass

KATHARINE BLODGETT WAS BORN on January 10, 1898, in Schenectady, New York. Her parents were Katharine and George Blodgett. Her mother was a homemaker and her father was a lawyer for General Electric. Sadly, her father died just weeks before Katharine was born. She had one brother, who was older.

KATHARINE BLODGETT GREW UP in the U.S. and Europe. Her mother moved the family to New York, then to Europe after her father's death. She wanted her children to learn languages, so they lived in Germany and France during Katharine's childhood. When she was eight, the family returned to America.

When she was little, Katharine showed a great interest in math and science. She actually knew the multiplication tables before she knew the alphabet. Her mother encouraged her bright daughter, and Katharine flourished.

KATHARINE BLODGETT WENT TO SCHOOL at the local public schools for one year, when she was nine. After that, she attended a private school in New York City. Katharine was an excellent student. She loved science especially. She graduated from high school at 15.

After high school, she attended Bryn Mawr on a scholarship. She did well in all her classes. Her math and physics professors thought she had great promise. She decided she wanted to become a scientist. Blodgett graduated from Bryn Mawr in 1917.

Blodgett visited the labs at General Electric (G.E.), where her father had worked. There, she met Irving Langmuir, who encouraged her to continue her education. So Blodgett went on to the University of Chicago to study for a master's degree. When she'd finished, Langmuir hired her. She became the first woman scientist hired by G.E. labs.

WORKING FOR GENERAL ELECTRIC: Blodgett began working for G.E. in 1918. She spent her entire career there. During most of that time, she worked with Langmuir, who became her mentor.

AN IMPORTANT INNOVATION IN THE GAS MASK: Blodgett's master's thesis had been about gasses. She started working for G.E. during World War I (1914 - 1918). In that war, weapons with poisonous gasses were being used. Based in part on Blodgett's research, the military developed gas masks that protected soldiers.

After six years at G.E., Blodgett decided to get a PhD in physics. She did her doctoral work at Cambridge University in England. In 1926, she became the first woman to receive a PhD in physics from Cambridge.

"THIN FILMS": Blodgett returned to G.E. and continued her work with Langmuir. Their special area of research was "thin films." These are thin layers of chemicals—some just a molecule thick. When added to a surface like glass, they add special properties to the material.

Blodgett worked for years researching how thin films develop. For example, a plate of glass dipped in an oily substance will form a layer that coats the glass.

Based on her research, Blodgett created a very important product. She developed a color gauge that measured the thickness of thin films. At that time, the best instruments could measure a thousandth of an inch of thickness. Blodgett's gauge could measure less than one millionth of an inch.

Blodgett's "color gauge" was immediately useful in scientific fields from chemistry to biology. And it led her to her most important invention.

INVENTING NON-REFLECTIVE GLASS: In an experiment, Blodgett coated a sheet of glass with 44 layers of liquid soap. Each was just one molecule thick. The soap layers didn't allow the glass to reflect light. The result was a non-reflective, "invisible" glass.

The discovery was a huge success. It was used in many different products. For the first time, people could look through glass—eyeglasses, windshields, cameras, telescopes—and see without glare or distortion. Blodgett received a **patent** for her invention in 1938.

Blodgett's invention was very useful to the military, too. In World War II (1939 - 1945) periscopes and aerial cameras with non-reflective glass aided troops. But her most important effort for the war was the development of smokescreens. She created a generator that provided huge billows of smoke to shield U.S. troops during invasions. Hundreds of lives were saved through her efforts.

OTHER SCIENTIFIC RESEARCH: Blodgett's later work included using thin films to create products that could de-ice airplane wings, making flight safer. In all, she received six patents for her work.

LATER LIFE: Blodgett retired from G.E. in 1963 as a well-known and respected scientist. She received many honors and awards. Colleges and universities gave her honorary degrees. She also became a member of several scientific societies. Her home town, Schenectady, even created a "Katharine Blodgett Day" in her honor.

KATHARINE BLODGETT'S HOME AND FAMILY: Blodgett never married or had children. She lived in a house close to her family's original home in Schenectady. She enjoyed gardening and travel and was active in her church. Katharine Blodgett died on October 12, 1979. She was 81 years old.

HER INVENTION: Blodgett's invention of non-reflective glass benefitted people all over the world. Windshields, eyeglasses, telescopes, microscopes—hundreds of products—became more useful because of her invention.

WORLD WIDE WEB SITES:

http://cwp.library.ucla.edu/Phase2/Blodgett_Katharine_Burr
http://jchemed.chem.wisc.edu/JCEWWW/Features/eChemists/Bios/
    Blodgett
http://web.mit.edu/invent/iow/blodgett.html

Louis Braille
1809 - 1852
French Educator
Inventor of the Braille System of Printing and Writing for the Blind

LOUIS BRAILLE WAS BORN on January 4, 1809, in Coupuray, France, about 25 miles from Paris. His parents were Simon and Monique Braille. Simon was a saddle maker and Monique was a homemaker. Louis was the youngest of four children. His parents named all their children after the kings and queens of France. So his brother was named Louis-Simon. His sisters were named Catherine Josephine and Marie Celine.

LOUIS BRAILLE GREW UP a curious child. He liked to spend time in the harness shop watching his father make saddles, reins, and collars. One day when he was three years old, Louis decided to try to punch a hole in a piece of leather, as he had seen his father do many times. He used a sharp tool called an awl.

Tragically, his hand slipped and the sharp tool went into his left eye. His mother and father rushed him to the village doctor. Medical care at that time was poor. Louis's eye became infected. Soon, the infection spread to his other eye. By the time he was five years old, he was completely and permanently blind.

BEING BLIND: In Braille's time, blind people were considered helpless. Blind children almost never went to school. Many never learned to read and write. Many blind people became beggars. When they could not beg enough money for food they ate garbage or went hungry.

Louis's parents refused to accept that life for him. They knew he was smart, so they sent him to school to learn what he could by listening. They made him do chores in the harness shop. They helped him learn to take care of himself.

Louis's father made him a long cane with a pointed tip. Louis learned to sweep it in front of him as he walked. When the cane hit something, Louis knew he had to stop and walk around the object. Without sight, Louis learned to tell where he was and what was going on by the sounds and smells around him.

EDUCATION—THE ROYAL INSTITUTE FOR BLIND YOUTH: At school, Louis kept up with the other children. By the time he was 10 he had learned most everything he could by listening. He needed a new way to learn.

Father Palluy, the village priest, told Louis's family about a special school in Paris. The Royal Institute for Blind Youth was the world's first school for the blind. They taught blind children arithmetic, geography, history, and music. They also taught them how to do many things with their hands. That way, they could earn money when they grew up.

Louis's parents couldn't afford to send him to the special school. But a wealthy villager offered to pay his way. On a cold day in February 1819, Louis boarded a stagecoach and rode off to Paris. He was excited to think that he was going to learn to read. At last, he would be able to find things out for himself.

AT SCHOOL: The school building was rundown, dark, and damp. The first day was filled with many new smells and sounds. When Louis went to bed that night he was homesick and cried. A boy from a bed nearby came over and sat with him. He talked to him in a friendly voice. He told Louis he would feel better the next day.

Louis loved his classes. Even though he was the youngest boy in the school, he was bright and often was at the head of his class. His favorite class was music. All the boys learned to play a musical instrument, but Louis learned to play piano, organ and cello. He had a special talent for piano. Since he could not "read" music, he memorized the notes. For the rest of his life, music was to be one of Braille's greatest loves.

One of the reasons Louis had been excited about school was that they had books especially for blind people. He wanted to read all of them. When he arrived at school, though, he was disappointed to learn there were only 14 books in the library.

At that time, books for the blind were made with raised print. That is, the individual letters in words were raised. Blind people read by feeling the letters, one by one. Not only were these books expensive to make, they were heavy to hold and hard to read. Some of the letters were hard to tell apart by feeling and it was slow going. Sometimes Louis forgot the beginning of the sentence before he came to the end.

He decided there had to be a way to make books for blind people. He was determined to figure out how.

READING AND WRITING IN THE DARK: In 1821, a captain from the French army came to Louis's school. His name was Charles Barbier and he had invented an alphabet code he called "night writing." This code was a series of raised dots and dashes punched on cardboard. It was used to send secret military messages that could be read at night, without light.

Captain Barbier had also invented a device that gave blind students a way to write. A piece of paper was fitted onto a slate and held in place by a locking bar. A sharp, pointed tool punched holes in the paper. Using the code of dots and dashes, words were punched onto the paper. Blind students "read" by feeling the holes with their fingers.

Louis began to learn the code. But he thought it was too hard to use. Also, the alphabet could not make capital letters or numbers.

And there was no way to make periods, commas, or exclamation points. Most of all, it was hard to learn and hard to feel. But Captain Barbier's alphabet was Braille's starting point. For the next three years, Louis worked to make the code easier to use.

THE BRAILLE ALPHABET: Braille spent all his free time experimenting with different patterns of dots. One day he had a new idea. What if the dots stood for the letters of the alphabet? This pattern of dots would be much easier to use and to understand.

After three years of work, at the age of 15, Louis finally found a solution. Using an awl from his father's workshop, the very tool that had made him blind in the first place, Louis Braille created an alphabet made up of combinations of six raised dots. By arranging the dots in 63 different combinations, he created the letters of the alphabet.

Louis returned to school with his new alphabet. His fellow students were delighted. Braille's alphabet was simple and easy to feel. Now they could write and keep diaries. They could take notes in class and read them later. But most of all, they could read books! Louis published the first book using his new alphabet in 1829.

The director of the school met with Louis. He was proud to think that one of his students had accomplished what people had been trying to do for many years. Unfortunately, the school was a charity school. It didn't have money to make books using the new alphabet.

The director began writing letters to anyone who might contribute money for making books. But he wasn't able to find the support they needed.

The Braille Alphabet

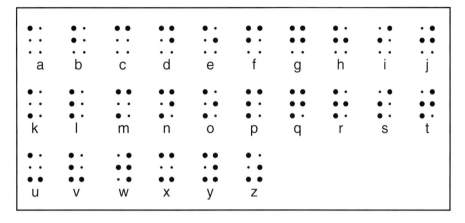

The Braille Cell

The basic unit of the braille system is the braille cell. A braille cell is a group of six dots.

The dots of the cell are arranged and numbered like this:

```
1 • • 4
2 • • 5
3 • • 6
```

A braille letter, number, or other character is made by raising one or more of the dots in the cell.

Braille graduated from the Institute when he was 19. He was invited to stay on and become a teacher. He accepted the job. He spent much of his time copying books into his code for his students to read. In 1837, he added new symbols for numbers and musical notes. Now blind students could learn math, and read and write music.

Around this time, Braille became ill with tuberculosis (TB). TB is a disease that destroys the lungs. Today, TB victims are treated with antibiotics. But in Braille's time, antibiotics hadn't yet been invented. Instead, many people died of the disease.

THE DEATH OF LOUIS BRAILLE: Braille's health grew worse. In 1844, he had to quit teaching. When he felt well enough, he was able to give a few piano lessons. But most of his time was spent in bed, where he continued to work on his alphabet. Although it wasn't yet widely used, Braille was certain it was a valuable tool for blind people.

Braille never lived to see how his alphabet changed the world for blind people. He died on January 6, 1852, at the age of 43.

HIS INVENTION: Although Braille was not well-known when he died, today his name is recognized around the world. Soon after his death, the use of the alphabet he designed, called the Braille alphabet in his honor, began to spread worldwide. Books began to be printed in Braille. His alphabet was translated into almost every known language.

Today, books in Braille are available in almost every nation. Public spaces and signs use Braille. His invention has allowed blind people to learn, achieve, and be active members of their societies. The house where Braille was born is a museum. There is a plaque on the wall honoring him. It says, "He opened the doors of knowledge to all those who cannot see".

WORLD WIDE WEB SITES:

http://afb.org/braille/louis_braille_bio.asp
http://www.louisbrailleschool.org.html

Rachel Fuller Brown
1898 - 1980
American Scientist
Co-Creator of the First Anti-Fungal Antibiotic

RACHEL FULLER BROWN WAS BORN on November 23, 1898, in Springfield, Massachusetts. Her parents were Annie Fuller and George Brown. Annie was a homemaker during Rachel's early years. Later, she worked as a secretary. George sold insurance and real estate. Rachel had a younger brother named Sumner.

RACHEL FULLER BROWN GREW UP first in Springfield, then in Webster Groves, Missouri. Her family had moved there when she was young. When she was 12, her father left the family. Rachel, her mother, and brother moved back to Springfield, Massachusetts.

RACHEL FULLER BROWN WENT TO SCHOOL at the public schools in Missouri and Massachusetts. She was a fine student. When it was time for college, a family friend paid for her to attend Mount Holyoke.

Brown originally planned to major in history. But after taking a chemistry class in college, she decided she really wanted to study that, too. So she took a double major, in history and chemistry. She graduated from Mount Holyoke in 1920.

Brown went on to graduate school at the University of Chicago. She earned her master's degree in chemistry, then began to teach at a girls' school. After finishing her master's she began her PhD. She finished her research for her doctoral degree in 1926. That same year, she began a 42-year career in medical research.

STARTING TO WORK IN MEDICAL RESEARCH: Brown's first job was as a chemist for the New York State Division of Laboratories and Research. For the first 20 years of her career, she focused on finding drugs to fight infections, like pneumonia. In 1928, **Alexander Fleming** discovered penicillin. It was the first effective and safe antibiotic. (An "antibiotic" is a drug that fights bacterial infections.) Medical researchers everywhere worked to create other antibiotics to fight life-threatening diseases.

WORKING WITH ELIZABETH LEE HAZEN: In 1948, Brown began a very important working relationship. While working as a chemist in

Dr. Brown (left) and Dr. Hazen (right) in the lab.

Albany, she was chosen to work with microbiologist **Elizabeth Lee Hazen** to develop a drug that would fight fungal infections. Fungi are found everywhere, especially in soil and plants. Like bacteria and viruses, fungi can cause serious, life-threatening infections. Fungi cause infections of the skin, mouth, throat, digestive system, and other areas of the body. Hazen was working in New York City identifying antifungal chemicals. The two worked together to develop the first antifungal antibiotic for human use.

Over the span of two years, the two scientists conducted long-distance research. Hazen collected samples of fungi found in soil. She grew cultures in her New York City lab. Then, she sent them to Brown in Albany in mason jars. In her Albany lab, Brown conducted experiments to determine the active agents in the samples. She'd identify the agents, then send them back to Hazen. Hazen would retest the sample, to see if the agent killed the fungi. If it did, she'd test the sample on animals to see if it was toxic.

The scientists faced a difficult problem. If an agent was effective against fungi, it could also be toxic to animals. To be safely used in humans, it first had to pass this important test. After two years of research, the scientists found a chemical that killed fungi, but was safe to use on animals. They named the drug Nystatin. (Named after "New York State.") Soon, it was tested on humans. It was a success. Hazen and Brown had done it. They'd invented a drug that successfully treated fungal infections.

Hazen and Brown received the **patent** for Nystatin in 1957. The drug made more than $13 million dollars in its first years. It is important to note that neither scientist ever earned money from their discovery. Instead, Hazen and Brown invested the money in a non-profit research foundation. That foundation still provides funding for medical research.

Nystatin proved to be effective in areas beyond human illness. It was used to fight infections in plants, like Dutch Elm Disease. Nystatin was also used to kill mold in old paintings and other art work.

Brown and Hazen continued to work together on antifungal research. In fact, they discovered two more antibiotics. The two scientists received many honors and awards, including the Chemical

Pioneer Award. It was especially important to Brown to provide scholarship and research money to deserving students. Brown continued to work at the New York State labs until she retired in 1968. A vaccine she developed to treat pneumonia is still used today.

RACHEL FULLER BROWN'S HOME AND FAMILY: Brown never married or had children. She died in Albany, New York, on January 14, 1980. She was 81 years old.

In a letter written the month she died, Brown stated her hopes for the future. She wrote that she wished for "equal opportunities and accomplishments for all scientists regardless of sex."

THEIR INVENTION: Hazen and Brown's invention of Nystatin is considered one of the major breakthroughs in 20th century medicine. Nystatin has been used millions of times to treat fungal infections worldwide. Hazen and Brown also inspired young women to become scientists.

In 1994, Hazen and Brown became the second and third women to enter the National Inventors Hall of Fame. They followed **Gertrude Elion**, who created many important and life-saving medicines.

WORLD WIDE WEB SITES:

http://web.mit.edu/invent/iow/HazenBrown.html
http://www.chemheritage.org/EducationalServices/pharm/
http://www.invent.org/hall_of_fame/75.html

William Seward Burroughs
1855 - 1898
American Inventor and Manufacturer
Inventor of the First Adding Machine

WILLIAM SEWARD BURROUGHS WAS BORN on January 28, 1855, in Auburn, New York. His parents were Edmund and Ellen Burroughs. Edmund was a model maker and Ellen was a homemaker. William was the third of four children.

WILLIAM SEWARD BURROUGHS GREW UP in Auburn, in upstate New York. He liked to tinker in his father's workshop.

WILLIAM SEWARD BURROUGHS WENT TO SCHOOL at the local public schools in Auburn. He only attended school until the age of 15. Then, he started to work.

FIRST JOBS: Burroughs's first job was as a clerk in a bank. At that time, there were no accurate adding machines. Earlier inventors had tried, but their machines often gave incorrect sums. Instead, clerks and accountants had to add long sums by hand, and they often made errors.

When Burroughs was 26, he moved to St. Louis, Missouri. There, he continued to work on his adding machine. His family had moved there, and he worked briefly in his father's shop.

INVENTING THE ADDING MACHINE: A local shop owner let Burroughs use his workshop to develop his machine. In 1884, Burroughs went into business with a partner, Thomas Metcalf. In 1886, the two created the American Arithmometer Company to produce their adding machine.

Burroughs's original design had a large key pad, used to enter the numbers. Pulling the handle entered the numbers and made the calculation.

Burroughs applied for a **patent** in 1885 for a "Calculating Machine." He received the patent in 1888. But there was a problem with the device. If the handle wasn't pulled just right, the calculations were incorrect. Burroughs made improvements over the next few years.

A Burroughs adding machine.

In 1893, he received a patent for an improved calculating machine. Burroughs also added a printing function that listed the items added. That allowed the user to easily check for accuracy. The user could check separate items, as well as the final calculation, on a paper tape.

The new machines were ready for production and sale. They were a great success. In 1895, the company sold 284 machines. In 1905, the company moved to Detroit, and was renamed the Burroughs Adding Machine Company. By 1928, the company had manufactured one million adding machines.

WILLIAM SEWARD BURROUGHS HOME AND FAMILY: Burroughs married Ida Selover in 1879. They had four children: Jennie, Horace, Mortimer, and Helen.

Burroughs had health problems all his life. He died on September 14, 1898, at the age of 43.

HIS INVENTION: Burroughs never lived to see the huge company that bore his name. The Burroughs Corporation became the largest adding machine company in the United States. His invention of the first reliable adding machine spurred the technology that led to electronic calculators and computers. He was elected to the Inventors Hall of Fame in 1987.

WORLD WIDE WEB SITES:

http://web.mit.edu/invent/iow/burroughs.html
http://www.invent.org.hall_of_fame/23.html

Carothers with Neoprene, c. 1930.

Wallace Carothers
1896 - 1937
American Chemist
Inventor of Neoprene, Synthetic Rubber, and
Nylon, the First Synthetic Fiber

WALLACE CAROTHERS WAS BORN on April 27, 1896, in Burlington, Iowa. His father, Ira, was a college teacher. Wallace was the oldest of four children. The family moved from Burlington to Des Moines, Iowa, when he was five.

WALLACE CAROTHERS GREW UP in Des Moines. As a boy, he loved to tinker with things. When he was in grade school, he built a crystal radio in a Quaker Oats box.

WALLACE CAROTHERS WENT TO SCHOOL at the public schools in Iowa. He was very smart. At Sabin Elementary, his friends called him "Doc." Wallace and his friends formed a club to experiment with electricity. His love of science continued in high school. While still a teenager, he turned his bedroom into a laboratory.

After high school, Carothers attended Capital City Commercial College, where he studied accounting. He finished his bachelor's degree at Tarkio College in Missouri. Still fascinated by chemistry, Carothers went to graduate school at the University of Illinois. He got his PhD in chemistry in 1924.

FIRST JOBS: After graduation, Carothers took a teaching job at Harvard. He taught for two years, then went to work for the DuPont chemical company

Carothers was a very shy man. He didn't like teaching and lecturing. He wanted to be involved in scientific research. He was happy to leave teaching and work for DuPont.

WORKING FOR DUPONT: At DuPont, Carothers headed up a lab devoted to studying "polymers." A polymer is a molecule made up of a string of smaller molecules called "monomers."

Polymers occur in nature. Carothers wanted to create them in the lab. He studied natural polymers, like the fibers cotton and silk. His search for synthetic (manufactured) polymers led him to several important inventions.

It's hard to believe that before the 1930s, people made things out of materials that had been around since the earliest humans. Wood, stone, and metals were used to make houses, buildings, ships, carts, cars, and other products. Plant and animal fibers—like cotton and silk—were used to make clothing and other items.

The new age of "synthetics"—manufactured materials—had begun. Synthetics could share the properties of age-old materials. And because they were created chemically, they wouldn't use up limited natural resources. They could also be made cheaply, so many people could benefit from them.

NEOPRENE—SYNTHETIC RUBBER: In 1930, Carothers's team developed its first major synthetic product. It was called "Neoprene," and it was synthetic rubber.

Natural rubber comes from the rubber tree plant, found in Asia. Neoprene had many advantages over natural rubber. It could be made in the lab, so it didn't have to be harvested and shipped from Asia to the U.S.

Neoprene also had qualities that made it better than natural rubber. It was heat resistant, and that made it a better material for things like tires. Tires on cars heat up from the friction created during driving. Neoprene tires resisted the heat created by friction. That made them more durable and efficient than natural rubber tires.

Neoprene became especially important after World War II began in 1939. During World War II, the U.S. and its allies fought against Japan, Germany, and Italy. The Japanese Army controlled the rubber plantations of Asia. They cut the U.S. off from its supply. So Neoprene provided a constant, inexpensive source of rubber.

NYLON—SYNTHETIC SILK: Carothers and his team next tried to create a synthetic version of silk. Silk had been used for clothing and other items for thousands of years. Silk is a natural product produced from a fiber made by silkworms. Silkworms use the fiber to make cocoons and webs. About 3,000 B.C. the Chinese discovered a way to weave the fibers into fabric. The fabric was a wonder: it could be washed and dyed, and was strong, durable, and beautiful.

Carothers's invention of Nylon led to the production of nylon stockings in 1938.

But silk was expensive. The silkworms created the fiber, then the fiber had to be made into cloth. The process made the price of silk very high.

Chemists had been trying to create synthetic silk for years when Carothers took on the task. Scientists and business people knew that the fiber would be a very successful product, for Du Pont and the world.

As happens so often with inventions, nylon was created by accident. One of the scientists working with Carothers was named

Julian Hill. One day Hill dipped a glass rod into a container containing the synthetic polymer they hoped would become the new silk. When Hill backed across the room, the polymer stuck to the rod and stretched like taffy.

The fiber was strong and elastic, but it couldn't stand up to soap or heat. So it couldn't be used for clothing. Carothers and his team went back to the drawing board. By 1935, they had developed a fabric that was strong, elastic, and could be washed and iron. They'd done it. They'd invented the first manmade fiber. They called it "nylon."

Nylon was a huge commercial success for DuPont. It was used in everything from toothbrushes to medical sutures. But the most famous product using the new fiber were nylon stockings. Women had bought expensive silk stockings for years. Now they could buy nylon hose, which were cheaper, easier to find, and more durable than silk.

Nylon stockings were a tremendous hit. When they went on sale in 1938, more than 5 million pairs were sold in just a few days. Soon nylon manufacture became a million dollar industry.

PATENTS: As a DuPont employee, Carothers filed the **patents** for Neoprene and nylon, but the patents belonged to DuPont. His inventions, funded by the company, reflected the research and work of his entire team. So while he is considered the inventor of nylon, the patent for the fiber belonged to DuPont.

In World War II (1939 - 1945) nylon was used to make everything from military clothing to parachutes to fuel tanks. After the war, sales for nylon products soared.

PERSONAL PROBLEMS: Despite his fame as a successful inventor, Carothers was a deeply unhappy man. His colleagues and friends had noticed that he was often depressed. Just days after he filed the patent for nylon, Carothers took poison and died. He was only 41 years old.

WALLACE CAROTHERS'S HOME AND FAMILY: Carothers married Helen Sweetman, who worked at Du Pont, in 1936. They had a daughter born after his death. Carothers died on April 29, 1937.

HIS INVENTION: Although he didn't live to see it, Carothers's invention of nylon brought about a new era in science. To this day, scientists are still developing new synthetic fibers. And nylon is still used in a wide variety of products, including clothing, home furnishings, and industry.

Carothers is also considered one of the most important chemists of his time. He was the first organic chemist elected to the National Academy of Sciences. At the time of his death, he'd filed more than 50 patents for his work at DuPont.

WORLD WIDE WEB SITES:

http://heritage.dupont.com/touchpoints/tp_1928/overview.shtml
http://www.invent.org/hall_of_fame/28.html
http://www.pbs.org/wgbh/aso/databank/entires/becaro.html

Willis Carrier
1876 - 1950
American Engineer and Inventor
"The Father of Air Conditioning"

WILLIS CARRIER WAS BORN on November 26, 1876, in Angola, New York. His parents were Elizabeth and Duane Carrier. They were farmers. Willis was an only child.

WILLIS CARRIER GREW UP in Angola, a small farm town in upstate New York. As an only child, he grew up surrounded by adults, including his grandparents. He was bright and inventive, and enjoyed making up games.

Carrier's mother was a special influence on him. She was very mechanical, and she could fix almost anything. She helped her young son understand fractions with a practical, simple idea. "My mother told me to bring up a pan of apples from the cellar," he recalled. "She had me cut them into halves, quarters, and eighths, then add and subtract parts. Fractions took on a new meaning. I felt as if no problems would be too hard for me. I'd simply break them down to something simple and they would be easy to solve."

WILLIS CARRIER WENT TO SCHOOL at the local public schools. He was an excellent student. He graduated from Buffalo General High School.

Carrier won a scholarship to Cornell University in Ithaca, New York. He studied mechanical engineering. At Cornell, he joined the cross country, rowing, and boxing teams. He also worked to pay for his room and board. He mowed lawns and created a student laundry for the school. He graduated in 1901.

FIRST JOBS: After college, Carrier got a job at the Buffalo Forge Company. He worked there as an engineer. His special area was heating systems. Carrier was always an innovative thinker. He realized that engineers didn't have reliable data to determine how to build dependable heating systems.

Carrier set to work developing tables, based on research data, for engineers. He started a research program that determined the quantity of heat needed to heat a specific space. Using Carrier's tables saved the company $40,000 in just one year.

Carrier became head of the experimental engineering department. His next innovation would truly change the world.

*The Sackett-Wilhelms Lithographing Company, of Brooklyn, New York,
the site of the first use of modern mechanical air conditioning, 1902.*

INVENTING AIR CONDITIONING: In 1902, Carrier was asked to solve a problem for a printing company. The Sackett-Wilhelms Lithographing Company of Brooklyn, New York had a heating—and cooling—problem. During the color printing process, the colors on the paper ran together, ruining the printed pages.

Carrier realized that uncontrolled heat and humidity in the plant caused the paper to expand and contract. When that happened, the color would run off the paper. He saw that the problem was controlling the humidity. Methodically, he determined what the humidity should be to prevent the paper from expanding and contracting. He even reviewed tables from the National Weather Service to determine the right humidity and temperature levels.

Using all that information, Carrier developed a cooling system that kept the temperature and humidity in the printing plant constant. The printing company's problem was solved. And in doing that, Carrier created the first scientific air conditioning system.

HOW DID IT WORK? Carrier's system was based on controlling the temperature of water that flowed through refrigeration coils. The coils released cooled air into a specific space. Carrier calculated the amounts of water necessary to cool the space.

Carrier continued to research and develop new systems to provide air conditioning. The demand for the service was tremendous. By 1914, he had developed air conditioning systems for all kinds of businesses, from bakeries to factories and stores.

But that year, the Buffalo Forge Company decided to get rid of his department. Carrier knew he had a good idea worth developing. He and a group of engineers pooled their money and started their own company, the Carrier Engineering Corporation.

THE CARRIER COMPANY: As head of the company, Carrier continued to develop innovative systems for air conditioning. By the 1920s, he'd created air conditioning for Madison Square Garden, the houses of Congress in Washington, D.C., even the White House. Soon, offices, theaters and stores were air conditioned. Then buses, railroad cars, and boats became air conditioned. Next, he expanded his service to homes. Now, most homes built have air conditioning. But then, it was a true innovation. Without air conditioning, the South, including Florida, Texas and Southern California, would never have been developed for homes and businesses the way they are today.

Carrier with air conditioning unit, 1922.

Air conditioning played a major part in conserving art and important documents, too. Rare books and manuscripts in libraries are kept from decaying with air conditioning. Michelangelo's frescos at the Sistine Chapel in Rome are protected from heat and humidity by a system designed by the Carrier company.

There have been controversies about Carrier's invention, too. The coolants used in most air conditioning systems are chlorofluorocarbons. Most scientists believe that they contribute to global warming. The Carrier company has produced more environmentally friendly coolants in response.

LATER LIFE: Carrier accumulated more than 80 **patents** for his air conditioning systems. He received many honors and awards in his lifetime. He was presented with important prizes in science and engineering. He received honorary degrees. Fifty years after his death, both *Time* and *Life* magazines named him one of "The Most Important People of the 20th Century." Carrier's company is still the number one producer of air conditioning equipment in the world.

WILLIS CARRIER'S HOME AND FAMILY: Carrier was married three times. He met his first wife, Edith Seymour, at Cornell. They married in 1902. Edith died in 1912. Carrier's second wife was named Jennie Martin. They were married until her death in 1939. In 1941, Carrier married Elizabeth Wise. Carrier had two adopted children. He died on October 10, 1950. He was 73 years old.

HIS INVENTION: Carrier created air conditioning systems that allowed homes, hospitals, schools, and factories to be kept at livable temperatures year round. His cooling systems affected business in many ways. Fresh produce and meats could be processed and transported to supermarkets all over the country. The modern computer industry relies on silicon chips. During manufacturing, these chips must be kept at a constant temperature. That would be impossible without air conditioning.

Prior to Carrier's inventions, summer heat in the South was so extreme that work and life would grind to a halt. With air conditioning, businesses and homes could expand in the South. The development of Florida, Texas, and other southern states for homes, vacation sites, and businesses would have been impossible without air conditioning. That is Carrier's legacy.

WORLD WIDE WEB SITES:

http://ah.bfn.org/h/carr
http://www.global.carrier.com/details
http://www.invent.org/hall_of_fame/29/html

George Washington Carver
1864(?) - 1943
American Inventor, Farmer, Educator, and Food Scientist
Created more than 300 Products Using Peanuts

GEORGE WASHINGTON CARVER WAS BORN in the Kansas Territory near Diamond Grove, Missouri. He was born a slave. George's mother, Mary, had been sold as a slave for $700 when she was 13. The German couple who owned her, Moses and Susan Carver, treated her as a farm hand rather than a slave. They gave Mary a small cabin on the farm.

Mary worked with Susan in the house and the garden. Because birth records were not kept on slaves, the exact date of George's birth is not known. However, it is likely he was born in 1864, near the end of the Civil War. There isn't a record of his father's name. It is believed that his father was a slave on a neighboring farm, who died in an accident shortly after George's birth.

At the beginning of the Civil War, in 1861, the South seceded from the Union. The country was divided, North and South, on the issue of slavery. The Northern states wanted to preserve the Union and abolish slavery. The Southern states wanted slavery to continue, and to extend into the territories. Because Missouri bordered states allied with both the North and South, soldiers from both sides fought bloody battles not far from Diamond Grove.

One night a band of soldiers rode onto Moses Carver's farm and kidnapped Mary and her baby, George. The soldiers took them to Arkansas. Moses Carver sent a man to find them but he returned with only George. No one ever knew what happened to Mary. George grew up never knowing his mother.

The Carvers had no children of their own. They raised George as their own son, even giving him their last name.

GEORGE WASHINGTON CARVER GREW UP where almost everything the family needed came from the farm. They grew fruits and vegetables, raised livestock, and spun fabric for clothing from flax and wool. Moses Carver was also a bee keeper with more than 50 hives.

George was a sickly child who suffered from breathing problems. He was also small for his age. He helped Susan plant and weed the gardens. He picked fruit, milked cows, and gathered eggs from the hens. He also helped in the house doing laundry, cleaning, and cooking.

George loved working in the garden and exploring the woods. He liked learning to do new things and was always asking questions.

THE PLANT DOCTOR: George developed a keen interest in plants at an early age. He wondered why some flowers grew in the sun and some in the shade. He noticed that plants with the same roots produced flowers that were different colors. He collected leaves, seeds, and tree bark. He took care of the flowers around the Carver house so carefully that people began asking him how they could make their own gardens thrive. "Love them," was his answer.

Soon people were bringing their sick plants to Carver. His careful attention to the details of nature helped him learn how to nurse sick plants back to health. He became known as "The Plant Doctor" in Diamond Grove.

EARLY SCHOOLING: Before the Civil War there were laws against teaching slaves to read and write. After the war, African-Americans supposedly gained the right to an education. But George was not allowed to attend the local school because he was black. Missouri's racist laws allowed schools to bar blacks from attending.

George taught himself to read from a copy of "Webster's Elementary Spelling Book." Moses Carver hired the village school teacher to tutor him. But George wanted more. So when he was about 12 years old, he left the farm and walked eight miles to Neosho, Missouri, where there was a one-room schoolhouse that he could attend.

In Neosho, George lived with an African-American couple, Andrew and Mariah Watkins, who had no children of their own. Andrew did odd jobs around town and Mariah worked as a midwife and laundry woman. When she had to leave home to help someone have a baby, George took over the cooking and the laundry. They lived next door to the school. During recess George didn't play with the other children. Instead, he walked home to help wash clothes.

In 1878, when he was about 14 years old, George earned a certificate of merit from the school. He moved to Fort Scott, Kansas, and began working for a family. In Fort Scott, he went to a school that was mostly white. One night he witnessed a brutal act of racist violence.

On March 26, 1879, George was running an errand when he saw an angry group of white people beat a black man to death. They dragged the body to the village square and set it on fire. It horrified George, and he feared for his own life. He left town that night. But he never forgot the hateful act of racism as long as he lived.

SCHOOLING: School continued to be important to George. When he left Fort Scott, he traveled to Olathe, Kansas. There, he became a housekeeper for the Seymour family and attended the local high school. When the Seymours moved to Minneapolis, Kansas, George moved with them. He attended school and opened his own laundry business. Although the students at school were mostly white and George was older than most of them, he got along with everyone. He finished high school in 1884, when he was 20 years old. It is not

Carver at his graduation from Iowa State, 1894.

known if he ever received a diploma.

In the town of Minneapolis there was another person with the name of George Carver. This is when George added a "W" as his middle name so people could tell the two men apart. When someone asked him what the "W" stood for, he replied "Washington." But he never used Washington as part of his name. He was always George W. Carver.

In 1885, Carver applied by mail to Highland College, in Highland, Kansas. He was accepted, but when he arrived on campus, college officials would not let him attend because he was black. Since he had spent all his money getting there, Carver had to stay and work to save up enough money to move on.

Once again, he did laundry and cooking until he'd saved enough money. Then, he moved to Beeler, Kansas. There he worked for a farmer and saved up enough money to buy some land. He built a sod house, with a special addition. On the south side he built a room with large windows where he kept a collection of plants he gathered from the woods.

Life was hard on the farm. After four years, Carver sold his homestead for $300 and moved east to Winterset, Iowa. There, he heard about Simpson College, 25 miles away in Indianola. Carver walked all the way, arriving with almost nothing. After he paid his tuition, he had 15 cents left. He set up a laundry service and made enough money to pay for his classes.

Carver studied art and music. He was a talented artist but his art teacher, Miss Etta Budd, worried that it would be hard for an African-American man to make a living as an artist. She encouraged Carver to study agriculture.

Luckily, Budd's father was a professor at the Iowa State College of Agriculture and Mechanical Arts. (It's now called Iowa State University). Budd and her father helped Carver change the course of his studies. He became the first black student at Iowa State College.

COLLEGE LIFE: At college, Carver continued to face racial prejudice. Because he was black, he wasn't allowed to stay in the dormitories. He wasn't allowed to eat in the dining hall with the other students.

Somehow, he was able to overcome the prejudice and eagerly took part in many college activities. He joined the debate club, trained football players, and joined the college militia. He worked at many jobs to pay his tuition. Over the years, he worked as a janitor, waiter, and gardener in the college farms.

Carver was a good student, especially in chemistry. He continued to study art outside of class. He loved painting the plants and flowers he studied in the fields. In 1893, his sketch of the rose *Yucca gloriosa* won first prize at the Columbian Exposition in Chicago.

Creamery operators class, Iowa State, 1894.
Carver is second from right in the back row.

CARVER THE TEACHER: In 1894, at the age of 30, Carver earned a Bachelor of Science degree in agriculture. He was offered a job working with a florist, but he decided to continue to study for a master's degree.

While working on his master's, Carver taught biology at Iowa State. He was also in charge of the greenhouse and worked in a lab where he studied plant diseases. He was the first African-American on the staff at Iowa State. Carver continued to make excellent drawings of plants. He completed his master's degree in agriculture in 1896.

TUSKEGEE INSTITUTE: That same year, Carver received a letter that would give him the chance to accomplish another of his goals:

to improve the lives and opportunities of his fellow African-Americans.

Booker T. Washington was a former slave who had founded the Tuskegee Institute in Tuskegee, Alabama, for African-American students. Like Carver, Washington wanted to help black people improve their lives by teaching them practical skills like carpentry and farming. Washington offered Carver a job at the Institute. Carver felt the offer was his chance to make a difference. He accepted the job and became head of the agricultural department at Tuskegee.

THE SCIENCE OF FARMING: When Carver arrived in Alabama, he was struck by the poverty of the former slaves. Although they were free, they had to rent land from white farmers and grow what the farmers told them to grow. In Alabama, that meant cotton. Carver also noticed that the land was worn out. Even with hard work, it was impossible to make the soil yield enough crops, so the farmers could make enough money to live. Carver decided to show these new farmers how to make a good living. He wanted to teach them that science could make farming more profitable.

Word of Carver's teaching quickly spread. In his first year at Tuskegee, he had only 13 students. By the second year he had 75. Using land given by the Alabama government, Carver and his students began experiments to rebuild the worn out soil.

CROP ROTATION: Carver knew that different plants required different types of soil. He taught his students his theory of "crop rotation." By alternating, or changing the plants grown each year, the soil could be made richer and better able to produce big and healthy crops. It was a breakthrough in farming.

Carver's first Faculty and Farmer's Institute, Tuskegee Institute.

FINDING THE FARMERS: Carver shared his knowledge with many local farmers. But he knew there were many more who needed to learn. He decided to travel around the South to reach them. In 1906, Carver created a moveable school. He called it the Jesup Wagon, named after Morris K. Jesup, a New York banker who gave him the money to pay for the traveling school. Carver and his students began giving demonstrations to farmers on weekends. They showed them tools to help with farming and shared techniques to help them increase their crop yields.

Traveling around Alabama, Carver noticed how different the farms were from the farm where he had lived as a boy. Farmers in Alabama only grew cotton. They didn't have vegetable gardens that would give them food. Most didn't raise chickens, pigs, and cows that could provide protein.

More than 2,000 farmers a month came to see Carver's demonstrations. He encouraged them to plant vegetable gardens and showed them how to preserve meat. He also told them to take pride in their farming. He encouraged them to save a little money each day so they could one day buy their own land.

FROM COTTON TO PEANUTS: Throughout his life, Carver learned the most by paying close attention to nature. He believed that nature was the greatest teacher. His experiments focused on improving soil, finding out about plant diseases, and finding new ways to use plants.

While Carver was experimenting with crop rotation, he discovered that peanuts put "nutrients" back into the soil that cotton took out. In other words, if a farmer planted cotton one year and peanuts the next, the soil would stay rich. Growing peanuts also gave southern farmers another crop to sell.

At first, farmers were not interested in growing peanuts. They didn't think there was much use for them and they knew they could sell cotton. Their minds changed when the boll weevil insect destroyed entire fields of cotton. With their cotton crop ruined, they looked to peanuts.

Soon farmers had more peanuts than they could use. They fed peanuts to their animals. But there were still storehouses filled with them. The extra crop lay rotting in the fields.

Carver devoted himself to finding a way to use peanuts. In his laboratory he separated the peanut into all its parts. He found

Carver working in the lab at Tuskegee Institute.

starches, oils, fats, and proteins. He then began experimenting, and discovered more than 300 products that could be made from peanuts.

OTHER DISCOVERIES: In addition to his work with peanuts, Carver used the clay soil of Alabama to create dyes. He created more than 60 products from the pecan nut and about 100 products from the common sweet potato. Studying soybeans, he discovered a crop that could be used to make many things, from oils to plastics. He also created what he called "fruit leathers" by mashing over-ripe fruit to a pulp, rolling it out like pie crust, drying it, and then cutting it into strips.

A GREAT HUMANITARIAN: Carver never got rich from his discoveries. His goal was to help farmers raise crops that would make money and give them healthy food to eat. News spread of his work and before long he became famous. He was invited to help out in nationwide efforts to increase crops, and in worldwide efforts to fight hunger.

In 1918 the U.S. government invited Carver to Washington, D.C., to discuss his discoveries. That year, U.S. troops were fighting in World War I in Europe. During the war, trade had broken off, and it was difficult to import dyes. Using American-grown products, Carver produced dyes that were used to make camouflage uniforms for soldiers. The government was also interested in his fruit leather because it was lightweight and easy to carry—perfect for soldiers. Because of the war there was also a world-wide food shortage. The U.S. government wanted to learn about the products Carver had created from peanuts, sweet potatoes, and other crops.

Thomas Edison was interested in Carver's work on producing rubber from the sweet potato. He offered him a large salary to come work in his lab in New Jersey.

Henry Ford was interested in using agricultural products in industry. This common interest led Ford and Carver to become friends. In addition, Carver was invited to speak all over the world.

During the last 20 years of his life, he shared his knowledge of plants to help improve crops and fight hunger.

LAST DAYS: In March 1941, the George Washington Carver Museum was opened in Tuskegee, Alabama. Mr. and Mrs. Henry Ford were there to dedicate the collection that included plants, minerals, products made from peanuts and sweet potatoes, original paintings, and equipment from Carver's first laboratory. By this time, Carver was weak and frail.

In July 1942, Carver traveled to Dearborn, Michigan, where Henry Ford had founded Greenfield Village. In the Village, Ford had included a replica of the log cabin where Carver had lived as a child. Carver spent several weeks in Dearborn before returning to Tuskegee.

One day in December 1942, Carver suffered a serious fall. He never really recovered. On January 5, 1943, he lay down for a nap and never woke up. He is buried next to his friend, Booker T. Washington, on the Tuskegee Institute campus.

GEORGE WASHINGTON CARVER'S HOME AND FAMILY: Carver never married because, he said, he "didn't have time." He left his life earnings to the Tuskegee Institute to build a research facility where his work could be carried on after he was gone.

HIS INVENTIONS: During his lifetime, Carver helped thousands of southern farmers improve their lives by using his system of crop rotation. He later developed peanuts as a major crop that led to discoveries in agriculture and industry. These innovations helped fight hunger throughout the world. Carver received many awards and honors during his lifetime. Nearly 40 years after his death, he was among the first individuals inducted into the Inventors Hall of Fame.

WORLD WIDE WEB SITES:

http://www.lib.iastate.edu/spcl/gwc/home.html
http://www.invent.org/hall_of_fame/30.html
http://www.nps.gov/gwca/expanded/auto_bio.htm

Jacques Cousteau
1910 - 1997
French Ocean Explorer, Film Producer, and Inventor
Inventor of SCUBA Diving Equipment

JACQUES COUSTEAU WAS BORN on June 11, 1910, near Bordeaux, France. His name is pronounced "zhahk koos-TOE." His parents were Daniel and Elizabeth Cousteau. Daniel was a lawyer and Elizabeth was a homemaker. Jacques had an older brother named Pierre.

JACQUES COUSTEAU GREW UP in many different places. His father's work took the family around the world. When he was eight, the family moved to New York for his father's job. They moved back to Paris two years later, but still continued to travel often.

Even when he was little, Cousteau loved the sea."When I was four or five years old, I loved touching water," he recalled. "Water fascinated me. First floating ships, then me floating."

He started inventing when he was just a boy, too. He built a model crane when he was 11. At 13, he designed a car that ran on batteries. He got a camera at 15 and started making movies.

JACQUES COUSTEAU WENT TO SCHOOL at schools in New York and France. He was very bright, but not very interested in school. He was expelled from one high school for bad behavior. Finally, when he entered the French Naval College, he was studying what he loved. He did very well. He graduated from the Naval College in 1933.

THE NAVY: As a young Navy seaman, Cousteau sailed around the world. He planned to become a Navy pilot, but a serious car accident ended that dream. Instead, he worked on Navy ships at sea for several years. He also began his lifelong career as a diver. He started to experiment with a breathing device that would let a diver stay underwater for long periods of time.

When World War II broke out in 1939, France came under control of the German Nazis. Cousteau was part of the "Underground." That was a group of people who fought to defeat the Nazis, within France. In 1945, Germany was defeated, and Cousteau received several awards for bravery.

Even during the war, Cousteau continued to dive and invent. He became an expert undersea diver and made underwater films. He also came up with one of the major inventions in undersea exploration.

INVENTING SCUBA: Cousteau was still trying to find a way for divers to breathe underwater. In 1943, he and a French engineer developed equipment now used worldwide: SCUBA. SCUBA stands for "self-contained underwater breathing apparatus." It was manufactured under the name "Aqualung."

This ground-breaking invention contained tanks of oxygen connected to a breathing device. It allowed divers to stay underwater for hours.

Cousteau's inventions didn't stop with SCUBA. He also developed ways to use a television camera underwater. He even created an underwater research colony. The Conshelf Program was a laboratory under the sea, where scientists lived and worked for months at a time.

In 1946, Cousteau bought the *Calypso*. He converted the boat into a floating exploration ship. It had a diving platform and an underwater observation chamber. And it became famous to viewers around the world. Cousteau began a series of journeys on the *Calypso*, which he captured on film. On his many expeditions he explored the world's oceans and the plants and animals living there. Combining his devotion to the oceans and to filmmaking, Cousteau produced several award-winning films. He also wrote several best-selling books about his adventures.

Cousteau looks out from a two-man underwater observation chamber, 1959.

Cousteau became the head of several important scientific groups. Through these, he developed research programs for scientists. He also started the Cousteau Society. It is a group devoted to the study and protection of the environment.

"THE UNDERSEA WORLD OF JACQUES COUSTEAU": In 1968, Cousteau brought the ocean world to television viewers all over the globe. That year, the first show in his series "The Undersea World of Jacques Cousteau" was broadcast. Using his skill as a filmmaker and his knowledge of ocean life, Cousteau brought the beauty and mystery of the seas to millions. Through the series, he also made people aware of the dangers of pollution.

Cousteau continued his travels, filmmaking, and writing until his death on June 25, 1997. He was 86 years old.

JACQUES COUSTEAU'S HOME AND FAMILY: Cousteau married his wife, Simone, in 1937. They had two sons, Jean-Michel and Philippe. Working with his father, Philippe became a diver and moviemaker. Sadly, he died in a plane crash in 1979.

HIS INVENTION: Using the equipment he invented, Cousteau made discoveries that changed the way we think about the undersea world. He brought that world alive to millions in his films. He presented the beauty and wonder of ocean life, while alerting the world to the dangers of undersea pollution. At his death, the chairman of the National Geographic Society, Gilbert Grosvenor, said, "The ocean environment has lost its greatest champion."

WORLD WIDE WEB SITES:

http://www.cousteausociety.org
http://marine.rutgers.edu/pt/home.htm

Seymour Cray
1925 - 1996
American Computer Designer
Inventor of the First "Supercomputer"

SEYMOUR CRAY WAS BORN on September 28, 1925, in Chippewa Falls, Wisconsin. His parents were Seymour and Lillian Cray. His father was an engineer and his mother was a homemaker. Seymour had one sister, Carol.

SEYMOUR CRAY GREW UP loving science and radio. He built his own telegraph machine when he was 10 years old. It could translate holes punched in paper into Morse code, which had been invented by **Samuel Morse.** His parents bought him a home chemistry set, and he made a lab in his basement. He said that he was a "nerd" before the word was invented.

SEYMOUR CRAY WENT TO SCHOOL at the local public schools in Chippewa Falls. He was an excellent student. In high school, he taught physics class when the teacher was absent.

WORLD WAR II: Cray was in high school when the U.S. entered World War II in 1941. He enlisted after he graduated, and worked as an Army radio operator in Europe. Then he went to the Philippines, where he helped break the Japanese Army's secret code. That helped defeat the Japanese and end the war.

After the war ended in 1945, Cray went back to school. He enrolled at the University of Wisconsin, then transferred to the University of Minnesota. He graduated from Minnesota in 1950, with a degree in electrical engineering. Cray decided to continue on and earned a master's degree in math in 1951.

FIRST JOBS: Cray's first job out of college was with Engineering Research Associates. There, he got a chance to work on the first commercial computers. These computers were far different from the ones we have today.

FIRST COMPUTERS: The first computers were huge machines. Just one computer could fill an entire room. And it didn't have the power or speed of just one of today's PCs.

But like today's computers, the early versions worked on the same principle.

A BRIEF HISTORY OF COMPUTERS: The root word of "computer" tells the origin of the machine. Computers "compute"—that is, they perform math calculations. The earliest "computer" was actually an adding machine. It was created in 1642 by Frenchman Blaise Pascal. Pascal's machine was simple. He entered numbers into a machine using dials. Inside the machine were cogs and wheels connected to the dials. They moved according to the numbers entered. The machine could add and subtract numbers.

The next major step forward happened in the 1800s. Charles Babbage, a British mathematician, designed a machine to process numbers. It had many of the features of a modern computer. It had an input mechanism (like a keyboard), storage (memory), a computing mechanism (CPU), and an output mechanism (a computer screen or printer). Babbage never built his machine. But his research was very influential.

The first modern computers were developed during World War II (1939 - 1945). Mathematician Howard Aiken developed the Mark 1, a computer that ran on electromechanical relays. It helped improve the accuracy of Navy artillery.

Another advance from the World War II era came about through the research of Alan Turing. Turing invented the "Colossus," a computer that broke the Nazi military code. It helped end the war in Europe. "Colossus" was important for another reason. It was the first computer to use vacuum tubes to store and process data.

The next major innovation in computers was the ENIAC. (That stands for the Electronic Numerical Integrator and Calculator). Previous computers were used for military purposes. The ENIAC was the first computer for general, commercial use. It was enormous: it weighed 30 tons, and used more than 17,000 vacuum tubes.

In 1948, John Bardeen, William Schockley, and Walter Brattain invented the transistor. It was another tremendous breakthrough. Transistors replaced vacuum tubes with smaller, cooler processors.

The integrated circuit, invented by Jack Kilby in 1958, introduced the true modern era in computing. Now one silicon microchip could hold millions of electronic components. It revolutionized the industry.

CONTROL DATA CORPORATION: It was in this era that Cray started his own computer company. He and William Norris formed Control Data Corporation (CDC) in 1957. Cray knew the advantages of the transistor, and he used it to make the CDC 1604. It was the first commercial computer to use transistors instead of vacuum tubes. The CDC 1604 was a success, and Cray was on his way.

But Cray didn't like the business-side of computers. He wanted to be off by himself, inventing. His business partner obliged. For the next several years, Cray spent most of his time in a lab where he designed the next generation of computers. These became the first "supercomputers."

THE CDC 6600: In 1963, Cray announced the CDC 6600. It was the most powerful computer that had ever been built. It could handle 3 million computations per second. He'd also designed it to use

Freon, a gas that could keep the 350,000 transistors that ran the computer cool.

The 6600 was the first of many machines Cray invented. Each was more powerful than the next. Each could handle even more computations. His next major supercomputer, the CDC 7600, could process 15 million computations per second.

Cray's machines were bought by the government for military use. They were purchased by weather forecasting organizations. They were used to predict storms and long-term forecasts.

Cray was ready to continue creating even bigger, more powerful machines. But CDC was going in a different direction. So he decided to leave and start off on his own again.

CRAY RESEARCH: In 1972, he started Cray Research. He wanted to create a machine so powerful it could create "simulations." At that time, computers were not powerful enough to provide the computer modeling we're used to today. These early Cray computers produced the first computer-generated 3-D models.

THE CRAY-1: The Cray-1 was the first computer Cray produced for his new firm. It came out in 1976, and was an amazing 10 times faster than any computer the world had ever seen. Cray sold one to the National Center for Atmospheric Research for $8.8 million. He sold another to the Los Alamos labs in New Mexico. That is where the first atomic bombs had been created, during World War II. The scientists at Los Alamos used the Cray-1 to create simulations of nuclear explosions.

Cray with the Cray-1 computer, 1976.

THE CRAY-2: Cray still drove himself to create faster computers. In 1985 he unveiled the Cray-2. It could process an incredible 1.2 billion operations per second. It could process data at a rate that was 50,000 times faster than the personal computers (PCs) of the era. The kinds of problems that used to take years to solve could be solved in one second on the Cray-2.

Cray's supercomputers changed the way science was done. One was bought by NASA to design components for spacecraft. Drug

The Cray-2 computer, 1984.

companies used them to create new, improved medicines. His company flourished, as four out of five supercomputers used worldwide were made by his company.

But the market, and technology, were changing. The PCs that were being produced by 1990 were capable of much faster processing. And scientists were learning that they could link PCs together and work on a problem. Cray rejected that thinking. He proposed an even more powerful supercomputer, the Cray-3.

THE CRAY-3: Once again, Cray wanted to devote himself to pure invention, not business. So he moved to Colorado Springs and

119

started to work on his new machine. But Cray faced problems that delayed the project. He missed an important deadline in 1991, and the buyer of the Cray-3 backed out. His company went broke.

SRC COMPUTER: Cray refused to give up. He started another new company, SRC Computer, in 1996. But he never realized his plans for the Cray-3. In September 1996, he was in a serious car accident. He never recovered, and died on October 5, 1996. He was mourned throughout the computer world.

SEYMOUR CRAY'S HOME AND FAMILY: Cray was married twice. He married his first wife, Verene, in 1947. They had three children, Susan, Carolyn, and Steven. They divorced in 1975. In 1980, Cray married his second wife, Geri Harrand.

HIS INVENTIONS: Cray designed and built the first supercomputers. He is considered one of the most important inventors and innovators in the history of computing. His supercomputers were able to advance science in areas as different as spacecraft, nuclear engineering, weather forecasting, and medicine. A year after his death, he was inaugurated into the Inventors Hall of Fame.

WORLD WIDE WEB SITES:

http://americanhistory.si.edu/collections/comphist/cray.htm
http://www.cbi.umn.edu/exhibits/cray/
http://www.invent.org/hall_of_fame/35.html

Gottlieb Daimler
1834 - 1900
German Engineer and Industrialist
Inventor of the First Four-Wheeled Automobile,
First Motorcycle and First Gasoline Engine

GOTTLIEB DAIMLER WAS BORN on March 17, 1834, in Schorndorf, Germany (near Stuttgart). His name is pronounced GOT-leeb DIME-ler. His parents were Johannes and Wilhelmine Daimler. His father was a master baker. He ran a bakery and tavern that had been owned by his family for generations. His mother was a homemaker. Gottlieb had three brothers, Johannes, Karl, and Christian.

GOTTLIEB DAIMLER GREW UP in Schorndorf. The family lived above his father's bakery.

EDUCATION: Gottlieb's father wanted his son to get a classical education and work in the civil service. But Gottlieb was interested in mechanics and engineering. In 1848, he went to a technical school in nearby Stuttgart. While he was studying, he also worked as an apprentice in a gun factory.

FIRST JOBS: In 1853 Gottlieb went to work at a steam engine factory in Strassburg. After four years, he went back to school, and finished his training as a mechanical engineer at the Stuttgart Polytechnic school. He returned to Strassburg and worked in the factory, but then became interested in alternatives to the steam engine.

In 1862 Daimler toured England and France. During his travels, he saw the new internal combustion gas engine that the Belgian inventor Etienne Lenoir (1822 - 1900) had built. When he returned to Germany, Daimler spent the next several years working as an engineer at a number of factories.

In 1872 Daimler went to work for Nikolaus Otto (1832-1891) at the Deutz Engine Works. There, he met another engineer named Karl Maybach. They soon became close friends. Together they worked on refining the new four-stroke engine that Otto invented. At the time, Otto's engine was considered the most advanced in the world. But it still used illuminating gas for fuel. This resulted in an engine that was big and heavy, and ran slowly. Daimler wanted to build a lightweight, high-speed engine.

THE INTERNAL COMBUSTION ENGINE: All engines require heat in order to work. Heat causes the gas in the cylinder to expand, which provides the force to move the piston. The steam engines created by **James Watt** and others are examples of "external combustion" engines. That means that the heat is produced away from the piston. In a steam engine the heat (or combustion) is applied to a

boiler, to make steam. The steam then goes to the cylinder, where the pressure moves the piston.

In an "internal combustion" engine, the heat (or combustion) takes place inside the cylinder. The first internal combustion engine used a gunpowder charge to move the piston. This wasn't practical. In 1860 Etienne Lenoir developed the first practical internal combustion engine. It used illuminating gas as the fuel. Illuminating gas, also called coal gas, is a mixture of hydrogen, methane, and ethylene.

The next major advance came in 1876, when Nikolaus Otto built the first four-stroke engine. The Otto engine operated in four separate steps, or strokes:

Intake stroke: The air-fuel mixture moves into the cylinder as the piston slides down.

Compression stroke: The piston slides up, compressing the mixture.

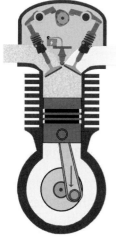   

Intake stroke   Compression stroke   Power stroke   Exhaust stroke

1886 Daimler Motor Carriage.

Power stroke: The mixture is ignited, and the pressure from the burning mixture pushes the piston back down.

Exhaust stroke: The exhaust fumes from the burnt mixture is pushed out of the cylinder as the piston slides back up.

This is basically the way most internal combustion engines work today. Otto's first engines still used illuminating gas as fuel. In 1882, Daimler and Maybach developed the carburetor, which made it possible for the engine to use liquid fuel (gasoline). They also developed an improved method for ignition. These refinements finally made it possible to build a lightweight and portable engine.

THE FIRST AUTOMOBILE: In 1882 Daimler and Maybach left the Deutz company and went to work on a light, high-speed gasoline-powered engine on their own. Its design was similar to the Otto four-stroke design, but it featured a new hot-tube ignition system.

Their first successful gasoline engine was finished in 1883. In 1884, they attached a small one-cylinder engine to a bicycle. It was the world's first motorcycle.

In 1886, Daimler and Maybach attached one of their engines to a horse carriage. Power was transferred to the wheels with a belt drive, and a tiller was added to steer the carriage. Daimler's motorized coach was the world's first four-wheel gasoline automobile. (His chief competitor, **Karl Benz**, had created the first three-wheel automobile in 1885.)

DAIMLER MOTOR COMPANY: The cost of running his workshop had used up most of Daimler's own money. He received financial support from wealthy partners and founded the Daimler Motor Company in 1890. They began building gasoline engines for use in cars, boats, and airships.

Disagreements with their partners led first Maybach, and then Daimler to leave the company. They continued to work together, refining the gasoline engine on their own. The company struggled financially without the leadership of its founders. The owners tried to rehire Maybach, but he refused to return unless they also hired Daimler. Finally, the two returned to Daimler Motor Company in 1895.

THE MERCEDES: In 1897 the company began receiving orders for automobiles from Emil Jellinek. Jellinek was a wealthy Austrian diplomat who lived in France, and was an early car enthusiast. He was interested in racing as well as driving, and kept demanding faster cars. In 1898, he bought two Daimler Phoenix models, which featured a front-mounted eight-horsepower engine. They were the world's first automobiles with four-cylinder engines.

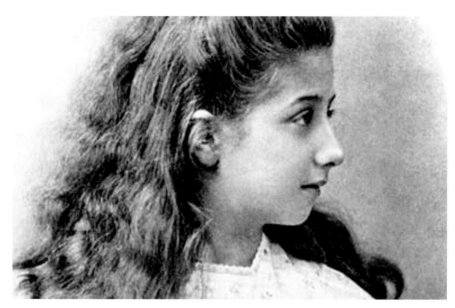

Mercedes Jellinek, for whom the Mercedes car was named.

These new models created a sensation. Jellinek became an automobile dealer, and ordered larger numbers of cars from Daimler to sell to his wealthy friends. He named these models after his daughter, Mercedes. By 1902, "Daimler-Mercedes" became an official product name.

Gottlieb did not live to see the success of the Mercedes. He suffered from heart disease for several years, and died on March 6, 1900. He was 65 years old.

GOTTLIEB DAIMLER'S HOME AND FAMILY: Daimler was married twice. He married his first wife, Emma Kurtz, on November 9, 1867. She died on July 28, 1889. In 1892, Gottlieb met Lina Hartmann in Italy, while he was recovering from a heart ailment. They were married on July 8, 1893.

MERCEDES-BENZ: Karl Benz and Gottlieb Daimler developed their vehicles within months of each other, and were rivals in the early

The first Mercedes, 1901.

automobile business. Although they were certainly aware of each other's efforts, they never met. Gottlieb Daimler died in 1900 just as the automotive industry was beginning to grow.

Germany faced an economic depression after World War I ended in 1918. In 1926, Benz & Co. merged with Daimler-Mercedes in order to increase their chances of survival. The new company was called Mercedes-Benz. Karl Benz served on the board of directors until his death in 1929.

HIS INVENTION: Gottlieb Daimler and his friend Wilhelm Maybach produced the first practical gasoline internal combustion engine. Its light weight and high speeds made it possible to power vehicles. They also built the first motorcycle, and the first four-wheel gasoline automobile.

It is interesting to note that Daimler's and Benz's automobiles had less of an impact on European society than **Henry Ford's**

Model-T did on American life. That is because their cars were more expensive and weren't mass-produced. So they didn't become a common purchase for most people at the time of their invention. It wasn't until after World War II that Europeans began to buy cars in similar numbers to Americans.

Almost 100 years after Daimler's death, the Mercedes-Benz company merged with the American car company Chrysler. The DaimlerChrysler Corporation is now one of the largest automobile manufacturers in the world. So Daimler's name lives on in the industry he helped create.

WORLD WIDE WEB SITES:

http://www.autonews.com/files/euroauto/inductees/daimler.htm
http://www.daimlerchrysler.com/emb_classic/
http://www.mercedes-benz.com/content/mbcom/international/

Damadian (left) with first MRI scanner, 1977.

Raymond Damadian
1936 -
American Inventor and Businessman
Invented the Magnetic Resonance Imaging (MRI) Scanner

RAYMOND DAMADIAN WAS BORN on March 16, 1936, in Forest Hills, New York.

RAYMOND DAMADIAN GREW UP a very curious child. He loved to learn how things worked.

RAYMOND DAMADIAN WENT TO SCHOOL at the local schools and did very well. He was an excellent violin player, too. For high school, Damadian attended the Julliard School. That's one of the finest music schools in the country, offering both high school and college degrees.

Damadian graduated at 16. At first he thought he would become a professional violinist. But when his beloved grandmother died of cancer, he decided to study medicine.

Damadian went to college at the University of Wisconsin. There, he studied math and physics. He graduated from Wisconsin in 1956. Damadian went to medical school at Albert Einstein College in New York. He finished medical school in 1960.

Damadian wanted to be a researcher, instead of a doctor who sees patients. He wanted to make medical discoveries that could help many people. Over the next 10 years he did research in kidney disease, physics, and chemistry. He worked at several places, including Washington University, Harvard, and the School of Aerospace Medicine.

FIRST JOBS: When his studies were over, Damadian served in the Air Force. When he was discharged, he became a professor at the State University of New York. He began to study the science of "magnetic resonance."

MAGNETIC RESONANCE: Magnetic resonance is a diagnostic technology. Like the x-ray, invented by **Wilhelm Roentgen**, magnetic resonance is an imaging technology that allows doctors to see inside the human body.

In magnetic resonance, a patient is scanned by a machine that sends out a powerful magnetic field. The body puts out magnetic signals in response to the rays. These signals create an image. This image is transferred to a computer. The computer then creates a three-dimensional image of the interior of the body.

INVENTING THE MRI SCANNER: Damadian had a theory. He thought that healthy organs would look different from diseased organs when scanned with magnetic resonance. He created the Magnetic Resonance Imaging (MRI) scanner to check for diseases.

Damadian built the first MRI scanner in 1977. It took seven years to complete, so he called it the "Indomitable." The first MRI scan was done on Damadian's assistant, Larry Minkoff.

THE FONAR CORPORATION: In 1978, Damadian founded the FONAR Corporation to build MRIs. But his scanner was not immediately successful. Damadian had a hard time getting funding to develop the scanner. He applied for a **patent** for the technology. Yet even though he received the patent for the MRI, Damadian had many other competitors who were also creating scanners. He was involved in patent infringement lawsuits against other companies that he claimed used his technology without the right to do so.

Damadian continued to make improvements to his scanner. As the technology improved, so did the abilities of the MRI scanner. Today's MRI scanners produce images of organs and tissues that are more detailed than x-rays. It can detect cancer and other diseases at earlier stages than other technology. By finding a disease early, doctors have a better chance of successfully treating it. Also, MRI scanners are not harmful to the body. X-rays can be harmful, because of the large doses of radiation they use.

Today MRI scanners, made by FONAR and other companies, are used in hospitals and laboratories around the world.

THE NOBEL CONTROVERSY: In 2003, the Nobel Prize committee awarded its prize in medicine to two scientists who had helped develop magnetic resonance imaging. But Damadian was not one of them. He was furious. He took out full-page ads in newspapers to bring the issue to the public.

Some scientists believed Damadian had been wrongly overlooked. Others thought that he did not deserve the prize. They thought that the two scientists who won, Paul Lauterbur and Peter Mansfield, had done more to develop the technology.

But Damadian has won other honors and awards. In 1989, he was inducted into the National Inventors Hall of Fame. In 2001, he was given the Lifetime Achievement Award for Invention and Innovation by the Lemelson-MIT Program.

Damadian continues to work and invent. He has over 45 patents to date. Most of his patents are improvements of the MRI technology.

HIS INVENTION: The MRI scanner has greatly improved medical diagnosis and treatment. It allows doctors to see inside the body and determine the location of cancer or other diseases. It can detect disease early, so a patient can receive treatment early. This has helped saved thousands of lives worldwide.

WORLD WIDE WEB SITES:

http://web.mit.edu/invent/a-winners/a-damadian.html
http://www.fonar.com/discovery.htm
http://www.invent.org/hall_of_fame/36.html

LEONARDO DA VINCI PITT. SCVL. E ARCHI.
FIORENTINO

L. da Vinci Pinſit   Colombini
                                                        56

Leonardo Da Vinci
1452 - 1519
Italian Artist, Inventor, Scientist, and Engineer

LEONARDO DA VINCI WAS BORN on April 15, 1452, in Vinci, near
Florence, Italy. His name means "Leonardo from Vinci." People of
his time didn't always have last names, the way we do now. Instead,
they were known by their first names.

His father was Ser Peiro da Vinci. He was a notary from a wealthy family. (A notary is an official who certifies public documents, like deeds.) His mother was a servant girl named Caterina. His parents never married. At that time, a child born to unmarried parents had a very limited future. Leonardo couldn't go to the best schools. He wasn't able to pursue whatever job he wanted, either.

LEONARDO DA VINCI GREW UP with his father. He learned to read, and read books from his father's library. From a very young age, Leonardo was an excellent artist. When he was 15, his father sent him to study with the famous Italian artist Andrea del Verrocchio. He was Verrocchio's apprentice for 10 years.

BECOMING AN ARTIST: With Verrocchio, Leonardo absorbed the spirit of the artistic movement known as the Renaissance. In that spirit, and with his own talent and vision, he created some of the greatest masterpieces in the history of art.

THE RENAISSANCE: The Renaissance was an era that began in the late 1300s in Italy, then spread throughout Europe. The word "renaissance" is French for "rebirth." It was a time of great social and artistic change. It was, in fact, a rebirth of ideas from ancient times.

Scholars of Leonardo's time rediscovered the great works of ancient Greece and Rome. These works of art and literature caused a change in people's way of thinking. In writers like Plato and Sophocles, they found ideas about art, society, and philosophy. In the sculptures of ancient Greece, they saw the celebration of the beauty of the human form.

Before the Renaissance, artists focused almost exclusively on religious subjects. The people in their paintings didn't look like real people. Instead, the works centered on the religious *story* of the art. The realistic picturing of the *people* in the art wasn't as important.

During the Renaissance, artists like Leonardo created art that reflected the real world. The people in their paintings and sculptures look like real people. The artists used human models. They painted and sculpted human figures that looked like their models in real life.

In subject matter, too, Renaissance artists took a new direction. Many paintings of the time still had religious themes. One of Leonardo's most famous paintings is "The Last Supper." It shows Jesus having his final meal with his disciples.

But Leonardo's most famous painting, "Mona Lisa," is the portrait of a real person. The subject of the painting was the wife of a businessman from Florence. She has fascinated people for 500 years because we see her as a real person, painted in a way that celebrates her humanness.

LEONARDO'S DEVELOPMENT AS AN ARTIST: While Leonardo studied under Verrocchio, his talent bloomed. A legend says that after viewing one of Leonardo's angels in a painting, Verrocchio gave up art himself.

After 10 years with Verrocchio, Leonardo went out on his own. In 1482, he started to work for the Duke of Milan. He produced art work that was commissioned, and paid for, by the Duke. He painted "The Last Supper" during these years. He started a huge sculpture of the Duke's father on horseback. He also designed costumes and sets for the Duke's theater productions.

INVENTIONS AND DRAWINGS: Leonardo told the Duke he was an engineer as well as an artist. Around 1485 he began to produce drawings for buildings and bridges. He also created drawings for machines and weapons unlike any seen before.

Leonardo drew flying machines and tanks, even a submarine. He had an incredible imagination—all of the natural world fascinated him. He left more than 4,000 pages of notes and drawings of plants, animals, dissected cadavers, and extraordinary machines.

Leonardo was not a trained scientist, and he didn't have the mathematical background of **Galileo** or **Isaac Newton.** But like them, he was fascinated by force and motion, and how they influence the shape of

Da Vinci's sketch for a helicopter-like "airship."

things, and their function. He studied the flow of water, then designed canals, swim fins, and a diving suit.

Leonardo was fascinated by flight. He studied birds' wings, and the flow of air around them, to understand lift. Nearly 400 years later, the **Wright brothers** would study bird's wings, too. He drew designs of gliders and flying machines. He designed a helicopter that had a screw as the propeller. Its design was similar to that of the first real helicopter, invented by **Igor Sikorsky**.

Leonardo also sketched an early tank, for use in war fare. It had multiple cannons, and was built on wheels. Leonardo drew a "crossbow machine." It was like a water wheel that shot arrows as it rotated. The machines were never built, and some of them are more fanciful than

Da Vinci's sketch for a tank.

practical. But they indicate the breadth of his interests and imagination.

Leonardo's notes are particularly interesting. They are written in "mirror writing." The words are all backwards, and can't be read unless held up to a mirror. No one knows why he wrote that way. He might have done it because he was left-handed. Or perhaps he didn't want other people to steal his ideas.

Milan was invaded by French forces in 1499, so Leonardo left for Florence. In 1503, he produced his famous "Mona Lisa." By now, Leonardo's fame had spread throughout Europe. He worked for a number of patrons over the next several years. One of his patrons was Cesare Borgia.

Da Vinci's sketch for a human crossbow.

While working for Borgia, Leonardo designed a bridge for Constantinople (modern-day Istanbul). It was a very ambitious project. It would have been one of the largest bridges ever built. Modern engineers have determined that Leonardo's design was accurate.

In 1513, Leonardo moved to Rome. There, he had a workshop and created art for a number of patrons, including the Pope. One of Leonardo's greatest champions was the King of France. In 1516, he offered Leonardo a position for life. He was named Premier Painter and Engineer and Architect of the King. Leonardo held the position until his death on May 2, 1519, in France.

LEONARDO DA VINCI'S HOME AND FAMILY: Leonardo never married or had children. He spent the last years of his life in France, in a home provided by the King.

HIS INVENTIONS: A creative genius unlike any other, Leonardo made major contributions in fields as different as art, science, and engineering. His designs for bridges have turned out to be accurately engineered. His early drawings of "air ships" are uncannily similar to the successful designs of 20th-century inventors. His study of bird wings and air flow anticipated the later studies of the **Wright brothers.** And 400 years after his death, **Igor Sikorksy**, influenced by Leonardo's designs, built the first working helicopter.

WORLD WIDE WEB SITES:

http://www.leonardo.net/
http://www.metmuseum.org/toah/hio/hi_ledv.htm
http://www.mos.org/leonardo/bio.html
http://www.museoscienza.org/english/leonardo/
http://www.nga.gov/cgi-bin/pbio?18300

John Deere
1804 - 1886
American Blacksmith and Businessman
Inventor of the Steel Plow

JOHN DEERE WAS BORN on February 7, 1804, in Rutland, Vermont. His parents were William and Sarah Deere. John's father was a tailor and his mother was a homemaker. Tragically, his father was lost at sea when John was four. That left his mother to raise her young family of six children.

JOHN DEERE GREW UP in the country. Even as a young boy he was interested in nature and the land. But he felt he had to help out his family, too. He ground bark and sold it. He made a little money, and got a suit of clothes and a pair of shoes in payment.

JOHN DEERE WENT TO SCHOOL in Rutland. He received only a very basic education.

When he was 17 years old, John became apprenticed to a blacksmith in Middlebury, Vermont. For the next four years John worked with Captain Benjamin Lawrence. By the time he was 21, John was a skilled blacksmith. Over the next 12 years, he traveled throughout western Vermont working in small towns. He became known as a careful and honest craftsman.

MOVING WEST: John married Demarius Lamb of Granville, Connecticut, in 1827. By 1836 the couple had four children and a fifth on the way. Then hard times hit the family. Deere's blacksmith shop was twice destroyed by fire. He became deeply in debt. Looking for better opportunities, Deere decided to pack up his tools and head west.

Leaving his wife and family in Vermont, he traveled to Grand Detour, Illinois. The small community needed a blacksmith. Deere decided to settle down. Within two days he had built a forge and was busy at work. He sent for his wife and children, who happily joined him.

PROBLEMS WITH PLOWS: As a blacksmith, Deere worked every day with local farmers. They told him about the troubles they were having plowing their fields. The land was very different from the land they'd left in the East. This prairie soil was tough, heavy, and

Deere demonstrating the first steel plow

full of clay. The wooden and iron plows that the settlers had brought didn't work well. They were slow, and dirt clung to the bottom. The farmers had to stop often and remove the heavy dirt by hand.

Deere wanted to make a plow that would work in the heavy dirt. He knew that if he could, the stubborn earth could be turned into farm land.

INVENTION OF THE STEEL PLOW: Deere began testing plow designs using different materials. Through trial and error, in 1837 he found something that worked.

Using an old saw blade made of steel, he designed a moldboard that was curved instead of flat. The curve of this new design pushed the dirt off to one side. Now it was no longer necessary to stop and remove the dirt by hand. And the plow could be pulled by horses rather than oxen, which the old plows had needed.

When Deere put his new plow to the test, he found that he was able to plow more than 10 rows without stopping. He and his partner, Leonard Andrus, made three of the plows and found they were just right for working the soil and preparing it for planting.

By 1839, Deere and Andrus were making and selling new plows at the rate of 10 per year. The next year, that number rose to 30. Then demand exploded. By 1846, Deere and Andrus were selling 1,000 plows a year.

The demand for the new plows was so great that Deere had to find a plentiful source for high quality steel. At first he got his steel from England, but later found a closer source, in Pittsburgh, Pennsylvania.

MOVING TO MOLINE: Deere decided he needed a better location for his business. In 1847, he sold his part of the business to Andrus and moved to Moline, Illinois. The new location was on the Mississippi River, and railroad routes. That made it easier to receive supplies and deliver plows. Moline also had better power resources for manufacturing the plows.

In 1848 John Deere made 1,000 plows in his new plant. He sent them all over the United States to see if the design was good enough to work in any soil. The response was positive. Next, he got serious about building plows.

By 1855, the John Deere Company was producing more than 13,000 plows a year. Many of them were purchased by pioneers

Deere factory workers with a sulky plow, c. 1900.

traveling westward and were carried across the country in covered wagons. People called the John Deere plow "the singing plow" because of the sound the blade made while it was pushing through the earth.

In 1858 John brought his son Charles into the business. Five years later, in 1863, his son-in-law, Stephen Velie, joined the firm. In 1868 the company changed its name to Deere and Company. It began to make other farm products, including cultivators and hay balers.

Over the years the company expanded its line of products to include wagons, carriages, and other agricultural equipment. Deere and Company was a prosperous and well-managed company, and used modern ways of selling and delivering its products.

Deere became active in local activities. He served as President of the First National Bank of Moline. He was also a director of the Moline Public Library and served as Mayor for two years. Deere remained president of his company until his death in 1886.

Today the John Deere Company is still a major supplier of farm machinery and equipment. The company has expanded to include the manufacture of lawn, construction, and forestry equipment. Many people think that it was because John Deere was such a fair and honest man that his company was so successful. He took pride in everything he did and made sure that everything he sold was of high quality. More than 150 years after Deere started his company, his tractors are used on farms all over the world.

JOHN DEERE'S HOME AND FAMILY: Deere married his first wife Demarius, in 1827. They had five children. Demarius died in 1865. In 1867, Deere married her younger sister, Lucinda. John Deere died at home on May 17, 1886, at the age of 82.

HIS INVENTION: John Deere's steel plows made it possible for pioneer settlers to turn hard earth into soil suitable for farming. Before his invention, many people gave up farming because the earth was too hard to cultivate. Those early settlers were able to survive, and thrive, because of John Deere's plows.

WORLD WIDE WEB SITES:

http://www.deere.com
http://www.invent.org/hall_of_fame/39.html
http://www.jdheritage.net/CEO_of_Deere/John_Deere.htm

Georges de Mestral
1907 - 1990
Swiss Inventor of Velcro

GEORGES DE MESTRAL WAS BORN on June 19, 1907, near Lausanne, Switzerland. He was a lively and curious boy. He loved to invent from an early age. At 12, he received his first **patent**—for a toy airplane.

GEORGES DE MESTRAL WENT TO SCHOOL at an engineering school in Lausanne. He graduated with a degree in electrical engineering.

FIRST JOBS: After getting his degree, De Mestral got a job in a machine shop. He was still curious, and always thinking about the world around him.

INVENTING VELCRO: One day in 1941, De Mestral was walking his dog in the Swiss mountains. As often happened, his pants, and the dog's fur, became covered with sticky burrs. De Mestral found the burrs annoying, but fascinating, too. He wanted to know what made them stick to fabric, to his dog's fur, and to anything else.

De Mestral decided to look at the burrs under the microscope. What he saw astounded him. The burrs had hundred of little hooks. The burrs are actually seed pods. By "hooking" the pods onto clothing or animal hair, the plant insured its seeds would be widely spread.

Those tiny hooks gave De Mestral an idea. He wanted to invent a fastener that did what the burrs did. "I will design a unique, two-sided fastener," he said. "One with stiff hooks like the burrs and the other side with soft loops like the fabric of my pants."

De Mestral thought his new invention would be more useful than the zipper as a fastener. It couldn't jam like a zipper. And it would be made out of fabric, not metal.

De Mestral's friend Alfred Gonet offered to help. De Mestral quit his job and borrowed money. He and Gonet started a company.

De Mestral worked for eight years on his invention. He tried different fabrics and designs. He finally found a weaver who came up with the winning design. He made two cotton tapes. One side was made of tiny hooks. The other was made of tiny loops. It worked well, but needed improvement. Finally, De Mestral discovered that nylon was the best fabric to use. When exposed to heat, the hooks were more durable. The invention was ready.

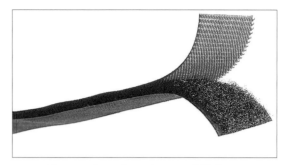

Example of a piece of Velcro.

De Mestral called his new invention "Velcro." It's a combination of the French words "velour" and "crochet." He applied for a **patent** in 1951. He and Gonet Formed Velcro Industries. The product was a great success. Manufacturers of all kinds of products began to use the new fasteners.

LATER YEARS: De Mestral sold the company in the 1970s. By that point, his patent had expired. Many other companies now make versions of his fastener. But Velcro sales are still going strong: more than 60 million yards of the fabric fastener are sold every year. The name is now also a registered trademark. De Mestral died in Switzerland on February 8, 1990, at age 82.

HIS INVENTION: Velcro is one of the most successful cloth inventions of the second half of the 20th century. It is used in many products including shoes, clothing, sporting goods, and office equipment. Its fasteners made from products like stainless steel and plastic are used in medicine and manufacturing. Velcro has even gone into space. When the astronauts travel, Velcro fasteners keep their tools—as well as plates and spoons—from flying away in zero gravity.

WORLD WIDE WEB SITES:

http://www.invent.org/hall_of_fame/37.html
http://www.VELCRO.com/kidzone.html

Rudolf Diesel
1858 - 1913
German Engineer and Industrialist
Inventor of the Diesel Engine

RUDOLF DIESEL WAS BORN on March 18, 1858, in Paris, France. His parents were Theodor and Elise Diesel. His father was a bookbinder. His mother was a teacher. They were born in Augsburg, Germany, and moved to Paris in 1850. Rudolf had two sisters, Louise and Emma.

RUDOLF DIESEL GREW UP in Paris. He lived in the apartment above his father's workshop. His parents were strict disciplinarians. They spoke French and German at home, but Rudolf's mother also taught him English. As a boy, Rudolf was shy, and had few friends. He became interested in technology at an early age.

RUDOLF DIESEL WENT TO SCHOOL first in France and then in Augsburgh, Germany. Rudolf's family was forced to leave France in 1870 during the Franco-Prussian War. His parents went to London, and Rudolf stayed with relatives in Augsburgh. He enrolled at the local industrial school. Rudolf was an excellent student. He decided he wanted to be an engineer. When he graduated in 1875, his final exam grades were the highest in the school's history.

His academic achievement earned Rudolf a scholarship to a technical college in Munich. He graduated in 1880 at the top of his class with a degree in civil engineering.

FIRST JOBS: One of Rudolf's professors in Munich was Carl von Linde, a leader in the fields of machine design and refrigeration science. After graduation, Diesel went to work at his professor's company, the Linde Refrigeration Company. In 1881, he invented an early ice-making machine. He also started his design for an economical internal combustion engine.

THE INTERNAL COMBUSTION ENGINE: All engines require heat in order to work. Heat causes the gas in the cylinder to expand, which provides the force to move the piston. The steam engines created by **James Watt** and others are examples of "external combustion" engines. That means that the heat is produced away from the piston. In a steam engine the heat (or combustion) is applied to a

boiler, to make steam. The steam then goes to the cylinder, where the pressure moves the piston.

In an "internal combustion" engine, the heat (or combustion) takes place inside the cylinder. The first internal combustion engine used a gunpowder charge to move the piston. This wasn't practical. In 1860 Etienne Lenoir developed the first practical internal combustion engine. It used illuminating gas as the fuel. Illuminating gas, also called coal gas, is a mixture of hydrogen, methane, and ethylene.

The next major advance came in 1876, when Nikolaus Otto built the first four-stroke engine. The Otto engine operated in four separate steps, or strokes:

Intake stroke: The air-fuel mixture moves into the cylinder as the piston slides down.

Compression stroke: The piston slides up, compressing the mixture.

Power stroke: The mixture is ignited, and the pressure from the burning mixture pushes the piston back down.

Exhaust stroke: The exhaust fumes from the burnt mixture is pushed out of the cylinder as the piston slides back up.

THE DIESEL ENGINE: Throughout the 1870s and 1880s many people worked on the development of a practical internal combustion engine. They believed these engines would produce power more efficiently than steam engines, which were big, heavy, and expensive. Nikolaus Otto built a successful engine in 1876 that ran on illuminating gas, and **Gottlieb Daimler** developed an engine that

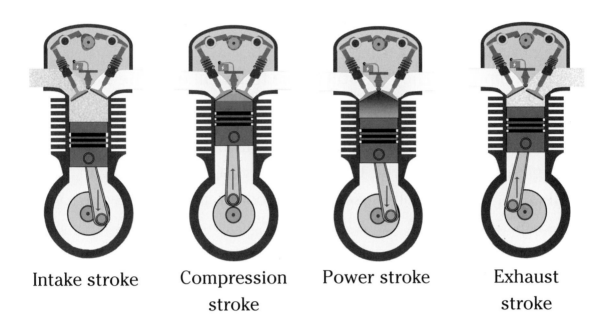

| Intake stroke | Compression stroke | Power stroke | Exhaust stroke |

ran on gasoline in 1882. Both of these engines required an ignition system (the method used to create a spark that ignites the fuel in the engine cylinder).

Diesel became interested in the science of thermodynamics. Thermodynamics studies the relationship between heat and energy. Using the theories developed by the French physicist Nicholas Carnot (1796 - 1832) he decided he could get the fuel to ignite by increasing the compression in the cylinder, without the use of an electric spark. That means that his engines did not require spark plugs.

Diesel worked on the design of his new engine for over ten years. Finally, in 1892 he received a **patent** for his innovative engine design. His first engines used powdered coal as the fuel. But in 1897 he introduced a newer design that ran on kerosene.

Diesel engines are heavier and more expensive than gasoline engines. However, they are much more durable, and cheaper to operate. They were first popular in stationary applications, and later were used to power boats, ships, locomotives, trucks, and heavy equipment. They are still in use today, all over the world.

Much of Diesel's later career was spent managing and protecting the licenses from his engine patents. In 1913 he traveled by ship to England to consult with the British Navy. On the evening of September 30, 1913, Rudolf Diesel fell overboard, and drowned. He was 55 years old.

RUDOLF DIESEL'S HOME AND FAMILY: In 1883, Rudolf Diesel married Martha Flasche. They had three children: Rudolph Jr., Hedy, and Eugen.

HIS INVENTION: Rudolf Diesel was a pioneer in the development of the internal combustion engine. He invented the first high-compression engine that did not require spark plugs. For his contributions to engineering, Diesel was named to the Inventors Hall of Fame in 1976.

WORLD WIDE WEB SITES:

http://www.invent.org/hall_of_fame/42.html
http://www.uh.edu/engines/epil1435.htm

Herbert Henry Dow
1866 - 1930
American Chemist and Inventor
Founder of the Dow Chemical Company

HERBERT HENRY DOW WAS BORN on February 26, 1866, in Ontario, Canada. His parents, both Americans, had moved to Canada so his father could find work. His father was named Joseph and his mother was named Sarah.

Dow's bromide plant, c.1905.

Soon after Herbert was born, the family moved back to the U.S. They settled in Derby, Connecticut, their hometown. His father had found work there as a mechanic. Herbert was the oldest of three children.

HERBERT HENRY DOW GREW UP first in Connecticut, then in Ohio. The family moved to Cleveland when Herbert was 12. By then, he had shown great gifts as an inventor and engineer. He invented a chicken egg incubator before he was 12. While still in high school, he and his father coinvented a steam turbine. The U.S. Navy used it to launch torpedoes.

The Dow family, 1921

HERBERT HENRY DOW WENT TO SCHOOL at the local public schools. He was an excellent student. He went on to college at Case School of Applied Science. (That school is now Case Western Reserve University.) He majored in chemistry, and his special interest was in "brines." Brines are naturally occurring salt water solutions.

In college, Dow researched brines in Ohio, Michigan, and other areas of the country. Brines and the chemicals that can be extracted from them would be the focus of his inventions.

FIRST JOBS: Dow graduated from college in 1888. That year, he studied ways to remove the chemical bromine from brine. Bromine was an important chemical used in medicine and photography. But bromine was expensive to extract from brine. Dow set out to find a way to make bromine extraction cheaper and easier.

FIRST INVENTION: In 1889, Dow created a process of extracting, or removing, bromine from brine. He added bleaching powder, then dripped the bromine over burlap sacks. The process, called "blowing out," then involved sending a current of air over the sacks.

MIDLAND, MICHIGAN: Dow moved to Midland, Michigan in 1890. There, he founded the Midland Chemical Company. Below the soil of Midland are vast reservoirs of brine. Scientists think they are the remnants of an ancient sea, formed millions of years ago.

Dow had found an endless supply of brine. He continued to improve his extracting process, turning the brine into valuable chemical products. In 1891, he'd created what's called the "Dow process." Using a generator, he applied electrical current to the brine, which extracted the bromine.

Dow knew that he could use the same process to extract other valuable chemicals. But he couldn't convince the company heads. In fact, he wound up losing his job, at the company he'd help create.

Dow went back to Ohio, where he used his new process on sodium chloride. The result was chlorine and caustic soda, two valuable chemicals.

FOUNDING THE DOW CHEMICAL COMPANY: Dow moved back to Midland and continued his extraction work. He founded Dow Chemical in 1897. In 1900, the Midland Chemical Company became part

Dow plant, night view, 1988.

of Dow. Under his direction, Dow Chemical became one of the most successful chemical companies in the world.

Dow's chemicals were used in medicine and industry. During World War I (1914 - 1918), Dow produced chemicals needed by the troops. In 1917, Dow invented synthetic indigo dye. Indigo blue, famous now because of its use for blue jeans, was a very popular dye. By making it synthetically, Dow was able to produce quantities cheaply, for use in cloth and clothing.

Dow next became involved in providing materials for the automotive industry. He created a lightweight metal, called Dowmetal. It was especially popular in racing cars, because it was light and helped the cars to run faster.

LATER LIFE: One of the last important achievements in Dow's career had to do with bromine. He'd discovered a way to extract bromine from sea water. The first plant to use the process opened in 1934.

Dow received many honors and awards in his career. He was a member of several scientific societies, including the American Association for the Advancement of Science. He also received the Perkin Medal, one of the highest honors in chemistry. In all, he received more than 100 patents for his chemical processes.

HERBERT HENRY DOW'S HOME AND FAMILY: Dow met his wife, Grace, in Midland. They married in 1892. They had seven children. Their sons were named Willard, Osborn, and Alden. Their daughters were Helen, Ruth, Margaret, and Dorothy. Dow was very involved with education and city life in Midland. Dow died in October 1930 of liver disease. He was 64 years old.

HIS INVENTIONS: Dow's invention of chemical processes like the extraction of bromine from brine provided chemicals for medicine and industry. Today, Dow Chemical still makes chemical products for use in medicine, farming, manufacturing, building, and home care.

WORLD WIDE WEB SITES:

http://news.dow.com/
http://www.chemheritage.org/expore/hhdow/HerbertDow.htm
http://www.invent.org/hall_of_fame/45.html

George Eastman
1854 - 1932
American Inventor and Businessman
Inventor of Rolled Photographic Film and the
Hand-Held Camera

GEORGE EASTMAN WAS BORN on July 12, 1854, in Waterville, New York. His parents were George and Maria Eastman. His father ran a plant nursery, then a commercial college. His mother was a home-maker, and later ran a boarding house. George had two sisters.

GEORGE EASTMAN GREW UP first in Waterville, then in Rochester, New York. His father moved the family to Rochester when George was five. There, he started a commercial college. Tragically, George's father died when he was eight. The family became poor.

GEORGE EASTMAN WENT TO SCHOOL at the Rochester public schools. He quit at the age of 14. He needed to help support his family.

FIRST JOBS: George took a job in the office of a local insurance company. He made $3 a week. He was hard working and smart. He learned the business, and started writing insurance policies as a teenager.

But the family needed more money. George studied accounting at night, and at 19, got a job in a local bank. He was making good money: $15 a week. He worked there in different jobs for the next several years. The job left evenings and weekends free to pursue his real love: photography.

Eastman loved to take pictures, and to develop them. But at that time, the process of developing film was time-consuming, expensive, and difficult. In the 1870s photographers used what's called a "wet plate" process. The image was projected on a glass plate coated with silver iodide, then exposed while still wet. After the plate dried, it was covered with film that contained the negative image.

Eastman set his mind to creating a cheaper, faster, easier process. He'd read about a process in England that used gelatin emulsions. Plates coated with the gelatin didn't have to be

A BRIEF HISTORY OF PHOTOGRAPHY: Capturing an image with a device, then reproducing it has always fascinated people. The original camera, called the "camera obscura," was in use in the 1500s. It was a light-proof box with a pinhole on one side, and a see-through screen on the other. When you looked through the hole at an object, it projected the image upside down. Artists used this first camera to trace objects.

In 1727, a German chemist discovered that the chemical silver nitrate darkened when exposed to light. In England in the early 1800s, Thomas Wedgwood and Humphrey Davy used silver nitrate to create "photograms." They placed objects on paper, then soaked the paper in silver nitrate. They exposed the paper to air. An image would appear—a photogram. But they didn't know how to stop the image from continuing to develop. The photogram would eventually disappear.

In France, Joseph Niepce made the first negative on paper in 1816. Niepce and fellow photographer Louis Daguerre worked together on trying to fix an image on a metal plate. In 1839, Daguerre developed a process to make an image on a silver plate. It was called a "Daguerreotype." Many of the first photographs seen by people around the world were Daguerreotypes. They were a sensation.

In England, Henry Fox Talbot had created a paper negative that could be used to make many copies of one image. He'd also found a way to stop, or "fix," the development process. He called his image a "calotype." Another early pioneer in photography was John Herschel. He found a way to use a chemical, hypsosulfite of soda, to fix images. Most historians consider Niepce, Daguerre, Talbot, and Herschel to be, together, the inventors of photography.

What happened next is a fascinating note in the history of invention and **patents.** The French government bought the photographic process created by Niepce and Daguerre. Then, they gave it to the world, without any patent.

developed immediately. They remained light sensitive after they dried. He decided to try to replicate the formula.

Eastman was still working in the day time at the bank. At night, he'd work on experiments in his mother's kitchen. He made chemical mixtures, poured them onto plates, then baked the plates in the oven. His mother remembered that sometimes he fell asleep on the kitchen floor, exhausted.

DRY PLATE PHOTOGRAPHY: Three years of hard work later, Eastman had invented a dry plate formula. In 1880, he **patented** the process, and also invented and patented a machine to create the plates for sale. That same year, at 26, he opened his own dry plate factory.

Eastman faced problems almost immediately. Some of the dry plates went bad. It was a costly mistake. Eastman replaced the plates, at his own expense. But, he recalled, "What we had left was more important—reputation." Then, competitors began producing dry plates more cheaply. Eastman's profits fell.

INVENTING ROLLED PHOTOGRAPHIC FILM: Then, Eastman had a great idea. He saw a way to make photography "an every day affair." He wanted to make "the camera as convenient as the pencil." He invented a lightweight, flexible paper-backed film, coated with emulsion. The film was rolled onto a holder that attached to the back of the camera. He patented the film in 1884.

THE HAND-HELD CAMERA: Next, he created a simple, hand-held camera that was easy enough to be used by anybody. In 1888, Eastman introduced it as the "Kodak" camera. It came loaded with the rolled film, and could take 100 photos. When users finished the roll, they sent the entire camera back to Kodak. The company developed the photos, and reloaded the camera with film. Then, Kodak mailed back the photos and reloaded camera back to the user.

Eastman self-portrait, c.1884

Eastman was a marketing genius. Often, he wrote the advertising slogans himself. The slogan for the first Kodak camera was: "You press the button, we do the rest."

The new camera was a success. In just one year, Kodak

163

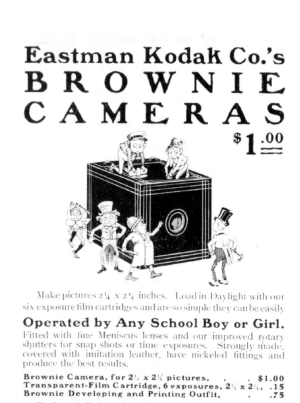

Early advertisement for

Kodak Brownie camera, c. 1900

sold 13,000 cameras. In just one day, they were processing 6,000 photographs. But there was one problem. The camera, priced at $25, was too expensive for most people.

In the 1890s, $25 was about two-months wages for the average worker. Eastman came up with another great idea. He developed the "Brownie" camera. When it came out in 1900, it sold for $1. It was a huge success. More than 100,000 Brownies were sold in the first year. Updated models of the camera sold for decades.

OTHER INVENTIONS: Eastman also invented film for use in motion pictures. He'd been asked by **Thomas Edison** to create the film, for Edison's new movie camera. For a while, motion picture film was Kodak's best-selling product.

GIVING A FORTUNE TO CHARITIES: Eastman became one of the wealthiest men in the country. He spent the last years of his life giving away most of his money. He gave the money to many universities, including the Massachusetts Institute of Technology and the University of Rochester. His gift to Rochester funded the Eastman School of Music, one of the finest music schools in the world. In all, he gave away more than $100 million.

GEORGE EASTMAN'S HOME AND FAMILY: Eastman never married or had children. With part of his vast fortune, he built a 50-room mansion. He loved music, and had a full pipe organ in his house, played by his private organist. In his later years, Eastman developed a painful spinal disease. He died on March 14, 1932, by his own hand. He was 77 years old. His former home is now a museum.

HIS INVENTIONS: Eastman's invention of easy to use and inexpensive film and cameras

Early advertisement for Kodak Brownie, c. 1900

made photography available to people everywhere. People all over the world could take pictures for their own use. His inventions spread what was previously an expensive process for a wealthy few into an everyday, affordable consumer item. His inventions helped develop the movie industry, too.

Today most people use digital cameras. But in the history of photography, few people made more important inventions and innovations than George Eastman.

WORLD WIDE WEB SITES:

http://www.invent.org/hall_of_fame/48.html
http://www.kodak.com/US-en/corp/kodakHistory.eastmanTheMan.
    shtml
http://www.pbs.org/wgbh/amex/eastman/

Thomas Edison
1847 - 1931
American Inventor of More Than 1,000 Items, Including the Incandescent Electric Lamp (Light Bulb), Phonograph, and Motion Picture Projector

THOMAS EDISON WAS BORN on February 11, 1847, in Milan, Ohio. His full name is Thomas Alva Edison. His parents were Samuel and Nancy Edison. He was the youngest of seven children. Only four survived to adulthood. He was always called "Al," or Alva, by his family.

Edison's father owned a lumber business. His mother was a former school teacher. After she married, she became a homemaker and mother to seven lively children.

THOMAS EDISON GREW UP active and curious. There are many interesting—and telling—stories of Edison's childhood. He was always asking questions. Once, he asked his mother why geese sat on eggs. She told him it was to make them hatch. He was found the next day in the neighbor's henhouse, sitting on the eggs.

When he was six, he set fire to his father's barn. He wasn't trying to get in trouble. He remembered that he just wanted to "see what it would do." The barn burned to the ground. When Tom did things like that, he'd get a spanking.

Milan was a town on a canal that led to Lake Erie. That's one of the Great Lakes, part of a great inland shipping pathway. At that time, Milan was an important shipping port. Farmers brought grain to the town, to ship throughout the Great Lakes. But soon the railroads became the preferred way to transport grain. Milan was no longer an important port. Samuel Edison's business began to fail. So in 1854, he moved the family to Port Huron, Michigan.

Around this time, Tom became seriously ill with scarlet fever. Scarlet fever is a serious infection that can damage the heart and other organs. Today it is treated with antibiotics. But there were no antibiotics to treat diseases then. Tom was ill for months. When he recovered, he had a hearing loss.

THOMAS EDISON WENT TO SCHOOL in Port Huron for a brief period of time. He hated school. He wanted to ask questions, and find answers. Instead, he was forced to sit and memorize. That wasn't learning to him. When he was nine, he decided he'd had enough. He left school for good.

Edison's mother decided to teach him at home. She was a former schoolteacher, and loved teaching Tom. She read him classic literature, including Shakespeare. That sparked his interest. Soon he was reading on his own.

One of the books he loved was on science. He recalled that it was the "first book I could understand." What fascinated him was the section on chemistry. It outlined all kinds of experiments. Tom decided to build a lab.

In the basement cellar, he experimented with chemicals. Sometimes, strange smells came out of the cellar. Sometimes, there were explosions. Edison's parents were concerned, but they let him continue.

Tom helped out on the family farm, too. He spent many hours plowing, planting, and harvesting. He also took the food to market, and sold it.

FIRST JOBS: When Tom was 13, he got his first job. There was a new railroad connecting Port Huron to Detroit. Tom got a job selling newspapers to passengers on the train.

Every day Edison rode the morning train from Port Huron to Detroit. He often spent the day at the Detroit Public Library. "I started with the first book on the bottom shelf," he recalled. "I went through the whole lot, one by one." He claimed later that he'd "read the whole library."

Every evening, Tom rode the evening train home to Port Huron. He sold his papers, and also got some space in the baggage car to

Edison and the first phonograph, c. 1878

continue his experiments. That ended after he caused an explosion and fire.

DEAFNESS: By this point, Edison had lost most of his hearing. He recalled the reasons differently at different times in his life. Certainly having scarlet fever affected his hearing. Also, he was struck in the ears by his angry boss after causing a fire onboard the train. And once, a conductor grabbed him by the ears and hauled him onto a moving train. All of these traumas led him to lose most of his hearing by the age of 13.

But his hearing loss didn't discourage his active curiosity. Like many people of his age, he was fascinated with the new technology of the era, especially the telegraph.

THE TELEGRAPH: The telegraph was invented by **Samuel Morse** in 1837. It was a sensation. Like the invention of the telephone and the World Wide Web, the telegraph represented a giant leap forward in communication.

Edison built his own telegraph set. He learned Morse Code. That's a system of clicks, made with the telegraph set, that represent the letters of the alphabet. The clicks were called "dots" and "dashes." A telegrapher (telegraph operator) tapped out the words of a message in Morse Code. The message was sent as an electric impulse through telegraph wires that linked cities across the country. Another telegrapher received and decoded the messages. It was the fastest way to communicate that had yet been invented.

Edison spent hours with his telegraph set. He became a fast and efficient telegrapher. He got a job with the Port Huron telegraph office. Then he was hired to work as a telegrapher for the railroad.

From 1864 to 1868, Edison worked for many different companies. He traveled around the country working as a telegrapher, learning all about telegraphs and the way they worked. This led him to learn all he could about

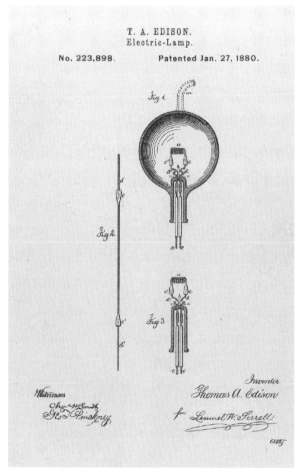

Edison's patent for the light bulb

electricity. Understanding electricity, and harnessing it for practical uses, became the focus of his life.

EARLY INVENTIONS: In 1868, Edison was working in Boston when he **patented** his first product. It was an electric vote recorder. He offered it to the Massachusetts state legislature. They weren't interested. Edison was a man known for his witty comments. He supposedly said of the experience that he'd

Edison's carbon filament light bulb

never again invent something people didn't want.

Edison moved to New York City. He got a job near Wall Street, then as now the home of the Stock Exchange. One day, the telegraph used at the Gold Exchange broke down. Stock trading ground to a halt. Edison fixed the machine, and the stock traders went back to work. The company hired him on the spot to run their telegraphic equipment.

Edison invented a stock ticker, the Edison Universal Stock Printer. It was a great improvement on the existing device. He sold the invention and related materials for $40,000. Now he had enough to start his first company.

In 1871, Edison built a factory and laboratory in Newark, New Jersey. Within three years, he'd perfected his most important early invention—a quadruplex telegraph system. It could send four messages at the same time, using just one wire.

MENLO PARK: Edison sold the invention to Western Union. He used the money to fund what he called his "Invention Factory." It was a new factory and lab in Menlo Park, New Jersey. It was the first company of its kind, and something of an "invention," too. It became the model for later research laboratories. Edison dedicated the rest of his life to inventing.

Edison had always been a hard worker. Now he worked around the clock. He'd spend up to 16 hours a day in his lab, stopping for quick meals and cat naps. He could be a difficult man to work for, too. He expected his employees to work as hard as he did. Edison married in 1871, and he and his wife had three children. But he spent most of his time in the lab.

One of the first inventions to come out of Menlo Park was an improvement to the telephone. **Alexander Graham Bell** had invented the telephone in 1876. But Edison's innovation—a carbon button transmitter—improved the quality of transmission. People's voices could be heard much more clearly, and the signal could travel farther, with Edison's invention. The carbon button transmitter, which is part of a phone's mouthpiece, is still in use today.

THE TIN FOIL PHONOGRAPH: Edison's first major invention developed at Menlo Park was the tin foil phonograph. It was the first device that could record sound, then reproduce it. Like many of his inventions, it was related to his earlier work. Working on the telephone made Edison think about how to capture sound, then play it back later. This made him think about the method, and the materials, that could first record, then reproduce sound.

Edison and others who worked on the wax-record phonograph, c.1892

The device he developed was a metal cylinder wrapped in tinfoil. A crank moved the cylinder along a screw. A cone attached to the cylinder had a diaphragm and needle. When someone spoke into the cone, the sound waves caused the diaphragm to vibrate. The vibration moved the needle up or down. That made dents in the tinfoil. The dents were like the grooves of a modern-day vinyl record. In those dents was the captured sound. Placing a needle in the grooves would play back the sounds.

Edison made the first recording in 1877. It was of him reciting "Mary Had a Little Lamb." The phonograph was a sensation. People all around the world were stunned at Edison's accomplishment. It made him a famous man. He became known as the "Wizard of Menlo Park."

THE INCANDESCENT ELECTRIC LAMP—THE LIGHT BULB: Edison next turned his attention to practical electric lighting. Many inventors had already made important discoveries in the field, especially **Nikola Tesla.**

Inventors like Tesla had already created outdoor lighting systems, such as arc lights. But there was nothing that could be used to light homes. Edison wanted to find a way to build a practical incandescent electric light—what we know as a light bulb.

Edison knew that he needed to create not just the lamp, or bulb. He needed to invent the entire system: how to *generate* the electricity, *transmit* the electricity, then use it to *light* the lamps. And it had to be done so that it was affordable.

Edison started with the light bulb. A major problem was finding the right "filament" for the glass bulb. The filament is the wire you can see inside a light bulb. It had to be durable, but also stable. It needed to be able to provide light for hours, when an electric current was run through it. Edison tested all kinds of materials— including fishing line and hair from a friend's beard. Finally, he found it. The perfect filament was carbonized thread.

Edison conducted the first light bulb tests in October 1879. The carbon-filament light bulb burned for 40 hours in the lab. Edison took his new invention on the road and gave public exhibitions showing its possibilities. The public eagerly anticipated Edison's new system.

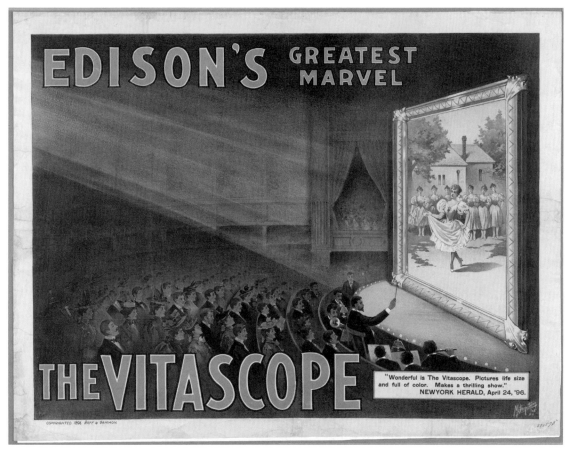

Poster for Edison Vitascope, 1896

THE FIRST COMMERCIAL ELECTRIC POWER STATION: Next, Edison got to work on the major part of the challenge: the electrical system. He based his model on the gas lighting systems already in use in major cities.

Gas had been used to light homes and businesses for years at that point. Gas was delivered from central stations, through an underground delivery system. In homes, gas was channeled into lamps. But gas was also dangerous. Gas fumes could kill people, and could catch on fire. Edison's electric system promised a safe, efficient alternative.

175

Edison began work on what would become the first electric power station in Manhattan. The facility was on Pearl Street, near Wall Street. He visited the local businesses in the area to understand their power needs.

Next, he built the station, then designed electric generators to create the power. Then, he designed a network for the distribution of the electricity.

Edison designed special dynamos to create the electricity. He helped design the fuses and light switches to be used in the new system. On September 4, 1882, the Pearl Street Station sent electricity to 25 buildings in a one-mile area of Manhattan.

It is important to note that Edison's system was a "Direct Current" system. This varied from the "Alternating Current" system designed by Tesla and **George Westinghouse**. The benefit of motors and generators using Alternating Current is their ability to send power over much greater distances than Direct Current. High Voltage Alternating Current can be sent hundreds of miles, while Direct Current could only be sent a few miles.

Edison could be a stubborn man. Even though it was a better system, he refused to build an Alternate Current system. It caused a great deal of problems in the electric company he'd founded. In 1889, several of the electric companies he'd founded merged to become Edison General Electric. There was another merger in 1892, and "Edison" was dropped from the company's name. He left the electric industry and moved on in the world of invention.

WEST ORANGE: In 1887, Edison built a huge new research complex in West Orange, New Jersey. It was 10 times the size of Menlo Park.

Edison and his original dynamo, c. 1906

It had five buildings, and labs for chemistry, physics, and metallurgy. Edison continued to invent, working on as many projects at once as he could.

As he had always done, Edison continued to create innovations to already existing products. He returned to the phonograph, and

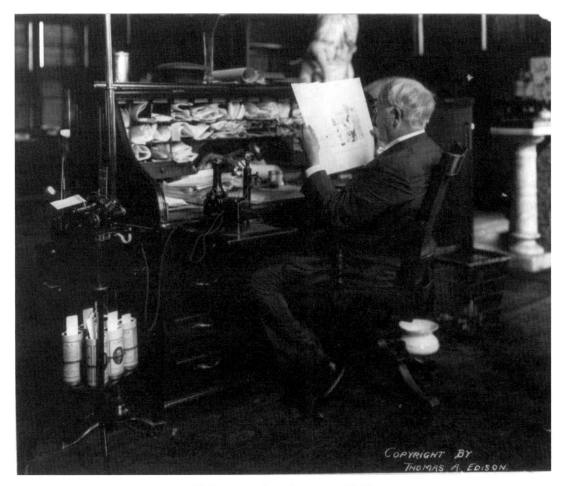

Edison at his desk, c. 1913

began to manufacture them for home use. He also created and sold wax records, recording equipment, and other items. His inventions were so important that he is credited with creating the recording industry.

MOTION PICTURES: Edison's next major invention was motion pictures. For Edison, it was a natural outgrowth of the phonograph. He said it "did for the eye what the phonograph does for the ear." Many of the innovations in motion pictures were a collaboration with W.K.L. Dickson, a photographer on his staff. Edison was the man with the vision, and the money, to fund the invention. He also drew on his knowledge from previous inventions. But Dickson, with his photography background, played a major role in developing the camera and other devices.

Edison and Dickson invented a motion picture camera in 1892. They also created a viewing device called the "Kinetoscope." In 1893, the invention was shown to the public. Once again, Edison captivated the world. And once again he played a major role in launching a new industry, the movies. The movie industry took off, with many others getting involved in the making and showing of films.

The Edison company continued to make advances and innovations in motion picture technology. In 1896, Edison launched the first successful American motion picture projector, the "Vitascope." It premiered in New York City in 1896.

HUGE SUCCESS—AND FAILURE, TOO: Not everything Edison created was a success. He spent years—and millions of dollars—to develop the mining industry in New Jersey. He wanted to find a source of iron ore to supply the steel industry. But he was never able to make the mines successful. He also started a cement company, but that was never a success, either. Still, Edison always felt there was a lesson in failure.

THE STORAGE BATTERY: Edison's last major invention was a storage battery. The battery was to be used to power electric vehicles. Edison started working on the battery in 1899. He was very enthusiastic about its possibilities. He thought that most cars in the future would run on electricity, rather than gas.

Edison knew that lead-acid storage batteries in use at the time weren't practical. He started with an alkaline battery, but the process was difficult. He worked on the project for nearly 10 years. Finally, in 1909, he'd invented a practical alkaline battery. But it was never used to power a car, as Edison had planned. By that time, **Henry Ford**'s Model-T had shown the world that gas-powered cars were the way of the future.

Edison's alkaline battery was still a huge success. It was used to light railroad cars, railroad signals, buoys, and underground lamps. And it proved to be his most profitable invention. Alkaline batteries in use today are based on Edison's original technology.

In 1911, Edison formed a corporation, Thomas A. Edison, Inc., to consolidate all his companies. He was the president, but by this time he had thousands of employees, working on hundreds of products. He was ready for another phase of his life.

Edison became more involved in service to the nation. He became head of the Naval Consulting Board in 1915. That was a group made up of science leaders who wanted to share technology to help the U.S. military.

HONORS, AWARDS, AND WORLD FAME: By the end of his life, Edison was a famous and honored man. He spent time with other famous inventors, like **Henry Ford**. Ford thought so much of Edison's inventions that he recreated his Menlo Park labs at his museum, Greenfield Village. In 1929, Edison traveled to Dearborn, Michigan, site of Greenfield Village. He took part in a celebration commemorating the invention of the light bulb, to national acclaim.

Edison in his lab, c.1920

Among his many awards was the Congressional Gold Medal of Honor. Edison received the medal in 1928. The citation noted that he "illuminated the path of progress by his inventions."

Edison had a home in Fort Meyers, Florida. He spent a good deal of time there, and even built a complete lab. He invented up until the end of his life. His last project, begun in 1927, was an attempt to make synthetic rubber from the goldenrod plant. He never lived to complete it.

THOMAS EDISON'S HOME AND FAMILY: Edison was married twice. He and his first wife, Mary Stillwell, married in 1871. They had three children, Marion, Thomas, and William. Edison nicknamed Marion "Dot" and Thomas "Dash." Mary died of scarlet fever

Edison and his dictating machine, c.1921

in 1884. In 1886, Edison married Mina Miller. They had three children, Madeline, Theo, and Charles.

Thomas Edison died on October 22, 1931, in West Orange, New Jersey. He was 84 years old. Tributes poured in from all over the world. Thousands lined the streets for his funeral. President Herbert Hoover asked all Americans to dim the lights in their homes on the evening of his funeral. It was a fitting tribute to the man who had brought electricity, and all its benefits, into homes across the world.

HIS MANY INVENTIONS: In his long and productive life, Edison patented 1,093 items. No other inventor has come close to that number. Many of his inventions, including the incandescent light bulb, the phonograph, and motion pictures, are so much a part of everyday existence that it seems impossible to imagine what life was like without them.

Part of Edison's genius was his ability to create practical, useful inventions. "I find out what the world needs, then I go ahead and try to invent it," he said. He was always optimistic, and never discouraged when an experiment failed. After months of working on the light bulb, he said, "If I find 10,000 ways something won't work, I haven't failed. I am not discouraged, because every wrong attempt discarded is often a step forward."

He believed in hard work. One of his many famous sayings is: "Genius is one percent inspiration and 99 percent perspiration." He didn't become an inventor to become rich. He made and lost millions over the years, driven by the desire to invent things, not to make a fortune.

Edison had one of the greatest inventive imaginations in history. He could look at a problem, and see many, interrelated parts that together form a solution. He didn't just create the incandescent light bulb. He created an entire electrical power system. He didn't just invent the phonograph. He invented the equipment and processes that became the foundation of the recording industry. This is his most important, lasting contribution to the history of invention.

WORLD WIDE WEB SITES:

http://edison.rutgers.edu/lamp.htm
http://www.invent.org/hall_of_fame/50.html
http://www.nps.gov/edis/
http://www.si.edu/lemelson/edison/000_story_02.asp

Gertrude Elion
1918 - 1999
American Scientist and Inventor of Life-Saving Drugs
to Treat Leukemia and Other Diseases
Winner of the Nobel Prize

GERTRUDE ELION WAS BORN on January 23, 1918, in New York City. Her parents were Robert and Bertha Elion. Her father was a dentist and her mother was a homemaker. Gertrude had a younger brother named Herbert.

GERTRUDE ELION GREW UP in the area of New York City known as the Bronx. She particularly loved the Bronx Zoo. She visited often, in the company of her beloved grandfather.

Gertrude was part of a loving family, and her parents nurtured her interests in reading and music. She remembered her father reading her "poetry, history, biography, and fiction." She especially loved the stories of famous scientists and people who "discovered things." Scientists like Marie Curie fascinated her.

Gertrude's mother was an important influence, too. When Gertrude was growing up, many girls were discouraged from choosing careers. But Bertha Elion encouraged her daughter to follow a career in science.

GERTRUDE ELION WENT TO SCHOOL at the local public schools. She was an outstanding student. She loved all her courses (except gym), and she got all "A's." She did so well in school that she skipped several grades. She graduated from high school at 15.

But the same year she graduated, tragedy struck. Her beloved grandfather died of cancer. Gertrude was terribly sad. But her grandfather's death made her resolve to study science and try to find a cure for a killer disease. "When I was 15, I already knew that I loved science," she recalled. "But that year I was so devastated by my grandfather's death from cancer that majoring in chemistry seemed the logical first step in committing myself to fighting the disease."

Elion studied biochemistry at Hunter College in New York City. She graduated in 1937 with highest honors. She wanted to go on to graduate school, but was rejected by all 15 colleges she applied to.

Elion knew it wasn't that she couldn't do the work. It was because those schools, and society in general, discriminated against women. "Nobody took me seriously," she said. "They wondered why in the world I wanted to be a chemist when no women were doing that."

But Gertrude Elion wouldn't give up. She tried to get a job in a laboratory. Once again, she faced discrimination. The companies she applied to wouldn't give her a chance. "I often wonder why I didn't give up then and there," she recalled. "I almost did. I actually went to secretarial school for six weeks." But then she was offered a job as a lab assistant. "I left secretarial school and never looked back," she said.

In 1939, Elion finally was admitted to New York University's graduate school. "I was the only female in my graduate chemistry class," she recalled. "But no one seemed to mind, and I didn't consider it at all strange." She studied chemistry while working two jobs to pay tuition. She received her master's degree in chemistry in 1941. Once again, she looked for a job as a scientist. But this time, she found work much more quickly.

GETTING WORK AS A SCIENTIST: Elion got her master's degree just as the U.S. was entering World War II. When the U.S. joined the war effort in 1941, millions of men left their jobs to fight.

"War changed everything," recalled Elion. "It was only when men weren't available that women were invited into the lab." For the first time, intelligent, able and educated women could find the jobs they wanted.

FIRST JOBS: Elion's first job was in a food company. She worked as a chemist, checking the quality of the foods the company produced. After a year in that job, she worked at Johnson and Johnson labs.

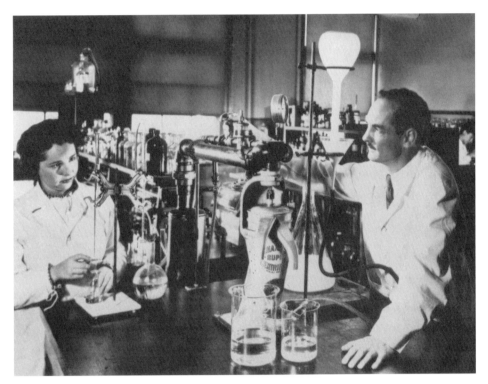

Elion and Hitchings, c. 1950

Next, she got a job at Burroughs Wellcome Laboratories. She was to remain there for the rest of her 40-year career in chemistry.

Elion was hired by George H. Hitchings. Over the next four decades, the two worked closely together. And together they developed some of the most important medicines of the 20th century.

THE CELL: Elion and Hitchings's focus was how diseases penetrated human cells. The cell is the basic unit of living things. All living things—plants, animals, and people—are made up of cells. Each cell contains the elements that allow the cell to live and reproduce.

When Elion and Hitchings began their work, drug research wasn't focused on the cell. At that time, most medical researchers started with an existing medicine that worked. Then, they would make some changes to it, and see if that improved the product.

Elion and Hitchings took a different path. They studied the differences between diseased and healthy cells. They looked at how cancer, bacteria, and viruses cause disease. Next, they developed drugs that would destroy the disease, without harming healthy cells.

DISCOVERING A DRUG TO TREAT LEUKEMIA: In the late 1940s, Elion began working on a drug to fight childhood leukemia. Leukemia is a type of cancer. At that time, it was nearly always fatal. By 1951, she had discovered a chemical that could fight leukemia.

The chemical compound that Elion created was called "6MP." That stands for "6-mercaptopurine." In its first trials, the drug helped leukemia patients live longer than they had on any previous drug. Soon, doctors were using 6MP with other drugs, plus radiation to fight leukemia.

The results of using 6MP were amazing. Cases of leukemia treated with the drugs disappeared. Leukemia soon became one of the most treatable cancers. Elion was overjoyed. "What greater joy can you have than to know what an impact your work has had on people's lives? The thrill of seeing people get well who otherwise might have died cannot be described in words." Today, nearly 80% of leukemia patients are cured.

Elion praised Hitchings as her mentor. "Dr. Hitchings permitted me to learn as rapidly as I could and to take on more and more responsibility," she said. She felt she could explore all areas of medical research. In addition to chemistry, she studied biochemistry, pharmacology, immunology, and eventually virology.

OTHER IMPORTANT DISCOVERIES: Another important discovery developed from Elion's work on 6MP. A new drug, Imuran, derived from 6MP, could fight the body's rejection of transplant organs, like kidneys. The body's "immune system" helps the body fight disease. But it also attacks anything "foreign" to the body, including an organ transplanted from another person.

However, if a patient received Imuran before transplant surgery, the body accepted the new organ. So another major medical breakthrough came about through Elion's research.

Next, Elion developed a drug to treat malaria. Malaria is a disease that kills millions of people every year. Most of its victims are in Africa and Asia. And most are infants and children. Elion's new drug saved many lives.

After Hitchings retired in 1967, Elion became director of Burroughs' Department of Experimental Therapy. Heading up the lab, she oversaw the creation of even more new drugs.

And on her own, she developed the first antiviral drug, acyclovir. The drug was used to treat diseases caused by viruses. It was especially important in the treatment of herpes, a disease group that includes chicken pox. She called it "my crown jewel. That such a thing was possible wasn't even imagined up until then."

Elion retired from Burroughs in 1983. But she continued to work with researchers and medical students. One of the teams she trained developed AZT, the first drug used to treat AIDS. Over the course of her career Elion received 45 **patents** for her work.

Elion and Hitchings, 1988, after winning the Nobel Prize

THE NOBEL PRIZE: In 1988, Elion received the Nobel Prize. That is one of the most important awards in the world. Her award came in the field of "Physiology or Medicine." She shared the award with Hitchings and a British scientist, James W. Black.

Elion was grateful for the Prize. But she was clear about what it meant to her. "People often ask whether it wasn't what I had been aiming for all my life. Nothing could be farther from the truth. My rewards had already come in seeing children with leukemia survive, meeting patients with long-term kidney transplants, and watching acyclovir save lives and reduce suffering. What we were aiming at was getting people well. The satisfaction of that is much greater than any prize you can get."

LATER YEARS: In 1991, Elion became the first woman named to the National Inventors Hall of Fame. "I'm happy to be the first woman," she said. "But I doubt I'll be the last." In fact, she was followed three years later by **Rachel Fuller Brown** and **Elizabeth Lee Hazen**, inventors of Nystatin.

After Elion retired, she often traveled to schools to visit young students. She encouraged them to study science. "The same thing that inspired me over the years inspires me now," she told them. "I want to get sick people well. I want to get children involved in science. I want them to have the same kind of excitement and fun I've had and do something useful with their lives."

Over the years, Elion received hundreds of letters from patients who were cured by her drugs. "I treasure those letters," she said. "I keep every one of them." Gertrude Elion died suddenly of a stroke on February 21, 1999. She was 81 years old.

GERTRUDE ELION'S HOME AND FAMILY: Elion never married or had children. In 1937, she met a fellow student named Leonard Canter. She and Leonard fell in love and became engaged. But, tragically, Canter died in 1941, of a heart infection. Throughout her life, Elion remained very close to her brother and his family.

HER INVENTION: Elion is considered one of the most important medical researchers of the 20th century. In her 40-year career, she invented some of the most important life-saving drugs of the era, including drugs for leukemia, kidney transplantation, and the herpes virus.

WORLD WIDE WEB SITES:

http://nobelprize.org/medicine/laureates/1988/elion-autobio.html
http://web.mit.edu/invent/iow/elion2.html
http://www.invent.org/hall_of_fame/51.html

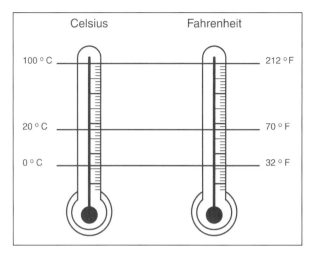

Fahrenheit and Celsius thermometers

Daniel Gabriel Fahrenheit
1686 - 1736
Dutch Instrument Maker
Inventor of the Mercury Thermometer

DANIEL GABRIEL FAHRENHEIT WAS BORN on May 14, 1686, in Danzig, Germany. His last name is pronounced FAIR-en-hite. His father was a successful businessman, and his mother was a homemaker. Daniel was the oldest of five children.

DANIEL GABRIEL FAHRENHEIT GREW UP in Danzig. His life was changed, tragically, when he was 15. His parents both died in an accident. He was sent away to Amsterdam, in the Netherlands, to learn a trade.

DANIEL GABRIEL FAHRENHEIT WENT TO SCHOOL until he was 15. After his parents death, his schooling ended.

LEARNING ABOUT SCIENTIFIC INSTRUMENTS: Fahrenheit didn't settle in the Netherlands. Instead, he traveled around Europe. He was fascinated by scientific instruments. He was especially interested in instruments that measured water, temperature, and air pressure. He studied with instrument makers and scientists wherever he traveled. That's what led him to his great invention, the mercury thermometer.

INVENTING THE MERCURY THERMOMETER: Galileo Galilei had invented the first thermometer in the early 1600s. Thermometers worked on a relatively simple principal. They were generally glass tubes, filled with a liquid. The tube had markings that measured the temperature. When the liquid was exposed to heat, it expanded and moved up the tube. When the liquid was exposed to cold, it contracted and moved down the tube.

While Galileo's thermometer was a groundbreaking invention, it needed improvement. Galileo's thermometer used a combination of water and alcohol. The temperatures measured using these liquids were inconsistent. That's because they couldn't record temperature accurately if air pressure changed, as it does during weather changes.

In 1714, Fahrenheit discovered a way to use mercury in thermometers. First, he developed a method for cleaning the mercury. That way, the metal would rise and fall in the tube, and not stick to the sides. Mercury was also a better choice because it could be read at higher and lower temperatures than alcohol. And it wasn't as sensitive to changes in air pressure as alcohol.

THE FAHRENHEIT SCALE: In addition to inventing the mercury thermometer, Fahrenheit developed a system, or scale, for measuring temperature. (At that time, there were several different temperature scales in use throughout Europe.)

WHO WAS CELSIUS? In the mid-20th century, most nations moved from the Fahrenheit to the Celsius temperature scale. The Celsius scale is named for Anders Celsius (1701 - 1744). Celsius was a Swedish astronomer. He created a hundred-point temperature scale. The freezing and boiling points of water are the constant temperatures at the top and bottom of the scale. Celsius did not *invent* the hundred-point scale, but he made improvements to it. It became the accepted temperature scale in 1948. It is now used throughout the world for the scientific measurement of temperature.

Fahrenheit used two basic measurements for the high and low end of his scale. For the high end of his scale, he used the normal temperature of the human body. At the low end, he used the temperature at which water froze. In his first scale, he determined the measurement for normal body temperature at 90 degrees, and freezing water at 30 degrees.

In 1717, he adjusted these measurements to 96 degrees for body temperature, and 32 degrees for freezing water. Over the next years, Fahrenheit did experiments to more accurately determine the exact temperature of freezing and boiling water. He determined that the boiling temperature of water was 212 degrees.

Fahrenheit made and sold his thermometers throughout Europe. They were widely accepted and a success. His temperature scale and thermometer became the accepted measurement systems. Later, the body temperature he'd defined was adjusted to the "98.6 degrees" we know today.

DANIEL GABRIEL FAHRENHEIT'S HOME AND FAMILY: Fahrenheit never married or had children. He died on September 16, 1736, in Amsterdam. He was 50 years old.

HIS INVENTION: Fahrenheit invented the first truly accurate thermometer, using mercury. From that invention, he worked out a temperature scale that was used worldwide until the mid-20th century. In most countries, the Celsius scale is now used to measure temperature. And most thermometers no longer use mercury. But in the U.S., it's the Fahrenheit scale that's used in doctor's offices, and the daily weather forecasts, to tell us the temperature.

WORLD WIDE WEB SITES:

http://chem.oswego.edu/chem209/Misc/fahrneheit.htm
http://www.bbc.co.uk/history/historic_figures/fahrenheit_daniel_ga
    briel.shtml

Philo Farnsworth
1906 - 1971
American Scientist and Inventor
Inventor of Electronic Television

PHILO FARNSWORTH WAS BORN on August 19, 1906, in Indian Creek, Utah. His parents were Lewis and Serena Farnsworth. They were farmers. Philo was the oldest of five children. He was named for his grandfather, who had moved to Utah as part of a group of Mormons, in the 19th century.

PHILO FARNSWORTH GREW UP in several places. The family moved often, in search of better farm land. His parents moved to a ranch in Rigby, Idaho, when he was 12. He was curious and smart, and fascinated by the world around him.

Philo loved to take apart farm machinery and see how it worked. He read all he could about science and electricity. When he was 13, he won a prize offered by a science magazine for inventing a car alarm. As a teenager, he came up with electrical gadgets—like an electric motor for the family's washing machine.

He decided early on he wanted to be an inventor. He loved learning about famous inventors, like **Alexander Graham Bell** and **Thomas Edison.** Like them, he was fascinated with the idea of sending messages through wires or airwaves.

PHILO FARNSWORTH WENT TO SCHOOL at the local public schools. The nearest school was four miles away, so he rode his horse. He was a brilliant student. When he was only 14, in 1920, he thought up the idea behind electronic television.

IMAGINING ELECTRONIC TELEVISION: Farnsworth thought about how he could convert moving images into electrical signals. He began to visualize how an electron beam could scan an image line by line. That image could then be transmitted, also line by line. The lines, when received, could be reconfigured to form the image. And that is the basis of electronic television.

Farnsworth wrote down his findings, with sketches, and shared them with his teacher. Later, during years of legal battles over who had invented television, his teacher testified about Philo's research.

When Farnsworth came up with his idea, there had already been early attempts at transmitting images. These used mechanical parts, including rotating disks, to produce rather poor, unstable images. The genius of Farnsworth's idea was that it was all electronic—there were no moving parts.

Farnsworth was so bright and so able that he only went to high school for two years. He applied and was accepted to Brigham Young University at the age of 15. He started college at 16, and spent two years there. He left college in 1924, after his father died. He worked for the next few years to support his family.

FIRST JOBS: Farnsworth worked briefly in Salt Lake City, then began his own company. He found financial backers willing to fund his experiments in television. They started a business, called Crocker Labs, in San Francisco. This eventually became the Farnsworth Radio and Television Corporation. He had recently married, and his wife, Pem, worked with him, along with a loyal band of assistants.

INVENTIONS AND INNOVATIONS IN TELEVISION: Over the next two years, Farnsworth developed all the basic components of the electronic television. These included an image scanner and camera tubes for transmission, and a receiver. Of key importance was what Farnsworth called the "image dissector." Following his earlier idea, the dissector could manipulate an electronic beam to scan the image, line by line, then stored it for transmission. He applied for a **patent** for his system in 1927, which he received in 1930.

THE FIRST ALL-ELECTRONIC TELEVISION IMAGE: Farnsworth introduced his invention on September 7, 1927. He transmitted an

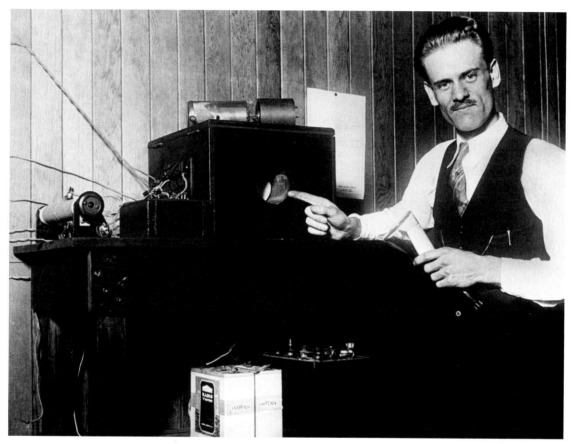

Farnsworth with the first electronic television, Sept. 10, 1928

image—a dollar sign. The assembled onlookers, his financial backers, were amazed. Television had been born. It was an amazing breakthrough.

In 1928, Farnsworth presented the first all-electric television system to the world. He became famous. Hollywood stars came to meet him.

RIVALS AND YEARS OF LEGAL BATTLES: Although Farnsworth didn't know it, there was another scientist, **Vladimir Zworykin**, at work on a television system.

Zworykin was developing what would be a competing system for RCA (Radio Corporation of America). RCA owned all the patents involved in radio. The head of RCA, David Sarnoff, wanted to own all the patents for television, too.

Zworykin went to San Francisco and visited Farnsworth in his lab. He said admiringly of Farnsworth "image dissector," "That's a beautiful tube. I wish I had invented it." Zworykin returned to RCA, with notes to help him replicate Farnsworth's tube.

In 1930 Farnsworth received his first patent for his electronic television system. Sarnoff decided to fight for the right to be first in all TV patents. He first offered to buy Farnsworth's patents and business for $100,000. But Farnsworth wanted to hold on to his rights as the inventor of the system. He wanted to license his invention, not sell it. When he refused to sell, Sarnoff used the power and money of RCA to fight him in court.

Farnsworth found a company, the Philco company of Philadelphia, that was willing to license his invention. He moved his family and business to Philadelphia. In 1934, at the Franklin Institute, Farnsworth presented the wonder of electronic television to the world. It was a great success. Visitors flocked to the museum to view the new technology.

A year later, Farnsworth won his first patent case against RCA. But his legal battles with RCA continued. Meanwhile, Farnsworth left Philco, and started his own company again. He traveled to England and licensed his television system to the British.

In 1936, Farnsworth also launched an early television station, W3XPF. Not many people had TVs then, because there were few broadcasts. Faced with continual lawsuits from RCA, he began to fall apart, mentally and physically. He left Philadelphia for a family home in Maine. There, he began to drink heavily and withdrew from the world.

In April 1939, Sarnoff and Zworykin triumphantly announced that RCA had created electronic television. They made their presentation at the New York World's Fair. There was no mention of Philo Farnsworth. His earlier demonstrations had been forgotten.

Just a few months later, in October 1939, after years in court, Farnsworth emerged the winner in his battles against RCA. He had finally proven that he had invented the idea of electronic television first. RCA had to pay Farnsworth licensing fees to use his inventions.

But Farnsworth never became a wealthy man from his invention. Instead, in 1941, all commercial television production stopped. That year, the U.S. entered World War II, and the government ordered a black-out of all commercial broadcasts. For the next four years, all television technology was centered on radar and other military defense.

During World War II, Farnsworth helped the war effort by creating radar and other devices for detecting enemy positions. At the end of the war, with his hard-won patents about to expire, he knew he would never make money from his invention. He sold his company to ITT in 1949.

LATER YEARS: Farnsworth continued to invent. He invented the first "cold" cathode ray tube, an early air traffic control system, and an early electron microscope.

Farnsworth devoted the last years of his life to the study of nuclear "fusion." That's a process to harness atomic energy safely, and without the problems of nuclear waste. He received two patents in contributing to the technology of nuclear fusion.

PHILO FARNSWORTH'S HOME AND FAMILY: Farnsworth married Pem Gardner in 1926. They had four children. Weakened and ill, Philo Farnsworth died on March 11, 1971, in Salt Lake City, Utah. He was 64 years old.

HIS INVENTIONS: When Farnsworth died, he held over 300 patents, worldwide. Though he is not well known, his inventions led to television as we know it today. His patents cover such basic TV processes as scanning, focusing, synchronizing, power, and controls. The story of his fight to hold on to the rights to his invention is a sad chapter in the history of inventors. He was inducted into the Inventors Hall of Fame in 1984. In 1999, *Time* magazine named him one of the most important people of the 20th century.

WORLD WIDE WEB SITES:

http://www.invent.org/hall_of_fame/56.html
http://www.sfmuseum.org/hist10/philo.html
http://www.time.com/time/time100/scientist/profile/farnsworth.html

Alexander Fleming
1881 - 1955
Scottish Doctor and Scientist
Discovered Penicillin, the First Successful Antibiotic
Winner of the Nobel Prize

ALEXANDER FLEMING WAS BORN on August 6, 1881, in Lochfield, Scotland. His parents were Hugh and Grace Fleming. They were farmers. Alexander, called Alec, was the seventh of eight children. These included two half-sisters and two half-brothers from his father's first marriage. His father died when Alec was seven. After that, his mother and oldest brother ran the farm.

ALEXANDER FLEMING GREW UP on the family farm. He and his siblings loved to roam the fields and study the world around them. "We unconsciously learned a great deal from nature," he recalled.

ALEXANDER FLEMING WENT TO SCHOOL in Dorval, four miles from home. He walked a total of eight miles a day, to and from school. He was an excellent student.

When Alec was 13, he moved to London. One of his older brothers, Tom, had become a doctor there. Alec went to live with him. He also began to study at a technical school. At that point, he planned a career in business.

STARTING TO WORK: After two years of business school, Alec got a job as a shipping clerk. The work wasn't very exciting.

When he was 19, Fleming joined the Army. He trained as a soldier, but never fought. The next year, an uncle died and left him about $500. Encouraged by his brother Tom, Fleming decided to go to medical school.

GOING TO MEDICAL SCHOOL: Fleming was always an outstanding student. He had the highest score on the medical school entrance exam. He attended St. Mary's Hospital Medical School. He won a scholarship that paid for his schooling.

In 1906, Fleming graduated from medical school. He began to work for St. Mary's in the lab. He remained there for the rest of his career.

FIRST JOBS IN MEDICINE: Fleming started working at St. Mary's in 1906. He also continued taking science courses at London

University. His first job at the lab was under the direction of a famous doctor named Almroth Wright. Wright's specialty was vaccines. Like **Edward Jenner**, he was interested in how the body could build its own defenses against disease.

When World War I began in 1914, Fleming became a captain in the army medical corps. In France, he worked in a lab created to treat wounded soldiers. Fleming saw first-hand the number of soldiers who died of bacterial infections, because there were no medicines to treat them.

At that time, Fleming and other scientists were studying antiseptics. These were chemicals that could stop some bacteria from growing. But they couldn't destroy the bacteria.

After the war ended in 1918, Fleming went back to St. Mary's. There, he continued to study antiseptics. He also studied how the body fights infections by itself. This led him to discover a naturally occurring chemical called "lysozyme." He noted that lysozymes occur in human blood, tears, and saliva. They could destroy harmless bacteria, but didn't affect bacteria that cause disease.

At that time, scientists knew that infections were spread by agents like bacteria, viruses, and fungi. But there was no successful drug that could kill these life-threatening agents. A simple bacterial infection—from a cut, or developing from a bad cold—could kill a person. Scientists everywhere were trying to come up with a drug that would kill infection. But the medicine had to be safe, too.

DISCOVERING PENICILLIN: In 1928, Fleming made a breakthrough discovery—penicillin. It happened by accident.

Fleming in his London laboratory, c. 1941

In September 1928, Fleming had several bacteria experiments growing in dishes. They were a type of bacteria called "staphylococcus" (staff-uh-low-COCK-us), or staph. Staph is a common bacteria that can cause serious infections.

Fleming left the dish out in the open air. He then went on a two-week vacation. When he returned, he looked at the dish. He was astonished by what he saw. The staph had continued to grow, but in one area of the dish, there was mold growing instead. And around the mold, the staph bacteria had been killed. He theorized that the mold had killed the bacteria.

Fleming analyzed the mold. He found it was from the family of molds called "Penicillium." Fleming had no idea how the mold had gotten into the dish. There was a mold laboratory downstairs from his lab. Perhaps it floated upstairs, and through the air.

But the mystery was even more fascinating—and astonishing. While Fleming was on vacation, London had one week of cold weather. That was followed by a week of warm weather. That made conditions perfect for first, mold to grow, then for the staph bacteria to flourish.

Fleming named the antibacterial mold "penicillin." He began working on the substance, trying to recreate it. But he couldn't produce enough pure, stable penicillin to test properly.

Nonetheless, Fleming wrote a scientific article about his findings. He presented the paper in 1929. But the article didn't draw much attention. That all changed in the late 1930s.

HOWARD FLOREY AND ERNST CHAIN: In the late 1930s, two chemists working in England came across Fleming's paper. Howard Florey and Ernst Chain were scientists working on developing a successful and safe antibiotic.

World War II was looming, and the English wanted to find an antibiotic to keep its troops safe from infection. Florey and Chain were trying to identify, then isolate, molds that could kill bacteria. After studying Fleming's paper, they decided to focus on penicillin.

Florey and Chain successfully isolated and purified the penicillin. Then, they tested it on mice, to make sure it was safe. It was both safe and effective. Next came trials in humans.

The results were amazing. Penicillin proved to be safe and effective in treating many different bacterial infections.

MASS-PRODUCING PENICILLIN: Laboratories in England and the U.S. began the mass-production of penicillin. By 1944, there was enough penicillin for all the troops, and for civilians, too.

For the first time in history, diseases that often ended in death were brought under control. Penicillin was effective against tuberculosis, pneumonia, scarlet fever, and infections of childbirth. Millions of lives were saved in just the first years of use.

Fleming, along with Florey and Chain, became famous. He was honored all over the world. But he remained a modest man. He also refused any money for his discovery.

THE NOBEL PRIZE: In 1945, just as World War II came to an end, Fleming won the Nobel Prize. That is one of the most important prizes in the world. He shared that year's prize in Medicine with Florey and Chain.

LATER WORK: Fleming continued to work at St. Mary's. His later work included studies in vaccines and bacteria. The lab where he made his great discovery was renamed the Wright-Fleming Institute in 1948. Today it is a museum devoted to educational programs about Fleming and medicine.

ALEXANDER FLEMING'S HOME AND FAMILY: Fleming married Sarah McElroy in 1915. They had one son, Robert. Sarah died in 1949. In 1953 he married Dr. Amalia Koutsouri-Voureka. She was a fellow researcher at St. Mary's.

Fleming retired from St. Mary's in 1954. He died on March 11, 1955. He was 73 years old.

HIS INVENTION: Fleming is remembered as the discover of penicillin. Although it took Florey and Chain to make a successful drug out of his discovery, Fleming's work blazed the trail. Millions of lives have been saved through his work. The discovery of penicillin is considered the most important medical breakthrough of the 20th century. In 1999, *Time* magazine named Fleming one of the most important people of the 20th century.

WORLD WIDE WEB SITES:

http:/nobelprize.org/medicine/laureates/1945/fleming-bio.html

http://www.chemheritage.org/EducationalServices/pharm/antibiot/
    readings/fleming

http://www.pbs.org/wgbh/aso/databank/entries/bmflem.html

http://www.time.com/time/time100/scientist/profile/fleming.html

Henry Ford
1863 - 1947
American Industrialist, Inventor, and Philanthropist
Developed Mass Production

HENRY FORD WAS BORN on July 30, 1863, Springwells, Michigan. His parents were William and Mary Ford. Mary was a homemaker. William was a successful farmer. Henry was the eldest of six children. His brothers were John, William, Jr., and Robert. His sisters were Margaret and Jane.

HENRY FORD GREW UP on his family's farm in what is now Dearborn, Michigan. People who knew him as a boy remembered that he didn't like the hard physical work of farming. He was always looking for easier and more efficient ways of getting his work done. He became interested in the machinery on the farm and helped his father keep them repaired.

Henry developed a keen interest in mechanics. When he got a new toy, he would take it apart to see how it worked, then put it back together. At Christmas his brothers and sisters would surround their toys and say, "Don't let Henry have them. He just takes them apart."

As Henry's mechanical skills grew, he became fascinated with clocks and watches. He learned how they worked, and how to repair them. He made his own set of tools and set up a small workshop in his house. Neighbors brought their broken clocks and watches to Henry. He fixed them for free.

HENRY FORD WENT TO SCHOOL at the Scotch Settlement School in 1871. It was a one-room schoolhouse near his family's farm. Children of all ages learned reading, writing, and arithmetic by memorizing and reciting at the school. The students read from McGuffey's Readers. These books taught reading skills while also providing moral lessons. Later in life, Henry said that these books were an important influence.

Henry was an average student. He did well in arithmetic. He would often fix his classmates' watches, when the teacher wasn't looking.

Henry was also famous for playing pranks on the other students. Once, he drilled two small holes in a classmate's seat. He put a pin in one hole, and ran a string through the other. From his desk, he pulled the string, causing his victim to jump from his seat with a shout.

FIRST JOBS: In 1879 Ford went to Detroit to become a mechanic. He was sixteen years old. He started as an apprentice at the Flowers Brothers machine shop for $2.50 a week. In 1880, he went to work at the Detroit Dry Dock Company, the largest shipbuilding factory in the city. He was paid only $2.00 a week, but he thought he would learn more. At night he made extra money repairing watches at a local jewelry store.

Ford returned to his family's farm every fall to help with the harvest. In 1882 John Gleason, a neighboring farmer, hired Henry to help him. He'd bought a **Westinghouse** steam engine to run his threshing machines, but he couldn't get it to work. "I have an idea he was afraid of his machine," Ford remembered. "To tell the truth I was frightened myself." Within a day Ford had the steam engine running. During the next few years, he used the engine to run farm machines and saw mills for Gleason and other farmers in the area. Westinghouse also hired him to repair and demonstrate its steam engines throughout Michigan.

In 1886 Ford started a lumber business on 80 acres of farmland his father gave him. With a rented steam engine and a saw, he harvested the timber on his land. During this time he developed an interest in the new gasoline engines that were beginning to appear. After seeing the Otto engine, he built his own version in his spare time. He saw the potential of gasoline engines as an alternative to

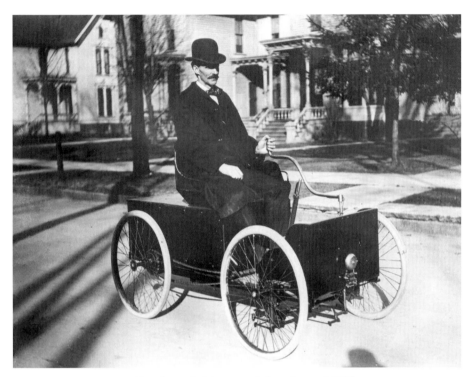

Ford and his quadricycle, c.1896.

heavy steam engines. He also started thinking about building a "horseless carriage" that could transport people under its own power. (See entries on **Karl Benz** and **Gottfried Daimler** for information on the first gasoline-powered automobiles.)

In 1891 Ford moved back to Detroit to work for the **Edison** Illuminating Company as an engineer and machinist. He was growing tired of rural life. He also decided he needed a better knowledge of electricity in order to build his "horseless carriage". At first, he ran the steam engines and generators in one of Edison's power plants. His skills and hard work impressed his bosses. By 1893 he had become one of the company's most valuable employees.

THE QUADRICYCLE: Ford built his first automobile while he worked at Edison. He set up a workshop in the shed behind his

213

house. Using scrap parts and pieces of pipe, he built a working gasoline engine. He worked on his automobile during his spare time over the next two years. It looked like a small buggy. It had a 2-cylinder motor that generated about 4 horsepower, a "steering bar", and bicycle wheels.

In 1896, Ford finished his Quadricycle. When he was ready for a test drive, he discovered that the vehicle wouldn't fit through the shed door. He took an ax and knocked out some bricks to make the door wider. Although it was not the first gasoline-powered car built in America, it had many important new features: it was light, inexpensive, and easy to repair.

STARTING IN THE AUTOMOBILE BUSINESS: In 1899, Ford left Edison to dedicate all of his time to building automobiles. He started the Detroit Automobile Company, with the financial backing of several wealthy Detroit businessmen. But he argued with his backers, and was unable to get a car into production. The company closed after one year.

In 1901, he started the Henry Ford Company with the support of a new group of investors. Once again he struggled to get an acceptable car into production. Like before, he argued with the other investors over the kind of car they should build. Ford left the company in 1902. The investors hired Henry Leland to run the company. They changed the name to the Cadillac Automobile Company. It was very successful, and became part of General Motors in 1909.

For the next few years, Ford dedicated his time to building race-cars. He thought racing provided a good way to develop better automotive designs. It also gave him plenty of free publicity. He

Ford with race driver Barney Oldfield and the "999" race car, c.1903

built his first successful racecar in 1901. It had a four-cylinder engine that produced 26 horsepower.

Ford challenged Alexander Winton to a ten-mile race. Winton was the country's leading race car designer and driver. His car was considered the "world's fastest automobile." Ford drove his car himself. After eight miles, he passed Winton, and ended up winning the race by a quarter mile. His victory made him a national celebrity.

Ford's racing successes continued over the next three years. One of his famous cars was called the "999", in which legendary driver Barney Oldfield won many races. Henry also broke the world speed record with an average speed of 100 miles per hour in 1904.

THE FORD MOTOR COMPANY: In 1903, at the height of his racing fame, Henry Ford started his next automobile company, the Ford

Motor Company. His partners included James Couzens and John and Horace Dodge. Couzens was a dynamic business manager, and the Dodge brothers would manufacture most of the parts for the early Ford cars.

In the early 1900s automobiles were considered playthings for the rich. They were big, heavy, complicated machines. The owner usually needed to hire a chauffer to drive and repair them. Ford went to work building an affordable car for the average American. His first cars sold well, and the company prospered. Each new model was named after a letter in the alphabet, starting with "A" and eventually going to "S".

THE MODEL T FORD: Ford introduced the Model T in 1908. He had finally realized his vision of producing a car that was light, simple, reliable, and inexpensive. He called it the "universal car." The first models sold for $850. At that time most other cars available cost $2,000 to $3,000.

The Model T was an instant success. Ford sold 8,000 Model T's in its first year, 1908. Sales grew dramatically over the next few years. He sold 18,000 in 1909, 34,000 in 1910, and 78,000 in 1911.

MASS PRODUCTION: In 1910, Ford opened a large new factory in Highland Park, Michigan (near Detroit). It was the first factory specifically designed for automobile manufacturing. There, Ford and his managers worked on new methods to increase car production.

THE ASSEMBLY LINE: Ford and his managers developed the moving assembly line, which revolutionized the automotive industry. On the assembly line, the car's frame starts at one end and moves

Model T Fords rolling off the assembly line, Highland Park, MI, c. 1917

along a conveyor. Workers stationed along the line add parts to the frame as it goes by them. Finally, the finished car rolls off the other end of the line. This method cut the time it took to build a car from 12 hours and 30 minutes to 1 hour and 30 minutes. The result was a rate of production that couldn't have been imagined before. In 1916 Ford built—and sold—730,000 Model T's.

The success of the Model T made Ford the largest automobile manufacturer in the world. By 1918, half of all the cars sold in the

United States were Fords. Between 1908 and 1927, when production of the model ended, Ford had sold 15,500,000 Model T's.

It is important to note that Henry Ford didn't invent mass production. Many of its principles had been in use for almost a century. In fact, **Eli Whitney** had developed mass production techniques around 1800. But it was Ford who first applied and refined these methods to automobile production. That allowed him to fulfill his vision of building cars for the masses. He is credited with beginning the age of "consumerism." Mass production made it possible for average people to be able to buy a wide variety products, like cars, refrigerators, washing machines, radios, and televisions.

The success of the Model T made Henry Ford a very wealthy man. He believed he should share his wealth with people who bought his cars and with the workers who made them. Ford constantly made improvements to the Model T, and kept lowering the price. In 1908 it cost $850. By 1927 some models were as low as $263.

In 1914, Ford decided to share his wealth with his workers. He doubled their pay from $2.50 an hour to $5.00, and cut the workday from 9 hours to 8 hours. Many industrial leaders called him "a traitor to his class," but most people regarded this as a great step forward for industrial workers. Ford's new policy led to many economic benefits. It lowered employee turnover, and raised the workers' morale, leading to even greater productivity. It also created a new class of consumers who could afford to buy the cars they built.

OTHER VENTURES: Although Henry Ford is most famous for his cars, he had many other interests. In 1917, he started the Henry

Ford & Son Company and began producing the Fordson tractor. Like the Model T car, it was lightweight and affordable. It made mechanized farming methods affordable for the small farmer.

Ford was also an innovator in the early aircraft industry. He built the Ford Tri-motor airplane in 1927. It was one of the first successful airliners.

Ford always loved the outdoors, and was an enthusiastic camper all of his life. His interest in camping led him to develop the charcoal briquette, which he processed from sawdust from his factories and lumber mills. Ford enjoyed camping with other famous Americans, including **Thomas Edison,** Harvy Firestone, and the naturalist William Burroughs. They called themselves the "Vagabonds."

In 1936, Ford created the Ford Foundation for the purpose of advancing human welfare. The Foundation is now one of the largest philanthropies in the world. It provides financial aid to people in need all over the world, as well as to educational and health programs. Ford also created Greenfield Village and the Henry Ford Museum, now called the Henry Ford. It is a collection of buildings and displays celebrating inventors and their inventions.

HENRY FORD'S HOME AND FAMILY: Ford married Clara Bryant in 1888. They first settled in a house that Henry built on his timber farm. Clara was a homemaker and gave Henry a lot of support during his early years in the automobile business. In 1916, they moved into Fairlane, a mansion that Ford built in Dearborn. Their only child, Edsel Bryant Ford, was born in 1893. Edsel was president of the Ford Motor Company from 1919 until his death in 1943. Henry Ford died at the age of 83 on April 7, 1947, on his Fairlane estate.

Ford and Thomas Edison, commemorating the first light bulb, at Greenfield Village in Dearborn, Michigan, 1929.

HIS INVENTION: Henry Ford developed mass production methods for the automobile industry. This made it possible for average Americans to own a car. Widespread car ownership was a major influence in 20th century American history. Highways, suburban communities, motels, and shopping centers were all brought about by mass car ownership.

WORLD WIDE WEB SITES:

http://www.ford.com/en/heritage/fordFamily/
http://www.hfmgv.org/exhibits/hf/
http://www.pbs.org/wgbh/aso/databank/entries/btford/hmtl
http://www.time.com/time/time100/builder/profile/ford.html

Benjamin Franklin
1706 - 1790
American Statesman, Printer, and Inventor of the Lightning Rod, the Franklin Stove, and Bifocals

BENJAMIN FRANKLIN WAS BORN on January 17, 1706, in Boston, Massachusetts. At that time, Massachusetts was a colony of Britain. His parents were Josiah and Abiah Franklin. Josiah was a soap and candle maker. Abiah took care of a household of 17 children.

Ben had seven sisters and nine brothers. His sisters were named Elizabeth, Hannah, Anne, Mary, Sarah, Lydia, and Jane. His brothers were Samuel, Josiah, John, Peter, and James. Four other brothers died as infants.

BENJAMIN FRANKLIN GREW UP in a large and lively family. He was a curious, outgoing boy. He had a natural inventiveness, too. He loved to swim, and spent hours at the sport. To improve his stroke, he created a pair of wooden swim paddles. He strapped them to his hands, and paddled in the water around Boston.

BENJAMIN FRANKLIN WENT TO SCHOOL at Latin School in Boston for one year. His father sent him to the school hoping Ben would become a preacher. But it was too expensive. So Ben was sent to another school. It was called "Mr. George Brownell's school for writing and arithmetic." Ben attended for two years, then left formal schooling for good. His father had decided it was time for him to work.

STARTING TO WORK: Ben started working for his father at the age of 10. He helped out in the soap and candle business. When he was 12, his father wanted him to become an apprentice. Ben wanted to be a sailor. But Ben's father had lost a son, Josiah, who drowned at sea.

Ben's father wanted him to became an apprentice to his brother James, to learn to be a printer. Ben didn't like the idea. He knew he'd learn the business quickly. In Franklin's time, a person had to spend years as an apprentice. An apprentice was in many ways a servant, tied to his master. Ben didn't want to spend years at one thing. He wanted to learn, and do, many things.

LEARNING THE PRINTER'S TRADE: Ben's father insisted, so despite his wishes, Ben became James's apprentice. He worked hard, and learned all about printing.

Ben spent his free time, and all his money, on books and reading. He enjoyed books on all topics. He read about vegetarianism (a diet that doesn't include meat). He decided it would be a healthful, and cheap, way to eat. Ben was always frugal with money, too. He became a vegetarian, then talked his brother into giving him the money he'd normally spend on meat for Ben's meals.

At that time, many printers were also newspaper owners. Ben wanted to write for his brother's paper. But James wasn't interested in his articles. So Ben sent pieces he'd written to the paper, using the pseudonym "Silence Dogood." A pseudonym (SOO-doe-nim) is a name an author chooses to write as, instead of his or her own.

Not knowing it was Ben's work, James printed the articles. When he found out the truth, he was furious. They argued, and Ben knew it was time for him to leave. He decided to run away. That was the only way he could escape spending years as James's apprentice.

MOVING TO PHILADELPHIA: At the age of 17, Franklin set out, alone, for Philadelphia. He found work with a printer, and soon was on his way. Within a few years, he bought his own press. Next, he bought a newspaper. It became a great success.

NEWSPAPERMAN: Franklin's newspaper was the *Pennsylvania Gazette*. It was full of lively, well-written stories. It brought a lot of attention to Franklin. He became the official printer for the colonies of Pennsylvania, New Jersey, and Delaware. That meant that he was

Franklin working as a printer.

responsible for printing government documents and money. Over the next several years, Franklin purchased papers in other parts of the colonies. He became a successful, wealthy, man.

POOR RICHARD'S ALMANAC: In 1732, Franklin began publishing the work for which he is most famous: *Poor Richard's Almanac*. At that time, most households had an almanac on hand. They came out every year, and contained information on holidays, weather, sunrises and sunsets, tides, and other data of general interest.

But Franklin's Almanac was special. It contained all kinds of witty sayings and predictions for the coming year. Famous phrases of Franklin's, like "a penny saved is a penny earned," first appeared in his Almanac. "Poor Richard" was Richard Saunders, another of Franklin's pseudonyms. Franklin published *Poor Richard's Almanac* for 25 years.

CITIZEN, INVENTOR, STATESMAN: By the time he was 42, Franklin had made his fortune. He decided to devote the rest of his life to other things. Over the next 40 years, this tireless, curious man distinguished himself as a citizen, inventor, and statesman.

As a citizen of Philadelphia, he created the city's first fire department, lending library, and postal service. As an inventor, he created the lightning rod, the Franklin stove, and bifocals. As a statesman, he helped bring about the birth of a new nation, the United States of America.

CREATING MANY FIRSTS FOR THE PEOPLE OF PHILADELPHIA: Franklin was dedicated to improving the life of the people of Philadelphia. In the 1700s, there was no fire department in the city. In 1736, Franklin started the first. There was also no fire insurance a homeowner could purchase to replace a home that had burned down. In 1752, Franklin started the first fire insurance company in the colonies.

In the 1700s, libraries were private. There was no such thing as a public lending library. Franklin loved books and reading. He thought that books should be available to all people. So, in 1731, he started the first lending library in the colonies. He also created a postal system and became the first Postmaster of Philadelphia.

SCIENTIST AND INVENTOR: Franklin was fascinated by science. He studied nature and developed theories about hurricanes, the gulf

Franklin opening the first public lending library.

stream, and other natural phenomena. Like many people of his day, he was particularly interested in electricity.

ELECTRICITY AND LIGHTNING: In Franklin's time, people didn't know where lightning came from. Some thought it was a mysterious force that came from the heavens. Franklin theorized that lightning was a form of electricity. How he proved that led to his first major invention.

In 1752, to test his theory, Franklin flew a kite in a thunderstorm. The kite had a pointed piece of metal at the top, connected to a key at the bottom of the kite string. During the storm, an electrical charge traveled down the string to the key.

When Franklin touched the key, he got a shock. He knew that meant he'd proved his theory. Lightning was a form of electric current. It was drawn to the metal at the top of the kite. The current traveled down the string, sending the electric charge to the key, and

Franklin's famous kite experiment, proving that
lightning is a form of electricity.

then into his hand. Franklin published his theories, and they made him a famous man, all over the world.

THE LIGHTNING ROD: Using the knowledge from his experiment, Franklin invented the lightning rod. The electrical current from lightning can cause fires and explosions. Franklin's device was a metal rod placed on the roof of a building. It was connected to a metal wire that ran down the side of the building and into the ground. It worked by drawing the electrical current away from the building and channeling it into the ground, making the current harmless. Lightning rods based on Franklin's original design are still in use today.

THE FRANKLIN STOVE: Another of his important inventions was the Franklin Stove. In Franklin's time, most homes were heated by fireplaces. Franklin's invention, from the 1740s, was an iron stove that produced more heat, cost less to run, and was more efficient than a regular fireplace. Like lightning rods, Franklin stoves are still in use today.

BIFOCALS: Franklin loved to read, and as he got older, he couldn't see as well. He needed two pairs of glasses: one for reading, and one for seeing at a distance. But he didn't like having two pairs. So he invented "bifocals." He had a glass maker cut the two pairs apart, then put them back together, with the lenses for reading on the bottom, and the one for distance on top. Bifocals, too, are still used today.

Franklin didn't believe he should profit from his inventions. He never applied for a **patent** for any of them. Instead, he chose to share his inventions with the world, for free.

TRAVELING TO ENGLAND: In 1757, the leaders of Pennsylvania sent Franklin to England. They wanted him to develop trade agreements between the colony and the British. Franklin would remain overseas for most of the next 18 years.

THE REVOLUTIONARY WAR: By the time Franklin left Pennsylvania, trouble was brewing between the colonies and Britain. At that time, the colonies were governed by England and King George III. Most American colonists believed that the colonies should have their own government, a government that they controlled. During his years in England, Franklin met the most important leaders of Europe. He kept a close eye on the developing political situation between England and his home land.

FOUNDING FATHER: Franklin headed home to Philadelphia in 1775. By the time he landed, the Revolutionary War had begun. Over the next 15 years, Franklin would serve as one of the Founding Fathers of his country.

In 1775, he was elected to the Continental Congress. As part of those duties, he helped write the Declaration of Independence. Published on July 4th, 1776, the Declaration outlined the ideas behind the Revolution. It was written in large part by Thomas Jefferson, but Franklin contributed his own ideas and wisdom to the document.

Next, Franklin was sent to France. The new United States needed France to provide money and military force in the war against England. Franklin did a splendid job. He won the aid and support of the French for the U.S. He also witnessed the flight of the first hot air balloon, invented by **Joseph and Jacques Montgolfier.**

When the Revolutionary War ended in 1781, the U.S. called on Franklin once again. He helped negotiate the treaty that ended the war, which he signed in 1783.

When he returned home, Franklin was named head of the Pennsylvania government. In 1788, at the age of 82, he performed his final service to the nation, as a delegate to the Constitutional Convention. He contributed to the writing of the Constitution, and, after it was written, argued passionately that the members pass it. The Constitution was passed, and Franklin signed it, on September 17, 1787.

Franklin is the only person to sign the four major documents establishing the United States. His signature appears on the Declaration of Independence (1776), The Treaty of Alliance with

France (1778), The Treaty of Peace (1783), and the Constitution (1787).

LATER YEARS: At the end of the Constitutional Convention, Franklin returned home and finished his famous *Autobiography*. He moved into the Philadelphia home of his daughter, Sarah. He died there on April 17, 1790, at the age of 84.

BENJAMIN FRANKLIN'S HOME AND FAMILY: Franklin married Deborah Read in September 1730. They had two children, Francis and Sarah. Francis died as a child. They also raised a son, William, whom Franklin had with another woman.

HIS INVENTIONS: The most important of Franklin's inventions were the lightning rod, the Franklin stove, and bifocals. All show his practical approach to solving problems. And, in a tribute to this great American, born 300 years ago, all are in use today.

Franklin was one of the most popular, and famous men of his time. He brought his special inventive gifts to devices of great practicality and institutions for the common good, and his genius to the creation of a great nation.

WORLD WIDE WEB SITES:

http://bensguide.gpo.gov/benfranklin/inventor.html
http://sln.fi.edu/franklin/birthday
http://www.english.udel.edu/lemay/franklin
http://www.pbs.org/benfranklin/13_inquiring_little.html

Robert Fulton
1765 - 1815
American Inventor and Engineer
Inventor of the First Successful Commercial Steamboat

ROBERT FULTON WAS BORN on November 14, 1765, in Little
Britain, Pennsylvania. His parents were Robert and Mary Fulton.

His father was a farmer and his mother was a homemaker.
Robert was one of five children. His father died when he was three.

ROBERT FULTON GREW UP in the city of Lancaster, Pennsylvania.
He had an early interest in how things worked, and began to invent

at an early age. He made his own lead pencils by hammering sheet metal. As a young teenager, Fulton designed and built guns. He assembled the guns, and produced accurate drawings, outlining his designs. He was also interested in boats. In fact, he made a model of a paddle-wheel boat as a teenager.

ROBERT FULTON WENT TO SCHOOL at the local schools for several years. But he wasn't that interested in school. He loved to draw, and was a gifted artist. He left school after a few years to try to make his living as an artist.

When he was 17, Fulton moved to Philadelphia and began to paint, draw, and sell his art. He did well enough that four years later, at 21, he returned to Lancaster and bought his mother a small farm. Then, in 1786, he decided to go to Europe.

TRAVELING TO EUROPE: Fulton first visited England, where his former neighbor, the artist Benjamin West, was living. Fulton studied painting with West, and also began to develop some ideas he had for inventions. In 1793, impressed by the steam engine of **James Watt**, he sketched plans for a steam-powered boat.

Over the next several years, Fulton designed and **patented** several different devices. In 1794, he patented a saw for cutting marble. He also developed a machine that spun flax into cloth, one that made rope, and a mechanical shovel. Fulton also designed cast-iron bridges.

Fulton was fascinated by ships and navigation systems. In 1795, he published a book on canal navigation. He proposed several innovations in the design and building of locks. Canals are systems of natural and man-made waterways. Locks are devices that control the flow of water in and out of canals, allowing boats to travel throughout a waterway. In 1794, Fulton patented a "double-inclined plane." It was a device that raised and lowered boats in canals.

In 1797, Fulton traveled to France. Over the next few years, he applied for patents for his devices in that country. He also began work on a design for a submarine. It was to be used to launch torpedoes and lay mines in the water.

At that time, France and England were at war. The French wanted to use Fulton's torpedoes against the British Navy, which had blockaded French ports. Fulton built a submarine that could, in theory, be used to carry and plant explosives in water. His first model didn't work properly. But he was convinced they could be effective in naval battles.

Fulton traveled back to England. The English government was also interested in his submarine. They wanted to know all about the technology, to use against the French. Fulton continued to work on his submarine, then decided to return home.

In 1802, Fulton returned to the U.S. Before he left England, he'd purchased a steam engine from James Watt. Now, he set out to put that engine to work in a boat.

BUILDING THE STEAMBOAT: Fulton returned to America with great ideas, and began to look for money to fund them. He found financial help from a wealthy man named Robert Livingston. Livingston had been the U.S. ambassador to France when Fulton lived there. He knew Fulton's abilities, and paid for the development of his first steamboat.

First voyage of Fulton's steamboat to Albany, 1807.

It is important to note that Fulton did not *invent* the steamboat. When Fulton was at work on his first boat, other inventors had already created steamboats. The best known of these early inventors was John Fitch. Fitch had successfully launched a steamboat in Philadelphia in 1785.

Fulton's first steamboat was the *Clermont*. It was 133 feet long and 18 feet wide. The hull of the boat was built following the design of ocean-going ships. The engine was placed in the hull, with the steam boiler behind it. Two 15-foot wide paddle wheels were placed on either side of the engine.

STEAM ENGINES: All steam engines work on a basic principle: they convert heat energy into mechanical energy. All steam engines have a boiler. The boilers of Fulton's time burned coal to boil water. When water is heated in a closed space and converted into steam, the pressure increases. When steam expands, it takes up many times the space of water. The force of the pressure of the steam drives the engine.

THE *CLERMONT*: The *Clermont* was launched on August 17, 1807, on the Hudson River. The ship traveled from New York to Albany, at about five miles an hour. The trip took 32 hours.

The voyage of the *Clermont* was a great success. Fulton and Livingston had proved that steamboats were reliable transportation. By the fall of 1807, the *Clermont* was making regular runs delivering goods and passengers between New York and Albany. It became the first successful commercial steamboat in the U.S.

For the rest of his life, Fulton devoted himself to improving his steamboat. He also was involved in ship building and establishing steamboat lines. And he continued designing boats and arms for naval warfare. During the War of 1812, he designed a huge steamboat to protect New York harbor.

ROBERT FULTON'S HOME AND FAMILY: Fulton married Harriet Livingston on January 8, 1808. They had four children. Fulton died on February 25, 1815. He was 50 years old.

HIS INVENTION: Although he didn't invent the steamboat, Fulton built the first commercially successful ship to run on steam. He showed that steamships were safe and reliable transportation. It was an important development for trade in the country. Later steamboats brought goods and people to the inland waterways of the U.S.

WORLD WIDE WEB SITES:

http://www.history.rochester.edu/steam/thurston/fulton
http://www.robertfulton.org/
http://xroads.virginia.edu/~HYPER/DETOC/transport/fulton.html

Galileo Galilei
1564 - 1642
**Italian Mathematician, Physicist, and Astronomer
Inventor of the Thermometer and the
First Practical Telescope
"Father of the Scientific Method"**

GALILEO WAS BORN on February 15, 1564, in Pisa, Italy. He is known to us by his first name only, Galileo. His parents were Vincenzo Galilei and Giulia degli Ammannati. Vincenzo was a musician.

Galileo was the oldest of six children. The family moved to Florence in the early 1570s.

GALILEO WENT TO SCHOOL at the University of Pisa. His father wanted him to study medicine. But mathematics fascinated Galileo. He studied math, and later became a professor at the University of Padua.

While still a student, Galileo began to study the movement of objects in space—physics. He noted the movements of a hanging lamp as it swayed. From its motion, he developed his concept of how a pendulum works. This influenced the first pendulum clocks.

FIRST INVENTIONS AND DISCOVERIES IN PHYSICS: Galileo studied the works of Euclid and **Archimedes.** In Padua, which is a port town, he studied how mechanical devices could move water. Like Archimedes, he developed a pump system to move water. He also developed a balance, or scale, based on Archimedes's theories.

In 1606, Galileo invented the first thermometer. He called it a "thermoscope." It was a bulb filled with a combination of water and alcohol that either expanded or contracted, based on changes in temperature. It was not as accurate as the mercury thermometer of **Daniel Gabriel Fahrenheit**. But it was one of the first devices of its type in the history of science.

Galileo also performed experiments to understand how gravity works. He rolled balls down a hill, examining whether their weight determined how quickly they moved. He also dropped objects of different weights from a standard height. This led him to his theory of gravity. He theorized that objects fall at a constant rate, no

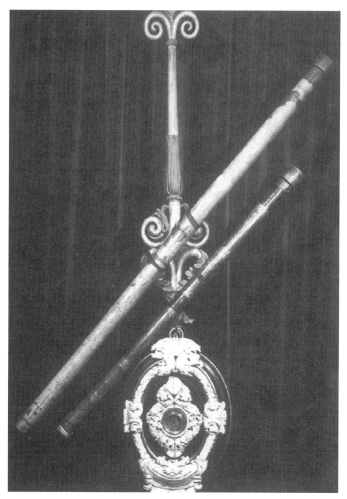

Replica of Galileo's telescope. c. 1609

matter what their weight. These theories greatly influenced **Isaac Newton**.

SCIENTIFIC METHOD: Galileo is considered the "father of the scientific method." He would first suggest a theory, then test it, based on experiments. He took a rational, ordered approach to science.

INVENTING THE FIRST PRACTICAL TELESCOPE: The first telescope had been patented by Hans Lippershay in 1608. In 1609,

Galileo invented his first telescope. It was a tremendous improvement on Lippershay's design.

Lippershay's telescope could magnify objects three times. Galileo's telescope could magnify objects 20 times. Through his telescope, he became the first person to see the surface of the moon. He saw that it had mountains and craters. He saw Jupiter, and Jupiter's moons. He could see the change of seasons on Venus. He saw sunspots on the surface of the sun.

Galileo's observation of the solar system led him to a ground-breaking conclusion. Like the scientist Copernicus (1473 - 1543), Galileo now believed that the Earth and other planets revolved around the sun. This theory is called the "heliocentric," or sun-centered, system of the universe. He published these findings in a famous book called *The Starry Messenger.* We know, of course, that Galileo's conclusion was true. But it was against the teachings of the most powerful political force of the time, the Catholic Church.

THE CATHOLIC CHURCH AND THE INQUISITION: The Catholic Church stated that the sun, and all planets, revolved around the Earth. This theory, called a "geocentric," or Earth-centered system, was part of the beliefs of the Church.

Galileo published his discovery that the Earth and planets revolved around the Sun. The Catholic Church considered these beliefs to be "heresy"—against the teachings of the Church. Galileo was called to Rome by the Inquisition. (That was the part of the Church that charged and tried heretics.)

People charged with heresy were sometimes condemned to death. Luckily, Galileo escaped that fate. But he was told he could

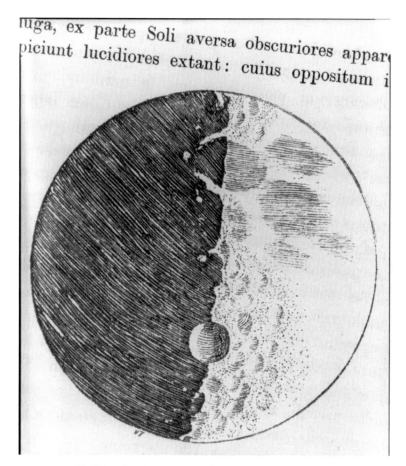

Galileo's drawing of the Moon, c. 1609.

not discuss or defend the theory that stated that the Earth moved around the sun.

Galileo continued his observations. He became more and more convinced that he was correct. In 1632, he published a book that stated his beliefs again. As a result, he was again called before the Inquisition.

BANNED FROM PUBLISHING AND PLACED UNDER HOUSE ARREST: This time the Church found Galileo guilty of heresy. Because of his age, he was placed under "house arrest." That meant that he could not travel or move freely. He was also banned from publishing anything ever again. Galileo remained under house arrest until his death in 1642.

GALILEO'S HOME AND FAMILY: Galileo never married. He did have three children, two daughters and a son, with a woman named Marina Gamba.

HIS INVENTIONS: Galileo is one of the most important scientists of all time. Using his telescope, he made observations that changed our knowledge of the universe. His development of the scientific method influenced the way research is done to this day. His studies in physics led to later discoveries by Newton and others.

WORLD WIDE WEB SITES:

http://galielo.rice.edu/bio/
http://starchild.gsfc.nasa.gov/

Bill Gates
1955 -
American Computer Software Pioneer
Co-Founder of Microsoft

BILL GATES WAS BORN on October 28, 1955, in Seattle, Washington. His full name is William Henry Gates III. His parents were William and Mary Gates. William is a lawyer. Mary, who died in 1994, was a teacher. She also worked with educational groups. Bill has two sisters, Kristi and Libby.

BILL GATES GREW UP in a close family. As a boy, he enjoyed all kinds of activities. He loved water sports and Boy Scouts. He had a paper route, and he liked to play tennis and baseball.

BILL GATES WENT TO SCHOOL at the local public schools until he was 12. He was a math whiz, but he didn't like school. He got in trouble, and his parents thought he could do better in school. They decided to send him to a private school called Lakeside.

Gates remembers that he didn't want to go at first. "I seriously considered flunking the entrance exam," he recalls. But he got into Lakeside, and things started to change.

STARTING TO WORK WITH COMPUTERS: At Lakeside, the school had rented computer time from a local company. At that time, there were no personal computers, or PCs.

FIRST COMPUTERS: The first computers were huge machines. Just one computer could fill an entire room. And it didn't have the power or speed of just one of today's personal computers.

A BRIEF HISTORY OF COMPUTERS: The root word of "computer" tells the origin of the machine. Computers "compute"—that is, they perform math calculations. The earliest "computer" was actually an adding machine. It was created in 1642 by Frenchman Blaise Pascal. Pascal's machine was simple. He entered numbers into a machine using dials. Inside the machine were cogs and wheels connected to the dials. They moved according to the numbers entered. The machine could accurately add and subtract numbers.

The next major step forward happened in the 1800s. Charles Babbage, a British mathematician, designed a machine to process numbers. It had many of the features of a modern computer. It had an input mechanism (like a keyboard), storage (memory), a computing mechanism (CPU), and an output mechanism (a computer screen or printer). Babbage never built his machine. But his research was very influential.

The first modern computers were developed during World War II (1939 - 1945). Mathematician Howard Aiken developed the Mark 1, a computer that ran on electromechanical relays. It helped improve the accuracy of Navy artillery.

Another advance from the World War II era came about through the research of Alan Turing. Turing invented the "Colossus," a computer that broke the Nazi military code. It helped end the war in Europe. "Colossus" was important for another reason. It was the first computer to use vacuum tubes to store and process data.

The next major innovation in computers was the ENIAC. (That stands for the Electronic Numerical Integrator and Calculator). Previous computers were used for military purposes. The ENIAC was the first computer for general, commercial use. It was enormous: it weighed 30-tons, and used more than 17,000 vacuum tubes.

In 1948, John Bardeen, William Schockley, and Walter Brattain invented the transistor. It was another tremendous breakthrough. Transistors replaced vacuum tubes with smaller, cooler processors.

The integrated circuit, invented by Jack Kilby in 1958, introduced the true modern era in computing. Now one silicon microchip could hold millions of electronic components. It revolutionized the industry.

Those early computers fascinated Gates. He used his math skills and natural curiosity to learn all he could about them.

One of his friends at Lakeside was a kid named Paul Allen. He loved computers, too. Allen and Gates learned how to "program" computers. That means that they created commands that could make the computer do tasks.

Gates and Allen learned enough to put the school's class scheduling system on the computer. They earned $4200 for that job. They also collected data on traffic and fed it into the computer. They sold the data to city and county governments. That job made them $20,000.

When Gates was 14, he and Allen were hired by another company. Their job was to review the electricity needs of the area. That's the kind of work done by large companies with college-educated staff. "No one knew we were just in the 9th and 10th grades," recalls Gates.

During the last half of his senior year, Gates began to work as a programmer full time. He finished his high school degree off-campus, graduating in 1973. Next, he went off to Harvard University. That's one of the finest colleges in the country.

But Gates wasn't very happy at Harvard. "At my high school I was kind of unique," he recalls. He didn't stand out among all the bright kids at Harvard.

THE ALTAIR 8800: In 1975 Gates got a call from Paul Allen. Allen had seen an article about the world's first personal computer, the Altair 8800. It was small and not very powerful. It had just 256 bytes of memory. (Most of today's PCs have 248,000,000 bytes of memory.)

But Gates and Allen saw the possibilities of the Altair 8800. They saw a way of making a computer for home and office use. The company that had developed the computer had only created the "hardware." That's the machine. They hadn't developed any "software." That's the programming that tells the machine what to do.

CO-FOUNDING MICROSOFT: Gates and Allen told the company that made the Altair 8800, MITS, that they had developed software for it. (They really hadn't done it yet.) MITS said they wanted to see it. So the two worked for weeks to develop the software.

They started out with an existing program, called BASIC. With it, they developed a special computer language for software to run on the Altair 8800. And it worked.

Gates dropped out of Harvard and started working with Allen. They formed their own company, Microsoft, in 1975. One of their first big contracts was with IBM.

MS-DOS: IBM had a new PC that needed an "operating system." An "operating system" is a series of commands, written in computer language. It controls the basic function of the computer. It also allows the "application software"—the programs for word processing, for instance—to work.

Gates and Allen developed the operating system for IBM in 1980. They called it MS-DOS. The letters stood for "Microsoft Disk Operating System." At that time, it was used on every computer that IBM made.

Gates with computer running Microsoft Windows XP

Gates, in a stroke of brilliance, didn't sell the program to IBM. Instead, he worked out an agreement in which Microsoft would get paid every time an IBM computer with MS-DOS was sold. Also, because IBM was the leading computer maker, MS-DOS was the most used system for PCs. It became the standard operating system used on almost all PCs. It made Gates, Allen, and Microsoft very, very rich.

Gates remembers those times. "Our vision was to put a computer on every desk and in every home. We'd eat pizza, drink Coke, and stay up all night. We'd write programs that would make computers more useful. When we weren't writing code, we were daydreaming about all the exciting things the computer might someday be able to do. People thought we were crazy."

But they weren't crazy. Instead, they were building one of the biggest companies in the world. In the early 1980s, over 90% of the world's PCs were running MS-DOS. And they were just getting started.

WINDOWS: In 1985, Microsoft announced "Windows 1.0." It is a software system that is very easy to use. At that time, most homes didn't have computers. Many businesses used them only for banking and finance.

Before Windows, computer users had to go through many complicated commands to start a program. There was no "mouse." Instead, the user pressed a number of keys to get into a program for a function like word processing.

Windows is based on the "point and click" idea. That means that a user can use a computer mouse to select a function, like word processing. The user points the mouse to the icon for that function on the computer screen, then clicks it. That "point and click" is all that's needed to make the function work. It made using a computer easier. Microsoft sold millions of copies. Gates was closer than ever to his goal of having "a computer on every desk and in every home."

Gates is a very competitive man. He wanted the computers on every desk to be running Microsoft software, too. So Microsoft created software for use at home, school, or office. Programs like Word for word processing and Power Point for presentations were packaged in the computers that were sold to millions of customers. They became the most common software used in homes, schools, and businesses. Microsoft products—and profits—grew enormously.

How people feel about Gates is another story. Some people love his products and services. Others think he is more concerned with

Gates with students at Chicago's Museum of Science and Industry

making money than making good products. Gates has also been ac-cused of unfair business practices to keep other companies from competing in the software market. That has led to lawsuits.

LEGAL PROBLEMS: In the 1990s, Microsoft got in trouble with the federal government. Some of Microsoft's competitors claimed that the company was blocking rivals from developing and selling simi-lar products. The Federal Trade Commission challenged Microsoft in court. The judge found Microsoft guilty of "anti-trust" violations.

That means that Microsoft has tried to keep other companies from selling their computer products fairly. Microsoft had to pay fines for its violations.

Today, Bill Gates is the wealthiest man in the world, with $60.5 billion. His job now is chairman and chief software architect at Microsoft. The company has more than 55,000 workers in 85 countries. Microsoft has also expanded into the Internet. Its Internet Explorer is the most used Web browser in the world.

THE BILL AND MELINDA GATES FOUNDATION: In the past few years, Gates has been spending more time—and money—on charity. He and his wife, Melinda, head a foundation that gives money away for health and education. They especially want to help improve the health of people in poor nations. They've given millions of dollars in aid to poor countries. They've helped vaccinate African and Asian children against diseases like polio.

They're also heading up programs to provide better educations to children in the U.S. They have scholarship programs for poor students. They also give free PCs and software providing Internet access to libraries all over the country.

BILL GATES'S HOME AND FAMILY: Bill Gates met his wife, Melinda, at work. She was an executive at Microsoft for several years. They married in 1994. They have three children, Jennifer, Rory, and Phoebe.

The Gates family lives in a huge house—it's 40,000 square feet. That's the size of about 20 regular houses put together. It's on a lake and has a huge pool. There's also a trampoline room and a movie theater. Bill and Melinda Gates are very private about their

Bill and Melinda Gates with young patients in Mozambique, Africa

family. They work hard to protect their privacy so their kids can have a normal childhood.

HIS INVENTION: Gates is one of the most important pioneers in the world of computers. His innovations in software have made it possible for computers to be used with ease in homes and businesses worldwide.

WORLD WIDE WEB SITES:

http://www.gatesfoundation.org
http://www.microsoft.comhttp://www.microsoft.com

King Gillette
1855 - 1932
American Businessman and Inventor
Inventor of the Safety Razor

KING GILLETTE WAS BORN on January 5, 1855, in Fond du Lac, Wisconsin. His parents were George and Fanny Gillette. He was one of five children, and had two brothers and two sisters. His full name is "King Camp Gillette." He got his unusual name from his parents. They chose his first name, King, in honor of a friend named Judge King. His middle name, Camp, was his mother's maiden name.

KING GILLETTE GREW UP in Wisconsin and Chicago. His family moved to Chicago when he was a boy. His parents ran a hardware store. King's mother was a great influence on him. She was very organized, and didn't like to waste time. She encouraged King to work hard, and to learn by doing.

KING GILLETTE WENT TO SCHOOL in Chicago at the public schools. When he was 16, his family's home and business were destroyed by the Great Chicago Fire of 1871. The family moved to New York City. King set out to make a living.

FIRST JOBS: Gillette worked at hardware stores in New York, Chicago, and Kansas City. Then he became a successful traveling salesman.

In the 1890s, Gillette became a salesman for the Baltimore Seal Company. Its president, William Painter, had recently invented the bottle cap. He gave Gillette a piece of advice. He told him to think of a product that was disposable. If people liked his product, they'd keep buying new ones, when the old ones were thrown away.

It took a few years, but Gillette finally came up with the perfect disposable product: the safety razor.

INVENTING THE SAFETY RAZOR: Before Gillette's invention, shaving was a dangerous activity. Although most men shaved daily, they had to use a razor that could have a deadly, sharp edge. And the blade became dull after each shave. So they had to keep sharpening it with a leather strap.

Gillette claimed the idea came to him one morning, in 1895, as he was shaving. "As I stood there with the razor in my hand, my

*Gillette Blue Blade
wrapper*

eyes resting on it as lightly as a bird settling down on its nest—the Gillette razor was born."

Over the next few years, Gillette worked with engineer William Nickerson to develop the product. He knew he wanted a disposable blade made of steel. It would be very thin, flexible, and very sharp on both sides. The razor handle itself held the blade in place. The razor would be purchased just once. But when the blade became dull, it was thrown away. Then, it was replaced with a new blade.

Gillette and Nickerson opened their factory in Boston in 1901. They began producing their disposable safety razors in 1903. They were an immediate success. They offered a safe shave, and blades could be replaced cheaply. By 1905, the Gillette Safety Razor Company had manufactured 90,000 razors. They'd made 12,400,00 disposable blades.

Gillette filed for a **patent** for his razor in 1904. He spent many years fighting competitors in court. Often, he'd buy the companies who made competing razors. So he was able to keep up with increasing demand, and handle competition.

Gillette was a marketing genius, too. He packaged the blades in wrappers with his picture on them. Soon, his was one of the most recognized faces in the world. During World War I (1914 - 1918), American soldiers went off to war with Gillette razors. In 1918, the

Army bought 3.5 million of his razors. When those men came home from the war, they continued to buy Gillette razors and blades.

Gillette became a rich, successful inventor. He and his product were famous all over in the world. "There is no other article for individual use so universally known or widely distributed," he said in 1926. "In my travels, I have found it in the most northern town in Norway, and in the heart of the Sahara Desert."

LATER LIFE: After the success of his razor, Gillette became an author. He had very strong beliefs about society and the economy. He wrote books about the evils of capitalism. He proposed that people live more cooperatively in communities. His ideas never caught on, however. He retired from the company in 1913. He spent his last years in California.

KING GILLETTE'S HOME AND FAMILY: Gillette married Atlanta Ella Gaines in 1890. They had one son, King Gaines Gillette. King Gillette died in California on July 9, 1932. He was 77 years old.

HIS INVENTION: Gillette's invention truly changed the way men shaved. He offered an inexpensive, useful product whose popularity spread all over the world. The Gillette company still produces popular razors used worldwide.

WORLD WIDE WEB SITES:

http://web.mit.edu/invent/iow/gillette.html
http://www.massmoments.org/moment.cfm?mid=329

Goddard with his first liquid propellant rocket, 1926

Robert Hutchings Goddard
1882 - 1945
American Physicist and Pioneer of Modern Rocketry
Invented the Liquid Fueled Rocket and
Gyroscopic Guidance for Rockets

ROBERT GODDARD WAS BORN on October 5, 1882, in Worcester, Massachusetts. His parents were Nahum and Fannie Goddard. The Goddards could trace their family roots in Massachusetts back to 1635. Fannie's father owned a knife manufacturing plant, where

Nahum worked. Nahum was a tinkerer and inventor and Robert took after him. Robert had a brother who died in infancy.

ROBERT GODDARD WENT TO SCHOOL first in the Boston area, where his father was working. In 1898, Robert's mother learned she had tuberculosis and the family moved back to Worcester. Tuberculosis is a disease that destroys the lungs. At that time, there were no antibiotics to fight the disease.

Robert himself was sickly, and did not do very well in school. When the family returned to Worcester, he began attending South High School and studied harder to improve his grades. He was sick, however, missing a lot of school and falling behind. Much of his time was spent at home where he would play with rifles and sling-shots, becoming fascinated with things forced into the air.

When Robert was 16 years old, he read *War of the Worlds,* by H. G. Wells. This and other works of science fiction would have an impact on the rest of his life.

On October 19, 1899, while climbing a cherry tree to trim dead limbs, he imagined "how wonderful it would be to make some device which even had the possibility of ascending to Mars, and how it would look on a small scale, if sent up from the meadow at my feet." Robert celebrated October 19th as his private Anniversary Day. For the rest of his life, whenever he was in Worcester on October 19th, he would visit that very same tree.

Because of illness, Robert did not graduate from high school until 1904, when he was 22 years old. He was the oldest person to ever graduate from South High School. But he graduated at the head of his class.

Goddard rocket with four rocket motors, 1936

At his graduation in June of 1904, he gave a speech entitled "On Taking Things for Granted." He told the audience, "It is difficult to say what is impossible, for the dream of yesterday is the hope of today and the reality of tomorrow."

COLLEGE AND RESEARCH: Robert went on to Worcester Polytechnic Institute, graduating in 1908 with a Bachelor of Science degree. He took a job teaching physics at Worcester Polytechnic, and continued to study for his master's degree at Clark University.

While working on his degree, Goddard began his rocketry research. He received his master's degree from Clark University in 1910. He continued on for his PhD, which he received in 1911. During the balance of his life, Robert would have a very strong

259

relationship with Clark University, first as a professor, then as head of the physics department and physical laboratories.

In 1913, Goddard became very ill. He was diagnosed with tuberculosis and given only two weeks to live. He surprised everyone by recovering enough to continue his work. By 1914, he had received **patents** for a two-stage rocket, a cartridge loaded rocket, and a liquid fueled rocket. The liquids, gasoline for fuel and liquid nitrous oxide for oxygen, were very hard to get at that time. Goddard did most of his rocketry with powder, just as the Chinese had for hundreds of years.

NEWTON'S THEORY AND ROCKETS: About this time, Goddard conducted an experiment that proved that rockets could be propelled into a vacuum—the vacuum of space. At that time, most people believed that rockets had to have air to push against in order to move. But Goddard proved that theory wrong. He based his theory on one of **Isaac Newton's** theory of motion.

In Goddard's experiment, he mounted a pistol with a rod through the trigger guard. He placed it in a glass jar and pumped out all of the air, to form a vacuum like that in space. He then remotely fired a blank cartridge from the pistol and watched it spin around on the rod. The experiment proved that thrust could be produced in a vacuum. That meant that space flight—sending a rocket into the vacuum of space—was possible.

When the United States became involved in World War I, Goddard did research for the government. He developed solid-fuel rockets that could be launched from hand-held devices or launching tubes. This research led to the development of the bazooka.

In 1919, Goddard published a paper titled "A Method of Reaching Extreme Altitudes." In it, he concluded that a properly fueled rocket could reach the moon. On January 12, 1920, the *New York Times* ran a front page story with the headline "Believes Rocket Can Reach Moon" citing the article. The following day, an editorial mocking the entire idea of rockets in space appeared in the *Times*. It said that Goddard "does not know of the relation of action to reaction, and the need to have something better than a vacuum against which to react." It claimed that Goddard "only seems to lack the knowledge ladled out daily in high schools."

The *Times* was proven wrong, and Goddard was proven right, within a few years of the article. But it took the paper a while to acknowledge its error. It was not until July 17, 1969, the day following the launch of Apollo 11 to the moon, that the *New York Times* printed a "correction." On that day, the *Times* wrote, "Further investigation and experimentation have confirmed the findings of Isaac Newton in the 17th century and it is now definitely established that a rocket can function in a vacuum as well as in an atmosphere. The *Times* regrets the error."

Goddard observes the launch site from his control shack, 1936

With funding from the United States government and foundations, Goddard continued his research.

LIQUID FUELED ROCKETS: In 1921, Goddard switched his focus to liquid fueled rockets. He used gasoline and liquid oxygen. Liquid oxygen was much easier to obtain than liquid nitrous oxide.

In 1924, Goddard married Esther Kisk. Esther had been a secretary at Clark University. Their marriage was to be a partnership of discovery for the rest of Goddard's life. Esther photographed, and recorded all his research from then on.

THE FIRST LAUNCH OF A LIQUID FUELED ROCKET: On March 16, 1926, 10 years after he first proposed it, Goddard launched the world's first liquid fueled rocket. It was about the size of a large salami. It only went up about 41 feet and then crashed into a cabbage field. The entire flight lasted about 2-1/2 seconds, but it was a very important moment in the history of rocketry.

Shooting off rockets in heavily populated Massachusetts was becoming dangerous. Goddard received a research grant in 1930

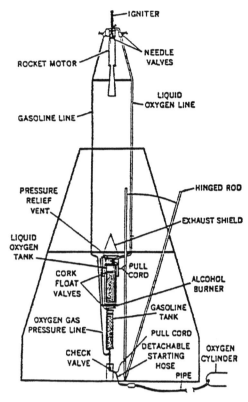

Goddard's liquid fueled rocket, 1926

that allowed him to move his operations to Roswell, New Mexico. He worked in Roswell off and on until the late 1930s. In New Mexico, he invented many items to help rockets attain greater altitude, but he was disappointed with his results. The highest altitude his rockets reached was about 9,000 feet.

WORLD WAR II: When World War II began in Europe in 1939, Goddard offered his services to the United States government. He wanted to help develop rockets that could be used as weapons. The government was not interested in that idea. But they did ask Goddard's help in making rockets to assist airplanes when taking off from aircraft carriers.

The Nazis, however used Goddard's designs in developing the V-2 rocket, which they used to bomb England. During World War II, a German spy was placed into the group of researchers that worked for Goddard. The spy kept the Germans informed of any advances Goddard made in rocketry.

When the United States entered the war in 1941, Goddard moved his research to Annapolis, Maryland. He continued his work until his death on August 10, 1945, just days before the war ended.

ROBERT GODDARD'S HOME AND FAMILY: Goddard married Esther Kisk in 1924. She assisted Goddard in his work for 40 years. In 1960, the U. S. government paid Esther Goddard and the Guggenheim Foundation $1 million for the rights to all of Goddard's **patents**.

HIS INVENTIONS: Goddard invented many parts of the rocket that would eventually lead to human space flight. He invented gyroscopic guidance, gimbals mounted rocket motors, parachute recovery systems and much more. He was awarded 214 patents for his work, many of them granted after his death.

On March 16, 1961, exactly 35 years after the first liquid fueled rocket flight, NASA dedicated the opening of the Goddard Space Flight Center in Maryland. It is a tribute to the man whose vision and work led to his unofficial title as the "father of modern rocketry."

WORLD WIDE WEB SITES:

http://www-spof.gsfc.nasa.gov/stargaze/Sgoddard.htm
http://www.clarku.edu/research/archives/goddard/
http://www.invent.org.hall_of_fame/67html
http://www.time.com/time/time100/scientist/profile/goddard.html

Charles Goodyear
1800 - 1860
American Inventor
Inventor of the Vulcanized Rubber Process

CHARLES GOODYEAR WAS BORN on December 29, 1800, in New Haven, Connecticut. He was the son of Amasa and Cynthia Goodyear. His father was an inventor and later owned a button factory. Charles was the oldest of six children. He had four brothers, Henry, Robert, Nelson, and Amasa, and one sister, Harriet.

CHARLES GOODYEAR GREW UP in New Haven. He was often sick as a child. He spent a lot of time with his father, watching him invent farm tools. One of Amasa Goodyear's best inventions was a steel hayfork.

CHARLES GOODYEAR WENT TO SCHOOL only briefly. He was not very interested in school. Instead, he worked in his father's button factory and studied at home. When he was 17, he moved to Philadelphia to learn the hardware business.

THE BEGINNING OF BUSINESS TROUBLES: Goodyear became a hardware salesman in a company started by his father. In 1826 he and his new wife, Clarissa, opened a hardware store in partnership with his father. But by 1830 the business failed, and father and son were bankrupt. Sadly, it was a pattern that would be repeated many times in his life.

BANKRUPTCY AND JAIL: For the next few years Goodyear spent time in and out of jail. In his time, if you couldn't pay your debts you went to debtor's prison. While in prison, Goodyear became fascinated with what was called "India rubber." He asked his wife to bring him a batch of rubber and her rolling pin. It was here, in jail, that he began his early experiments with the sticky, gummy substance.

THE HISTORY OF RUBBER: Native tribes of Central and South America were using the sticky sap of trees by the time the first explorers reached the New World in the late 1400s. Those explorers noted that the "Indians" as they called them, made shoes of this gummy sap. Spanish soldiers used it to rub on their cloaks to keep out the rain.

In 1770, the English scientist Joseph Priestly made another discovery. He found that this gum would erase pencil marks. Because it came from the "Indies" and was used by "rubbing," it became known as "India rubber."

So in the early 1800s, people began to experiment with rubber. It was useful for the soles of shoes, for suspenders, and for waterproofing fabrics. One famous example was the "Macintosh." It was a waterproof raincoat made with rubber, created by Charles Macintosh.

DAYS OF RUBBER FEVER: Caught up in the "rubber fever" of the day, Goodyear invented an improved valve for a rubber life preserver. He took the new preserver to the owner of the Roxbury India Rubber Company in New York City, hoping to sell it. The owner told Goodyear it wasn't the valve that needed improvement. It was the rubber itself.

One of the biggest problems with rubber was that it could not hold up under extreme temperatures. In the heat of summer it became soft and almost liquid. In the cold of winter it became hard and stiff.

Goodyear believed that God had called him to the task of searching for the way to perfect rubber. Luckily, his experiments did not require expensive equipment. Fingers were the best tools to use when working with the gum.

While in prison, Goodyear was allowed to have a bench and a marble slab. This "equipment," together with his wife's rolling pin, allowed Goodyear to begin the quest that would eventually lead to the "recipe" for useful rubber.

EXPERIMENTS WITH RUBBER: Goodyear began mixing the raw gum with other substances. He tried magnesia but found the result too sticky. He tried nitric acid and thought he had discovered the secret. With a partner he leased an abandoned rubber factory. But his company went broke when his partner lost all his money. Once again Goodyear was penniless.

Still dedicated to his experiments, Goodyear found another partner. They set up shop in a deserted plant in Roxbury. Goodyear received an order for mail bags from the government. For the first time, he received publicity and interest from manufacturers across the country. But by the time all the bags were completed, the rubber in the earliest batch had deteriorated. The mail bags were ruined. Goodyear had failed again.

SUCCESS AT LAST: One day, in 1839, Goodyear finally discovered the secret to making rubber stronger, and resistant to heat and cold. As happens so often in the history of invention, it happened by accident.

Goodyear was experimenting with a batch of rubber mixed with sulphur. He spilled a lump of the mixture onto a red hot stove. To his surprise, the mixture didn't melt. Instead, it instantly hardened. And it was resistant to heat and cold. Now Goodyear worked on how much sulphur (the formula) and how much heat (the process) would insure a uniform product.

In 1844 Goodyear was satisfied with the formula and the process. He applied for a **patent** for his rubber-making process.

THE VULCANIZATION OF RUBBER: The term Goodyear used for the process of turning raw tree gum into usable rubber was "vulcanization." He named it after the Roman god of fire and forge—Vulcan.

PATENT BATTLES AND BAD BUSINESS DECISIONS: Goodyear spent most of the rest of his life trying to defend his patents. "Patent pirates," as they were called, stole his ideas. When he challenged them in court, he paid more in legal fees that he recovered.

Goodyear made bad business decisions, too. As the owner of the patent for vulcanized rubber, he could have made a lot of money licensing his process. But instead, he allowed manufacturer's to purchase licenses at very low prices.

In 1851, Goodyear spent $30,000 for an extravagant display at the London Crystal Palace exhibition. He placed a similar display at a Paris exhibition. The exhibits earned him nothing but more debt. He returned to the United States in 1858 a broken man.

Goodyear died in poverty in 1860. He was 60 years old. At the time of his death, he was more than $200,000 in debt.

CHARLES GOODYEAR'S HOME AND FAMILY: Goodyear married Clarissa Beecher in 1824. They had 12 children; only six lived to adulthood. The family often lived in poverty and faced hunger on a daily basis. They often lived on charity, while Goodyear lived in debtor's prison.

HIS INVENTIONS: Although Goodyear died in poverty, his discoveries led to the creation of the modern rubber industry. The vulcanization process produced rubber that was elastic, and resistant to heat and cold. It was airtight and watertight. Rubber became a widely used product for commercial and industrial use. With the advent of the car industry, demand for rubber skyrocketed.

In 1898, Frank Seiberling founded the Goodyear Tire & Rubber Company. He named the company after Charles Goodyear, as a tribute to the inventor of the vulcanization process.

WORLD WIDE WEB SITES:

http://www.goodyear.com/corporate/history/history_story.html
http://www.invent.org/hall_of_fame/68.html

Gould holding the notebook pages that proved his patent claims.

Gordon Gould
1920 - 2005
American Scientist and Inventor
Inventor of the Laser

GORDON GOULD WAS BORN on July 17, 1920, in New York City. His full name was Richard Gordon Gould, but he was called Gordon. His parents were Kenneth and Helen Gould. His father was an editor for Scholastic Magazine. His mother was a homemaker.

GORDON GOULD GREW UP thinking of how to make things work. **Thomas Edison** was his hero, both because he was a great inventor, and because he made money at it. His mother recognized his talent and encouraged him. She gave Gordon an Erector set to develop his mechanical ability.

GORDON GOULD WENT TO SCHOOL at the public schools. He was an excellent student. In high school, he ran track, played in the band, and sang for his church choir.

Gordon wanted to attend the Massachusetts Institute of Technology, but his family couldn't afford it. Instead, in 1937 he enrolled at Union College in Schenectady, New York. At Union, one of his professors stirred his interest in physics. He also visited the labs of nearby General Electric Co. There, he could see industrial applications of science at work.

Gould remembered getting a lot of personal attention in college. "I did some experiments as an undergraduate that you wouldn't normally do," he recalled. He received a bachelor of science degree in physics in 1941.

Gould continued his studies at Yale University. It had a well-known program in spectroscopy. That's the study of how light is made up of various color elements, called spectra. He completed his master's degree in physics at Yale in 1943.

WORLD WAR II: The United States entered World War II in December 1941. While at Yale, Gould was recruited for the Manhattan Project. That was a secret project that developed the first atomic bomb. Gould worked for the project in New York City until 1945. While in New York, he attended meetings of the Communist Party with a girlfriend. This got him into trouble. He lost his job with the Manhattan Project because he was considered a security risk.

FIRST JOBS: Gould went to work as an engineer for a glass company in New York City after the war. He also taught classes at the City College of New York.

GRADUATE YEARS AT COLUMBIA: In 1949 Gould decided to pursue a doctorate in physics at Columbia University in New York. There he studied under several of the major scientists in the field.

At Columbia, Gould learned of the work of Charles H. Townes. Townes had invented a device called a maser, which stimulated microwave energy. Maser stands for "microwave amplification by stimulated emission of radiation." Townes and Gould discussed the maser. Townes considered it valuable only as a research tool.

A FLASH OF INSPIRATION: Thinking about the maser, Gould began to think about applying similar principles to visible light.

Both visible light and microwaves are forms of energy made up of particles called photons. But every photon of visible light has many thousands of times more energy than a microwave photon. In November 1957, Gould woke up with the inspiration of how to stimulate the emission of visible light.

He got up and recorded his ideas in a notebook. He referred to his idea as a "laser." The name referred to the maser and to "light amplification by stimulated emission of radiation." Gould knew he had thought of something very important. He had the pages of his notebook verified and dated by a notary public on November 13,

1957. (A notary public is a person who is authorized to authenticate documents and verify people who wrote them.)

Gould also knew his idea could be worth a lot of money. He spoke to an attorney about applying for a **patent**. The attorney gave him bad advice. He told Gould that he needed a working model of his laser to file for a patent. So Gould did not submit his work to the U.S. Patent Office.

Meanwhile, Townes and Arthur Schawlow of Bell Laboratories published an article on what they called an "optical maser," which used visible light waves. They patented their plans in 1960. That same year, Theodore Maiman of Hughes Aircraft Co. produced the first working model of a laser.

LASER TECHNOLOGY: We are all familiar with light from the sun, the spectrum of colors in a rainbow, and artificial light from light bulbs. Laser light is different. It focuses and aligns the individual photons of light of a single color, so they form a thin beam. Laser light is said to be "coherent." That means that all the light waves are aligned, and are of a single frequency. The result is a kind of light with intense energy. In fact, a powerful laser beam can melt steel, and can even create temperatures as hot as the surface of the sun.

PATENT WARS: Gould felt certain that he had the idea for the laser first. But he failed to be the first to file for a patent. He was also in need of money. He left Columbia, without completing his doctorate. He went to work for a company called Technical Research Group (TRG) in 1958.

He hoped to develop a working laser at TRG, with the help of corporate funding. In 1959 Gould filed several patent applications for his laser developments. His work came to the attention of the U.S. military. They awarded Gould's company a million-dollar grant, hoping the laser could be developed into a "death ray."

OTHER PROFESSIONAL PROBLEMS: Gould's research was hampered because of his earlier Communist contacts. After World War II, the U.S. and Soviet Union were embroiled in the Cold War. Americans who had any affiliation with Communism were questioned about their backgrounds. Some lost their jobs. And some, like Gould, were haunted by their pasts for years.

Gould was unable to get a security clearance to work on his own project. His work at TRG bogged down. Meanwhile, the Townes and Schawlow patent led to the first practical uses of the laser in industry.

Gould's patent applications were challenged because he had filed them later than others. He was also scorned by the scientific community because he hadn't completed his doctoral degree. The outlook was bleak for Gould.

But he didn't give up. Through the 1960s, he continued to seek recognition for his patents. He took a job teaching at the Polytechnic Institute of Brooklyn. His teaching job ended in 1968, and Gould struggled to support himself on personal investments. By 1974 he had run out of money. He then signed a partnership arrangement with Refac Technology Development Corporation to pursue his patent fight. Over the years they spent more than $2.5 million in attorney's fees fighting Gould's case.

BREAKTHROUGH: Finally, things started to turn brighter for Gould. In October 1977, one of his patents was granted. By this time the technology had already caught on in many industries, and large corporations were using lasers in many applications.

That meant that the invention was making money—in fact, millions of dollars. Gould and his partner company continued their patent suits, against corporate giants like General Motors and AT&T.

The tide began to turn as several court decisions came out in favor of Gould. He won on the strength of the notarized pages of his notebook. They clearly showed that his ideas had preceded other patents. Court decisions recognizing his patents went in favor of Gould in 1979, 1982, and 1985. And in 1989, Townes admitted that he himself had seen Gould's notebook prior to filing his own patent.

Gould's 30-year struggle to have his patents recognized made him a wealthy man. The laser was in widespread use by the late 1980s. So he was able to collect licensing fees from more than 200 corporations. The patents he was finally awarded account for more than 80% of all laser designs currently in use. Even after sharing his earnings with his corporate partner, Gould personally made more than $30 million.

LATER YEARS: In his later years, Gould worked on refinements to the laser and filed additional patents. He was pleased that he had succeeded as an inventor, and that his long patent battles had paid off. In 1985 he retired.

Gould donated money to his alma mater, Union College, to establish a professorship in physics. The college honored him with an honorary doctorate in 1978. In 1991 he was named to the National Inventors Hall of Fame.

In 1984 Gould benefitted from his own invention. That year, he underwent successful laser eye surgery. He spent his last years dividing his time between homes in Colorado and New York. He died on September 16, 2005. He was 85.

GORDON GOULD'S HOME AND FAMILY: Gould was married three times. In 1947 he married Glen Fulwider. They were divorced in 1953. His second marriage, to Ruth Hill, ended in 1955. He married Marilyn Appel in 1992.

HIS INVENTION: Though notable scientists and major corporations fought his claims as the inventor of the laser for decades, Gould persevered, clinging to the proof contained in his notebook. Finally he was awarded patents that recognized his development of gas-discharge lasers and optically-pumped lasers, as well as other refinements.

Lasers are now in everyday use, from supermarket scanners and laser pointers to CD and DVD players and surgical instruments. In industry they are used to weld metal, cut fabrics, and in fiber optic communications. Applications in science and the military include precise interplanetary measurements of distance and weapons guidance systems.

WORLD WIDE WEB SITES:

http://www.edisonexploratorium.us/GordonGould.html
http://www.invent.org/hall_of_fame/69.html
http://web.mit.edu/Invent/iow/gould.html

Temple Grandin
1947 -
American Animal Scientist and Inventor
Creator of Equipment for
Humane Treatment of Livestock
Author of Books on Her Life with Autism

TEMPLE GRANDIN WAS BORN on August 29, 1947, in Boston, Massachusetts. Her parents are Richard and Eustacia Grandin. Richard sold real estate and Eustacia was a singer and actress. Temple is the oldest of four children. She has two sisters, Isabel and Katherine, and a brother, Richard.

TEMPLE GRANDIN GREW UP in Massachusetts. But she didn't have a regular childhood. When Temple was just six months old, her mother noticed changes in the way she acted. When her mom tried to touch her or pick her up, Temple would stiffen. She hated being touched. It was clear something was wrong.

Temple's parents had her tested by doctors. The doctors told her parents that Temple was autistic.

WHAT IS AUTISM? Autism is a disorder of the nervous system. Doctors aren't sure exactly what causes autism. But they know it has to do with the part of the brain that controls the senses, language, and how we interact with others.

A person with autism is very sensitive to touch, sight, sounds, and smells. They are overwhelmed when their senses are stimulated. That is why Temple couldn't stand to be touched, even as an infant. Instead, she began to withdraw from the everyday world.

Many autistics withdraw so much that they never learn to speak. They also have difficulty understanding relationships. They have trouble "reading" people's emotions.

Temple wanted to be alone. She couldn't speak, and she appeared to be deaf. She also had terrible temper tantrums. "Loud noise hurt my ears," she remembers. "and I withdrew from touch to avoid overwhelming sensation. My hearing is like having a hearing aid with the volume control stuck on 'super loud'."

When Temple was growing up, very little was known about autism. Most autistic children were sent away from their families, to institutions. But Temple's mother wanted to raise her at home. She

"I hardly know what to say about this remarkable book.... It provides a way to understand the many kinds of sentience, human and animal, that adorn the earth."
— Elizabeth Marshall Thomas, author of *The Hidden Life of Dogs*

THINKING IN PICTURES

AND OTHER REPORTS FROM

MY LIFE WITH AUTISM

TEMPLE GRANDIN

WITH A FOREWORD BY OLIVER SACKS

did everything she could to make Temple's childhood as normal as possible.

Still, Temple had a terribly hard time dealing with "normal" life. "I wanted to feel the good feeling of being hugged," she recalls. "But when people hugged me the stimuli washed over me like a tidal wave." Learning to speak was also a huge challenge. "If adults spoke to me, I could understand everything," she says. "But I could not get my words out. It was like a big stutter. My mother and teachers wondered why I screamed. Screaming was the only way I could communicate."

Her mother decided to find a school and a private care giver for Temple. She began daily speech therapy. Her care giver made sure that Temple had plenty to do each day. They played games and did activities with other children. That way, Temple stayed active in the world of other people.

TEMPLE GRANDIN WENT TO SCHOOL at a local private school for normal kids. She was a good student, but had some problems with math. Junior high was more difficult. Temple went to an all-girls private school. Some of the girls were cruel. They said hurtful things, and Temple often lost her temper. She was expelled for throwing a book at a student who called her names.

Temple's next school was the Hampshire Country School. That's a special school for kids who are gifted, and also have emotional problems.

Temple thrived there. She enjoyed her classes, and she spent time horseback riding, which she loved. She had a science teacher in particular who helped her. His name was William Carlock. Mr. Carlock helped Temple understand her autism. He also helped her create a machine to help ease some of her symptoms. It was the "squeeze machine."

FIRST INVENTION—The Squeeze Machine: From the time she was little, Temple knew that she didn't want to be touched. But she also knew that pressure—an all-over squeezing sensation—made her feel more relaxed.

The idea for a "squeeze machine" first came to her when she spent time on her aunt's cattle ranch. At the ranch, the cattle were placed in a "squeeze chute" when they got their vaccines. The movable sides of the chute would gently press on the cattle's bodies, holding them still as they received their shots. Grandin noticed that the animals relaxed when they were "squeezed."

Temple wanted to try the squeeze chute on herself and see if it helped her anxious feelings. To her great relief, it did.

"For about an hour afterward I felt very calm and serene," she recalls. "My constant anxiety had diminished. This was the first time I ever felt really comfortable in my own skin."

Animals in
Translation

Using
the Mysteries
of Autism
to Decode
Animal
Behavior

"Deeply moving and
fascinating."
—Oliver Sacks

Temple Grandin and Catherine Johnson
author of **Thinking in Pictures**

Back at Hampshire, Mr. Carlock helped Grandin build a "squeeze machine" of her own. It worked well, and it helped her enormously. She wasn't as anxious or angry. She did better in school. She got along better with the other kids, too.

The "squeeze machine" became Grandin's first invention. It's helped other children with similar problems. Today it's used to help kids with autism, attention-deficit hyperactivity disorder (ADHD), and other conditions.

Grandin graduated from Hampshire and went to Franklin Pierce College. There, she studied psychology. She did very well, and she also began to develop more social skills. She got to know other students, and felt she fit in.

After graduating from college, Grandin decided to go to graduate school at Arizona State. She'd begun to work with livestock and she wanted to learn more about animals.

BECOMING AN ANIMAL SCIENTIST: Grandin has a deep closeness and understanding of animals. She got a job working a cattle chute. She observed the animals closely. She became "more tuned in to the animals and their feelings of pain and anxiety."

Grandin completed her master's degree in animal sciences. Her special area of interest was animal handling. She went on to work on a PhD at the University of Illinois in the same subject. She also worked several jobs in the livestock industry.

INVENTOR: Grandin started her own company, Grandin Livestock Systems. She began to develop new equipment for handling livestock. She created corrals, pens, chutes, feedlots, and other systems. All of them shared a purpose: to treat livestock humanely.

Grandin's systems have been so successful that one third of the livestock in the U.S. use units she created. The same systems and techniques are used by horse trainers and zoo keepers, too.

"THINKING IN PICTURES": As an autistic, Grandin processes the world in a unique way. She says that she "thinks in pictures." She designs animal systems in her head, picturing each piece of the process. "I visualize the animal entering the chute from different angles," she says. "Or I turn myself into an animal and feel what it would be like entering the chute."

"Animals are a lot like autistics," she claims. Both "communicate by focusing on the visual." She notes that migrating birds appear to use the same system. "Consider how a whooping crane only has to be shown once how to migrate and they will know it for the rest of their lives."

WRITING AND SPEAKING ABOUT AUTISM: In addition to her work with animals, Grandin has another important role. She has become a spokesperson on autism.

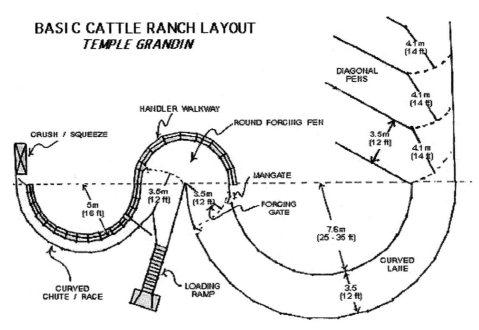

A cattle ranch system designed by Grandin.

Grandin is one of the first people with autism to write about it. And she's one of the first people to talk about autism from an *autistic* point of view. She's written several books and gives many speeches every year. She talks to parents, scientists, and others interested in autism. She shares with them the techniques that helped her learn to communicate and succeed. She helps parents understand their children, and teachers help their students. She hopes to continue her work for years to come.

TEMPLE GRANDIN'S HOME AND FAMILY: Grandin lives in a townhouse in Fort Collins, Colorado. She's a professor of animal behavior at Colorado State University. She isn't married and doesn't have children. She decided long ago that it would be very difficult to form those kinds of relationships. Instead, she focuses on her work with animals and autism. "My work is my life," she says.

HER INVENTION: Grandin's inventions of humane livestock systems, and her research into animal behavior, have changed the way people think about animals. She has brought ground-breaking insights into animals' emotional and physical needs.

WORLD WIDE WEB SITES:

http://www.grandin.com
http://www.templegrandin.org

Greatbatch holding a cardiac pacemaker

Wilson Greatbatch
1919 -
American Inventor and Engineer
Inventor of the Implantable Cardiac Pacemaker

WILSON GREATBATCH WAS BORN on September 6, 1919, in Buffalo, New York. His parents were Walter and Charlotte Greatbatch. His father was a construction worker and his mother was a homemaker. Wilson was an only child.

WILSON GREATBATCH GREW UP fascinated with the way things worked. He recalls making "rubber-band guns and having neighborhood 'wars' with them." He took apart his father's Model T Ford, to examine the magnet.

Even as a child, Greatbatch was fascinated with electricity. "There was something going on that you couldn't see. You had to use a meter, or a neon bulb, to see what was going on," he said. He also loved the radio. "I built my own short-wave receivers and transmitters," he recalls. He also got his ham radio license when he was 16.

WILSON GREATBATCH WENT TO SCHOOL at the local public schools. He played football in high school, and was a Boy Scout. In 1939, Greatbatch joined the Navy. When the U.S. entered World War II in 1941, Greatbatch worked as a radio operator. He also worked on radar and other communication systems, and flew combat missions.

After the war was over in 1945, Greatbatch returned to New York. He went to college at Cornell, where he studied electrical engineering. He took courses in math, physics, and chemistry. He also completed a master's degree in electrical engineering from the University of Buffalo.

It was at Cornell that Greatbatch found the area he would specialize in. At the college there were scientists studying heart disease. They were working with animals, trying to understand what happens when the heart doesn't work properly.

The doctors were studying "heart block." That's what happens when the "beat" signals in the heart don't work correctly. Irregular heart rhythms can lead to death. Greatbatch knew exactly what he needed to do.

"When they explained it, I knew I could fix it with an implantable device," he recalled. "But not with the vacuum tubes and storage batteries we had at the time."

At that time, it took a large machine to "shock" the heart back into proper rhythm. In the late 1950s, John Bardeen and others invented the transistor. The transistor revolutionized electrical devices. Among its many properties, it allowed the storage of electricity in small batteries. It was the technological advance Greatbatch had been waiting for.

In 1958, he was working with a transistor that could record the sound of heartbeats. But at first he used the wrong transistor. Instead of *recording*, it produced a current that *mimicked* a normal heart rhythm. "I stared at the thing in disbelief," recalls Greatbatch. "This was exactly the properties of a pacemaker."

INVENTING THE CARDIAC PACEMAKER: Greatbatch quit his job and went to work in his barn workshop. He invested his own money—$2000—into building his first cardiac pacemaker. "I built 50 pacemakers there in two years," he recalls.

The cardiac pacemaker is built to be implanted into the chest of a patient. It is a device with a main battery and wires that are attached to the heart. If the heart goes into a life-threatening rhythm, the pacemaker sends an electrical current through the wires to "shock" it into beating properly.

Working with two heart specialists, Greatbatch implanted the first cardiac pacemaker into a dog in May 1958. Using the information from animal experiments, Greatbatch readied his device for humans. In 1960, the first pacemakers were implanted in 10 patients. All of them had serious heart disease. "The thing worked," recalled Greatbatch.

Greatbatch received a **patent** for his invention. Then, to produce the pacemaker, he licensed it to Medtronic, a medical device manufacturer. They made 300 the first year. By 2000, some 3 million patients around the world have had pacemakers implanted. It's estimated that millions of lives have been saved thanks to Greatbatch's invention.

Greatbatch formed his own company, Greatbatch, Inc. It's in upstate New York, near Buffalo. The company produces medical devices, including the batteries that power the implantable pacemakers. One of the benefits Greatbatch gives his employees is education. The company's more than 500 employees all can go to college for free, as can their children.

OTHER INVENTIONS: Greatbatch has more than 150 patents to date. He has developed products that make his pacemaker even more useful. These include batteries made of lithium. He's also interested in exploring energy sources for other projects, like space travel. He says he wants to explore "the energy that will power the Earth for this century and get us to the Moon."

Working with other scientists, Greatbatch has created methods that help stop the AIDS virus. He's also done work to stop an AIDS-like virus that affects cats. In his 70's Greatbatch invented a solar-powered canoe.

HONORS AND AWARDS: Greatbatch has received many awards in his long career. He was named to the Inventor Hall of Fame in 1986. That same year, he received the National Medal of Technology. In 1996, he won the Lemelson-MIT Lifetime Achievement Award.

WILSON GREATBATCH'S HOME AND FAMILY: Greatbatch met his future wife, Eleanor Wright, in the early 1940s. They married in 1945, when he returned from World War II. They had five children.

Greatbatch is still at work inventing. He's also given generously to educational groups and charities. Greatbatch enjoys speaking to students at schools all over the country. For all his accomplishments, he's a modest man. "Don't fear failure," he tells students. "Don't crave success. The reward is not in the results, but rather in the doing."

HIS INVENTION: Greatbatch's cardiac pacemaker has saved millions of lives worldwide. In 1983, the National Society of Professional Engineers gave him a special award. They named the pacemaker one of most important engineering contributions of the previous 50 years.

WORLD WIDE WEB SITES:

http://web.mit.edu/invent/a-winners/a-greatbatch.html
http://www.invent.org/hall_of_fame/70.html
http://www.si.edu.lemelson/centerpieces/ilives/lecture09.html

Johannes Gutenberg
1400 (?) - 1468
German Printer and Inventor
Inventor of the Movable-Type Printing Press

JOHANNES GUTENBERG WAS BORN around 1400 in Mainz, Germany. His father was named Freile zum Gensfleisch. His mother was named Else zum Gutenberg. Johannes took his mother's last name. His name is pronounced "yo-HAHN-ess GOOT-en-burg."

Very little is known about Gutenberg's early life and education. Historians believe he must have studied Latin, the language of books and documents of the time. He learned goldsmithing, gem cutting and metal working as a young man. Gutenberg moved from Mainz to Strasbourg around 1430. He moved back to Mainz around 1448.

LEARNING THE PRINTING TRADE: Gutenberg learned to be a printer during the time he lived in Strasbourg. At that time, printing was a slow and difficult process. Printers worked from woodblocks. Each woodblock included an entire page of type. The block was covered in ink, then a sheet of paper was laid over it. Then the impression of the page was rubbed into the ink.

INVENTING THE MOVABLE-TYPE PRINTING PRESS: Gutenberg came up with a new idea. Instead of cutting a woodblock of an entire page, he created metal type of individual letters, upper and lower case, and punctuation marks. He cast the letters in metal, using lead, tin, and antimony. The metal characters cooled quickly, and were very durable.

Gutenberg made many copies of each letter. The letters were cast as type in reverse. The individual cast letters were placed next to each other to form words. The words were placed into composing sticks to form whole lines, with filler between the words.

The lines were put together into columns or pages on a wooden board. This was called a "galley." The page was lined up, with exact amounts of space between the lines.

A Gutenberg press.

These woodcuts from 1568 show the steps in creating a page of text.

*A typesetter assembles
a page.*

*The page is positioned
over the type-area*

*The type-area is dyed
with printer's ink*

The page of type was then covered in ink, applied with a leather ball. Gutenberg made his ink from lampblack, linseed oil, and egg white. A sheet of moist paper was then placed into a cover over the type page, fixed to it with pins. The paper was pressed between the plate of the press and the type page. The press distributed the ink equally and evenly over the paper.

The results were remarkable. Gutenberg had invented a manufacturing method that consistently produced pages of high quality. The metal letters could be used again and again. Each element in the process—from the metal letters to the press—were durable, and created a uniform look to the type.

For the first time in history, books could be mass-produced and purchased by common people. Gutenberg had started a revolution.

THE GUTENBERG BIBLE: One of Gutenberg's first projects was a Bible, which he began around 1452. It was the first book to be mass-produced using the movable-type method.

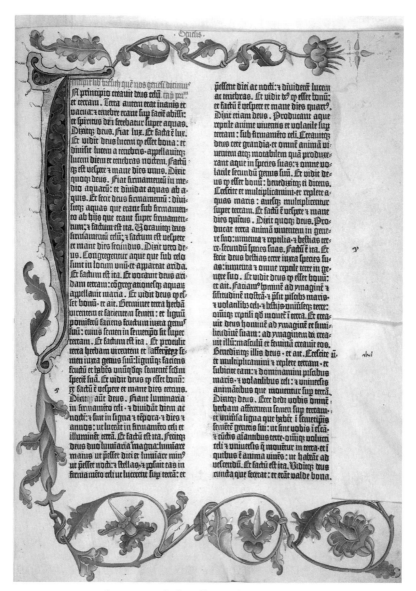

A page of the Gutenberg Bible.

The Gutenberg Bible was an enormous project. The first printing was for 180 copies, and each Bible was 1,282 pages long. Gutenberg set the pages in two columns, with 42 lines on each page. As his text, he used the Latin translation of the Bible. That's why it's sometimes called the "42-Line Latin Bible."

Gutenberg cast 100,000 letters for the project. Up to 12 printers worked on six presses to complete the first printing. The entire project took three years. But that was a great improvement on the previous technology. It used to take one scribe three years to complete one copy of the Bible by hand.

There are now 48 remaining Gutenberg Bibles. They are treasured works in the collections of museums and libraries all over the world. There are several copies in U.S. libraries, including the Library of Congress in Washington, D.C.

The Gutenberg Bible was also a glorious work of art. Using the medieval illuminated bibles as their model, artists painted decorations on the pages that glowed with color.

But Gutenberg's Bible was more than a beautiful book. It was the first book printed with a process that made books affordable for the common people of Europe. Before Gutenberg, books had been so expensive that only the rich could afford them. They were created and copied by hand, or printed using the slow and expensive woodblock process. Now there was an affordable way to print books and all kinds of documents. Newspapers, court records, hymnals, as well as books, got into the hands of everyday people.

BUSINESS PROBLEMS: Despite his revolutionary invention, Gutenberg had business problems. Around 1450, he built a printing plant, with money he borrowed from Johann Fust. He also borrowed money from Fust to print the Bible. Fust and Gutenberg quarreled about Gutenberg's use of the money. Fust sued, and they went to court. Gutenberg lost. He had to hand over the printing workshop and half the Bibles to Fust.

Fust continued to run the workshop. Gutenberg was forced to find work with another printer. Not much is known about the later years of his life. In 1465, he appealed to the bishop of Mainz for financial help. He received a small salary from the church for the last few years of his life, along with clothes, food, and wine. Gutenberg died in Mainz on February 3, 1468.

HIS INVENTION: Many people consider Gutenberg's creation of the movable-type printing press to be the most important invention in history. It made books affordable and available to people of all backgrounds. People learned to read, and education and knowledge spread to all the people of Europe, and the world.

The concept of movable type was the basis of all typesetting until the 20th century. In the late 20th century, computer typesetting took the place of movable type. But it was Gutenberg's invention that allowed the printed word to extend around the world.

WORLD WIDE WEB SITES:

http://web.mit.edu/invent/i-main.html
http://www.gutenberg.de/english/
http://www.gutenbergdigital.de/
http://www.uh.edu/engines/epu753.htm

Elizabeth Lee Hazen
1885 - 1975
American Scientist
Co-Creator of the First Anti-Fungal Antibiotic

ELIZABETH LEE HAZEN WAS BORN on August 24, 1885, in Rich, Mississippi. Her parents, William and Maggie Hazen, were farmers. They died when Elizabeth was three. She had one sister named Annis. Elizabeth and Annis were raised by an aunt and uncle, Laura and Robert Hazen.

ELIZABETH LEE HAZEN GREW UP in her aunt and uncle's house in Mississippi.

ELIZABETH LEE HAZEN WENT TO SCHOOL at the local public schools. She was an excellent student, and her relatives encouraged her to go to college. She attended what is now Mississippi University for Women. She graduated with a bachelor of science degree.

After teaching high school science, Hazen went back to school. She took classes at the Universities of Tennessee and Virginia, and Columbia University in New York City. She got her master's degree in biology from Columbia, then began working on her PhD.

SCHOOL AND MEDICAL RESEARCH: Hazen interrupted her studies during World War I (1914 - 1918). She left Columbia and served in an army lab. After the war ended, she headed a lab in a West Virginia hospital.

Hazen returned to Columbia in 1923 to continue her studies. In 1927, she received her PhD in microbiology. Microbiology is the study of living things on the smallest—microscopic—level.

In 1931, Hazen took a job with the New York Department of Health. She headed up the Bacterial Diagnostic Lab. She spent most of the next ten years studying infectious diseases. At that time, **Alexander Fleming** had discovered penicillin. The medical world became committed to finding more antibiotics to treat bacterial diseases.

STUDYING FUNGI: Hazen became fascinated with fungi (plural of "fungus"). Fungi are found everywhere, especially in soil and plants. Like bacteria and viruses, fungi can cause serious, life-threatening infections. Fungi cause infections of the skin, mouth, throat, digestive system, and other areas of the body.

Scientists were just learning that antibiotics could actually do harm as well as good. That's because antibiotics kill the "good" bacteria in the body that help fight infection. A patient taking an antibiotic could develop a fungal infection. And at that time, there was no treatment.

In 1944, Hazen became head of an investigation into fungi that caused disease. In a few years, she'd identified anitfungal agents that occurred in soil. These natural agents could kill fungi. Now she needed to find a chemist to test the antifungal agents.

WORKING WITH RACHEL FULLER BROWN: In 1948, a very important working relationship began. Hazen was working in New York City identifying antifungal chemicals. **Rachel Fuller Brown**, a chemist in Albany, New York, was chosen as her partner to develop the first antibiotic to fight fungal infections.

Over the span of two years, the two conducted long-distance research. Hazen collected samples of antifungal agents found in soil. She grew cultures in her New York City lab. Then, she sent them to Brown in Albany in mason jars. In her Albany lab, Brown conducted experiments to determine the chemical agents that killed fungi in the samples. She'd identify the agents, then send them back to Hazen. Hazen would retest the sample, to see if the agent killed the fungi. If it did, she'd test the sample on animals to see if it was toxic.

The scientists faced a difficult problem. If a chemical agent was effective against fungi, it could also be toxic to animals. To be safely used in humans, it first had to pass this important test.

Dr. Hazen (right) and Dr. Brown (left) in the lab.

Finally, in 1950, the scientists found an agent that killed fungi, but was safe on animals. They named the drug Nystatin. (Named for "New York State.") Soon, it was tested on humans. It was a success. Hazen and Brown had done it. They'd invented the first antibiotic drug that successfully treated fungal infections.

Hazen and Brown received the **patent** for Nystatin in 1957. The drug made more than $13 million dollars in its first years. It is important to note that neither scientist ever earned money from their discovery. Instead, Hazen and Brown invested the money in a

300

nonprofit research foundation. That foundation still provides funding for medical research.

Nystatin proved to be effective in other areas, too. It was used to fight infections in plants, like Dutch Elm Disease. Nystatin was also used to kill mold in old paintings and other art work.

After their work with Nystatin, Hazen and Brown continued to work together. They discovered two more antibiotics. Hazen also returned to teaching at Columbia. She continued doing medical research until she was 87.

ELIZABETH LEE HAZEN'S HOME AND FAMILY: Hazen never married or had children. She retired to Seattle, Washington, in 1973, to be near her sister. She was in frail health, and died on June 24, 1975. She was 89 years old.

THEIR INVENTION: Hazen and Brown's invention of Nystatin is considered one of the major breakthroughs in 20th century medicine. Nystatin has been used to treat fungal infections worldwide. The two scientists received many honors and awards, including the Chemical Pioneer Award. Hazen and Brown also inspired young women to become scientists.

In 1994, Hazen and Brown became the second and third women to enter the National Inventors Hall of Fame. They followed **Gertrude Elion**, who created many important and life-saving medicines.

WORLD WIDE WEB SITES:

http://web.mit.edu/invent/iow/HazenBrown.html
http://www.chemheritage.org/EducationalServices/pharm/
http://www.invent.org/hall_of_fame/75.html

Elias Howe
1819 - 1867
American Inventor of the
First Practical Sewing Machine

ELIAS HOWE WAS BORN on July 9, 1819, in Spencer, Massachusetts. Very little is known about his early life. He grew up helping out on the family farm and mill.

ELIAS HOWE WENT TO SCHOOL at the local public schools. Like many people of his era, he attended only through grade school.

FIRST JOBS: At 16, Howe became an apprentice in a machinist's shop. His next job was in a cotton factory in Lowell, Massachusetts. He lost that job in 1837, during an economic downturn.

Howe moved to Boston, where he got a job as a machinist. During his free time, he loved to tinker. Howe began to work on his famous invention: a mechanized sewing machine.

INVENTING THE SEWING MACHINE: It is hard to imagine that in Howe's time, all clothing was made by hand. Using only a needle and thread, people sewed everything they wore: dresses, pants, and shirts.

Inventors had tried to create a sewing machine before Howe. In France, a man named Thimonnier came up with a model in 1830. But the new machine caused the tailors of France to riot. They worried that a sewing machine would put them out of work. So the tailors destroyed Thimonnier's factory and all his machines.

While watching his wife sew, Howe came up with an idea. He created a sewing machine powered by a hand crank. His design used thread coming from two sources, one above and one beneath a piece of cloth. The thread from above the cloth was placed through a needle. The one underneath came from a shuttle. The needle, with thread through its eye, pushed one piece of thread through the cloth from above. Underneath, a shuttle put another thread through the loop formed by the thread in the needle. The two pieces formed a "lock stitch."

Howe introduced his invention to the public in 1845. People were amazed at its speed. It could make 250 stitches per minute.

Howe's sewing machine, 1845.

Howe got a **patent** for his sewing machine in 1846. But it would be years before he would make any money from his invention. He tried to find investors so he could fund the manufacture of his machine. But no one in America was interested.

Howe moved to England with his family to try to find financing. He found someone who bought the patent rights, but Howe still didn't make much money. He wound up working for about $5 a week, making improvements to the machine.

Broke and discouraged, Howe sent his family back to the United States. He followed later, only to discover that his wife was dying. It was a time of personal and professional loss for Howe.

He discovered that while he'd been in England, several people had stolen his ideas. There were now several companies manufacturing sewing machines obviously based on his patented ideas. Howe spent the next several years in court fighting for his rights.

Finally, in 1854 Howe's patent rights were upheld. One of the manufacturers who'd violated Howe's patent was Isaac Singer. (He was the founder of the Singer Sewing Machine Company.) The court ruled that Singer had to pay Howe $15,000 for infringing on his patent. Another agreement stated that Howe would receive money for every sewing machine sold in the U.S.

A seamstress using an early sewing machine, c. 1853.

At long last, Elias Howe made money from his important invention. He became a very wealthy man. During the Civil War (1861 - 1865) Howe supported a Union regiment with his money. After the war, he founded the Howe Machine Company, in Connecticut. He died in 1867, at the age of 48.

ELIAS HOWE'S HOME AND FAMILY: Howe married in 1841. He and his wife had three children.

HIS INVENTION: By inventing the first practical sewing machine, Howe changed many lives. His invention allowed people to make clothes faster. It helped spur a booming industry in clothing manufacturing in the U.S. and Europe.

The sewing machine was also the first widely used mechanical home appliance. Later innovations in power led to the treadle sewing machine (powered by pedals, like a player piano). The sewing machines used in industry and homes today are powered by electricity. But it was Howe who first saw a practical way to power a process that had been done by hand for thousands of years.

WORLD WIDE WEB SITES:

http://memory.loc.gov/ammem/today/jul09.html
http://www.americaslibrary.gov/cgi-bin/page.cgi/jb/nation/howe_1

Edward Jenner
1749 - 1823
English Physician and Inventor of Vaccination
"The Father of Immunology"

EDWARD JENNER WAS BORN on May 17, 1749, in the town of Berkeley, in Gloucestershire, England. His parents were Stephen and Sarah Jenner. Stephen was a minister. Sarah was a homemaker. Edward was the eighth of nine children. When he was five, his parents died. He was raised by his older sister and her husband.

EDWARD JENNER GREW UP in Berkeley, in western England. As a young boy, he loved to explore the natural world. He especially liked to collect fossils. He also studied birds.

EDWARD JENNER WENT TO SCHOOL in Wotton-under-Edge and Cirencester. When he was 14, he became an apprentice to a surgeon named Daniel Ludlow. With Ludlow, Jenner learned the basics of medicine.

STUDYING MEDICINE: In Jenner's time, it didn't take years of college and medical school to be a doctor. Instead, an apprentice assisted a doctor for several years. Jenner learned about the human body, diseases, and treatments.

When he was 21, Jenner moved to London to complete his training. He worked with Dr. John Hunter, a famous surgeon. After studying with Hunter for two years, Jenner was ready to begin his own practice. He moved back to Berkeley in 1772 and became a country doctor.

SMALLPOX: When Jenner began his medical career, smallpox was one of the deadliest diseases in the world. The disease was ancient: smallpox scars were found on Egyptian mummies from 1100 B.C. It had spread around the world, from Asia to Europe to Africa and the New World. European explorers brought smallpox with them to America, killing untold thousands of native peoples.

Like cancer and heart disease today, smallpox was the major killer of its time. Most of its victims were infants and children under five. The disease began with fever and chills, then a rash would appear on the body. The rash would turn into blisters. The blisters would dry up and fall off, leaving deep, ugly pock marks on the skin. There was no medicine to control the disease. Some patients recovered; many died.

Jenner treated many patients with smallpox. He was determined to understand the disease. He thought smallpox was close to cowpox, a disease that affects cows. He noted that milkmaids, who milked cows, often developed a mild form of cowpox. After that, they appeared to be "immune," or resistant to, smallpox.

VACCINES: Jenner experimented with making a "vaccine" out of cowpox. (Jenner actually developed the word. "Vaccine" is formed from the Latin word for cow: "vacca.")

A vaccine is a form of a bacterial or viral disease that can help the body create antibodies to fight the disease. Jenner created the vaccine from material taken from a milkmaid who had a mild form of cowpox. He first injected the vaccine into an eight-year-old boy, James Phipps. James became slightly sick with cowpox. Next, he exposed James to smallpox. The boy didn't come down with the dread disease. Instead, the cowpox had made him immune to smallpox.

Jenner's experiment worked. Next, he had to present his findings to the world. Many were skeptical.

In Jenner's time, people had experimented with live smallpox serum. They called the process "variolation." When injected into a healthy human, the live serum caused an outbreak of the illness. This would make that person immune, or resistant to, smallpox. But the serum could be deadly, too. There was no

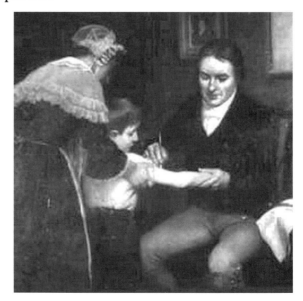

Jenner vaccinating a child.

Cartoon of Jenner vaccinating a child.

exact science to the method. When injected with live serum, many people came down with a full-blown case of smallpox, and died.

Still, Jenner had to convince the world that his vaccine worked. He continued to use the vaccine on patients. He kept careful records of his results. He published his research in 1798. It confirmed that cowpox did protect against smallpox.

Other doctors were willing to try the cowpox-based vaccine. They ordered cowpox samples from Jenner. Some of these became contaminated and patients died. That made people afraid of vaccines.

Yet the success of Jenner's discovery was undeniable. He continued to vaccinate patients and published his results. From 1798 to 1800, 12,000 people in England were vaccinated. Smallpox deaths dropped by two-thirds.

A FAMOUS DOCTOR: These results vindicated Jenner. He became a famous man. He was honored all over the world for developing a vaccine against a terrible disease. Countries all over the world began vaccination programs. Smallpox began to disappear around the world.

In 1980, the World Health Organization declared that "Smallpox is Dead." The work Edward Jenner had begun in the 1790s had led to the end of one of the oldest and deadliest diseases known to humankind.

EDWARD JENNER'S HOME AND FAMILY: Jenner married Catherine Kingscote in 1788. They had three children, Edward, Catherine, and Robert. His wife died in 1815. On January 26, 1823, Jenner died after a stroke.

HIS INVENTION: Jenner is known as the "Father of Immunology." He created a way to immunize and prevent disease by using the body's own defenses to develop resistance. On the web site for the Jenner Museum in England is the following statement: "It has been estimated that the task he started has led to the saving of more human lives than the work of any other person."

Scientists of Jenner's time didn't know it, but they were actually working with a virus. It took several hundred years of research and understanding of viruses on the microscopic level for the age of vaccines to come about. Scientists who followed in Jenner's footsteps include **Louis Pasteur** and **Jonas Salk**. Jenner was the pioneer in what is now one of the most important areas of medicine.

WORLD WIDE WEB SITES:

http://www.jennermuseum.com
http://www.sc.edu/library/spcoll/nathist/jenner.html

Steven Jobs
1955 -
American Computer Pioneer
Co-Founder of Apple Computer
Head of Apple and Pixar

STEVEN JOBS WAS BORN on February 24, 1955, in San Francisco, California. His birth mother was an unmarried college student. When he was a few days old, he was adopted by Paul and Clara Jobs. He has one sister named Patty.

STEVEN JOBS GREW UP first in San Francisco, then in Mountain View, California. Mountain View is in an area south of Palo Alto. It's now called "Silicon Valley" because it became the center of the computer industry. (Silicon is one of the main materials used to make computer chips.) Jobs has been part of that world from the time he was a child.

Steve was something as of a loner. He swam competitively, but he really wasn't into sports. Instead, he spent time with the Hewlett-Packard Explorer Club. Hewlett-Packard was one of the first, and most successful, electronics companies in Southern California. The club was run by engineers who encouraged kids to get interested science.

At one of the meetings, Jobs saw his first computer. "I was maybe 12 at the time," he recalled. "I remember the night. They showed us one of their new desktop computers and let us play on it. I wanted one badly. I thought they were neat. I wanted to mess around with one."

STEVEN JOBS WENT TO SCHOOL at the local public schools. He didn't like school at all. He didn't get along with other kids, and, at one point, he wanted to quit. His parents moved to another district, and he started going to Homestead High School. He graduated from Homestead in 1972.

Jobs went on to Reed College in Portland, Oregon. But college just wasn't for him. He dropped out after six months. He worked briefly at Atari, designing video games. With the money from that, he traveled to India.

STARTING APPLE IN HIS PARENT'S GARAGE: In 1975, Jobs was back in California living with his family. He joined a group of early computer lovers called the Homebrew Computer Club. Through the group he met **Steve Wozniak,** who would become his partner in Apple Computer.

Jobs and "Woz" decided to try their hand at building their own computer. Working in the Jobs's garage, they got started in 1975.

FIRST COMPUTERS: The first computers were huge machines. Just one computer could fill an entire room. And it didn't have the power or speed of just one of today's personal computers.

But like today's computers, the early versions worked on a basic principle.

A BRIEF HISTORY OF COMPUTERS: The root word of "computer" tells the origin of the machine. Computers "compute"—that is, they perform math calculations. The earliest "computer" was actually an adding machine. It was created in 1642 by Frenchman Blaise Pascal. Pascal's machine was simple. He entered numbers into a machine using dials. Inside the machine were cogs and wheels connected to the dials. They moved according to the numbers entered. The machine could accurately add and subtract numbers.

The next major step forward happened in the 1800s. Charles Babbage, a British mathematician, designed a machine to process numbers. It had many of the features of a modern computer. It had an input mechanism (like a keyboard), storage (memory), a computing mechanism (CPU), and an output mechanism (a computer screen or printer). Babbage never built his machine. But his research was very influential.

The first modern computers were developed during World War II (1939 - 1945). Mathematician Howard Aiken developed the

Mark 1, a computer that ran on electromechanical relays. It helped improve the accuracy of Navy artillery.

Another advance from the World War II era came about through the research of Alan Turing. Turing invented the "Colossus," a computer that broke the Nazi military code. It helped end the war in Europe. "Colossus" was important for another reason. It was the first computer to use vacuum tubes to store and process data.

The next major innovation in computers was the ENIAC. (That stands for the Electronic Numerical Integrator and Calculator). Previous computers were used for military purposes. The ENIAC was the first computer for general, commercial use. It was enormous: it weighed 30 tons, and used more than 17,000 vacuum tubes.

In 1948, John Bardeen, William Schockley, and Walter Brattain invented the transistor. It was another tremendous breakthrough. Transistors replaced vacuum tubes with smaller, cooler processors.

The integrated circuit, invented by Jack Kilby in 1958, introduced the true modern era in computing. Now one silicon microchip could hold millions of electronic components. It revolutionized the industry.

When Jobs and Wozniak started out, there were no computers for personal use. The large computers made by **Seymour Cray** or IBM were used by governments, corporations, and universities. Jobs and Woz had another idea. Why not build a computer for the average person to use?

APPLE COMPUTER: Jobs and Wozniak founded Apple Computer in 1976. They built their first computer, the Apple I, that year. It wasn't anything like the computer of today. It was just a circuit board.

There was no keyboard, monitor, power source, or software. But it was a start.

APPLE II: In 1977, Jobs and Wozniak created a revolution in the computer industry. They released the Apple II. It was the first desktop personal computer, for the general user. It was small—it could fit on a desktop. It took up about the same space as a typewriter, with a screen, keyboard, speaker, and power supply.

The Apple II was a huge success. The company made more than $1 billion in just five years. The two friends continued to work together, in the roles that best suited them. Wozniak was the engineer and designer of the computers. Jobs was the marketing genius. He could see the potential of the Apple. Like **Bill Gates**, who became his fierce rival, he could see that computers could be used in every home, and in every business. He was able to convince investors, too. That way, Apple had the money to continue to develop and grow.

THE MACINTOSH: Apple's next major release was the Macintosh, or Mac. It came out in 1984, and it was incredibly easy to use. Before the Mac, users still had to enter long, complicated commands into a computer to tell it what to do.

The Mac used what's called a "GUI" (pronounced "gooey") interface. That means that it featured pictures—the icons now familiar on computer screens. The icons stood for commands, like "print" or "save." Using another new computer innovation, the mouse, users pointed to the function they wanted, then clicked the mouse. This "point and click" technology was first developed for the Mac.

Jobs with the new Apple II, 1977.

People loved the Mac. It was immediately popular, and hugely successful for Apple. They had created a product that made personal computers easy and a part of all aspects of life. Bill Gates's Windows came soon after, and used the same "point and click" technology. PCs using Microsoft's Windows system began to dominate the market. Things were changing, and Apple wasn't the place that Jobs and Wozniak had started.

317

GETTING FIRED: Wozniak left the company in 1985. Jobs hired a manager, John Sculley to run Apple. Soon, Sculley and Jobs were locked in a power struggle for control of the company. Jobs lost. He was fired from the company he'd formed and led to success. The success of Apple had made him a multimillionaire. He had money, and he wanted to stay in the computer world.

NEXT: Jobs wouldn't give up. In 1985, he started NeXT, to build a new type of computer. He wanted to create a computer capable of high quality graphics and sound. But the NeXT computers never took off. Jobs's next business venture would bring him back to the greatest heights of success.

PIXAR: In 1986, Jobs bought Pixar. The design and animation studio was owned by director George Lucas. The company had recently hired a talented young animator named John Lasseter. Pixar animators were among the first to use computer graphic imagery (CGI) technology. With CGI, Pixar artists could create vivid, lifelike animation.

With Jobs's innovative vision, and Lasseter's creative talent, Pixar became one of the most successful studios in the country. Their hits include *Toy Story, Bug's Life, Finding Nemo,* and *The Incredibles.*

BACK TO APPLE: In 1996, Jobs sold NeXT to Apple, and began to work as a consultant for the company. Apple was facing some difficult times financially. With Jobs back, things began to change. He rejoined the company officially, and began to turn things around.

Jobs has always had a flair for design, and it shows in the visual impact of Apple products. He's also a genius at marketing. He has

Jobs (left) with Pixar staff, including John Lasseter (second from left).

an ability to anticipate what people want in a product. What will appeal to them, from a practical point of view, is most important. But the way something looks, and how that will draw a customer in, is important, too. That helped make blockbusters of two recent Apple products, the iMac and the iPod.

The iMac is a beautifully designed personal computer, and a popular one, too. Apple's Powerbook notebook computer was another great success for the company. But Apple's biggest recent hit is the iPod.

IPOD: The iPod is a portable music player that has become one of the most popular consumer products of recent times. It's available in several versions, and can hold from hundreds to thousands of

319

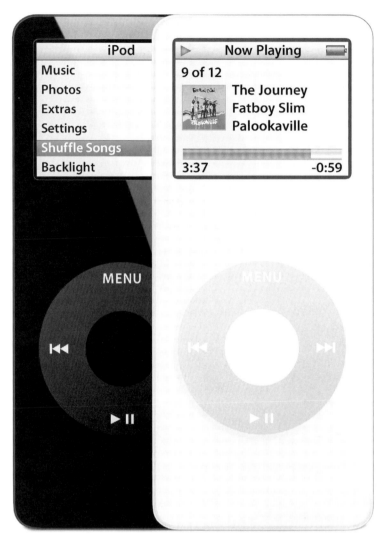

The Apple iPod.

songs. It has a sleek design, and it's easy to use. And it made $1 billion for Apple in just three years.

To go with the iPod, Jobs created iTunes. It's software that stores millions of songs that are downloadable from Apple's iTunes Music Store.

FACING CANCER: In 2004, Jobs learned that he had a rare form of cancer. He had surgery, and was back at work a month later. He says the experience has made him more focused on what matters. He's fine now, and back to work creating new, innovative products. He plans to do that for years to come.

STEVEN JOBS'S HOME AND FAMILY: Jobs lives with his wife, Laurene, and two children in Palo Alto, California. He has another daughter, Lisa, who was born to Jobs and a former girlfriend in the 1970s. In recent years, they have gotten to know each other. Lisa lived with Jobs during her high school years.

HIS INVENTION: In helping create the personal computer, Jobs brought about a major change in our daily lives. PCs are now present in all aspects of life—home, school, and work. His creativity in design and marketing continues in film, music, and continued innovation in the computer industry.

WORLD WIDE WEB SITES:

http://news-service.stanford.edu/news/2005/june15/
     jobs-061505.html
http://www.apple.com/pr/bios/jobs.html

Dean Kamen
1951 -
American Inventor, Physicist, and Engineer
Inventor of the AutoSyringe, Portable Kidney Dialysis Machine, the iBOT, and the Segway

DEAN KAMEN WAS BORN on April 5, 1951, in Rockville Center, New York. His parents are Jack and Evelyn Kamen. Jack was an illustrator for *Mad* magazine. Now, he illustrates Dean's inventions. Evelyn was a teacher. She now works as an accountant for Dean. Dean has one older brother, Barton.

DEAN KAMEN GREW UP on Long Island, New York. He was a curious and inventive kid. He claims to have created his first invention at five. "I figured out a way to make my bed without having to run from one side of the bed to another," he says.

DEAN KAMEN WENT TO SCHOOL at the local public schools. He hated school and remembers being bored. Outside of class, he read books by such great scientists as **Galileo** and **Isaac Newton.**

Kamen went to college at Worcester Polytechnic Institute. He was not a very serious student. After five years, he left without a degree.

STARTING TO INVENT: By the time he left college, Kamen was already earning a good living as an inventor. As a teenager, he developed light and sound systems for the Hayden Planetarium in New York City. Around the same time he came up with his first major invention: an automatic medication pump.

THE AUTOSYRINGE: Dean's brother Barton was a medical student. He told Dean that patients needing regular medicine injections often spent their days going to and from the hospital. That gave Dean the idea for the AutoSyringe. It is a device that automatically injects medicine into a patient at specific times.

The AutoSyringe is a small, portable device. It is worn by a patient, allowing a more normal life. It was a great success for Kamen. He founded his own company, called AutoSyringe, to manufacture and sell the device. In 1982, he sold the company for millions of dollars.

OTHER MEDICAL INVENTIONS: Kamen has also invented a "stent" that's used in patients with clogged arteries. The stent opens up the arteries, without surgery. Vice President Dick Cheney currently has an implanted stent made by Kamen's company.

Another of Kamen's important inventions is a portable dialysis machine. Patients whose kidneys do not work must have their blood filtered regularly. That procedure is called "dialysis." It used to have to be done in hospitals. But Kamen invented a portable dialysis device. Patients can now have dialysis done outside of hospitals.

FOUNDING DEKA: Kamen started his current company, DEKA, in 1982. He built the company in the old mill town of Manchester, New Hampshire. There, his employees work on developing his many inventions.

THE iBOT: Kamen's next major invention was the iBOT. It is a wheelchair unlike any other. It can climb curbs and stairs. It can lift a person in a wheelchair to a standing position. The iBOT makes life much easier for a wheelchair-bound person. It allows patients to go over all kinds of terrain. And patients aren't limited to places that have ramps, because the iBOT can climb stairs. Kamen even took it up the Eiffel Tower in Paris.

THE SEGWAY: In 2002, Kamen came out with a new invention called a "Segway." Kamen calls it a "human transporter." It's a two-wheeled vehicle that is self-balancing. It uses a complex computer that mimics the body's own balancing ability.

"All of the knowledge that went into knowing how to walk is transferred to this machine," said Kamen. The Segway travels at

Kamen sits in an iBOT—a wheel chair that can climb stairs

about 12 miles per hour, and it's very responsive to the rider. To go forward, the rider leans a bit forward. To go in reverse, the rider leans backward.

Kamen is hoping the Segway will catch on with businesses and the public, worldwide. Already, some police departments and the U.S. Post Office are giving it a trial run. Kamen hopes it's successful in Asia, where there are large populations in large cities. It allows people to move quickly and efficiently. It costs only about 5 cents to power a Segway all day.

But some city planners aren't sure about the Segway's safety. They're not sure that city sidewalks can handle both pedestrians and Segway riders. Time will tell if the Segway will catch on, in the U.S. and worldwide.

US FIRST: One of Kamen's proudest creations is US FIRST. It is an organization for kids. The letters stand for **F**or **I**nspiration and **R**ecognition of **S**cience and **T**echnology. He started it to get kids excited about science careers. He wanted them to know that they could make great contributions to the world—and make money—through science.

Every year, FIRST sponsors a robotics competition. Kids team with engineers to build a robot. The competition is like a sports event, with cheerleaders and announcers.

A police officer in Worcester, MA, on a Segway.

"The only young and exciting people young kids see are athletes and movie stars," says Kamen. "It's wrong. So I said, let's use that model and show them the NFL, the NCAA of young, enthusiastic scientists and engineers." He hopes that, with programs like FIRST, kids will "know of a world-famous scientist or Nobel Prize-winning physicist."

DEAN KAMEN'S HOME AND FAMILY: Kamen's inventions have made him a very wealthy man. He has a huge 30,000 sq. ft. home in New Hampshire, near DEKA. He flies to work in one of the helicopters he designed. He has a garage full of cars and he owns an island off the coast of Connecticut, too.

Kamen isn't married and doesn't have children. He says it's just not the life for him. "I can start the biggest project in the world," he says. "But I think getting in relationships is riskier, and to me scarier."

For Kamen, work is life. "To me, a vacation is to go from one project to another." He has over 150 **patents**, in the U.S. and worldwide, for his many inventions.

Kamen has received many honors and awards for his work. He was inducted into the Inventor's Hall of Fame in 2005. He received the Lemelson-MIT Prize for invention. He's also received the Heinz Award in Technology.

But it's not the awards that keep him going. Kamen loves to take on new ideas and new challenges. And he's not afraid of failure. "Most people define success as a lack of failure," he says. "But if you start to do things you've never done before, you're probably going to fail at least some of the time. And I say that's OK. **Thomas Edison** said he never failed. He just found 14,000 ways not to build a lightbulb."

HIS INVENTIONS: Kamen's medical inventions, like the Autosyringe and the portable dialysis machine, have allowed patients to live more normal lives. His iBOT has allowed wheelchair-bound patients greater mobility. And the Segway has provided inexpensive, energy-efficient transportation for pedestrians.

WORLD WIDE WEB SITES:
http://www.dekaresearch.com/aboutDean.html
http://www.invent.org/hall_of_fame/222.html
http://www.thefutureschannel.com/kamen_conversation.htm
http://www.usfirst.org/about/bio_dean.htm

W.K. Kellogg
1860 - 1951
American Businessman and Cereal Manufacturer
Inventor of Corn Flakes

WILLIE KEITH KELLOGG WAS BORN on April 7, 1860, in Battle Creek, Michigan. His parents were John Preston Kellogg, a broom maker, and Ann Janette Kellogg, a schoolteacher. Willie Keith's father and mother followed the religious way of the Seventh-day Adventists.

Kellogg as a broom salesman, c.1878

They had moved to Battle Creek because it was home to the Adventist Tabernacle (or church), the Health Reform Institute, and the publishing headquarters for this faith. Willie was the seventh of 16 children. He never liked the name Willie, and asked that people call him "W.K." instead.

W.K. KELLOGG GREW UP in a small town of Seventh-day Adventists who lived a strict and simple life. They were very interested in health and paid close attention to the food that they ate. As a young child, W.K. had little time to play. In spring and summer, he tended his family's many vegetable gardens. Starting at age seven, W.K. worked in his father's broom factory after school and on weekends.

W.K. KELLOGG WENT TO SCHOOL at the local schools. He wasn't a very good student. The real problem, as he learned later, was that he needed glasses. That's why he couldn't see the blackboard. W.K. quit school at 14 and began selling brooms for his father. For about eight years he traveled central Michigan as a salesman and became quite successful. One day, he was asked to help manage a broom factory in Texas. He did an excellent job.

But W.K. was homesick for Battle Creek, and for his girlfriend, who later became his wife. He returned to Battle Creek with $500 in his pocket.

WORKING WITH HIS BROTHER: In 1880 married Ella Davis. He also completed a business course in Kalamazoo, Michigan, and took a job at the nationally famous Battle Creek Sanitarium. For more than 25 years, W.K. worked as a bookkeeper, cashier, shipping clerk, and business manager helping his brother, Dr. John Harvey Kellogg, run the sanitarium. W.K. worked long and hard at "the San." But he barely earned enough money to support his family, which grew steadily as he and Ella had five children.

Dr. John Harvey Kellogg, a physician, had taken over the Adventist Health Center and re-named it the Battle Creek Sanitarium. In keeping with Seventh-day Adventist teachings, Dr. Kellogg believed that good health came from healthy eating. He conducted many experiments with nuts and grains. He tried to create tasty food that people could eat instead of meat and potatoes. Dr. Kellogg wrote books about healthy diets and a medical newsletter. He tried to tell people the benefits of vegetarianism, a diet that does not include meat.

CORN FLAKES BY ACCIDENT: Sometime in the fall of 1895, W.K. was conducting an experiment for his brother. Late one night, he accidentally left out a batched of cooked wheat. When he returned the next morning, the wheat had dried out. W.K. tried to put the dried wheat through the rollers that they usually used on moist grains. As it was rolled, each dried grain of wheat turned into a large, crispy flake.

W.K. encouraged John to bake the flakes and serve them with milk to the San's patients. The wheat flakes were a great success. The patients loved them immediately. After they went home, the former patients ordered the flakes by mail.

The brothers continued to experiment using other grains. In 1898, they were the first to introduce corn flakes to the world.

John and W.K. Kellogg both believed strongly in the good work of the San. Yet they often disagreed about business operations. One person described them "as like two fellows trying to climb the same ladder." Oftentimes, Dr. Kellogg treated W.K. more like a low-ranking secretary than a business partner. Battle Creek residents would see Dr. Kellogg pedaling his bicycle to work, as W.K. jogged beside him, taking notes.

Dr. Kellogg was a nationally famous physician, but it was W.K.'s business skills that helped the San run smoothly. W.K. wanted to produce more flaked cereal and sell it in stores nationwide. Dr. Kellogg wasn't interested in doing that.

During the 1890s, a patient named Charles William Post visited the San. He saw at once the value of flaked cereal. He soon created his own company and began selling boxes by the train load. The Kelloggs may have invented flaked cereal, but it was C.W. Post who first sold it widely.

THE BATTLE CREEK TOASTED CORN FLAKE COMPANY: At age 46, W.K. was finally ready to start his own business. With money from friends and business associates, he established The Battle

Creek Toasted Corn Flake Company. Later, it would become the famous Kellogg Company.

From the start, Kellogg was confident that his company would succeed. Even in 1907, after his one-year-old factory was destroyed by fire, he was undaunted. With the ruins still smoking, he brought an architect to the site and began building a new and bigger building.

Kellogg also had a good eye for advertising. His company was the first to use an electric billboard in New York's Times Square. He packaged his cereal in boxes that carried the Kellogg's name in bright, red lettering. The famous painter Norman Rockwell designed paintings for some of the boxes. Each box carried these words: "None Genuine Without This Signature—W.K. Kellogg."

THE KELLOGG EMPIRE: By the late 1930's, Kellogg's cereal boxes were recognized all across America, England, and even Australia. He became a millionaire and began to share his wealth.

Kellogg was involved in many things that helped others. He was known for giving large sums of money to charity, many focused on children. He believed that the most good could be accomplished by helping young children. In 1925, he established the Fellowship Corporation. In 1930, he established the W. K. Kellogg Child Welfare Foundation to help handicapped children receive better health care and services.

Within a few months, the foundation changed its name to the W.K. Kellogg Foundation. Its new focus was to help people around the world to improve the quality of their lives. To finance the foundation's work, Kellogg donated most of his fortune: $66 million.

Kellogg with his family

Kellogg also gave generously to local causes in Battle Creek, including a school where disabled children and non-disabled children could be taught side-by-side. (The first U.S. school of its kind to do so.) W.K. also donated money to build a city auditorium, junior high school, and youth recreation center.

W.K. KELLOGG'S HOME AND FAMILY: Kellogg married Ella Davis in 1880. They had five children. Kellogg worked such long hours that he often went days without seeing his family. Ella died in 1912. In 1918, he married Dr. Carrie Staines, a physician at the San.

Both Kellogg's son and grandson worked for Kellogg Company and they were good at what they did. His son invented the practice of using wax paper for packing cereal, to maintain freshness. His grandson developed the process of "puffing" the corn grits and making a cereal like Rice Krispies. As a father, Kellogg believed that his relatives should work as hard—and even harder—than anyone

Kellogg in front of his Foundation, c. 1940

else. Later, both his son and grandson left the Kellogg Company after disagreements with him. Yet he always felt sad that a Kellogg couldn't take over the business after him.

Kellogg loved to spend time on his country homes, in Michigan and California, where he kept horses and other animals. He built a ranch in Pomona, California, and raised some of the finest Arabian horses in the world there.

Late in life, Kellogg developed glaucoma, which caused him to slowly lose his vision. During his last 10 years he was totally blind. W.K. Kellogg died on October 6, 1951.

HIS INVENTION: The cereals of W. K. Kellogg changed the way many people eat breakfast. More than 100 years after their invention, corn flakes and other Kellogg products are sold in stores around the world. The Kellogg Foundation continues to support programs in health and education.

WORLD WIDE WEB SITES:

http://www.learningtogive.org/materials/foundations/kellogg.asp?
http://www.wkkf.org/WhoWeAre/Founder.aspx
http://www.wkkf.org

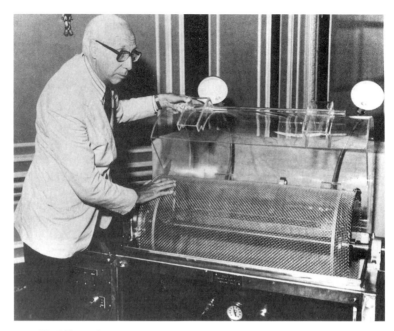

Kolff with his original artificial kidney machine.

Willem Kolff
1911 -
Dutch-Born American Doctor and Inventor
Inventor of the Artificial Kidney Machine and
Other Artificial Organs

WILLEM KOLFF WAS BORN on February 14, 1911, in Leyden, Holland. His parents were Adriana and Jacob Kolff. Adriana was a homemaker and Jacob was a doctor. Jacob ran a tuberculosis hospital. At that time, tuberculosis was a deadly lung disease.

WILLEM KOLFF GREW UP with many interests. He says that he didn't see himself as an inventor. "But I always wanted to make something." Willem had a great love for animals. "I had rabbits, pigeons, pheasants," he recalls. "I had a sheep, guinea pigs, and so on."

Kolff recalls that his father had a great influence on him. He sometimes visited his father's hospital. At that time, tuberculosis was a deadly disease. There were no antibiotics to control it, and patients often died. Seeing his father's devotion to his patients made Willem want to become a doctor, too.

WILLEM KOLFF WENT TO SCHOOL at the local schools in Holland. He says he wasn't a good student, in part because he has dyslexia. He had to struggle to read, and he still reads slowly. Dutch schools are also much harder than American schools. In high school, he took six classes, including four foreign languages. He had hours of homework in every class. He worked hard and did well.

Kolff went to college at the University of Leiden. There, he studied medicine.

After receiving his degree, he took a teaching job at the University of Groningen. He worked under a wonderful instructor there named Professor Daniels. Daniels let his students pursue their own interests. "He set us free," recalls Kolff. "All my life I've tried to follow that example."

At Groningen in the 1940s, Kolff was responsible for several patients. One was a young man suffering from kidney failure. The kidneys are among the most important organs in the body. Every day, they filter over 400 gallons of blood, taking out all liquid waste. If the kidneys fail, toxins build up in the body. Before the artificial kidney, patients with kidney failure died.

When Kolff's young patient died, it inspired his first invention.

INVENTING THE AFTIFICIAL KIDNEY MACHINE: Kolff developed a simple, but effective machine to filter the blood of patients whose kidneys had failed. That process is called "dialysis."

In that first dialysis machine, tubes channeled blood from the patient to a device that had cellophane tubing. "Cellophane tubing looks like ribbon, but it's hollow," Kolff remembers. "It's artificial sausage skin, an excellent membrane for dialysis." Kolff also used a car water pump he found at a local factory.

The cellophane tubing was wrapped around a cylinder. The cylinder was in a bath of cleansing fluid. The blood drawn from the patient flowed through the cellophane tubing into the bath. The fluid filtered out the toxins, then the blood was returned to the patient. In September 1945, the new dialysis machine saved its first patient, a 67-year old woman. Since then, artificial kidney machines have saved millions of lives.

MOVING TO THE UNITED STATES: Kolff and his family moved to the U.S. in 1950. He took a job at the Cleveland Clinic in Cleveland, Ohio. There, he became head of the artificial organ department. He later became a U.S. citizen.

ARTIFICIAL HEART: Over the next several years, Kolff concentrated on developing an artificial heart. Finally, in 1957, the first artificial heart was implanted in a dog.

In 1982, after years of research, the first artificial heart was implanted into a patient named Barney Clark. Clark had been suffering from heart disease, and the artificial heart improved his condition. Clark lived for 112 days. He became a famous patient whose experience brought a lot of public attention to artificial organs. Artificial hearts are still being improved. Today, most are used to keep patients alive until a donor organ can be found.

WORK ON OTHER ARTIFICIAL ORGANS: In 1967, Kolff moved to the University of Utah. He became the director of biomedical research and artificial organs. Since then, he has developed many different artificial organs, including an artificial eye, ear, and, recently, a portable artificial lung.

STILL INVENTING: At the age of 95, Kolff is still inventing. He lives in a one-room studio apartment in a retirement home. He uses the art room of the retirement home for his research.

Kolff recently explained his philosophy. "There are a lot of people that are a great deal smarter than I am. So I have to work very hard. But I'm extremely persistent. If I cannot get there one way, I try another way."

His advice to young people is simple and direct. "First, simplify what you want to do, and see whether or not you can do it. If you see a possibility, take it on."

HONORS AND AWARDS: Kolff has received many awards throughout his long and productive life. In 1985, he was inducted into the Inventors' Hall of Fame. In 2002, he received the Lasker Award for clinical medical research. That's one of the highest honors in medicine. In 2003, he received the Russ Prize. He used the award money, $500,000, to help develop his artificial lung.

WILLEM KOLFF'S HOME AND FAMILY: Kolff and his wife, Janke, married in 1937. They have five children. Three of them followed their father's career, and are doctors.

HIS INVENTIONS: Kolff is considered the "father of artificial organs." His inventions have extended the lives of more than 20 million people worldwide. In the U.S. today, more than 240,000 people are regular dialysis patients. *Life* magazine named him one of "The 100 Most Important Americans of the 20th Century."

WORLD WIDE WEB SITES:

http://web.mit.edu/invent/iow/kolff.html
http://www.achievement.org/
http://www.invent.org/hall_of_fame/88.html

Stephanie Kwolek
1923 -
American Chemist and Inventor
Inventor of Kevlar

STEPHANIE KWOLEK WAS BORN on July 13, 1923, in New Kensington, Pennsylvania. Her parents were John and Nellie Kwolek. John worked in a foundry and Nellie was a homemaker. Stephanie has one brother, who is younger.

STEPHANIE KWOLEK GREW UP loving to explore the outdoors. She and her father took nature walks. "I remember trudging through the woods near my house with him looking for snakes and other animals," she recalls. They also collected and saved "wild plants and leaves and seeds." Tragically, her dad died when she was 10.

Stephanie's mom had to go to work in a factory. The family didn't have money for toys, but that didn't bother Stephanie. She remembers "drawing fashionable clothes for my paper dolls." She'd also use her mother's sewing machine to make doll's clothes.

Even though her mother was gone a lot, she had a great influence on Stephanie. "She was an intelligent woman of great determination," she recalls. "Yet she had a great sense of humor. I've always admired her. I think she was very significant in molding my character and ability to do the things I later did."

STEPHANIE KWOLEK WENT TO SCHOOL at the local public schools. She was an excellent student. She went to college at Margaret Morrison Carnegie College. That's now part of Carnegie Mellon University, one of the nation's finest schools for science. Kwolek studied chemistry. She wanted to be a doctor, but when she graduated in 1946, she couldn't afford medical school. She went to work instead, planning to return to school later.

WORKING AT DUPONT: Kwolek took a job at DuPont. That's one of the largest chemical companies in the world. She interviewed with inventor W. Hale Charch. The interview went well. Charch told her he'd get back to her in a few weeks. Kwolek wanted the job. She told him she needed to know right away, because she'd had another offer. He hired her on the spot.

Kwolek began what would be a 40-year career at DuPont. She found the work so fascinating that she decided against medical school. Like her fellow DuPont chemists, Teflon inventor **Roy**

Plunkett, and nylon inventor **W.H. Carothers,** Kwolek worked on polymers. A polymer is a molecule made up of a string of smaller molecules called "monomers." Over the years, she worked on polymers used to create fabrics like Lycra and Spandex. But she is best known for the invention of Kevlar.

INVENTING KEVLAR: In the 1960s, Kwolek was working as part of the Pioneering Research Laboratory. Their goal was to develop new high-performance fibers. At that time, there was a gas shortage. Kwolek's team was trying to find a fiber that was strong but lightweight, to use in tires. Cars using tires that were strong but light would need less gas.

No one on Kwolek's team was very interested in the project. "So I was asked if I would do it," she recalls. Working on her own, she made an important discovery. The polymer solution she was working on was different. Instead of being thick, it was thin and cloudy. The solution formed liquid crystals. That hadn't happened before. And there were other strange features. When the polymers were forced through a "spinneret"—a device with many tiny holes—the straight fibers arranged themselves in parallel lines.

The result was a strong, stiff fiber. Kwolek sent the fiber for testing. The results amazed her. She sent them back to the lab for more testing. She wanted to be absolutely sure of her discovery. "The strength was above the standard fiber," she recalled. "But what shocked me was the stiffness." The new fiber was nine times stiffer than anything she'd worked on.

Kwolek let her co-workers know about her amazing discovery. They were delighted. They could see it had great potential in a variety of products.

Kevlar fibers being manufactured.

In 1971, DuPont introduced Kevlar. It is truly an amazing product. It is heat resistant, five times stronger than steel, and lighter than fiberglass. It has been used in more than 200 products: spacecraft, bridges, boats, fiber optic cables, tennis rackets, and hockey equipment all contain Kevlar. One of its most important, lifesaving uses has been in bullet-proof vests. Police officers and soldiers

Police officer wearing a Kevlar vest. More than 2,800 officers have survived because of Kevlar vests.

wear Kevlar vests every day. Thousands of lives have been saved because of Kwolek's invention.

Kwolek has received many honors and awards. She was elected to the Inventor's Hall of Fame in 1995. She's also a member of the National Academy of Sciences. In 1996, she received the National Medal of Technology. Kwolek was honored with the Lifetime Achievement Award from the Lemelson-MIT program in 1999. When

345

she retired from DuPont in 1986, she had received 28 patents, dating from 1961 to 1986.

STEPHANIE KWOLEK'S HOME AND FAMILY: Kwolek didn't marry or have children. She lives in Delaware and has remained very active since her retirement. She still does consulting work for DuPont and serves on the National Research Council.

Kwolek also enjoys visiting schools to talk about science. Many students ask her about her inventions. She's happy to share her love of science with them. In her free time, Kwolek likes to garden, read, and she still likes to sew.

HER INVENTION: Kevlar has proven useful in more than 200 products. Its use in bullet proof vests has saved thousands of lives. Kwolek is modest about her accomplishment. But she is passionate about science.

"I love doing chemistry. And I love making discoveries. I discovered over the years that I seem to see things that other people did not see. If things don't work out, I don't just throw them out. I struggle over them, to try and see if there's something there."

WORLD WIDE WEB SITES:

http://web.mit.edu/invent/www/ima/kwolek_bio.html
http://chemheritage.org/classroom/chemach/plastics/kwolek.html
http://www.invent.org/hall

L.AENNEC.

Rene Laennec
1781 - 1826
French Doctor and Inventor of the Stethoscope

RENE LAENNEC WAS BORN on February 17, 1781, in Quimper, France. His parents were Michelle and Theophile Laennec. Michelle was a homemaker and Theophile was a lawyer. His last name is pronounced "lah-en-neck." Rene had one brother named Michaud.

RENE LAENNEC GREW UP in the French countryside near the Atlantic Ocean. His mother died of tuberculosis when he was six.

His father sent Rene and his brother to live with an uncle, who was a doctor.

RENE LAENNEC WENT TO SCHOOL in the city of Nantes, where his uncle lived. He was an excellent student. He studied Greek, Latin, and English, as well as chemistry and physics. He was also a very good flute player, and enjoyed art and dancing.

STUDYING MEDICINE: When he was 14, Rene began to study medicine as his uncle's assistant. He was weak and sickly, but he was determined to study hard. In 1801, when he was 20, Laennec went to Paris. There, he went to medical school.

He studied with a famous doctor named Corvisart. Corvisart's method of diagnosing patients was very new. He told his students to closely observe their patients. Then, the students were to try to link the symptoms to diseases.

Laennec was an excellent medical student. He graduated with several awards in 1803. By then, he was writing important papers for medical journals.

Laennec's special interest was diseases of the heart and lungs. One of the most deadly and common diseases of his time was tuberculosis (TB). TB is a disease that destroys the lungs. It is very contagious, and people can become infected just by breathing in the germs of a TB victim. Today, TB victims are treated with antibiotics. But in Laennec's time, antibiotics hadn't yet been invented. Instead, many people died of the disease.

Laennec's mother had died of TB, and in 1810, his brother Michaud died of it, too.

Laennec became a doctor and treated many patients. He also continued to work and to teach in hospitals.

INVENTING THE STETHOSCOPE: In 1816 Laennec created an invention that changed medicine. He was faced with a problem. He had a young female patient whom he knew had heart disease. At that time, doctors listened to a patient's heart by putting their ear to the patient's chest. But this patient was a young woman, and she was very fat. So the traditional way of listening to her heart wouldn't work. He didn't want to embarrass her. But he needed to listen to her heart. That's when he came up with the idea for a stethoscope.

Laennec remembered that a piece of wood could convey sound. He recalled watching children play on a teeter-totter. One child would scratch on one end of the wooden beam, while another placed an ear on the other. The sound would travel through the wood and be easily heard.

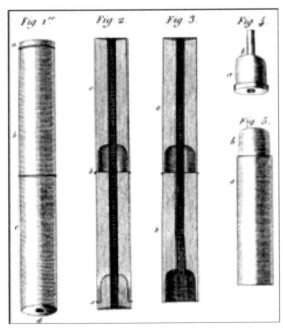

A drawing of Laennec's stethoscope. c. 1819.

Laennec thought the same idea could help him solve his problem. He recalled it later this way. "I then tightly rolled sheets of paper, one end of which I placed over the patient's chest, and my ear to the other. I was surprised and elated to be able to hear the beating of her heart." The results were excellent. He could hear the patient's heart more clearly than ever before.

Laennec made a wooden model of his invention. He carved a foot-long cylinder of wood, and bored a hole through the center. He called his invention a "stethoscope." The word comes from the Greek for "chest" and "observe." (The modern stethoscope—with ear pieces—was developed about 30 years later by George Cammann.)

HOW IT WORKED: The stethoscope works on a simple scientific principle. Sounds are made by vibrations. The vibrations move by sound waves. Sound waves can be carried through the air, or through a material. Laennec's stethoscope guided the sound waves made by the heart or lungs from the patient, through the wooden tube, and to the doctor's ears.

Laennec's invention was immediately successful. For the first time, doctors could listen to hearts and lungs. They learned how healthy hearts and lungs sound. Then they learned how diseased hearts and lungs sound. By comparing them, doctors could accurately diagnose, then treat their patients. It was one of the most important breakthroughs in medicine in history.

Laennec spent the next few years writing about his findings. He wrote several important books describing and explaining the sounds made by diseased lungs. These are considered the foundation of modern understanding of lung disease. He called his method "auscultation." His purpose was "not merely to listen, but to listen carefully."

Laennec also worked to improve his stethoscope. His books on the lungs were sold with a stethoscope. But his hard work had exhausted him. Frail and often ill, he spent several years in the country trying to regain his strength. Later, he returned to Paris to teach and practice medicine.

OTHER CONTRIBUTIONS TO MEDICINE: Laennec's powerful abilities of observation led him to other medical discoveries. He was the first scientist to identify the skin cancer melanoma. He also identified the liver disease known as cirrhosis. He was an important medical teacher, too. Students came from all over the world to learn his diagnostic techniques.

RENE LAENNEC'S HOME AND FAMILY: Laennec didn't marry until he was 43. On December 16, 1824, he married Jacqueline Argou. They were married for less than two years. Tragically, like his mother and brother, Laennec had tuberculosis. He died of the disease on August 17, 1826. He was 45 years old.

HIS INVENTION: Laennec's invention of the stethoscope revolutionized medicine. It enabled doctors to hear the action of the lungs and heart. It provided a way to diagnose, and treat, deadly diseases. Even though the modern stethoscope looks different from Laennec's original, it's based on the same concept. And it is still used by doctors everyday, all over the world.

WORLD WIDE WEB SITES:

http://doctorsecrets.com/amazing-medical-facts/stethoscope
http://www.ncbi.nlm.nih.gov/

Edwin Land
1909 - 1991
American Physicist, Inventor, and Businessman
Inventor of Instant Photography and Founder of Polaroid

EDWIN LAND WAS BORN on May 7, 1909, in Bridgeport, Connecticut. His parents were Harry and Martha Land. His father had a scrap metal business and his mother was a homemaker.

EDWIN LAND GREW UP an energetic and curious child. He loved to take things apart to understand how they worked. Once, he took apart his family's beautiful wooden clock. His father was angry, and took the parts to a repair shop. Edwin was disappointed. He knew he could have put it back together, correctly, all by himself. Later, his father let him have a lab in the basement.

One of the many things that fired Edwin's curiosity was electricity. He learned all he could about it. By the age of 12, he had such a sure understanding of how it worked that he installed the electrical wiring at his summer camp. He was also fascinated by photography, which grew from a hobby to his profession.

EDWIN LAND WENT TO SCHOOL at the public schools in Bridgeport for several years. Then, he went to a private school, Norwich Academy. He was an excellent student. He loved science, particularly chemistry and physics.

After graduating from Norwich, Land went to college at Harvard University. But he left after one year. Land had become fascinated with "polarized" light. He took a leave from Harvard, and devoted the next three years to studying on his own.

POLARIZED LIGHT: Light is made up of electromagnetic waves. Waves of ordinary light, from the sun or a lamp, vibrate in many different directions. Polarized light rays all vibrate in the same direction. Ordinary light becomes polarized when it is passed through a polarizing filter. The structure of the filter blocks all but the polarized light.

STARTING HIS OWN LAB: Land wanted to understand everything about polarized light. He moved to New York City and set up a lab in his apartment. He spent days in the library, reading, and nights in his lab, experimenting. His goal was to create a special filter that would polarize light rays.

Land was inspired in part by the work of a German scientist, William Herapath. Herapath had discovered that combining iodine and quinine produced crystals that could polarize light.

FIRST INVENTION: Working in his lab, Land invented a synthetic sheet polarizer. The polarizer was made of ground crystals in a chemical solution, that was exposed to a magnetic field. A plastic sheet dipped in the solution became the first-ever synthetic sheet polarizer. Land **patented** the polarizer in 1929.

Land returned to Harvard and continued his studies. One of his professors, George Wheelwright, was amazed at what Land had accomplished. He was also convinced the idea had great business potential. He became Land's partner.

LAND-WHEELWRIGHT LABORATORIES: Land left Harvard in 1932, when he and Wheelwright started their own lab. The business started in a barn in Wellesley, Massachusetts, near Boston. In 1934, they received their first big order. **George Eastman** wanted to use Land's polarizer in Kodak's photographic light filters.

Another major buyer of Land's technology was the American Optical Corporation. They wanted to use polarized glass to produce nonglare sunglasses. The company became a financial success. The two owners decided to form a new company, the Polaroid Corporation.

POLAROID: The Polaroid Corporation was founded in 1937. The company bought all of Land's patents, and he became the

Courtesy the Polaroid Collections

Land demonstrating instant photography, c. 1947

president. Over the next 43 years, he led the company as president and head of research.

During World War II (1939 - 1945), the Polaroid company made many important products for the military. They developed infrared night vision devices, gun sight filters, and aerial surveillance cameras. But Land is best known for his invention of instant photography.

A BRIEF HISTORY OF PHOTOGRAPHY: Capturing an image with a device, then reproducing it, has always fascinated people. The original camera, called the "camera obscura," was in use in the 1500s. It was a light-proof box with a pinhole on one side, and a see-through screen on the other. When you looked through the hole at an object, it projected the image upside down. Artists used this first camera to trace objects.

In 1727, a German chemist discovered that the chemical silver nitrate darkened when exposed to light. In England in the early 1800s, Thomas Wedgwood and Humphrey Davy used silver nitrate to create "photograms." They placed objects on paper, then soaked the paper in silver nitrate. Then, they exposed the paper to air. An image would appear, which they called a photogram. But Wedgwood and Davy didn't know how to stop the image from continuing to develop. The photogram would eventually disappear.

In France, Joseph Niepce made the first negative on paper in 1816. Niepce and fellow photographer Louis Daguerre worked together on trying to fix an image on a metal plate. In 1839, Daguerre developed a process to make an image on a silver plate. It was called a "Daguerreotype." Many of the first photographs seen by people around the world were Daguerreotypes. They were a sensation.

In England, Henry Fox Talbot had created a paper negative that could be used to make many copies of one image. He'd also found a way to stop, or "fix," the development process. He called his image a "calotype." Another early pioneer in photography was John Herschel. He found a way to use a chemical, hypsosulfite of soda, to fix images. Most historians consider Niepce, Daguerre, Talbot, and Herschel to be, together, the inventors of photography.

Courtesy the Polaroid Collections

Land with an early Polaroid camera, c. 1948

What happened next is a fascinating note in the history of invention and **patents.** The French government bought the photographic process created by Niepce and Daguerre. Then, they gave it to the world, without any patent.

In the 1880s and 1890s, **George Eastman** developed both rolled film and an easy to use camera that became a common item in most homes. First, he invented a dry plate process to develop film. Next, he invented a lightweight, flexible paper-backed film, coated with emulsion. The film was rolled onto a holder that attached to the back of the camera. Then, he created a simple, hand-held camera that was easy enough to be used by anybody.

INVENTING INSTANT PHOTOGRAPHY: By the time Land invented instant photography, consumers were used to an easy to use, affordable camera. But what Land came up with was special.

The inspiration for Land's invention was a comment from his three-year old daughter, Jennifer. The family was on vacation, and Land was taking photos. He took a picture of Jennifer, and she asked to see it. She couldn't understand why she had to wait for the photo to be developed and printed.

Land was suddenly struck by an idea. He walked off, thinking. "Within the hour, the camera, the film, and the physical chemistry became so clear to me," he recalled. What he'd come up with was the first instant camera.

The inspiration appeared in a flash. "I suddenly knew how to make a one-step dry photographic process," he remembered. The research and design took five years. When it came out, Land's instant photography captivated the world.

The Polaroid Land Camera was a camera, developer, and printer, all in one. Using special, chemically treated paper, it could produce a photograph in 60 seconds. It was a huge success. In the 1960s, half of all homes in the U.S. had a Polaroid instant camera. The technology was useful in science and business, too.

OTHER RESEARCH: Land continued to make improvements to instant photography. He also worked for many years to develop an instant home movie camera. But despite spending close to $70 million on the project, it never became a product. Land retired from the company in 1980.

EDWIN LAND'S HOME AND FAMILY: Land met his wife, Helen, when they worked together in New York. They married in 1929 and had two daughters, Jennifer and Valerie. Land died after a long illness on March 1, 1991. He was 81 years old.

HIS INVENTION: Land's invention of instant photography was a great commercial success. The camera and film were affordable, and allowed consumers to have an "instant" look at their snapshots.

WORLD WIDE WEB SITES:

http://www.invent.org/hall_of_fame/91.html
http://www.polaroid.com/

Jerome Lemelson
1923 - 1997
American Inventor of More than 500 Items

JEROME LEMELSON WAS BORN on July 18, 1923, on Staten Island, in New York City. His father was a doctor and his mother was a teacher. Jerome, called Jerry, had two younger brothers named Howard and Justin.

JEROME LEMELSON GREW UP on Staten Island. He loved football and baseball and playing with this friends. He was bright and curious and started inventing when he was very young. His first invention was a lighted tongue depressor he made for his dad.

Jerry and his brother Howard were fascinated with airplanes. They read airplane magazines for much older readers, and started to build planes themselves. These were gas-powered model airplanes, which they sold to other kids.

JEROME LEMELSON WENT TO SCHOOL at the public schools on Staten Island. After high school, he went to college at New York University in Manhattan. He studied aeronautical (airplane) engineering.

Soon after Lemelson started college, the U.S. entered World War II. He left college to serve in the Army Air Corps. During the war, he designed weapon systems. When the war ended in 1945, he returned to college. He also began to work for the Navy, developing engines for rockets. Lemelson graduated from college in 1951. He earned a bachelor's degree in aeronautical engineering and two master's degrees, one in aeronautical and one in industrial engineering.

FIRST JOBS: After graduating, Lemelson worked as an engineer for several different companies. He also started to invent things in his spare time. He began to apply for **patents**.

DECIDING TO BECOME A FULL-TIME INVENTOR: Over the span of his career, Lemelson applied for and received over 500 patents. That effort took a tremendous amount of time and energy.

Lemelson with the toy race track involved in his patent suit with Mattel

By 1957, Lemelson decided he wanted to invent full-time. He quit his full-time job and started a home office and laboratory. "I wanted to invent, design, and develop a product," he said.

FIRST INVENTIONS: Lemelson's inventions cover a wide range of products. He never devoted himself to one area. Instead, he invented products, improvements, even processes. "My ideas seem to come from constantly looking for problems to solve," he said. He wrote down notes all day long. At night, he'd keep paper and pen by his bed. He'd wake up and jot down notes for new inventions.

Some ideas evolved from other inventions. Once, his wife came home with a new belt with a Velcro fastener. (See the entry on Velcro's inventor, **Georges De Mestral**). Lemelson immediately had an idea. He invented a dart game with Velcro on the dart tips. It was a great success.

Lemelson also created inventions for computers. Some of these were used to automate factory production. These included computerized robots that could do work quickly and efficiently. He also invented systems for bar-code scanners. But Lemelson faced a problem common to small businesses. He didn't have enough money to see his ideas through the process of production. Still, he was able to make some important, and money-making, inventions.

MOST IMPORTANT INVENTIONS: One of Lemelson's most important inventions is called a "flexible manufacturing system." It is actually a process involving tools controlled by a computer. The computer controls the manufacturing process of a product, as it is sent down an assembly line. It proved to be successful in many factories, particularly in the auto industry.

Lemelson also invented parts of many consumer products used everyday. Computers, VCRs, audio systems, and other products contain parts invented by Lemelson. The first Sony Walkman included a miniature cassette tape drive Lemelson invented. Also, companies like IBM paid him to use his inventions in their computers. They were great successes for him.

DEFENDING HIS INVENTIONS IN COURT: The incredibly productive Lemelson submitted almost one invention a month to the U.S. patent office. But over the years, something happened that stunned and angered him. Companies "infringed" on his patents. That is, they began making products based on his designs. But they did it illegally. They didn't ask Lemelson for permission, to license his

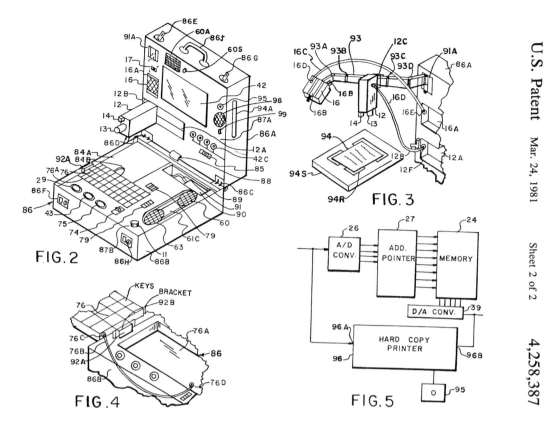

U.S. Patent   Mar. 24, 1981   Sheet 2 of 2   4,258,387

A patent diagram for Lemelson's design for a video telephone.

products, so that he would be paid for his invention. He decided to take them to court.

Over the years, Lemelson spent a great deal of time and money to defend his inventions in court. Sometimes he won, sometimes he didn't. It occupied time he would have rather spent inventing. But he felt he needed to protect himself and other independent inventors.

One famous case involved the Mattel toy company. They copied Lemelson's design for a toy race track. They produced it as part of their Hot Wheels toy car systems. Lemelson took Mattel to court, and won. But that ruling was challenged on appeal, and Lemelson lost the appeal. But it didn't stop him. He continued to fight the infringements on his patents for many years.

ENCOURAGING OTHER INVENTORS: Over the years, Lemelson's inventions made him a very wealthy man. He decided to start a foundation devoted to encouraging new inventors. He also partnered with the Massachusetts Institute of Technology (MIT) to educate young people about invention. Prizes and scholarships awarded through these programs have helped many young people get their ideas off the ground.

JEROME LEMELSON'S HOME AND FAMILY: Lemelson married Dorothy Ginsberg in 1954. Dorothy was an interior designer who provided for the family during Jerry's earliest years as in independent inventor. They had two sons, Eric and Robert.

Jerome Lemelson remained an active inventor until his death from cancer on October 1, 1997, at the age of 74.

HIS INVENTIONS: Lemelson is remembered as one of the most productive inventors of all time. Even after his death, his inventions continued to be patented. His foundation and program with MIT continue to inspire inventors, young and old.

WORLD WIDE WEB SITES:

http://web.mit.edu/invent/w-lemelsonbio.html
http://www.lemelson.org/about/bio_jerry.php

Joseph Lister
1827 - 1912
English Surgeon
Created the Antiseptic Technique,
Making Surgery Safe

JOSEPH LISTER WAS BORN on April 5, 1827, in Essex, England. His parents were Joseph and Isabella Lister. Joseph was a wine merchant and an amateur physicist. He created a special lens for the microscope. Isabella was a homemaker.

JOSEPH LISTER GREW UP in a family that believed in the importance of education. The Listers were also devout members of the Quaker faith.

JOSEPH LISTER WENT TO SCHOOL at a number of Quaker schools. He was an excellent student. He attended University College in London. He received his medical degree in 1852.

EARLY MEDICAL CAREER: Lister worked as a surgeon in London, then in Edinburgh, Scotland. When he began his career, nearly 50% of patients died after surgery. They died because their surgical wounds became infected. The death rate was so high that most doctors amputated injured limbs instead of trying to operate.

Lister noted that if a patient had a simple fracture—which did not break the skin—the patient often healed. But if the patient had a fracture that broke the skin, the wound became infected and the patient usually died. Lister wanted to change that. First, he had to determine why patients got infections so easily.

LOUIS PASTEUR: Lister studied the work of **Louis Pasteur**. Pasteur had found that bacteria are carried in the air and cause disease in people, plants, and animals. Lister thought about this in relation to surgery. He theorized that germs, carried in the air, entered the wounds of patients and spread infection. That's why so many surgical patients died.

Pasteur had killed bacteria with high heat. Lister couldn't do that with patients. Instead, he searched for a chemical that would kill germs before and after surgery. He decided to try carbolic acid. Lister also sterilized all medical instruments before surgery.

Painting showing Lister using antiseptic surgery.

Following Pasteur's methods, the materials were boiled in water, which killed the germs.

The first patient to receive an operation with the new methods was a child. On August 12, 1865, 11-year-old James Greenlees was brought to the hospital. He'd been run over by a wagon and broken his leg. Lister poured carbolic acid over the open wound. Then he set the leg, using sterilized instruments.

Six weeks later, James was just fine. His wound and fracture had healed, and he walked out of the hospital. Lister's method was a success.

Lister's results were immediate and dramatic. Deaths from post-surgical infections dropped from nearly 50% to less than 15% in a few years.

ANTISEPTIC TECHNIQUE: Lister called his methods "antiseptic." The word soon came to mean any chemical that stops the growth of bacteria, and disease. Some doctors didn't believe Lister. But after so many surgical patients survived using the antiseptic method, they were convinced.

LATER YEARS: In his later years, Lister was a surgery professor at King's College, London. He became a famous man for his successful new methods.

LISTERINE: In the 1890s, when an American company was trying to sell its mouthwash, they decided to call it "Listerine." It was named for a man who had brought the idea of "antiseptic"—germ-killing— to medicine.

JOSEPH LISTER'S HOME AND FAMILY: Lister's wife was named Agnes. She was the daughter of Dr. James Syme, the chief surgeon at Edinburgh hospital where Lister worked. They had no children.

Lister retired from medicine in 1893. He died on February 10, 1912. He was 84 years old.

HIS INVENTION: Lister is called the "Father of Modern Surgery." He was one of the first doctors to recognize the importance of antiseptic techniques in surgery. His methods have saved millions of lives.

It is hard to believe that before Lister doctors didn't wash their hands or their instruments. People didn't know to wash a cut or wound, either. And a simple infection could actually lead to death. But once people understood the relationship between bacteria and infection, it was a giant step forward in health of people everywhere. Lister helped the world take that step.

WORLD WIDE WEB SITES:

http://web.ukonline.co.uk/b.gardner/Lister.html

http://www.historylearningsite.co.uk/joseph_lister.htm

http://www.surgical-tutor.org.uk

Guglielmo Marconi
1874 - 1937
Italian Scientist and Inventor
Inventor of Successful Long-Distance
Transmission of Radio

GUGLIELMO MARCONI WAS BORN on April 25, 1874, in Bologna, Italy. He was the second child of Giuseppe Marconi, a country landowner, and Annie Jameson Marconi, who had come to Italy from Ireland to study opera. Marconi's father was wealthy enough to afford a country estate, in the town of Pontecchio, 11 miles from Bologna. Guglielmo had two brothers, Luigi and Alfonso.

GUGLIELMO MARCONI WENT TO SCHOOL at private schools in Bologna. At 12 he attended the Technical Institute in Livorno, where he studied physics.

Marconi never completed a degree, but continued to study on his own. He conducted his own experiments with electricity at his father's villa, helped by his brother, Alfonso. His mother also arranged for a neighbor, a physicist named Augusto Righi, to tutor her son.

EARLY INFLUENCES: Marconi was fascinated by developments of other scientists in the 1800s. These included British physicist James Clerk Maxwell (1831 - 1879), who demonstrated the existence and properties of electromagnetic radiation in the 1860s. (Electromagnetic radiation is energy of many kinds that travels in waves, such as visible light, ultraviolet light, magnetic fields, and X-rays.)

In 1887, German scientist Heinrich Hertz (1857 - 1894), following on Maxwell's work, produced an oscillator that generated electromagnetic waves from electric sparks. He also made a receiver made from looped wire that detected them. The scientific community called this transmittable, invisible radiation "Hertzian waves."

USING MORSE CODE: When he was 20 years old, Marconi read about Hertz's work. He decided to reproduce Hertz's devices and experiment further with the transmission of Hertzian waves. By the next year, 1895, working at his father's villa, he had sent signals over a distance of 1½ miles.

Marconi generated signals in Morse code, a system used by the telegraph industry for many years, which sent sequences of dots and dashes by wire. The patterns of dots and dashes were decoded into alphabetic messages. Morse code was invented by **Samuel F.B. Morse**, and was the standard for telegraphic messages from the 1840s.

"WIRELESS": What Marconi was developing in his experiments was a way to send Morse code wirelessly. In fact, Marconi's system was referred to as "wireless telegraphy," or simply "wireless." A major improvement to the system was Marconi's invention of an electrically insulated and grounded antenna. It made reception of the signals much better over longer distances.

Marconi's father saw the genius of his son's work. He tried to interest the Italian Minister of Post and Telegraph in the invention. When he showed no interest, Marconi decided to move to England. There, with his mother's help and connections, he hoped to interest the British government. At that time Britain was the strongest naval power in the world, and had a global empire.

SUCCESS IN ENGLAND: In 1896, a relative introduced Marconi to Sir William Preece, Engineer-in-Chief of the British Post Office. Preece had been investigating wireless telegraphic experiments in England. He saw that Marconi's method was superior to tests he had seen. He championed Marconi's system. In December 1896 Preece gave a lecture in London called "Telegraphy Without Wires," which received worldwide attention. Preece had successfully tested the Marconi system on Salisbury Plain in central England, sending messages wirelessly over ¾ of a mile.

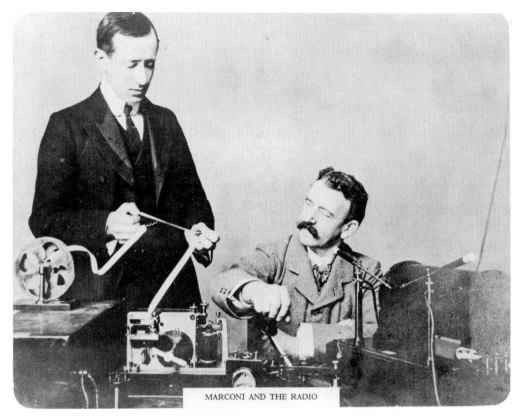

MARCONI AND THE RADIO

Marconi looking at telegraph tape, with an assistant, c. 1901.

Marconi continued to improve his system. Soon he was able to send messages at greater and greater distances: nine miles across the Bristol Channel in England, and 31 miles across the English Channel to France.

STARTING HIS OWN COMPANY: Marconi realized that for further funding and development he needed to establish a company. In 1897 he formed The Wireless Telegraph & Signal Company Limited. In 1900 its name was changed to Marconi's Wireless Telegraph Company Limited. ("Limited" is used by British companies, and is similar to "Incorporated" in the U.S.) His company offered its services for paid wireless transmissions.

In 1899, Marconi's company successfully transmitted news of the Kingstown regatta (boat race) in Ireland to London for Britain's Queen Victoria. He received huge publicity. In 1900 his company received a **patent** for his wireless system from the British government.

WIRELESS CROSSES THE ATLANTIC: Marconi had experimented early on with transmissions over hilly terrain. He was convinced that his wireless signals would carry hundreds or even thousands of miles. To prove his theory, he set up a transmitting station in Cornwall, on the west coast of England, and a receiving station on Cape Cod in Massachusetts. Before he could perform his first test, high winds destroyed the antennas on both sides of the Atlantic. The station in Cornwall was quickly repaired, but he decided to set up a new station at St. John's, Newfoundland, on the east coast of Canada.

There he launched an antenna 550 feet long on a kite. Assistants at the Cornwall station were instructed to send signals at pre-arranged times. Just after midnight, on December 12, 1901, Marconi received the first transatlantic wireless transmission, three "dots," Morse code for the letter "S." He heard the message in his headphones as he listened in St. John's. The signal had traveled more than 2,100 miles.

SKEPTICISM: The announcement of his achievement in newspapers on December 16, 1901, brought Marconi international attention. But scientists and critics doubted that he'd actually sent and received a wireless signal such a great distance. Many thought that the curvature of the Earth would prevent a wireless signal from traveling beyond the horizon. Also, the only witness was Marconi's assistant,

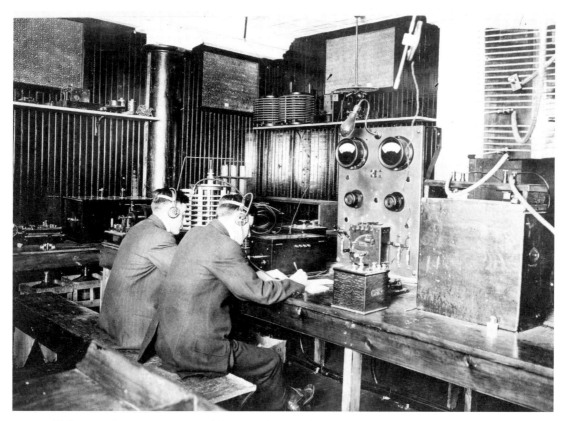

Telegraph operators at Marconi's wireless school, New York, c. 1912

George Kemp. The inventor of the telephone, **Alexander Graham Bell**, remarked, "I doubt Marconi did that. It's an impossibility."

PROVING THE DOUBTERS WRONG: Marconi needed to recreate his long-distance wireless transmission for objective observers. He'd already established the American Marconi Company in the U.S. He'd also conducted demonstrations. He'd reported the 1899 America's Cup yacht race to New York newspapers from ships at sea. But now the stakes were higher. Scientific proof was needed to save his reputation and bring business success.

Some had speculated that Marconi had received random electrical discharges from the atmosphere, not the signals sent from his

Cornwall station. So he set up receiving apparatus on the U.S. ocean liner *Philadelphia*, which sailed westward from England to America in February 1902. During the week of February 22, at pre-arranged times, Marconi received complete telegraphic messages from his Cornwall station, 1,551 miles away, as the *Philadelphia* steamed westward at twenty knots. Later he received signals from a distance of 2,099 miles. The messages were recorded by the ship's telegrapher, and witnessed by the captain.

"Can you read? Will they say now I was mistaken in Newfoundland?" a proud Marconi told a reporter on the *Philadelphia*.

Although Marconi didn't know it, physicists later found that wireless signals, also called radio waves, could bounce off a layer of the atmosphere called the ionosphere, which begins about 30 miles above the surface of the Earth. Radio waves of sufficient strength, tuned properly, would eventually be able to reach around the world, in a series of bounces back and forth to Earth.

FURTHER ADVANCEMENTS: Marconi continued to develop his system. He **patented** an improved radio wave detector, a horizontal directional antenna, and a system for generating continuous waves. In 1918 he sent the first wireless message from England to Australia.

His companies installed wireless sets for ships, and set up business to transmit and receive wireless messages. In the 1920s widespread radio transmissions began, including voice communication. The first commercial radio station in the U.S. was KDKA in Pittsburgh, Pennsylvania. It began operating experimentally in 1920, transmitting the results of the presidential election of November 1920. By 1922 there were up to a million radio receiving sets in the U.S. alone.

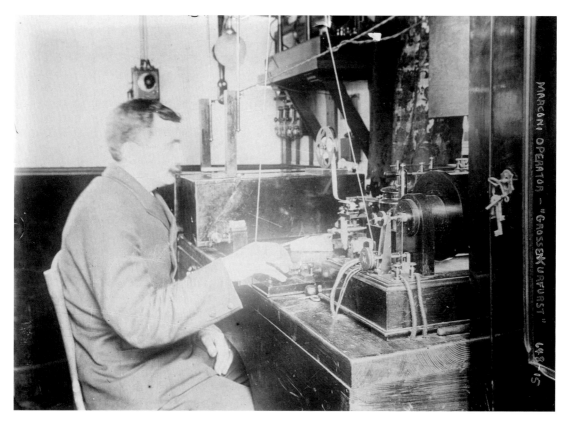

Telegraph operator aboard ship, c. 1912.

NOBEL PRIZE: In 1909 Marconi was awarded the Nobel Prize for physics. He was the first Italian to receive the award in this field. He shared the Nobel with German physicist Karl Ferdinand Braun (1850 - 1918). Braun had worked on wireless telegraphy independently of Marconi. He refined ways of strengthening and tuning wireless signals, which became very important in the history of radio. Marconi met Braun and acknowledged the contributions he made to the new technology.

LATER LIFE: With his fame assured, Marconi continued to work on radio technology. He served Italy as a technical consultant during World War I (1914 - 1918). He also experimented with shortwave radio, which generated signals that could be heard worldwide. By 1927 shortwave made possible worldwide radio communication.

In the 1930s, Marconi experimented with microwave radiation. Microwave radiation uses waves much shorter than radio short-waves, and is the basis of radar. In 1934, on board his yacht the Elettra, Marconi piloted the boat into a harbor using directed microwaves.

Marconi met such famous inventors as **Thomas Edison** and **Orville Wright**. He received honorary doctorates from several universities and won many awards. He was decorated by the King of Italy, the Tsar of Russia, and made an Honorary Knight of the Royal Victorian Order.

MARCONI'S HOME AND FAMILY: Marconi was married twice. He married Beatrice O'Brien in 1905. The couple had two daughters, Degna and Gioia, and a son, Giulio. They divorced in 1927. Later that year he married the Countess Bezzi-Scali of Rome. The couple had one daughter, Elettra.

FINAL YEARS: In the 1930s Marconi became caught up in the political turmoil of Italy. He moved to Rome in 1935, and never left his home country again. In the early 1930s he did further experiments with microwaves. But his health began to decline. After a series of heart attacks, Marconi died on July 20, 1937, at age 63. In tribute, all radio stations around the world observed two minutes of radio silence.

HIS INVENTIONS: Marconi cannot be called the sole inventor of radio. Many others, especially **Nikola Tesla**, contributed to its development. But he pulled together the necessary technology, demonstrated the functionality of wireless, and made a business success with it. He also refined it in ways so important that it is impossible to think of radio developing without him. In addition, his experiments with microwaves led to the invention of radar.

More importantly, wireless technology is a direct precursor of many of today's technologies. These include satellite communications, wireless modems, cell phones, and MP3 players. Even WiFi hotspots that laptop computers use to access the World Wide Web from "wireless" locations are directly linked to Marconi's invention.

WORLD WIDE WEB SITES:

http://www.marconiusa.org/index.html
http://www.marconifoundation.org/index.html
http://www.marconi.com/Home
http://nobelprize.org/physics/laureates/1909/marconi-bio.html
http://www.pbs.org/wgbh/aso/databank/entries/btmarc.html
http://www.invent.org/hall_of_fame/97.html

Cyrus McCormick
1809 - 1884
American Inventor and Businessman
Inventor of the Mechanical Reaper

CYRUS McCORMICK WAS BORN on February 15, 1809, in Rockbridge County, Virginia. He was the son of Robert and Mary Ann McCormick. They were farmers. Cyrus had seven brothers and sisters. In his early years they lived with his grandfather in a log home.

CYRUS McCORMICK GREW UP in the country hills of Virginia. When he was 10 years old, his father bought 532 acres from his grandfather, and the McCormick family moved to a farm they called "Walnut Grove." All the children helped with the farm chores. They helped out in the shop where their father experimented with improving farm machinery.

CYRUS McCORMICK WENT TO SCHOOL but only finished elementary school. At a young age he showed a talent for mechanics. He spent much of his time learning from his father, as he tried to create machines that would make farming easier. Robert had already patented a thresher and other farm machines. He'd also invented a hill plow and had tried to build a mechanical reaper—a machine that could cut grain—but gave up before he had figured it out.

THE IMPORTANCE OF A MECHANICAL REAPER: In the early 1800s, pioneers were moving West to claim land and begin to farm the Great Plains. With the invention of **John Deere**'s steel plow they were able to cultivate and plant large areas of land. Wheat was one of the major crops that they planted, along with oats and other grains.

When it was time to harvest (or reap) the wheat, it took many people to cut, sort, and bundle it by hand. Farmers had a hard time finding enough people to help with the harvest. Because of this, farmers either didn't plant as much wheat as their land could produce, or they watched it spoil in the fields.

CYRUS McCORMICK AND THE REAPER: In 1831, when McCormick was 22 years old, he began to work on a new reaper design. In July 1831 he demonstrated his machine to a group of farmers in Virginia.

At first, most farmers didn't believe his machine would be helpful to them. McCormick believed in it, however, and kept working on his machine.

A RIVAL WITH A REAPER: Another man named Obed Hussey had designed his own reaper. In 1833 he demonstrated his machine near Cincinnati, Ohio. Hussey **patented** his reaper in 1833. When McCormick learned of it, he patented his own reaper in 1834. For the next ten years these two men were in competition with each other. In those early years, Hussey actually sold more reapers than McCormick.

There were several reasons McCormick's early reapers didn't sell well. He had joined his father in an iron furnace business but it went broke. Also, his father had given him his own 400-acre farm, and he was busy trying to make it profitable. Most importantly, McCormick was still working to perfect his reaper.

In 1840 McCormick turned his full attention back to making reapers. By then, Hussey had been selling his machine for six years, but was having trouble maintaining quality. By 1845, McCormick was producing 150 reapers a year, in his Virginia and Ohio workshops. And they were a success.

One farmer who bought a McCormick reaper made a statement that would become the sales slogan for the company. He said, "My reaper has more than paid for itself in one harvest." The farmer had cut 175 acres of crops in just one week.

MOVING TO CHICAGO: McCormick saw that there was a market for his machines, and decided to move to Chicago. He knew that in the West, land was flat, farms were cheap, and workers were hard

McCormick's reaper

to get. He thought that by moving to Chicago and building his own factory he could make the most out of his business.

Chicago was a small town when McCormick moved there. There was only one school, one fire engine, and the police force had only six men. Because he needed money to begin his business, he went into partnership with the mayor of Chicago, William B. Ogden. Ogden lent McCormick $25,000. In 1847, he built his first factory on the north shore of the Chicago River. In 1849 McCormick had enough money to buy out Ogden's part of the business and became the sole owner.

In 1851 both Hussey and McCormick traveled to London for the World's Fair. They put their reapers into a contest. The Virginia McCormick Reaper won the Gold Medal. It was a big boost for McCormick and helped make his reaper the one farmers wanted to buy.

PATENT PROBLEMS: It is important to remember that Hussey and McCormick weren't the only ones making reapers. And when McCormick's first patent expired in 1848, he wasn't given another one. Although patents were given for *improvements* on existing inventions they did not bar others from using the previously protected idea.

It was hard for McCormick to protect the rights to his invention. He spent much time and money in court. New competitors were inventing and producing better machines more quickly. By 1864 there were more than 50 reaper manufacturers in the United States.

Now with each harvest farmers had many choices. To try and keep the favor of the farmers, McCormick bought competitors' reapers every year. He had them shipped to his factory in Chicago. He'd study the new models, and try to replicate their innovations, always mindful not to infringe on others' patents.

McCormick's hard work paid off. He became a very wealthy man. In 1856 alone, his company made more than one million dollars. He sold reapers in the U.S. and Europe, and also bought real estate in Chicago. He invested money in the new railroads of the United States and mines in South America.

INNOVATIVE BUSINESS IDEAS: McCormick was a shrewd businessman. He used ideas and strategies that are still important today. He was one of the first businessmen to guarantee his product. He promised his customers "15 acres a day or your money back." He gave this guarantee in writing to each farmer who bought a reaper.

McCormick's forge shop

He allowed farmers to buy on credit. He asked them to pay $30 when they took the reaper home. They would pay $90 later if they saw that the reaper lived up to its promise.

He set up sales offices in towns all over the country. His staff showed farmers how the reaper worked, and helped them with repairs. The offices had spare parts and mechanics on duty. The farmers felt sure that if they had any trouble there would be someone to help them.

McCormick believed in advertising. He used the positive comments he received from farmers to help with sales. He traveled to Europe to show people there how his reaper worked.

McCormick himself traveled the countryside to see how his machines were doing during the harvest season. Mechanics traveled with him, to repair reapers right in the fields.

By 1860 McCormick was producing about 4,000 reapers each year. But in 1871, the Great Chicago Fire destroyed his factory, along with almost everything else in the city. Though devastated by the loss, McCormick rebuilt his factory. He also paid to rebuild many of the other buildings that had been destroyed. Because of that, there are several Chicago landmarks named for him today, including the McCormick Convention Center.

A FAMILY BUSINESS: As the business grew, McCormick hired members of his family. His wife helped with paperwork, his brother Leander was in charge of factory operations, and another brother, William, handled business operations. In 1879 the company was reorganized with the brothers as partners and was renamed the McCormick Harvesting Machine Company. That same year, his son, Cyrus McCormick Jr. finished college and joined his father and uncles in the business.

McCormick was the president of the company until his death in 1884. He was 75 years old. By the time of his death, his company had produced almost six million reapers.

CYRUS McCORMICK'S HOME AND FAMILY: Because he spent so much time on his work, McCormick didn't marry until he was 49 years old. His wife's name was Nettie Fowler. Together, they had seven children. McCormick was very religious. He liked to spend his free time discussing religion with friends and ministers. He gave much of his fortune to the Presbyterian church.

In 1902 the McCormick Harvesting Machine Company was combined with four other small harvesting machine companies and became the International Harvester Company. Today, the company is known as Navistar.

HIS INVENTION: McCormick's mechanical reaper is one of the most important innovations in the history of farming. Using his reaper, crops were harvested in less time, using fewer workers. Farmers doubled their harvests. They produced so much grain that the Midwest became known as the "breadbasket of the nation."

During his lifetime, McCormick received many awards for his contributions to agriculture. He was elected to the French Academy of Sciences for "having done more for agriculture than any other living man." He was one of the first individuals inducted into the Inventors Hall of Fame in 1976.

WORLD WIDE WEB SITES:

www.invent.org/hall_of_fame
www.anbhf.org/laureates/mccormick.html
www.pbs.org/wgbh/amex/chicago/peopleevents/p_mccormick.html

Elijah McCoy
1844(?) - 1929
Canadian-Born American Inventor
Inventor of the Automatic Lubricating Cup
"The Real McCoy"

ELIJAH McCOY WAS BORN in Colchester, Ontario, Canada. The exact year of his birth isn't known for sure, but is thought to be either 1843 or 1844. His father, George, and his mother, Mildred, were fugitives slaves from Kentucky. They had escaped to Canada using the Underground Railroad.

In 1837, war broke out between the French-speaking people of Upper Canada and the English-speaking people of Lower Canada. George McCoy enlisted in the army and served with the English-speaking forces. When the war ended, he was given 160 acres of farmland near Colchester for his service. That's where Elijah was born.

ELIJAH McCOY GREW UP and went to the local public school for black children in Colchester. As a boy, he showed great interest in the machines and tools that were used on the family farm. He loved to take things apart and put them back together. His parents recognized his mechanical talents. They saved enough money to send him to school in Edinburgh, Scotland.

ELIJAH THE ENGINEER: At the age of 15 Elijah went to Scotland to learn about mechanical engineering. He spent five years studying in Edinburgh. He returned to Canada as a master mechanic and engineer.

When the American Civil War ended in 1865, the McCoy family moved back to the U.S. They settled in Ypsilanti, Michigan. Elijah tried to find work as an engineer, but because he was black there were not many jobs available to him.

He finally got a position as a fireman and oiler on the Michigan Central Railroad in 1870. This was a good job because many times the firemen were promoted to locomotive driver.

Physically, it was hard work. As the fireman, McCoy had to shovel two tons of coal into the firebox of a locomotive engine every hour. And as the oiler, he had to grease the moving parts of the locomotives every few miles. That meant that the trains had to stop frequently, just to be oiled.

McCoy's quick mind and engineering background led him to think of a better way to oil the moving parts of the locomotives. If there were some way to automatically drip oil onto these screws, axles, and bearings when it was needed, the trains would not have to stop every few miles for lubrication by hand.

THE AUTOMATIC LUBRICATING CUP: For two years McCoy experimented with a design in a home-made machine shop in Ypsilanti. When he was finished, he had created a special cup that held oil. The cup used steam pressure to push a piston and allowed oil to be released into tubes that carried the oil to the engine's operating parts.

On June 23, 1872, McCoy was issued a **patent** for his invention. He took his lubricating cup to the engineers of the Michigan Central Railroad, Soon the cups were installed on locomotive engines. Now the engines didn't have to stop every few miles to be oiled by hand. Not only was the lubrication process easier, but the lubricating cups made the engines last longer and need fewer repairs.

McCoy's cup also allowed machines to remain in motion while they were oiled. This completely changed the railroad industry. It could also be used in factory machinery.

There were some who thought that a black man could not make a worthy invention. They tried to discourage others from buying McCoy's cup. But the engineers at Michigan Central Railroad gave him a chance. They hired McCoy to teach the engineers and

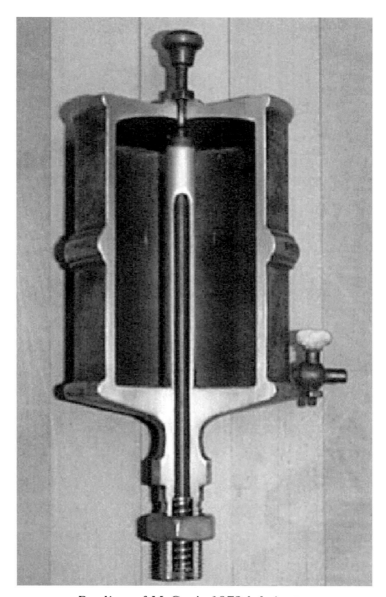

Replica of McCoy's 1872 lubricator

technicians how to use the oil cups. Before long McCoy's cups were being installed on locomotives, steamships, and heavy machinery.

Between 1872 and 1876 McCoy was granted six patents for lubricators and one for a folding ironing board.

THE REAL McCOY: As McCoy's lubricating cup became popular, others tried to copy his design. None of them were able to produce an oil cup that was as reliable as McCoy's. It is said that buyers began to ask, "Is this the real McCoy?" The expression continues to be used today when people want to make sure they are getting the genuine item.

McCOY IN DETROIT: In 1882 McCoy moved to Detroit, Michigan. He continued to work on inventions and also offered expertise and advice to the Detroit Lubricator Company and other firms. Between 1886 and 1926 McCoy was granted more than 45 patents. All but eight were for lubricating devices.

As the railroads began to carry more materials and passengers across the land it became clear that they needed larger locomotives. To power these engines a superheated steam process began to be used. While superheating allowed the engines to go more miles on less coal, it also caused new problems in lubrication.

In April 1915, McCoy was granted a patent for what he called his best invention, the "Locomotive Lubricator." This was a lubricator that used oil mixed with powdered graphite. McCoy's lubricator was effective and efficient and helped keep the superheated engines running smoothly while using less fuel.

THE McCOY MANUFACTURING COMPANY: To make and sell his locomotive lubricator, McCoy established his own business in 1920. By 1923 he had become well known in the manufacturing industry. He was still active at 80. He spent time working with young people in Detroit, encouraging them to work hard so that they, too, could have productive lives.

LAST YEARS: In 1923 Elijah and his wife, Mary, were involved in a car accident. Mary never fully recovered from her injuries and died shortly afterward. After her death, Elijah's health began to fail as well. He died on October 10, 1929.

ELIJAH McCOY'S HOME AND FAMILY: In 1868 Elijah married Ann Elizabeth Stuart. She passed away four years later. In 1873 he married Mary Eleanora Delaney Brownlow. She became his partner for the next 50 years. They had one child.

HIS INVENTIONS: Elijah McCoy never became rich from his inventions. He sold some of his important patents, but never received much money from the companies who profited from his creations.

McCoy contributed to the success of steam engines during the years when they were the main source of transportation. His contribution to the lubrication of machinery changed the way factories were run. Besides his famous lubricators, McCoy invented the first folding ironing board and also a lawn sprinkler. He is credited with inventing a buggy top support, a tread for tires, scaffold support, a rubber heel and a steam dome for locomotives.

Versions of McCoy's original lubricating cup are still in use today in factories, mining machinery, construction equipment, naval boats, and space craft.

WORLD WIDE WEB SITES:

http://www.africawithin.com/bios/elijah_mccoy.htm
http://www.blackhistorysociety.ca/EmcCoy.htm
http://www.blackinventor.com/pages/elijahmccoy.html

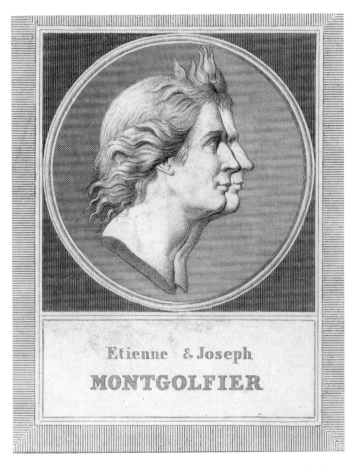

Etienne & Joseph
MONTGOLFIER

Joseph-Michael Montgolfier
1740 - 1810

Jacques-Etienne Montgolfier
1745 - 1799
French Inventors
Invented the First Practical Balloon,
Making Possible the First Human Flight

JOSEPH-MICHAEL MONTGOLFIER WAS BORN on August 26, 1740, in Annonay, France.

JACQUES-ETIENNE MONTGOLFIER WAS BORN on January 6, 1745. Their last name is pronounced "mawn-gol-fee-YAY."

They were two of 16 children born to Pierre Montgolfier. Pierre was a successful paper manufacturer.

GOING TO SCHOOL: The brothers went to school and studied chemistry, physics, and architecture. They both worked in the family business. There, they learned about manufacturing paper. That was important for the making of their first balloons, which were made of paper.

GETTING INTERESTED IN FLIGHT: The brothers were fascinated by flight. They began doing experiments in the 1770s.

While observing a fire, Joseph noted how the sparks and smoke rose. He made a small balloon out of silk. He placed the balloon over a fire in the fireplace. The balloon rose.

The brothers went outside and tried the experiment again. They placed the balloon over a fire of wood and straw. Again, the balloon rose. It reached a height of 70 feet, then drifted to the ground.

The brothers thought they had discovered a new gas. They called it "Montgolfier gas." They didn't realize that the balloon rose because heated air is lighter than cool air. But not knowing the science behind rising air didn't stop them.

FIRST BALLOON FLIGHT: In 1782, the Montgolfier brothers became the first people to fly a balloon using heated air. They launched a balloon made of fabric, filled with air heated over a fire. The balloon rose 3,000 feet, and traveled for about a mile. It stayed in the air for 10 minutes. The Montgolfiers knew they were ready to demonstrate their invention to the public.

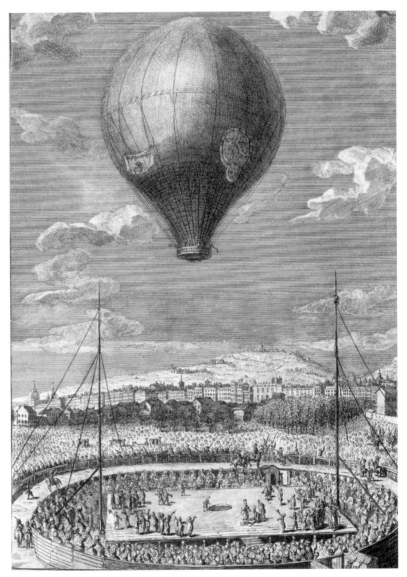

A drawing of one of the Montgolfier's balloons, from 1784.

JUNE 1783: On June 4, 1783, the Montgolfiers demonstrated their feat to the public. In their hometown of Annonay, they launched a 35-foot balloon made of silk and lined with paper. It was filled with gas heated by a wood fire. The balloon rose to 6,000 feet and traveled over a mile, in a flight lasting 25 minutes.

The Montgolfiers' flight was a sensation. Next, they wanted to show their new invention to the King of France.

A drawing of balloons and airships from 1885.
One of these is the 1784 Montgolfier balloon.

SEPTEMBER 1783: On September 19, 1783, the Montgolfiers demonstrated their hot-air balloon in Paris. Before King Louis XVI, they launched a balloon that included the first living creatures. They weren't human, though. The first passengers aboard an airship were a sheep, a duck, and a rooster. The brothers wanted to test the affects of flight on animals, before trying it with humans.

The balloon floated over Paris at a height of 1,000 feet, for eight minutes, traveling about two miles. When the balloon landed, the brothers discovered that all the animals were fine. Now it was time to try human flight.

NOVEMBER 1783: On November 21, 1783, the Montgolfiers launched the first humans into the air. Two men, Pilatre de Rozier and Francois Laurent, flew a Montgolfier balloon over Paris. The balloon traveled over five miles, for 25 minutes, at a height of 1,000 feet. It was the first human flight, more than 100 years before the **Wright brothers.**

The Montgolfier brothers became famous men. They were honored by French scientific societies. They continued to study flight, but then both returned to the paper business. Curiously, they didn't spend much time in the air themselves. Joseph flew just once in one of their balloons. Jacques never flew.

LATER YEARS: Jacques worked in the family paper business until his death on August 2, 1799. Joseph invented other devices, including a hydraulic ram and a temperature gauge. He died on June 26, 1810.

THEIR INVENTION: The Montgolfier brothers proved to the world that human flight was possible. Their accomplishment influenced aviation for years. It led to further innovations in balloon flight, including the development of hydrogen balloons. Today, balloons are still used by scientists to study the atmosphere. They are descendants of the first Montgolfier balloons.

WORLD WIDE WEB SITES:

http://allstar.fiu.edu/aero/montgolfiers.htm

http://www.centennialofflight.gov.essay/Dictionary/Montgolfier/
    D135.htm

http://www.chm.bris.ac.uk/

http://www.sciencemuseum.org.uk/on-line/flight/flight/mont.asp

Garrett Morgan
1877 - 1963
American Inventor of the Traffic Signal and the Gas Mask

GARRETT MORGAN WAS BORN on March 4, 1877, in Paris, Kentucky. His full name was Garrett Augustus Morgan. His parents were Sydney and Elizabeth Morgan. Sydney was a farmer and Elizabeth was a homemaker. Garrett was the seventh of 11 children.

GARRETT MORGAN GREW UP in the small town of Paris. His family was very poor. Both of his parents had been slaves. They were freed in 1863 during the Civil War, which lasted from 1861 to 1865. Yet even after the Civil War, when all blacks were free, they faced discrimination. It was hard for African-Americans to get a good education, a good job, or good housing. Many black families, like Morgan's, were poor.

GARRET MORGAN WENT TO SCHOOL at an all-black school in Kentucky. He only finished the fifth grade. At the age of 14, he decided to leave home and move north. He hoped to find more opportunity and build a new life.

MOVING NORTH: With very little money, but with ambition and hope, Morgan moved to Cincinnati, Ohio, in 1891. There, he found work as a handyman for a wealthy white landowner.

After four years in Cincinnati, Morgan moved to Cleveland, Ohio. He wanted to find better work for better pay. In Cleveland, he found a job repairing sewing machines.

BECOMING AN INVENTOR: Morgan discovered that he had a knack for fixing things. He liked to take machines apart and figure out how they could work better. In doing that, he made his first invention. It was a part for a sewing machine, and it made him $50.

In 1907, Morgan opened his own sewing machine shop. The store was very successful, and he made good money. He was able to buy a house and get married.

Morgan next opened a tailor shop, where he and his workers made clothes. While working in the tailor shop one night, he created another product. He accidently used a cloth made of curly pony fur to wipe polish off his hands. Several hours later, he noticed that the fur was straight.

Morgan was excited by his newest discovery. He knew that the polish could be used as a hair straightener. He used it on his neighbor's wiry-haired terrier, and it straightened the dog's hair. Morgan next tried it on his own hair, and it straightened that, too. Soon Morgan had another moneymaking business on his hands, as many curly-haired people bought his product to straighten their hair.

THE GAS MASK: Morgan's next invention was the gas mask. At that time, there was nothing that could protect firefighters or others who work with harmful smoke or gasses. The "Morgan helmet" was a helmet connected to a long hose. The end of the hose was lined with material that could absorb harmful gases.

In 1912, Morgan applied for a **patent** for his breathing device. His gas mask was a terrific success. He sold it through a new company he created called the National Safety Device Company. Morgan also brought in white partners to help sell the device. Sadly, racism was still a major force in America. Some people would not buy a product created by a black person.

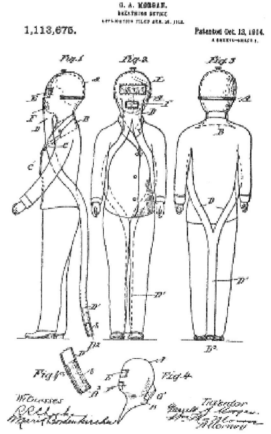

Morgan's first safety helmet. (Courtesy of Garrett A. Morgan, Jr.)

Patent drawing for Morgan's gas mask, 1914.

A HERO: On July 24, 1916, Garrett Morgan became a hero. There was a huge explosion in a tunnel below Lake Erie that trapped several workers. The gasses released during the explosion could kill the trapped men.

Morgan, his brother Frank, and two other rescue workers put on Morgan's gas masks and rescued the trapped workers. All of Cleveland honored Morgan as a hero. He was named the city's "most honored and bravest citizen."

Morgan's gas mask also saved the lives of thousands of soldiers during World War I (1914 - 1918). The German army used poison gasses against American soldiers and their allies. Thanks to Morgan's invention, those soldiers' lives were saved.

THE THREE-LIGHT TRAFFIC SIGNAL: Morgan's next major invention came about in the 1920s. By that time, there were many automobiles and horse-drawn carriages crowding the streets of America. But there was no organized way of controlling traffic.

What concerned Morgan most was the accidents that occurred at intersections. Where traffic from one street ran into traffic from another street, there was no way of determining who had the right of way.

So Morgan invented the traffic signal. It controlled stop-and-go traffic at intersections. Morgan created a "three-way signal." It had three arms that swung out in turn, with the words "Stop," "Go," and "Caution." Later, after traffic signals became electric, those signals became our modern "Red," "Green," and "Yellow" lights.

Morgan's invention made streets safer all over the world. His traffic signal was also used to control train traffic.

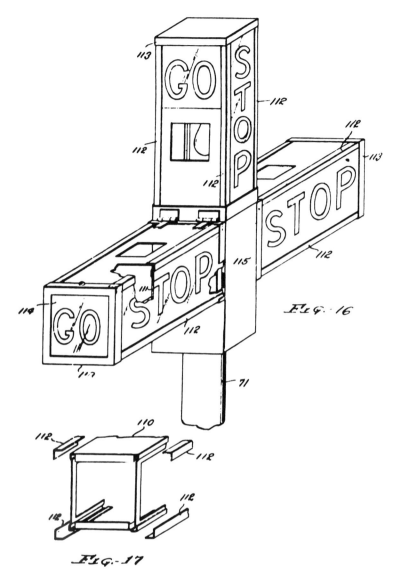

Patent drawing for Morgan's traffic signal, 1923.

Morgan received a **patent** for his traffic signal in 1923. He sold the patent to the General Electric Company for $40,000. That was a great deal of money at that time.

Morgan also devoted much of his life to improving the treatment of blacks in American society. He started a newspaper, called the *Cleveland Call*, that covered news about African-Americans. He was also active in political organizations that promoted equality for blacks.

After a long and productive life, Morgan died in 1963, at the age of 86.

GARRETT MORGAN'S HOME AND FAMILY: Garrett Morgan married his wife, Mary Anne, in 1908. They had three sons, John, Garrett Jr., and Cosmo.

GARRETT A. MORGAN TECHNOLOGY AND TRANSPORTATION FUTURES PROGRAM: The U.S. Department of Transportation has a program named after Garrett Morgan. The purpose of the program is to get young people interested in the field of transportation. It encourages them to study transportation and take jobs in the field.

HIS INVENTIONS: Through his invention of the traffic signal, Morgan made a major contribution to public safety. His name lives on in a program devoted to helping others through education and job opportunities. His invention of the gas mask also saved thousands of lives in World War I. He was inducted into the Inventors Hall of Fame in 2005.

WORLD WIDE WEB SITES:

http://education.dot.gov/aboutmorgan.html
http://web.mit.edu/invent/iow/morgan.html
http://www.invent.org/hall_of_fame/224.html
http://www.sciencemuseum.org/uk/on-line/garret-morgan/
http://www.uh.edu/engines/epi1624.htm

Samuel F.B. Morse

1791 - 1872
American Inventor and Artist
Inventor of Morse Code and the
First Practical Electric Telegraph

SAMUEL FINLEY BREESE MORSE WAS BORN on April 27, 1791, in Charlestown, Massachusetts. His parents were Jedidiah and Elizabeth Morse. Samuel was one of eleven children. Only three survived to adulthood. Samuel's two surviving brothers were Sidney and Richard.

Jedidiah Morse was a Congregational minister and a noted geographer. He published *Geography Made Easy* for use in schools, and a much larger work, *American Geography*. His books were highly successful. Jedidiah came to know other famous Americans, such as **Benjamin Franklin,** James Madison, and Noah Webster.

SAMUEL MORSE WENT TO SCHOOL at a private school, Phillips Academy, in Andover, Massachusetts. He graduated in 1805. He went on to college at Yale.

At Yale, Morse became interested in art, and began painting miniatures. His parents, who were strictly religious, did not approve of their son's interest in art. But Samuel's talent had earned the attention of two renowned artists, Gilbert Stuart and Washington Allston. Morse graduated from Yale in 1810.

ARTISTIC STUDIES: Stuart and Allston's attention to Morse's art impressed his parents. With his father's approval, he sailed to England with Allston to study painting at the Royal Academy in London. He studied under American painter Benjamin West. Some of Morse's early works received prizes in London. He returned to America in 1815, confident that he could achieve artistic success.

Back in America, Morse worked as an artist. He learned quickly that portrait painting was the most likely way to earn a living. He traveled the country to find commissions, building his reputation painting portraits. His most famous work from this era were a portrait of President James Monroe and a painting of the House of Representatives.

Morse moved to New York City in 1823 and set up his studio. He lived and worked there for most of the rest of his life. In 1825 he was elected president of the New York Drawing Association. The next year he became founder and first president of the National Academy of Design.

Just when Morse seemed to be headed towards success, three members of his family died. In February 1825 his wife died suddenly at the age of 25. In June 1826, Morse's father died. His mother passed away in May 1828. Morse was grief-stricken by these losses. Seeking relief, he decided to travel to Europe. Leaving his children in the care of family members, Morse visited museums in London, Paris, and Italy.

While returning to America in 1832, Morse met Dr. Charles T. Jackson. Jackson described recent European experiments with the electromagnet, invented in 1825 by British scientist William Sturgeon. An electromagnet is a device, usually made of iron, around which copper wire is wrapped. When a current of electricity is passed through the wire, the iron becomes magnetic. This is "electromagnetic induction." The electrical current in the wire is said to "induce" magnetic force in the iron. With a strong enough current, an electromagnet has far more magnetic force than a simple magnet of the same size and weight.

CHANGING CAREERS: Jackson told Morse that electrical impulses could travel great distances by wire. Morse realized that the transmission of varying electrical impulses would make possible communication by wire. From this time on his goal became to develop a practical way to use electrical impulses to send messages.

WORKING ON THE TELEGRAPH: Morse was not the only person, or the first person, who thought of the electrical telegraph. And he was not really suited for technical work. His entire career had been as an artist. He lacked the scientific knowledge and the financial means to be an inventor. But he still was devoted to developing the telegraph.

He returned to New York and to his art. In 1835 he became an art professor at what is now New York University. While teaching, he also kept up his studies in the telegraph.

At the university, he found help from a professor of science, Dr. Leonard Gale. The two produced a working model of the telegraph by late 1837. A demonstration of the device, which sent signals over ten miles of cable, convinced Alfred Vail to join them as a partner. Vail brought technical skills and financial resources.

FRUSTRATIONS: Morse and his partners were seven years away from achieving real success. First, they faced legal challenges, in America and Europe, over the invention of the telegraph. Several others fought Morse over a **patent**, each seeking exclusive rights to make money from selling telegraphic systems. Second, Morse and his partners needed financing to demonstrate a working system.

In 1838 Morse successfully demonstrated working models of his telegraph to a committee of scientists in Philadelphia, to a congressional committee, and to President Martin Van Buren. A bill to grant Morse money to develop the project was introduced in Congress in 1838. But it never came to a vote.

Meanwhile, he continued to develop his invention. Morse received an American patent in 1840. But it took 14 years, until 1854,

Morse's telegraph key, 1843

and a ruling by the U.S. Supreme Court, to dismiss all other challenges to his patent. While waiting for the outcome of his legal battles, Morse decided to use his fame and connections to obtain a congressional grant for a telegraph line from Washington to Baltimore, Maryland. In March 1843, the bill for Morse's funding was passed.

"WHAT HATH GOD WROUGHT": With a $30,000 federal grant, Morse set to work. The line was set up on poles between Washington and Baltimore, a distance of about 40 miles. On May 24, 1844, from the chambers of the U.S. Supreme Court in Washington, Morse sent a telegraphic message. He used a special coded alphabet he had invented (see accompanying table).

The message was "What hath God wrought," a quotation from the Bible. Vail received the message in Baltimore, and returned the same message to Morse. Morse's great achievement had now been proven over an intercity line.

Morse Code uses a sequence of dots and dashes, sent by telegraph operators letter by letter, to form words and sentences. Morse had worked out this code in the late 1830s. He checked with a printer to find out which letters were most commonly used in writing, and assigned these the simplest codes.

Usually messages were tapped out by the sender using a telegraph key, which looks like a single, large key on a computer keyboard. Each tap transmits a short electrical impulse for a dot, or a long one for a dash. The code is received and recorded at the other end of the line on paper tape, using a device that Morse developed. The message can also be heard as it is coming in, allowing those familiar with Morse Code to "read" messages as they hear them. The paper tape records the message so it can be checked and then read by others.

The Morse Code Alphabet

A .-	H	O ---	V ...-
B -...	I ..	P .--.	W .--
C -.-.	J .---	Q --.-	X -..-
D -..	K -.-	R .-.	Y -.--
E .	L .-..	S ...	Z -.-..
F ..-.	M --	T -	
G --.	N -.	U ..-	

There are also codes for numbers and basic punctuation marks. With practice, telegraphers can send messages at more than 40 words per minute. The messages can be read at the other end immediately by a good telegrapher, and recorded on tape or written out. Since the message is sent using electricity, it travels at nearly the speed of light. Communication is nearly instantaneous, even over hundreds or thousands of miles.

FAME AND FORTUNE: Although Morse still faced legal battles over patent claims, he won out, not only with the 1854 Supreme Court ruling, but because his system was the simplest, including his code for sending messages. A single wire from place to place was all the Morse telegraph needed, besides the proper devices for sending and receiving.

Morse formed the Magnetic Telegraph Company, and made money selling his system. With success over his patent, both in U.S. and Europe, the Morse system quickly caught on. Morse's company earned money by licensing his invention. Other companies put up telegraph cables between cities, usually along railroad lines. By 1861, the entire American continent was connected by telegraph. In 1866 Morse sold interest in his company to Western Union, which still operates today.

With money from his invention, Morse built an estate called Locust Grove in Poughkeepsie, New York. Today his former home is a historic site.

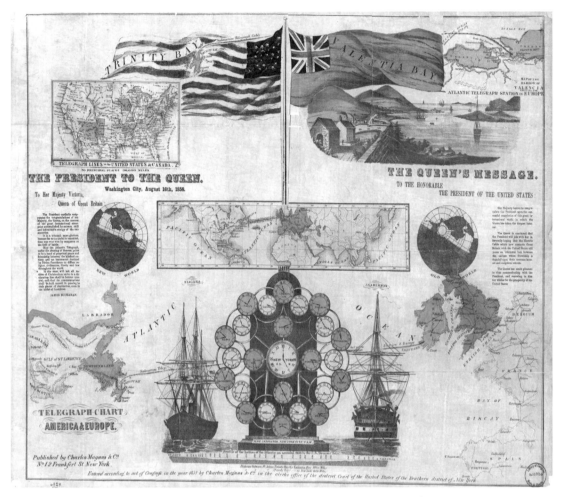

Telegraph chart, America and Europe, 1858.

Though he had put his artistic career behind him, Morse experimented with daguerreotypes, an early form of photography. (See entry on **George Eastman**.) In 1857 he helped in a project to lay a telegraphic cable underwater across the Atlantic.

HONORS AND AWARDS: Morse was recognized around the world for his invention. A group of European nations awarded him a large cash prize. A statue of him was erected in New York's Central Park.

Morse spent his final years involved in several charities. He helped found Vassar College in 1861. He also donated money to

Yale, and supported poor artists. He lived his final years in Poughkeepsie and New York City. Morse died of pneumonia on April 2, 1872, at the age of 80.

SAMUEL MORSE'S HOME AND FAMILY: Morse was married twice. In 1818, he married Lucretia Pickering Walker. He and Lucretia had three children: Susan, Charles, and James. Lucretia died in 1825. In 1848 Morse married Sarah Elizabeth Griswold. They had four children: Samuel, Cornelia, William, and Edward.

HIS INVENTIONS: Morse did not invent the principles for the telegraph, or even the first working model. He perfected a system that was simple, needing only a single wire, and invented Morse Code, which became the international standard. No longer was the world limited to messages relayed by horse or by foot, or using lights and signals sent from mountaintops.

The reliability, accuracy, and immediacy of Morse's telegraph linked cities, states, and countries. With the telegraph in place nationwide, it became possible to synchronize watches in different places. From that time zones were established, which was important for railroad travel. In future years the use of electrical impulses over wires led to the telephone, and eventually to electronic devices such as computers and cable TV.

WORLD WIDE WEB SITES:

http://www.morsehistoricsite.org/
http://memory.loc.gov/ammem/atthtml/mrshome.html
http://www.invent.org/hall_of_fame/106.html

Isaac Newton

1642 - 1727
English Physicist, Mathematician, and Inventor
Formulated Key Laws of Motion and Invented the
Reflecting Telescope

ISAAC NEWTON WAS BORN on December 25, 1642, in Woolsthorpe, Lincolnshire, England. His parents were Isaac and Hannah Newton. His father died before he was born.

ISAAC NEWTON GREW UP on his family's estate in Woolsthorpe. When Isaac was three, his mother remarried and moved with her new husband to another village. She left Isaac to be raised by his grandmother. Isaac didn't get along with his stepfather. After his stepfather died, his mother and his three half-siblings moved back to the house in Woolsthorpe.

ISAAC NEWTON WENT TO SCHOOL at the Free Grammar School, five miles from home. That was a great distance in his time. So Isaac lived with a family close to school. He wasn't a very good student. His teachers said he had trouble paying attention.

Isaac's mother decided he should move home and manage the family farm. But he showed no skill in that, either. One of his uncles decided Isaac should go back to school. So Isaac returned to the Grammar school. This time, he lived with the head of the school. And this time, he showed a great ability to learn.

In 1661, at the age of 19, Newton went to Cambridge University. At first he thought he'd become a lawyer. But after reading **Galileo**'s work, he became fascinated by astronomy. He studied the most advanced math theories of his time. That inspired him to theories of his own.

Newton graduated from Cambridge in 1665. He wanted to continue studying, but had to leave Cambridge. That year, there was an outbreak of the bubonic plague. When epidemics of this deadly disease swept through towns, people fled to the country.

THE FALLING APPLE: Newton returned to his family estate. Over the next two years, he continued to read and study. These were incredibly important years for Newton, and led to several major discoveries.

In 1666, he made a discovery that changed the way we think about the world. The story is now part of legend, but Newton claimed that it really happened.

While sitting in an orchard, Newton watched an apple fall to the ground. He was suddenly struck by an idea. He thought about the *force* that drew the apple to the ground. He theorized that the same force kept the Moon in orbit around the Earth. That force was gravity. He set out to prove his theory using math.

GRAVITY: Newton outlined his theory of gravity in his famous work, *Principia*. It is considered the most important science book ever written. In it, Newton claimed that gravity controlled not just the moon, but the motion of all the planets.

Newton outlined three important laws of motion. The first law says that a body at rest remains at rest, and a body in motion stays in motion. The second says that a force is equal to an object's mass multiplied by its acceleration. The third states that for every action, there is an equal and opposite reaction.

Newton's gravity theories dealt with determining the strength and weakness of the gravitational force. He outlined how those forces changed as the distance between objects—like planets—changed.

Newton's work changed the way people understood the physical world. Before Newton, people accepted the theories of the Greek philosopher Aristotle. Aristotle thought that each of the

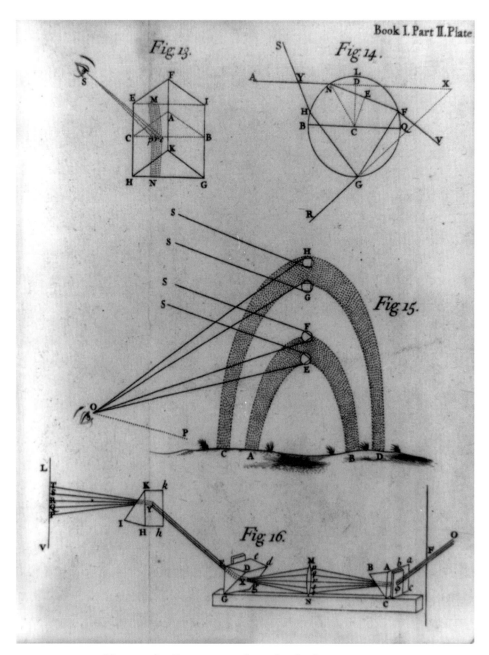

Newton's diagrams of optical phenomena,
including a rainbow and prism, 1704.

planets obeyed its own physical laws. Newton proved that was wrong. He showed how certain physical laws, like gravity, were constant throughout the universe. These findings made him the most famous scientist of his time.

OPTICS: Newton also did important work in the field of science known as "optics." Optics is the study of light. Newton studied the way light breaks down when passed through a prism. He experimented over several years, and discovered that white light is actually made up of the spectrum of colors. He showed how this is evident in nature, as in rainbows. It was one of his most famous discoveries.

INVENTING THE REFLECTING TELESCOPE: In 1667, Newton returned to Cambridge. He became a professor of mathematics. He continued his studies, and also worked on an important invention. He designed and built a reflecting telescope that used a lens made from a mirror instead of glass.

Newton's telescope was a great improvement on earlier devices of **Galileo** and others. That's because the mirror, as it reflects and magnifies the image, also makes it clearer. Newton's telescope was more powerful, and could reach farther into space.

CALCULUS: Newton made important contributions to mathematics, too. He developed mathematical solutions to important problems in analytical geometry. This is called "calculus." It is a complex method of calculating motion: changing, instead of fixed, amounts.

Some of Newton's findings made him a controversial man. Some scientists and mathematicians challenged his work. He also accused others of stealing his ideas. But regardless of any controversy about him, Newton is considered a scientific genius.

LATER LIFE: In his later years, Newton moved to London. He served in Parliament, and was made head of the Mint (where money is made). He was made a member of the Royal Society and served as its president. He also continued to write about science, history, and religion.

ISAAC NEWTON'S HOME AND FAMILY: Newton never married or had children. He was knighted by Queen Anne in 1705. He was the first scientist to receive that honor. He continued to work until his death on March 20, 1727. He was 84 years old.

HIS INVENTIONS: Newton is one of the most important scientists of all time. He invented a reflecting telescope that is still a model for modern instruments. His creation of the laws of gravitation and motion, and his studies in light and calculus, truly changed the way we understand the world.

WORLD WIDE WEB SITES:

http://galileoandeinstein.physics.virginia.edu/lectures/newton
http://www.newton.cam.ac.uk/newtlife.html
http://www.newtonproject.ic.ac.uk

Alfred Nobel
1833 - 1896
Swedish Scientist, Inventor, and Businessman
Inventor of Dynamite
Creator of the Nobel Prizes

ALFRED NOBEL WAS BORN on October 21, 1833, in Stockholm, Sweden. His parents were Immanuel and Andriette Nobel. Immanuel was an engineer and inventor. Andriette was a homemaker, and for a while ran a grocery store. Alfred had two older brothers, Robert and Ludvig, and a younger brother, Emil.

ALFRED NOBEL GREW UP first in Sweden, then in Russia. His father's business failed in 1837. Immanuel left Sweden to begin a new business in Russia. His company made explosives, including mines and ammunition. While he was setting up his new business, Andriette started a grocery store to support the family.

When Immanuel's business was established, he sent for his family. Andriette and the boys joined their father in St. Petersburg, Russia, in 1842.

ALFRED NOBEL WENT TO SCHOOL at home. He had private tutors who taught him science, languages, and literature. By the time he was 17, Alfred could speak five languages: Swedish, Russian, French, German, and English.

Alfred was an excellent student. He loved chemistry, physics, and literature. His father wanted him to study engineering and join the family business. So Alfred went to France. In Paris, he studied in the lab of a chemist named T.J. Pelouze. Through him, Nobel met a chemist named Ascanio Sobrero.

Sobrero had invented nitroglycerine. Nitroglycerine was one of the first powerful explosives. But it was unstable. Nobel could see that it had great practical value. It could be used to blast rocky land at construction sites. That way, bridges and buildings could be built on flat ground. But first, he had to find a way to make the chemical more stable.

FIRST JOBS: Nobel returned to St. Petersburg to work with his father. But the family business was failing. In 1863, the family returned to Sweden to start again. There, Alfred began work on what would become his most important invention, dynamite.

Nobel in 1853, at age 20.

INVENTING DYNAMITE: Back in Sweden, the Nobels worked to harness the power of nitroglycerine for commercial use. But the experiments led to a tragedy. Alfred's brother Emil was killed in an accidental explosion during an experiment. His death affected Alfred deeply.

The Swedish government wanted to prevent any further accidents. They banned experiments involving explosives within

Stockholm. So Nobel moved his experiments to a "floating lab," a boat on a nearby lake.

By 1864, Nobel had found a way to produce nitroglycerine for commercial use. He also found a way to make it more stable. He combined the chemical with sand, and shaped the compound into rods. In the rods, he inserted a fuse, and a blasting cap. He had invented dynamite.

In 1866, Nobel applied for a **patent** for his invention. Dynamite became a great success for the company. It was used to prepare level ground for construction. It was also used to create commercial mines for coal and other minerals. And it was used to blast tunnels in the sides of mountains, so that train tracks could be laid for railroads.

Nobel built 90 factories around the world to manufacture dynamite. He became a very wealthy man. He was one of the richest men of his day. Nobel also continued to experiment in other areas of science. He was especially interested in artificial fabrics, like synthetic rubber and silk. He received 355 patents for his inventions in chemistry, biology, and medicine.

ALFRED NOBEL'S HOME AND FAMILY: Nobel never married or had children. He was a very shy man and was often ill. He died on December 10, 1896, at the age of 63. After his death, the world learned of the incredible generosity of Alfred Nobel.

ESTABLISHING THE NOBEL PRIZES: In his will, Nobel stated that most of his vast fortune—worth millions—would go to fund annual awards. These awards were to be given to individuals in the areas of physics, medicine, chemistry, literature, and peace.

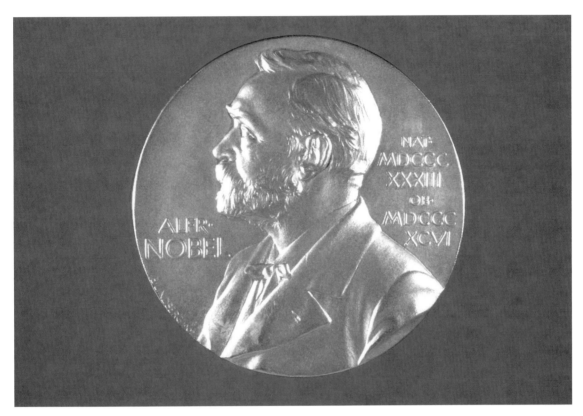

The Nobel Medal.

The award categories reflect Nobel's own deep beliefs. While he was a manufacturer of explosives, he valued them for their constructive, not destructive potential. He loved literature, and read the great books of the past and present. He wanted individuals who made great advances for the betterment of humankind to be recognized and rewarded.

It is interesting to note that members of Nobel's own family opposed his wishes. They challenged his will. It took five years to resolve the problem. The first Nobel Prizes were finally awarded in 1901.

HIS INVENTIONS: Nobel was an important inventor who created the explosive dynamite. But he is known to the world as the man who created the Nobel Prizes. These great humanitarian awards are his true legacy.

WORLD WIDE WEB SITES:

http://nobelprize.org/nobel/alfred-nobel/biographical/
    life-work/gradeschool.html
http://www.invent.org/hall_of_fame/112.html
http://www.nobel.no/eng_com_will1.html

Ellen Ochoa
1958 -
American Astronaut and Engineer
Inventor of Optic Systems Used in Space Flight

ELLEN OCHOA WAS BORN on May 10, 1958, in Los Angeles, California. Her parents are Joseph and Roseanne Ochoa. Joseph was a store manager. Roseanne was a homemaker, then a journalist. Ellen is one of five children. She has a sister, Beth, and three brothers, Monte, Tyler, and Wilson.

ELLEN OCHOA GREW UP in La Mesa, California. La Mesa is a suburb of San Diego. The family moved there when Ellen was one.

When Ellen was in junior high, her father left the family. Roseanne Ochoa always valued education. So when Joseph left, she went back to work and back to school. While Ellen was growing up, Roseanne was busy studying right along with her kids.

The experience made a lasting impression on Ellen. "My mom's been a big influence on me. She had to raise five kids on her own. And she stressed that education is important and that it opens up a lot of options. We were all encouraged to do whatever we wanted to do."

ELLEN OCHOA WENT TO SCHOOL at the local public schools in La Mesa. She was always an excellent student, and she especially loved math. Ellen was a fine musician, too. Everyone in her family played an instrument, and Ellen chose the flute. She played throughout elementary school, high school, college, and even in space.

In junior high, Ellen won the San Diego spelling bee. Her outstanding school career continued in high school. She took all the challenging courses she could, and also played in the band. She graduated from Grossmont High School at the top of her class.

Ochoa went to San Diego State University for college. She took courses in many different fields, including music, business, and science. She finally decided to major in physics. And she continued to play her flute, in the marching band and wind ensemble. She graduated from San Diego State with a bachelor's degree in physics in 1980.

Ochoa went on to graduate school at Stanford University. There, she studied electrical engineering. Still playing the flute, she was named top soloist in the Stanford Orchestra. She received her master's degree in 1981 and her doctorate in 1985.

FIRST JOBS: Ochoa found a job out of college at Sandia Laboratories in New Mexico. There, she did research in the area of optics. "Optics" is the field of science that explores how light, as energy, is transmitted. Ochoa's special field is optical systems and the way they transmit information. Laser beams and holographic images are two examples of optical transmission systems.

At Stanford, Ochoa had begun research into optical systems. She was especially interested in the way optical beams can detect problems in materials and objects.

BECOMING AN INVENTOR: Her study in optics led Ochoa to three inventions. She earned three **patents** for her work in these fields. Ochoa's inventions help scientists use the images that come from space. These devices are object-recognition and noise-reduction systems. The systems inspect and identify objects. Then, they take out any distortion. In helping to filter the images sent from space, they make data more accurate, and useful.

NASA: Although she'd never planned on becoming an astronaut, Ochoa took a job at NASA (the National Aeronautics and Space Administration) in 1988. She researched optical image and data systems for use in space. Heading a team of 35 scientists, she designed computers for the U.S. space program.

BECOMING AN ASTRONAUT: After two years with NASA, Ochoa applied to become an astronaut. She was accepted in 1989, and began her training. She studied geology and astronomy. She also

Ochoa parasails during training.

practiced landing with a parachute and rode in the space flight simulator. In July 1991, she became the first official Hispanic-American woman astronaut.

FOUR MISSIONS IN SPACE: To date, Ochoa has flown four missions aboard the space shuttles, logging nearly 1,000 hours in space. In April 1993, Ochoa flew in space for the first time. She was a mission specialist on a nine-day trip aboard the shuttle *Discovery.* She and the five-person crew did research into the affect of the sun's activity on Earth. Ochoa operated a robotic arm that released a satellite to collect data about the sun.

On her next mission, in November 1994, Ochoa served as Payload Commander. On that 11-day flight aboard the *Atlantis,* she continued to study the affects of the sun. This time, she both released and retrieved a satellite.

Ochoa was back in space in May 1999. This time, on a 10-day mission aboard the *Discovery,* she and the crew docked with the International Space Station. The Space Station is maintained by several countries. Each sends astronauts to run experiments in space. Ochoa helped deliver four tons of food, water, and equipment to the station. Those supplies were used by the first astronauts to live aboard the station.

Ochoa aboard the space shuttle Atlantis, 1994

In April 2002, Ochoa flew back to the Space Station. On this 11-day mission, Ochoa helped install new equipment. She also used the robotic arm to move crew members during their space-walks outside the station. Even in the upper atmosphere, Ochoa made time for music. "I even played the flute once in space," she says.

THE VIEW FROM SPACE: Ochoa says the view of Earth from space is "spectacular." "I never got tired of watching the Earth, day or night, as we passed over it. It's the one thing we all miss when we return to Earth."

Currently, Ochoa is the Deputy Director of Flight Crew Operations at NASA. In that job, she's involved with planning NASA programs. She's very excited about the future of the Space Station. "What the station will bring us is an orbiting lab that you can work in much as you would a lab on Earth."

Ochoa and crew of Discovery, 1999.

THE IMPORTANCE OF SPACE EXPLORATION: Ochoa is a champion of the U.S. space program. "Part of our role as a nation is to explore new territories and to understand more about science. If we didn't have an agency such as NASA committed to exploration and scientific development, then we'd stop growing. We would not be moving forward in areas of technology we have always wanted to pursue. It would change the whole character of the United States and what we think is important."

VISITING SCHOOLS: Ochoa visits schools to encourage kids to study math and science. She tells them that no matter what they do later, it's important to get a good education. "You may not know what you want to do right now or your interests may change. But it is important to keep your options open. For this reason, it is important to study math and science in school. With a good foundation in these areas you will be able to choose many different career paths."

ELLEN OCHOA'S HOME AND FAMILY: Ochoa married Coe Miles on May 27, 1990. Coe is a computer engineer with NASA. They have two children. The family lives in Houston, Texas. In her free time, Ochoa likes to play with her kids, bicycle, and read.

HER INVENTIONS: Ochoa's inventions in the field of optics have been important to space exploration and other fields.

WORLD WIDE WEB SITES:

http://invention.smithsonian.org/centerpieces/ilives/
http://web.mit.edu/invent/iow/ochoa.html
http://www.jsc.nasa.gov/Bios/htmlbios/ochoa.html

Louis Pasteur
1822 - 1895
French Chemist, Biologist, and Inventor
Pioneer in Microbiology and Immunology
Invented the "Pasteurization" Process

LOUIS PASTEUR WAS BORN on December 27, 1822, in Dole, France.
His name is pronounced "LOO-ee pass-TUR." His father, Jean
Joseph, was a tanner. (A tanner treats animal skins for use in
clothing and other items.) His mother, Jeanne, was a homemaker.

Louis had three sisters. The family lived in rooms above the tannery.

LOUIS PASTEUR GREW UP in Dole for his early years. When he was four, the family moved to nearby Arbois, a wine producing town. They lived in a stone house on the Cuisance River. Jean Joseph built pits for soaking animal skins in solutions that preserved them from rotting. Louis's father wanted his son to do better than he had. He sent him to school with the hope that he would one day become a teacher.

LOUIS PASTEUR WENT TO SCHOOL at the public primary school in Arbois. He was not an outstanding student. He preferred fishing and drawing over the other school subjects. He was a very talented portrait artist.

Louis's pastel portraits of family members were detailed and true-to-life. For a while his family expected him to become an artist. This talent was explained by one of Louis's teachers in a way that predicted his future. The teacher said that Louis appeared slow in his work because of the careful attention he gave to every detail.

When Louis was 16, he left Arbois to go to Paris to study. But he became so homesick that he returned after only a month. He did pastel portraits of his parents, the mayor, a nun, a barrel-maker, and other local citizens.

After a while, Louis decided to return to school. He wanted to attend the Ecole Normale Superieure in Paris. That is one of the finest colleges in France. He wanted to become a science teacher.

In October of 1842, now almost 20 years old, Louis returned to Paris to study. He was determined to do well, and go to the Ecole Normale. In Paris, he met Charles Chappuis. Charles became his constant companion and would continue to be his best friend for life.

At age 21, Pasteur passed the entrance examinations and began to attend the Ecole Normale. He spent 12-hour days at lectures and in the laboratory.

THE PATH OF DISCOVERY: Pasteur took courses in chemistry and physics. He also discovered that he loved laboratory work. In 1846, he finished his degree in physics. Soon he was offered a teaching job. He refused it, because he loved his work in the lab. One of his teachers, Antoine Balard, didn't want to lose his promising student. So he hired Pasteur to be his assistant. Over the next few years, he completed two doctoral degrees, one in chemistry and one in physics, while working in the lab.

Pasteur's journey of scientific discovery began in a new branch of chemistry. He studied "organic chemistry," which focuses on the structure of plants and animals. Pasteur was especially fascinated by crystals.

It was known at the time that substances, such as sugar and salt, were made of crystals. Their unique structure was invisible to the eye. They could only be seen under a microscope. Scientists were beginning to study the structure of crystals. They wanted to understand their building blocks—the arrangement of atoms and molecules.

At the age of 24, Pasteur created a simple, yet important experiment. First, he separated crystals in tartaric acid. He discovered that crystals made up of the same chemical formula could exist in different arrangements. Pasteur discovered that some crystals had two identical halves. Other crystals were "asymmetrical"—the halves were mirror images of each other.

This discovery answered a question that had puzzled scientists for years. It also launched the career of Pasteur, making him a leading scientist of the day.

In 1849 Pasteur was offered a position as a professor of chemistry at Strasbourg University. That same year he met and married Marie Laurent. Over the years, they had five children. Marie knew from the start that Pasteur's first love was his work. She dedicated much of her time to helping him prepare papers and assisting him in the lab.

In 1854, the family moved to Lille, where Pasteur became chemistry professor and dean of the Faculty of Science. One day the father of one of his students came to see him. Lille was an important center for the manufacture of wine. The man was having problems. Something was going wrong. His wine was turning sour. It didn't "ferment" properly.

FERMENTATION AND AIRBORNE MICROBES: At that time, scientists knew that organic materials in plants and animals are constantly changing. But they didn't understand what brought about the changes. The process of "fermentation" describes the chemical action that makes sweet milk sour and changes grape juice into wine. It was believed to be the result of chemicals decaying.

Pasteur began working on the winemaker's problem. He studied the wine solution under a microscope. He found clues that led him to believe that tiny living microorganisms were entering the wine and dividing and multiplying. He began to see that fermentation was a "living" process.

Over the next several years, Pasteur identified the organisms, which he called *microbes*. He was able to prove that when they entered an organic substance, such as milk, butter, beer, wine, and vinegar, they changed and contaminated the substance. That's what caused the man's wine to turn sour. He also discovered that if the milk or wine were heated to high temperatures for a few minutes, these microorganisms were killed. He had discovered the scientific source of the problem, and solved it, too.

PASTEURIZATION: The process of heating, or sterilizing, organic substances to prevent spoiling is known as *pasteurization*. It was named in honor of the man who was able to solve the mystery. You can still see the word on milk cartons everywhere.

SPONTANEOUS GENERATION: For thousands of years, people, including scientists, believed that certain forms of life developed from nonliving things. They thought that creatures like flies and worms just grew out of dirt. This belief was known as "spontaneous generation." In 1859, Pasteur began to explore the concept.

Pasteur's work with fermentation had shown him that microorganisms could enter organic matter from the outside. For example, microbes in the air could contaminate milk. He designed an experiment to show that microorganisms are present in ordinary air.

He boiled sugared yeast water to kill any microorganisms, then sealed the liquid into two sterilized flasks. After a few weeks, the flasks were checked and found to contain no microbes. Next, Pasteur opened up one of the flasks to the air. A few weeks later, Pasteur took a sample from each flask. He examined them under a microscope. He found what he'd expected. There were no microbes in the sealed flask, but there were microbes in the one that had been exposed to air.

These results disproved the theory of spontaneous generation. Pasteur proved that living things can only come from other living things.

As a result of this experiment, Pasteur began to wonder if microbes were the cause of disease in humans and animals.

HUMAN DISEASE AND SILK WORMS: In the 1860s, the French silk industry was being destroyed by a disease affecting silk worms. Because of Pasteur's work with microbes, silk businessmen believed he might figure out what was happening to the worms.

During this time, Pasteur suffered several personal tragedies. First, his father died. Then, in 1865 his two-year old daughter Camille died from a mysterious liver disease. Early the next year, his 12-year-old daughter Cecile died from typhoid.

It took all his determination, but Pasteur returned to his study of silkworms. First, he identified the bacteria that caused the disease. Then, he discovered the way it was transmitted. Pasteur found that the disease was transmitted to healthy worms through contact with sick worms. Healthy worms could also sicken from eating leaves contaminated with a sick worm's droppings. Getting rid

Painting showing Pasteur in his laboratory.

of the bacteria, then separating the healthy worms and the sick worms, would get rid of the disease.

Pasteur shared his findings with the silkworm farmers. He told them to keep the breeding nurseries clean and dry with plenty of fresh air. His work saved the silk worm industry in France.

THE GERM THEORY: Pasteur's discoveries with silk worms and fermentation led him back to disease in humans. What if micro-organisms, or germs, were also the cause of disease and illness in people?

As Pasteur walked through hospitals he became convinced that infections were spread by doctors and nurses from sick to healthy patients. It seemed like human disease was spread the same way as silkworm disease.

Pasteur explained his theories to doctors. There was much they could do to stop the spread of infection. They could sterilize instruments, sponges, and bandages by exposing them to high temperatures. That would kill the germs that spread disease. Even though he wasn't a doctor, Pasteur revolutionized the practice of medicine with his theories.

In England, Pasteur's work was studied by **Joseph Lister**. He was a surgeon, and he knew that Pasteur was right. He began using antiseptic techniques in surgery.

Pasteur realized that there were many kinds of germs. What made each disease different was the kind of germ that caused it. During his career, Pasteur identified and isolated the microbes that cause anthrax, cholera in fowl, childbirth fever, and pneumonia.

VACCINES: Pasteur also did pioneering work on vaccines. An earlier scientist, **Edward Jenner**, had developed a vaccine for smallpox. Pasteur understood the scientific theory behind it. A vaccine is a form of a bacterial or viral disease that can help the body create antibodies to fight the disease. By exposing the body to a weakened form of a disease, the body's own immune system will fight it.

Pasteur's important discovery in vaccines came about by accident. First, he identified the microbes that caused chicken cholera. A culture dish of the microbes was left to grow for several days. Then, Pasteur injected the microbes into a chicken to see what happened. Although the hen became mildly ill, it didn't die. Pasteur decided that an old culture of germs must be weaker than a new one. He injected several more chickens with the old culture, and they all lived.

Next, Pasteur injected the same chickens with a fresh culture of cholera germs. Normally, that would kill them. But the chickens all survived. The earlier injection, with a weakened dose, had helped them develop antibodies to the disease.

Next, Pasteur injected chickens who had not received the weak dose with a fresh dose of cholera germs. They all died. This proved his theory that a weak dose of a disease would build an immunity to the disease. Using similar testing techniques led Pasteur to develop a vaccine for anthrax in sheep.

The most famous success of Pasteur's vaccination theory was with rabies. Rabies is a terrible disease that causes inflammation of the brain, and often a slow, painful death. It is spread through the bite of a diseased animal. Rabies affects many kinds of animals. It is most harmful to humans when it occurs in dogs, because so many people have dogs as pets.

After working for more than five years, Pasteur and his assistant, Pierre Roux, isolated a vaccine that used extracts from rabies-infected rabbits. They used the vaccine on dogs, and it prevented them from getting rabies.

Pasteur received much attention and publicity. But he was afraid to try the vaccine on humans because he couldn't be sure of its safety.

An emergency, however, put his vaccination to the test. On July 6, 1886, a mother rushed into his lab with her young son. He had been attacked by a rabid dog. Although he was unsure of the result, Pasteur decided to give the boy the vaccine. It worked. The boy never came down with rabies. He recovered completely.

As word spread of the rabies cure, people came to Paris from around the world. In the first month following his success,

68 people received the vaccine. In the first year, 2,490 people from 18 countries received it. But there were those who criticized Pasteur. Some said he had treated people who didn't really have rabies. Others claimed he had not tested it enough before using it on humans. People in the medical community criticized Pasteur because he wasn't a doctor. How could one learn about disease in a laboratory?

Nonetheless, the pioneering work done by Pasteur changed the world of medicine. His discoveries in microbiology and immunization became accepted and won him honors around the world.

LATER YEARS: In 1888 the Pasteur Institute opened in Paris. It was funded by contributions from people all over the world to honor Pasteur. It provided him with a center to continue his research and teaching. Although he wanted to take part in setting up the institute, Pasteur was in poor health. He had suffered a stroke in 1868, and another in 1887. By the time the building opened, his son had to read his speech for him.

In the speech, Pasteur urged students and scientists to hold on to "rigorous standards of scientific proof." He believed that led to the "joy of certainty."

Pasteur and his wife moved into quarters in a wing of the new building. There, he spent time with his children and grandchildren. Although he was old and ill, he still missed his work.

On his 70th birthday, December 27, 1892, Pasteur was honored with a grand celebration in Paris. Scientists and dignitaries from all over the world came to honor him and his achievements.

Although his research days were ended, before his death Pasteur was able to see important results of his germ theory. In 1894, his assistants Pierre Roux and Alexandre Yersin developed a treatment for diphtheria. At that time, it was a life-threatening disease, particularly for children.

Pasteur died in Paris on September 28, 1895. He was 72 years old. He received a hero's funeral at Notre Dame Cathedral in Paris. He is buried in the chapel at the Pasteur Institute.

LOUIS PASTEUR'S HOME AND FAMILY: Pasteur married Marie Laurent in 1849. They had five children.

HIS INVENTION: Pasteur is one of the most important scientists in history. He made important discoveries in medicine, chemistry, and business. His work led to understanding, preventing and curing diseases and saved millions of lives. The discovery of vaccines for diseases like cholera, malaria, tetanus, measles, polio, mumps, and tuberculosis would have been impossible without his work.

WORLD WIDE WEB SITES:

http://accessexcellence.org/RC/AB/BC/Louis_Pasteur.html
http://ambafrance-ca.org/HYPERLAB/PEOPLE/_pasteur.html
http://www.invent.org/hall_of_fame/
http://www.labexplorer.com/Louis_pasteur.
http://www.historylearningsite.co.uk/Louis_pasteur.htm

Roy J. Plunkett
1910 - 1994
American Chemist and Inventor
Inventor of Teflon

ROY J. PLUNKETT WAS BORN on June 25, 1910, in New Carlisle, Ohio. Very little information is available about his early life.

ROY J. PLUNKETT GREW UP on a farm in rural Ohio. His family was very poor.

ROY J. PLUNKETT WENT TO SCHOOL at the local public schools. He was an excellent student. After graduating from high school, he went to Manchester College. He majored in chemistry and graduated in 1932. He went on to graduate school at Ohio State University. He received his master's degree in chemistry in 1933, and his PhD in 1936.

WORKING FOR DUPONT: Plunkett's first job out of graduate school was with DuPont. That's one of the largest chemical companies in the world. He joined the company in 1936, and worked there for the next 39 years.

Plunkett started off as a research chemist. He worked in the department specializing in chemicals used in refrigerator systems. These chemicals are called "refrigerants." At that time, some were dangerous to health and safety. Plunkett worked to develop safer refrigerants.

INVENTING TEFLON—BY MISTAKE: On April 6, 1938, Roy Plunkett made an amazing discovery. He and his assistant were reviewing a failed experiment with refrigeration gas. They cut open the cylinder that contained the failed experiment.

Inside was a white, waxy substance. The gas had solidified. Plunkett wanted to know the properties of the new compound. In studying it, he discovered that it was incredibly slippery—other chemicals just rolled off of it—and it had a high melting point. Plunkett had invented Teflon.

Plunkett discovered that during the experiment, the gas had "polymerized." That means that the molecules had bonded, forming a resin. The resin was a PTFE type. Its full name is "polytetrafluoroethylene." He had been able to make the PTFE resin in the lab. It was an important moment for invention, and for DuPont.

Plunkett, right, recreates the invention of Teflon.

The new resin was tested for several years. In 1941, DuPont patented the new substance, and officially named it Teflon. Although today we think of cooking pans and utensils when we think of Teflon, that wasn't its first commercial use. It was first used in weapons for the military and industry.

Teflon became a tremendously popular product in the 1960s, when it was first used to make nonstick cookware. Today, it is used in all kinds of products, from cloth to metal, and from cookware to medicines.

LATER YEARS AT DUPONT: Soon after his amazing discovery, Plunkett moved on to another division at DuPont. He became Chief Chemist of chemical lead manufacture at DuPont's Chambers Works

447

plant. After several years in the job, he became assistant manager. Over the years, he continued to rise within DuPont. From 1960 to 1975, he directed the division that developed products made of Freon.

Plunkett received many honors and awards in his long career. He was named to the Inventors Hall of Fame, the Plastics Hall of Fame, and the Engineering and Science Hall of Fame. He won awards from the Chemical Pioneering Society and the Modern Pioneers in Creative Industry. DuPont created a special scholarship in his honor. The DuPont Plunkett Student Award for Innovation with Teflon provides scholarship money for college students.

ROY J. PLUNKETT'S HOME AND FAMILY: Plunkett's wife was named Lois. They had two sons, Michael and Patrick. After his retirement in 1975, Plunkett moved to Corpus Christi, Texas. He enjoyed golfing, fishing, and other activities. Roy J. Plunkett died on May 12, 1994. He was 83 years old.

HIS INVENTION: Today, Plunkett's invention is used in many industries, in thousands of products. Teflon is used in industries as different as aerospace, electronics, and architecture. It's used in products as different as satellites, buildings, electronic equipment, and, of course, cookware.

WORLD WIDE WEB SITES:

http://heritage.dupont.com/touchpoints/tp_1938/depth.shtml
http://web.mit.edu/invent/iow/plunkett.html
http://www.chemheritage.org/classroom/chemach/plastics/
    plunkett.html
http://www.invent.org/hall_of_fame/121.html

Wilhelm Roentgen
1845 - 1923
German Physicist
Inventor of the X-Ray

WILHELM CONRAD ROENTGEN WAS BORN on March 27, 1845, in Lennep, Germany. His name is pronounced "VIL-helm RENT-guhn." His parents were Friedrich and Charlotte Roentgen. His father was a cloth salesman. His mother was a homemaker. Wilhelm was an only child.

WILHELM ROENTGEN GREW UP first in Germany, then in Holland. His family moved to Apeldoorn, Holland, when he was three. Later, they became Dutch citizens.

Wilhelm loved to roam the countryside. He loved nature, and he also loved to tinker. From a young age, he enjoyed putting things together.

WILHELM ROENTGEN WENT TO SCHOOL at the public schools in Holland. He also went to a private boarding school. When he was 17, Wilhelm began classes at the Utrecht Technical School. He was expelled two years later, accused of drawing a cartoon of a teacher. Wilhelm claimed he hadn't made the drawing. But the teachers didn't believe him.

Roentgen then went to Switzerland, where he studied at the Polytechnic Institute. He took courses in math, physics, and engineering. He got his degree in mechanical engineering in 1868. He continued his studies and finished his PhD in 1869.

WORKING IN PHYSICS: Roentgen concentrated his studies in physics. That's the study of matter and energy. Physics covers many fields of study. Roentgen was especially interested in heat, electricity, magnetism, and radiation.

After finishing his PhD, Roentgen worked as an assistant to a physicist named August Kundt. The two worked together for many years. First, they worked in Zurich. In 1871, they moved to the University of Wuerzburg. After several years there, Kundt and Roentgen went to the University of Strasbourg.

Roentgen became a professor of physics at the University of Strasbourg. He did research in gases, crystals, and electromagnetism. But it was his work with cathode ray tubes that led to his amazing discovery. (Cathode rays are beams of electrons, streamed through a vacuum tube.)

DISCOVERING X-RAYS: One day, Roentgen was experimenting, sending electric current through a cathode ray tube in a darkened room. There was a paper covered with barium lying some distance from the tube. All of a sudden, the paper began to glow. Roentgen recalled that it "lit up with brilliant fluorescence." He was amazed. The tube was covered in black cardboard. So whatever rays were coming through could penetrate the dark covering.

Roentgen came up with a theory. He thought that when the rays hit the walls of the tube, it created a new form of radiation that penetrated the covering. This new radiation traveled across the room and struck the barium crystals, causing them to glow.

Roentgen did experiments on the rays. They showed that

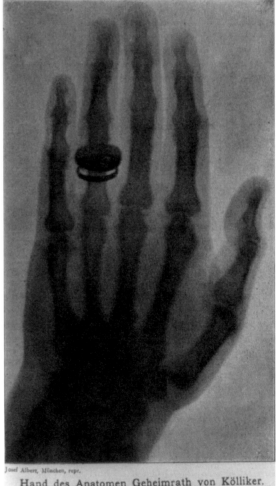

The x-ray of Roentgen's wife's hand, 1895

451

the new rays could go through paper, wood, skin, and other materials. But they didn't penetrate bone. It also made an image on a photographic plate. This meant that scientists could take pictures of things not visible to the eye.

Roentgen called his discovery "x-rays," because the source of the rays was unknown. One of the first x-rays Roentgen made was of his wife's hand. The picture showed the bones in her hand, and her wedding ring. He described it: "If a hand be held before the fluorescent screen, the shadow shows the bones darkly," he wrote. The hand itself was a shadow, showing "only faint outlines of the surrounding tissue."

The new x-rays were a sensation. People all over the world were fascinated with them. Soon, doctors saw their tremendous value in diagnosing patients. With an x-ray, doctors could see inside a patient. Previously, the only way to see inside the human body was through surgery. With x-rays, doctors could diagnose diseases, analyze a fracture, or note the size and shape of a tumor. Dentists could use them, too, to find cavities in teeth.

THE NOBEL PRIZE: In 1901, Roentgen became the first person to receive the Nobel Prize in Physics. He was such a shy man that he didn't give the usual speech at the award ceremony. He also gave the cash prize away to his university, for research.

Roentgen never patented the x-ray. He believed that scientific discoveries belonged to all humanity. Roentgen continued to research and teach for the next 25 years. He retired from the university in 1920.

WILHELM ROENTGEN'S HOME AND FAMILY: Roentgen married Anna Ludwig in 1872. They had no children. They adopted Anna's niece, Josephine, in 1887.

Roentgen always loved the outdoors, and the family had a home near the Alps. He was an active man and loved to mountain climb. Roentgen died on February 10, 1923. He was 72 years old.

HIS INVENTION: Roentgen's discovery of x-rays changed diagnostic medicine. Doctors could look inside a patient, identifying diseases and disorders as never before. Today, x-rays are still used all over the world. They help doctors diagnose disease so that patients receive treatments quickly and effectively.

Roentgen's name lives on as part of his discovery. When someone gets an x-ray, the radiation is measured in "roentgens," abbreviated as "R."

WORLD WIDE WEB SITES:

http://imagine.gsfc.nasa.gov/docs/people/Wilhelm_Roentgen.html
http://nobelprize.org/physics/laureates/1901/rontgen-bio.html

Jonas Salk
1914 - 1995
American Physician and Scientist
Developed the First Polio Vaccine

JONAS SALK WAS BORN on October 28, 1914, in New York City. His parents were Dora and Daniel Salk. Dora was a homemaker. Daniel worked in New York's garment district, where clothing is made. Jonas was the oldest of three boys.

JONAS SALK GREW UP in the Bronx section of New York City. He was very thin and small and didn't enjoy games very much. But he loved studying and was an excellent student. His parents encouraged him from the start, especially his mother.

From a very young age, Jonas knew he was born to make a difference. "Someday I shall grow up and do something in my own way, without anyone telling me how," he remembered thinking. He thought of childhood as "a period of patient waiting."

JONAS SALK WENT TO SCHOOL in the Bronx. He attended regular public schools until he was fourteen. That year, he was sent to the Townsend Harris High School for gifted boys. After high school, he attended City College of New York, where he planned to study law. But when he got a part-time job in a lab, he changed his major to science.

After receiving his bachelor's degree in 1934, Salk went to medical school at New York University (NYU). From the very start, he knew he was interested in research rather than treating patients.

FIRST JOBS: Salk received his medical degree in 1939. He then spent a year studying bacteriology at NYU. That same year he completed his internship at Mt. Sinai Hospital in New York. His co-workers were impressed with his abilities. "Nobody ever saw Jonas ruffled," remembers one doctor. "You told him to do something and he got it done. It got done and so did a dozen things you hadn't thought of."

LEARNING TO FIGHT DISEASE—VIRUSES, VACCINES AND THE IMMUNE SYSTEM: Salk knew that he wanted to study the human "immune" system. That's the system that helps the body fight disease.

Most diseases are passed on by bacteria or viruses. Salk's special interest was viruses and how they worked in the human body. In particular, he wanted to know how vaccines worked. He was following the work of previous scientists, like **Edward Jenner** and **Louis Pasteur**. In the 1700s Jenner developed a vaccine to fight the viral disease smallpox. At that time, smallpox was common, and deadly, all over the world. Pasteur developed several important vaccines, including one for rabies.

"LIVE" AND "DEAD" VACCINES: A vaccine is a form of a bacterial or viral disease that can help the body create antibodies to fight the disease. Vaccines come in two forms. In "live" vaccines, the bacteria or virus that is injected into people has been weakened but not killed. In "dead" vaccines, the bacteria or virus has been killed, but can still create immunity.

Before Jenner, people had experimented with live smallpox serum. When injected into a healthy human, it caused an outbreak of the illness. This would sometimes make that person immune, or resistant to, smallpox. But the serum could be deadly, too. There was no exact science to the method. When injected with live serum, many people came down with a full-blown case of smallpox, and died.

Jenner thought smallpox was close to cowpox, a disease that affects cows. He experimented with making a vaccine out of cowpox. He injected the vaccine into humans. It worked, helping humans create an immunity, or resistance, to smallpox. Scientists of Jenner's time didn't know it, but they were actually working with a virus. It took several hundred years of research and understanding of viruses on the microscopic level for the age of vaccines to come about.

In the 1930s, when Salk was in medical school, science still had much to learn about vaccines. He was sitting in class one day, listening to a lecture on bacterial vaccines, when an idea hit him "like a bolt of lightening." The professor said that *bacterial* diseases could be prevented with a vaccine using dead bacteria. In the next class, he was told that *viral* diseases worked differently, and that vaccines could not be developed to fight them.

That didn't make sense to Salk. "Both statements can't be true," he said to himself. He set out to prove his theory.

FIRST JOBS: After medical school, Salk worked at the University of Michigan. His job was to develop a flu shot to protect U.S. soldiers fighting in World War II (1939 - 1945). Flu epidemics had killed millions of people over the years. One of the worst outbreaks happened at the end of World War I, in 1918. In only a few years, the Spanish flu killed more than 40 million people worldwide.

Flu, short for "influenza," was caused by a virus. Salk's job was to develop a flu vaccine to protect soldiers fighting in World War II. He was successful, and his flu shots saved many lives in the 1940s. Salk also discovered that just one flu vaccine could contain many different virus types. That meant that just one shot could help the body create antibodies for a number of different strains of flu.

Next, Salk moved on to the University of Pittsburgh. There, he directed the Virus Research Laboratory. He got the chance to work on one of the most important medical projects of the century—the search for a polio vaccine.

POLIO: Polio, short for poliomyelitis, is an ancient viral disease. Egyptian skeletons from 1700 B.C. show limbs crippled by the disease. In the 1940s when Salk began his research, people were terrified of polio. Polio epidemics regularly swept the globe, claiming thousands of victims. It caused crippling, paralysis, and death. It was particularly deadly in the summer. And it affected young people especially.

It is hard for young people today to imagine the fear that people lived with then. One polio victim remembered it vividly. "The rules were: don't play with new friends, stick with your old friends, whose germs you already have. Stay away from crowded beaches and pools, especially in August. Never use another person's eating utensils or toothbrush or drink out of the same Coke bottle or glass. Don't get overtired or strained. If you get a headache, tell your mother."

People were afraid of getting polio anywhere crowds gathered. So city dwellers fled to the country. There, innkeepers were unwilling to rent to people who might have brought the dreaded disease from the city.

Early symptoms of polio are usually mild. Once the virus gets into the body, it produces the aches and pains of a regular flu. In most cases, victims recover in a few days. The body then develops an immunity because the system has built up antibodies to fight the disease.

But sometimes polio travels to the spinal cord. There, it attacks the nervous system and the brain. Polio then destroys muscles and paralyzes the arms and legs. Often, within 24 hours after coming down with the disease, a patient can't walk.

Sometimes the muscles around the chest are affected, and the polio victim loses the ability to breathe. In the late 1940s and early 1950s, polio victims such as these were placed in "iron lungs." These great iron cylinders performed the job of the ruined lungs,

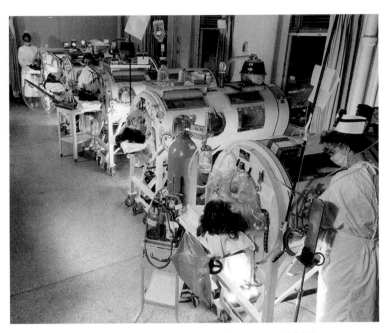

Polio patients in iron lungs, c, 1950.

pressing and releasing the chest to force air into the body. Photos of hospital wards full of children as young as four or five in iron lungs are one of the most painful memories of the time.

SALK'S VACCINE: Salk approached the March of Dimes, an organization devoted to fighting polio. He got funding and set to work on a vaccine using a "killed" form of the virus.

Humans and monkeys both get polio. So Salk and his fellow researchers used monkeys to test their vaccines. After two years of research, Salk had been able to identify three strains of polio. He developed a "killed virus" vaccine to treat all three forms.

To make the vaccine, Salk killed the viruses using formaldehyde. He mixed it with mineral oil to make an injectable vaccine. The first polio vaccination was actually a series of four shots. These helped the body develop immunity to all three strains of polio.

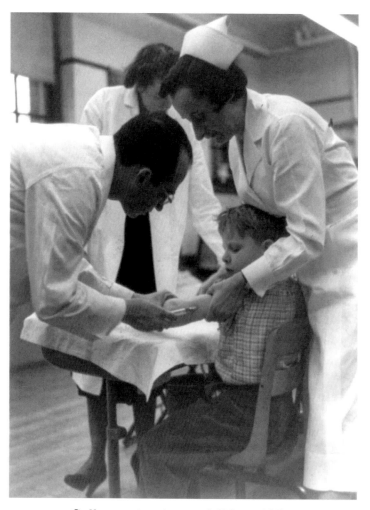

Salk vaccinating a child, c. 1954.

Next, it was time to test the vaccines on humans. Among those first vaccinated were Salk and his family. "You wouldn't do unto others that which you wouldn't do unto yourself," he said.

In 1952 Salk vaccinated a group of children who'd already had one strain of polio. The vaccine worked. It gave them immunity to the other forms. But polio still raged in the population. That same year, 1952, there were 57,000 cases in the U.S. alone.

"THE POLIO PIONEERS": It was time for a large national test of the vaccine. In 1954, 1.8 million children, ages six to nine, were chosen to take part. Called "The Polio Pioneers," they were divided into three groups. One group, numbering 650,000, got the vaccine. Another group, including 750,000, received a "placebo." That's a medicine that *looks* like a regular drug but in fact is not. The last group, of 430,000, acted as a "control" group, and did not receive the vaccine.

It was necessary to use the three groups to truly test the effectiveness of the vaccine. Only if you have people who take a medication, then compare them to a group who do not, can you have factual, scientific results. Doctors followed the "Pioneers" for a year. Then they studied the results. It was time to celebrate.

On April 12, 1955, the results were announced. Before huge crowds, and millions listening on radio, the world heard the joyous news. The vaccine worked, and it was safe.

The country celebrated, and Salk became a hero. He didn't like being famous. He said, "To a scientist, fame is neither an end nor even a means to an end." He received many honors and awards. He refused some, too. One company wanted him to endorse a line of children's pajamas that read "Thank you, Dr. Salk." He said no.

Across the country millions of people lined up for the free vaccine. And the results were astounding. In the years before the vaccine, polio cases averaged 45,000 per year in the U.S. By 1962, that number had dropped to 910.

It is important to note that Salk never patented the vaccine, and didn't make any money from his discovery. It was his wish that it be distributed as widely as possible.

CONTROVERSY: The success of those early years was dimmed by tragedy and controversy. One manufacturer of the vaccine didn't follow Salk's directions. A batch of vaccine containing a live virus caused 204 children to come down with polio. 150 were paralyzed and 11 died. Salk was devastated. He worked to ensure it never happened again.

ALFRED SABIN: Dr. Alfred Sabin (1906 - 1993) had also devoted his life to the creation of a polio vaccine. His vaccine was based on a "live" but weakened virus. Sabin claimed it was better than Salk's.

Also, Sabin's vaccine could be given by mouth, instead of in a shot. It didn't need to be kept cold, as Salk's did. Sabin did trials of his vaccine in Russia and Africa. It was a great success. By the early 1960s, Sabin's vaccine had replaced Salk's in most parts of the world.

But most importantly, the work of these two men has led to the near-end of polio. Just 50 years after Salk's vaccine appeared, this dreaded disease is about to disappear. Thanks to international vaccination programs, polio has been wiped out in the Americas.

By 1988, there were 350,000 cases of polio reported worldwide. By 2000, that number was down to 2,880. Scientists believe that the disease will be wiped out in the next several years.

THE SALK INSTITUTE: In the early 1960s, Salk was ready for a new challenge. He wanted to build an institute devoted to the study of the biological sciences. In 1963, he founded the Salk Institute in La Jolla, California. He brought scientists from all over the world. They worked on ways to prevent and cure some of the most devastating diseases of our time. Today, the Institute's scientists research cures for cancer, diabetes, birth defects, AIDS, and other diseases.

Salk himself worked on developing a vaccine for cancer and AIDS. He also wrote several books. He was still engaged in science when he died on June 23, 1995. He was 80 years old.

JONAS SALK'S HOME AND FAMILY: Salk was married twice. He and his first wife, Donna Lindsay, were married in 1939. They had three sons, and all of them grew up to become doctors. The marriage ended in 1968. His second wife, Francoise Gilot, was an artist. They lived in a house near the Salk Institute.

HIS INVENTION: Salk's vaccine helped bring an end to one of the world's deadliest diseases. Before his vaccine, millions suffered and died from polio. In 2004, fewer than 1,200 cases were reported worldwide. In 1999, *Time* magazine named him one of the top 100 people of the 20th century.

WORLD WIDE WEB SITES:

http://americanhistory.si.edu/polio/
http://www.achievement.org/autodoc/sal0bio-1/
http://www.salk.edu/
http://www.time.com/time/time100/scientist/prfile/salk.html

Patsy Sherman
1930 -
American Chemist and Inventor
Co-Inventor of Scotchgard Fabric Protector

PATSY SHERMAN WAS BORN on September 15, 1930, in Minneapolis, Minnesota. Sherman became her last name when she married. Her name when she was born was Patricia O'Connell.

PATSY SHERMAN GREW UP in Minneapolis. She loved science from a very young age. In fact, she and her dad did experiments in the kitchen. One day, they were heating some chemicals on the stove and caused an explosion.

PATSY SHERMAN WENT TO SCHOOL at the local public schools. She was an excellent student. Even so, she was discouraged from becoming a scientist. There was widespread prejudice against women when Patsy was growing up. Her high school counselor encouraged her to be a housewife instead of scientist. But Patsy didn't listen to her.

Sherman went to Gustavus Adolphus College in St. Peter, Minnesota. She majored in math and chemistry. After graduating from college in 1952, Sherman started working at 3M. She would spend the next 40 years there.

STARTING AT 3M: Sherman started working at 3M in 1952. "3M" stands for the Minnesota Mining and Manufacturing Company. Her first job there was as a research chemist. In that job, Sherman worked on a team to develop rubber to be used in jet fuel hoses. Her special area of research was fluorochemicals.

MEETING SAM SMITH: In her early years at 3M, Sherman began working with Sam Smith. They would be research partners for years. In fact, it was with Smith that Sherman made her first invention—Scotchgard.

INVENTING SCOTCHGARD - BY MISTAKE: One day, Sherman and Smith were working on a new chemical compound. By accident, a lab assistant dropped the beaker with the chemical on the floor. When the beaker broke, the contents spilled onto a technician's new sneakers.

They tried and tried, but they couldn't get the chemical off the shoes. Water, soap, solvents, just ran off the shoe's surface. It was "like water off a duck's back," Sherman recalled.

Sherman and Smith were fascinated by the properties of the compound. They began working on it. They wanted to create a product that could repel water and oil from fabric. The result was Scotchgard.

Sherman and Smith worked on the compound for several years. They wanted to improve its repellency, and lower the cost. By 1956, they were satisfied. That year, Scotchgard Protector became a successful consumer product. And Sherman and Smith received a **patent**.

Soon, fabrics of all kinds, from clothing to carpets to furniture to car interiors, were treated with Scotchgard. And just as it had with the tennis shoes, water, oil, food, and other liquids rolled off fabric treated with Scotchgard.

HOW IT WORKS: Scotchgard is a fluorochemical compound. When it's put on cloth, the chemical surrounds the fibers in the fabric with a fluorochemical shield. The shield keeps liquid—and dirt—from penetrating the fabric.

Scotchgard became a tremendous success for 3M. Sherman and Smith continued to work on new improvements for the product. For example, when permanent press fabrics became popular in the 1970s, they reworked the formula so it made the new fabric stain resistant, too.

Other uses for the protector have come about over the years. For instance, it's used to protect photographic and motion picture

Sherman and Sam Smith working at 3M labs.

film. Scotchgard is still a very important product for 3M. It brings in more than $3 million to the company each year.

LATER CAREER: Sherman had several jobs in her long career at 3M. She became a research specialist, then manager of 3M's Technical development. Sherman is a strong believer in continuing education. So she started a program that updates the education and training of staff.

Sherman continued to work with Smith, too. Together, they hold 13 patents for various fluorochemical polymers. Sherman retired from 3M in 1992, after 40 years with the company.

To acknowledge their contributions, Sherman and Smith were inducted into the Inventors Hall of Fame in 2001.

PATSY SHERMAN'S HOME AND FAMILY: Patsy O'Connell married Hubert Sherman in 1953. They have two daughters. Now in retirement, Patsy Sherman still enjoys meeting students and speaking at schools.

HER INVENTION: Sherman invented one of the most successful consumer products of the modern era. Fabrics treated with Scotchgard are used in many kinds of products all over the world.

Sherman is often asked for advice from students who'd like to be inventors. She tells them: "Keep your eyes and minds open. And don't ignore something that doesn't come out the way you expect it to. Just keep looking at the world with inventor's eyes!"

WORLD WIDE WEB SITES:

http://web.mit.edu/invent/iow/sherman.html
http://www.invent.org/hall_of_fame/160.html
http://www.mmm.com/about3M/pioneers/sherman.html
http://www.si.edu/lemelson/centerpieces/ilives/lecture11.html

Christopher Sholes
1819 - 1890
American Printer, Inventor, and Politician
Inventor of the First Practical Typewriter
and the "QWERTY" Keyboard

CHRISTOPHER SHOLES WAS BORN on February 14, 1819, in Danville, Pennsylvania. Very little is known about his young life.

CHRISTOPHER SHOLES GREW UP in Pennsylvania. He became a printer's apprentice when he was a teenager. He moved to Wisconsin in his late teens.

FIRST JOBS: In Wisconsin, Sholes worked as a printer and also ran a newspaper. He was the editor of the *Wisconsin Enquirer* for several years, then decided to enter politics.

POLITICAL CAREER: Sholes served in the Wisconsin state legislature for a few years. He was active in the Republican Party. That led President Abraham Lincoln, a Republican, to name him to be the head of customs at the port of Milwaukee.

STARTING TO INVENT: While working in Milwaukee, Sholes began to invent. With a friend, Samuel Soule, he created a page numbering machine. Sholes received a **patent** for the device, and kept on inventing.

INVENTING THE TYPEWRITER: Sholes's next project was a letter printing machine—the typewriter. He created a keyboard that was arranged alphabetically. Each key was attached to a metal rod with a letter on the end. The metal rod struck a surface with paper on it, leaving the imprint of the letter.

Sholes received a **patent** for his "type writing machine" in 1868. He knew he had a good idea, and he tried to start a business. But Sholes had too much trouble raising money to develop and market the machine. He wound up selling his patent rights to the Remington Arms Company in 1873.

Remington became the successful manufacturer of Sholes's invention. Sholes continued to contribute important innovations. The most important of these is the "QWERTY" keyboard.

THE QWERTY KEYBOARD: Sholes originally designed his typewriter with the keys arranged alphabetically. But when people used

Early Sholes typewriter, c. 1870.

the typewriter, the keys would jam. That's because an alphabetical arrangement puts the keys used most often too close together.

Sholes studied the problem and came up with a great solution. He changed the arrangement of the keys on the keyboard to place the keys most frequently used far apart. That prevented key jams. The top line of keys contained the letters Q, W, E, R, T, Y in a row. It was a great success. This arrangement became known as the "QWERTY" keyboard.

Sholes made other improvements to the typewriter, too. The first typewriters printed only capital letters. Sholes created two

471

Example of "QWERTY" keyboard.

typewriter keys for each letter, one upper case (all capital letters), and one lower case. Then he created a "shift" key, used to select either upper or lower case.

Sholes's typewriter design was the basis for all typewriters produced for 100 years. In the 1980s, people began to use computers instead of typewriters to create written documents. Typewriting became "word processing." But Sholes's influence continues into the present day. That's because we still use his QWERTY keyboard every day when we use our computers.

HIS INVENTION: Sholes "QWERTY" arrangement is the same one used on every English keyboard sold with every computer. So even though he's unknown in the modern era, computer users around the world use Sholes's invention every day.

WORLD WIDE WEB SITES:

http://www.invent.org/hall_of_fame/168.html
http://www2.milwaukee.k12.wi.us/sholes/CLShores.html

Igor Sikorsky
1889 - 1972
Russian-Born American Engineer and Inventor
Inventor of the Helicopter and the
First Multimotor Airplane

IGOR SIKORSKY WAS BORN on May 25, 1889, in Kiev, Russia. (It is now known as Ukraine.) His parents were Ivan and Zinalda Sikorsky. Ivan was a psychology professor and Zinalda was a doctor. Igor was the youngest of five children.

IGOR SIKORSKY GREW UP fascinated by flight and dreaming about flying. He studied the drawings of **Leonardo Da Vinci**. Leonardo's sketches for a helicopter-like airship sparked his imagination. He knew he wanted to design—and fly—aircraft.

IGOR SIKORSKY WENT TO SCHOOL at the Imperial Naval College in St. Petersburg, Russia. (It was called a "college," but was really a high school.) He graduated in 1906. He went to college at the Polytechnic Institute in Kiev.

Around this time, Sikorsky learned of the great achievements of the **Wright brothers**. He studied everything he could about their designs and technologies. He left Russia in 1909 to study engineering in Paris.

DESIGNING AIRCRAFT: In Paris, Sikorsky sketched an early model for a helicopter. At that point, he couldn't figure out how to power the craft so it could lift its weight to become airborne.

THE FIRST MULTIMOTOR AIRPLANE: Sikorsky decided to focus on regular, winged aircraft. In 1911, a plane he designed, the S-5, reached a record 70 miles per hour. In 1913, he designed and flew the first multimotor airplane. Sikorsky built the plane for the Russian Army, just as the country entered World War I.

World War I took place between 1914 and 1918 in Europe. In the war, Great Britain, France, and Russia went to war against Germany and Austria. (The U.S. entered the war in support of Great Britain, France and Russia in 1917.) Sikorsky's plane proved valuable in Russia's fight against Germany.

Composite illustration showing several
Sikorsky helicopter models.

Sikorsky's first multimotor airplane was called the "Ilya Mourometz." It was one of the largest aircraft of its time. It had four engines and could stay in flight for five hours, at 85 mph. It held a crew of five and even had sleeping berths.

The "Ilya" was the first bomber. It was powerful enough to fight off five German fighter aircraft, and bomb targets. The war ended with Germany and Austria's defeat in 1918.

THE RUSSIAN REVOLUTION: By the time the war was over, Sikorsky had to flee Russia. The Russian Revolution of 1917 brought the Communists to power. Sikorsky had been loyal to the toppled Tzar. He left Russia and emigrated to the U.S.

COMING TO AMERICA: Sikorsky arrived in New York City in March 1919. He'd had to leave almost everything behind when he left Russia. He entered the U.S. a poor man. He wanted to get back into aviation, but couldn't find a job. Instead, he taught math to Russian immigrants to get by.

In 1923, Sikorsky found people willing to lend him money to start his own business. He started his new company, Sikorsky Aero Engineering, on Long Island, New York. That year, he also became a U.S. citizen.

SEAPLANES: Sikorsky developed airplanes for commercial use. In 1928, he produced his most successful plane to date. The S-38 could transport 10 people, and could take off and land in water. It was the first successful commercial seaplane.

Sikorsky sold his seaplanes to Pan American, one of the first passenger airlines in the country. He kept improving the design and power of his seaplanes. In the 1930s, he produced the S-40.

Known as the "Clipper," it became the model for the first flights to cross the Atlantic and Pacific Oceans. For the first time, people began to fly between Europe, Asia, and the U.S. The age of passenger airlines had begun, thanks in part to Sikorsky's innovations.

HELICOPTERS: Sikorsky had never forgotten his dream of building a helicopter. In the 1930s, he began designing the first practical helicopter. His first model was called the VS-300. It made its first flight on September 14, 1939. It had an open cockpit and ran on a 75 horsepower motor.

Sikorsky's helicopters had a single-rotor design. The "rotor" on a helicopter is the propeller on the roof of the aircraft. The rotor was the sole source of controlled power for the craft. Sikorsky was delighted with his new invention. In describing that first flight, he outlined all the features of his new aircraft:

The Sikorsky S-42, one of his "Clipper"
amphibian flyer boats from 1934.

"It is a dream to feel the machine lift you gently up in the air, float smoothly over one spot for indefinite periods, move up or down under good control, as well as move not only forward or backward but in any direction."

The U.S. Military saw how useful the helicopter could be for its purposes. They asked Sikorsky to design another helicopter. In 1942, the aircraft, called the R-4, was in use.

Even in its early days, the helicopter was used to help victims of natural disasters. These peaceful uses for his craft pleased Sikorsky. "It was a source of great satisfaction that the helicopter started its practical career by saving lives and helping man in need rather than by spreading death and destruction," he said.

By the 1950s, Sikorsky helicopters were being used in the military, and also for passenger transportation. In addition to transporting military troops and wounded, helicopters became useful for transporting people short distances. In the 1960s, helicopters were first used for relaying traffic reports. Later, they became an important way to transport people with medical emergencies.

Sikorsky received several **patents** for his helicopters and innovations to aircraft. He became an honored inventor and businessman. He received the National Medal of Science and the Collier Trophy, given to aviation pioneers. He was named to the Inventors Hall of Fame in 1987.

IGOR SIKORSKY'S HOME AND FAMILY: Sikorsky married Elizabeth Semion in 1924. They had five children. Sikorsky continued to work in the aviation business until his death on October 26, 1972, at the age of 83.

HIS INVENTIONS: Sikorsky is one of the most important inventors in aviation. He created the first multimotor airplane and the first practical helicopter. His multimotor aircraft led to trans-Atlantic and trans-Pacific passenger flights. Helicopters are used all over the world, for civilian and military purposes. And his innovative single-rotor design is still used in helicopters today.

WORLD WIDE WEB SITES:

http://www.invent.org/hall_of_fame/135.html
http://www.sikorskyarchives.com/

Percy Spencer
1894 - 1970
American Scientist and Inventor
Inventor of the Microwave Oven

PERCY SPENCER WAS BORN on July 19, 1894, in Howland, Maine. His father died when he was 18 months old. After his father's death, his mother left home. Percy was raised by an aunt and uncle on their farm.

PERCY SPENCER GREW UP an active, curious child. He worked hard around the house, chopping wood and helping in the garden and with the farm animals.

PERCY SPENCER WENT TO SCHOOL only through elementary school. He left school to make money to help out at home.

FIRST JOBS: By the age of 12, Percy was working in a local thread mill. Always curious, when the mill converted to electricity in 1910, he helped with the wiring.

JOINING THE NAVY: After the *Titanic* sank in 1912, Spencer was inspired by the wireless operators and their role in rescuing survivors. He wanted to learn all about radios. He joined the Navy, and while serving, he studied radio transmission.

Spencer was devoted to educating himself. Even though he'd had to leave school at a young age, he continued to learn. "I just got hold of a lot of textbooks," he recalled. "I taught myself while I was standing watch at night." Over the years, he studied, on his own, calculus, chemistry, and physics.

After he left the Navy, Spencer got a job in Boston, at a radio company. The company provided radio and telegraph equipment to the U.S. troops in World War I (1914–1918).

WORKING FOR RAYTHEON: Spencer got a job at Raytheon in the 1920s, where he worked researching radar systems. Specifically, he worked with a type of vacuum tube called a magnetron.

MAGNETRONS: Magnetrons are vacuum tubes that can generate high-power electromagnetic signals at microwave frequencies. They are the power tube used in radar and weapons systems. In the early years of World War II, the German Army began bombing raids on Britain. At Raytheon, Spencer headed a team to create magnetrons needed for radar systems to detect and destroy incoming German fighter planes. How he did it was typical of his skill and ingenuity.

Spencer worked seven days a week, 52 weeks a year during the war years, 1939 - 1945. Raytheon received a model magnetron from the British. At that time, magnetrons were produced at the rate of 17 per day. Spencer figured out a way to increase production by making the magnetron from a combination of copper and silver-solder. Then, he created a conveyor belt assembly process that sped up production to 2,600 magnetrons per day.

It was an incredible feat of engineering. Thousands of magnetrons were used by the U.S. and British in the war, and it was a crucial part of the Allied war effort. For his innovative work, Spencer received one of his more than 150 **patents.**

INVENTING THE MICROWAVE OVEN—A MELTED CHOCOLATE BAR: In 1945, Spencer created the microwave oven—by accident. One day, as he stood in front of a magnetron, he noticed that the chocolate bar in his pocket was starting to melt. The curious Spencer had to know why it happened.

He put popcorn kernals in front of the device. They popped. He put a raw egg, still in its shell, near the magnetron. The egg exploded, as the yolk cooked faster than the outside of the egg.

Spencer saw the possibilities of using microwave radiation—the energy power generated by the magnetron—to prepare food. His team at Raytheon created the first microwave oven in 1947. It was

Spencer's first microwave, five times the size as modern versions.

huge: 5 ½ feet tall and weighing 750 pounds. Those first microwaves were used in restaurants and other places that prepared food commercially. In the 1950s, Raytheon developed a microwave for home use, but at $1,300, it was too expensive for many families.

In 1965, Raytheon acquired the Amana appliance company. Amana was already a well-known name in kitchen appliances, with a

Spencer, center, with the Amana Radarange,
the first popular microwave for home kitchens.

network of distributors. Raytheon developed the first countertop microwave, for use in home kitchens. They sold it as part of the Amana line, at a cost of just $500. Interest in the home microwave exploded, and the product became a great success. By the 1980s, it was as familiar in kitchens as a conventional oven.

LATER YEARS: By the time of his death in September 1970, Percy Spencer was best known to the world as the inventor of the microwave. But he was also an honored scientist. One said of him, "He has the respect of every physicist in the country, not only for his ingenuity but for what he has learned about physics by absorbing it through his skin. He is not merely a good experimenter and a good designer. He has become, in his own right, one of the recognized individuals in a very difficult field."

HIS INVENTIONS: Spencer's discovery of an efficient way to manufacture magnetrons led to important innovations in radar. He is best known today as the inventor of the microwave oven. More than 90 percent of American homes now have microwaves, and their popularity continues to grow worldwide.

WORLD WIDE WEB SITES:

http://web.mit.edu/invent/iow/spencer.html
http://www.invent.org/hall_of_fame.136html
http://www.inventionatplay.org/inventors_spe.html

George Stephenson
1781 - 1848
English Engineer and Inventor
Pioneer of the First Successful
Steam-Powered Locomotive

GEORGE STEPHENSON WAS BORN on June 9, 1781, in Wylam, England, near Newscastle. His father was Robert Stephenson. Robert worked as a steam-engine keeper for the local mine, the Wylam Colliery.

GEORGE STEPHENSON GREW UP fascinated with machines and how they worked. His home was right next to the Wylam Wagonway. "Wagonways" were wooden railways. They were often used to transport coal from mines to distribution areas, or ports. Horses pulled the coal wagons, on the tracks, from the mines to a river or harbor. In Wylam, the wagons took coal from the mine to the Tyne river.

GEORGE STEPHENSON WENT TO SCHOOL at night school, where he studied reading and writing. He started working at a very young age, first herding cows, then in the mines.

GOING TO WORK IN THE MINES: Stephenson began to work in the mines when he was 14. He helped his father with the steam engines. His father was an "engineman." That means he was in charge of tending the mine's steam engines.

STEAM ENGINES: All steam engines work on a basic principle: they convert heat energy into mechanical energy. All steam engines have a boiler. The boilers of Stephenson's time burned coal to boil water. When water is heated in a close space, like a boiler, and converted into steam, the pressure increases. When steam expands, it either takes up many times the space of water or increases the pressure. The force of the steam forces a piston to move in a cylinder.

In 1802, at the age of 21, Stephenson became an "engineman" himself. Still fascinated by all aspects of steam engines, he took them apart completely to understand how they worked. The engines he worked on had been made by **James Watt**.

Stephenson's next job took him to Killingworth Colliery. He became "enginewright" of the mine in 1812. That means he was in charge of actually building the mine's engines.

Stephenson's Locomotion engine, 1825.

BUILDING A LOCOMOTIVE: It is important to note that Stephenson did not invent the steam-powered locomotive. That development is usually credited to Richard Trevithick.

In 1814, Stephenson convinced his boss to let him build a new steam-powered machine. The result was a locomotive that could pull 30 tons of coal up a hill at 4 miles per hour. He called it "The Blutcher." Its engine had two vertical cylinders. The pistons inside the cylinders were connected to rods that drove the gears that turned the wheels. The Blutcher had "flanged" wheels. Those are the kinds of wheels with a rim that can fit on railroad tracks.

Stephenson continued to develop new engines, 16 in all, over the next several years. The owners of the Killingworth mines next

RICHARD TREVITHICK

Richard Trevithick (1771 - 1833) was an English engineer. When **James Watt's** patents expired in 1800, Trevithick built one of the first high-pressure steam engines. Trevithick used this technology to build one of the first locomotives. On Christmas Eve in 1801, Trevithick's steam locomotive became the first steam-powered carriage to transport passengers. In 1804, another Trevithick engine became the first steam locomotive used on a railway. His inventions greatly influenced Stephenson.

asked Stephenson to build a railway between Hetton and Sunderland. He built eight miles of track linking the two cities.

Stephenson was next hired by the railway company Stockton and Darlington. They wanted him to build a line linking the mines at West Durham and Darlington to the Tees River.

Stephenson made an important discovery while building the railway. He learned that a smooth, level track could move more weight, more efficiently than one that had to go over uneven ground. So Stephenson designed tunnels and flattened the land for rail beds to make the railroad routes as level as possible.

ROBERT STEPHENSON AND COMPANY: In 1825, Stephenson formed a company with his son, Robert, to produce steam-powered locomotives. It was called Robert Stephenson and Company, and it was the world's first locomotive factory. Their first product was an engine they called "Locomotion."

LOCOMOTION: The Locomotion ran on the new Stockton and Darlington line on September 27, 1825. It pulled 36 wagons filled with coal and flour. And it was a sensation. Crowds lined the track as the locomotive moved along the nine-mile stretch of track at a speed of 4 ½ miles per hour. The first voyage of the Locomotion proved that locomotives could be used to efficiently transport coal and other goods.

The success of his locomotives and rail lines made Stephenson and his son in demand. They continued to develop and refine their steam-powered locomotives.

THE ROCKET: The Stephensons had another triumph with their "Rocket" locomotive. They entered the engine in a contest held by the owners of the Liverpool and Manchester railway. The winner would create the engine used on the route between the two cities. It was an especially important route, because it would link a major industrial region with a major seaport.

The contest was held in October 1829. The Rocket won, hauling three times its weight, and reaching a speed of 36 miles per hour. It became the model used by the Liverpool and Manchester railway. And that railway became the first passenger railroad.

CHIEF ENGINEER: The success of the Rocket led to further success for Stephenson. He was named chief engineer of four major railways. He became a very wealthy man. He continued to create innovations to his engines and railways, then retired in 1840.

GEORGE STEPHENSON'S HOME AND FAMILY: Stephenson married Frances Henderson in 1802. They had one son, Robert, who later went into business with his father. Frances died in 1806. Stephenson later married Elizabeth Hindley; she died in 1845.

After his success in the railroad business, Stephenson bought a home, Tapton House, in Chesterfield, England. He invested in mines and also experimented with breeding farm animals. He died at his home on August 12, 1848. He was 67 years old.

HIS INVENTION: Stephenson contributed innovations that made the steam locomotive a useful, practical mode of transportation. He also used his knowledge to design railway lines. This led to the development of railroads first in England, then throughout the world. Soon, railroads brought people and products to the far reaches of the world. It brought about trade and transportation that had been unimaginable before. For his achievements, Stephenson is known as "The Father of the Railways."

WORLD WIDE WEB SITES:

http://www.britianexpress.com/History/bio/stephenson.htm
http://www.cottontimes.co.uk/stephenson.htm
http://www.spartacus.schoolnet.co.uk/RAstephensonG.htm

Levi Strauss
1829 - 1902
German-Born American Inventor of Blue Jeans

LEVI STRAUSS WAS BORN on February 26, 1829, in Buttenheim, Germany. His parents were Hirsch and Rebecca Strauss. Hirsch sold cloth and other goods to make clothing. (The products were known as "dry goods.") Levi's original name was Loeb. He was the youngest in a large family that included brothers Jacob, Jonas, and Louis, and sisters Rosla, Mathilde, and Fanny.

LEVI STRAUSS GREW UP in Buttenheim, in the part of Germany called Bavaria. Hirsch Strauss died in 1845. Around that time, Jonas and Louis went to America. They settled in New York City. Like their father, the boys set up a business selling dry goods.

COMING TO AMERICA: In 1847, Levi came to the U.S. with his mother and sisters. They reunited with his brothers in New York. Soon, Levi joined the family dry good business.

In 1848, gold was discovered at Sutter's Mill in Coloma, California. Soon, the area was swamped with prospectors who'd come to find their fortune in the Gold Rush. Many businesses sprung up to meet the needs of the miners. One of these was a dry goods firm called "Levi Strauss."

Strauss moved to San Francisco, California, in 1853. That same year, he became a U.S. citizen and opened his business at 90 Sacramento Street. There, he sold goods for his own company, and for his brothers' firm in New York.

Levi was a "wholesale" merchant. That means that he didn't have a traditional store where he sold cloth to individual customers. Instead, his company sold dry goods through salesmen who supplied stores in the Gold Rush country, and all over the West.

Soon, his sister Fanny and her husband, David Stern, moved to California and joined the company. Over the years, Strauss became a successful businessman, and "Levi Strauss & Co." was a prosperous firm. Yet despite his accomplishments, Strauss always remained a humble man. He insisted his workers call him by his first name, "Levi."

INVENTING BLUE JEANS:
There are many legends and myths surrounding the invention of blue jeans. But the real story is as fascinating as any myth.

The first pants similar to what we know as jeans came about in the 1870s. Jacob Davis was a tailor in Nevada. He'd bought cloth from Strauss for years. Davis had a customer who kept ripping his work pants. The tailor set to work to find a way to strengthen the trousers he made. Finally, he came up with a way to do just that. He developed a process using metal rivets to strengthen the pockets of work pants.

Strauss as a young man.

In 1872, Davis wrote Strauss a letter. He didn't want anyone to steal his idea, so he wanted to **patent** his riveted pants. But he couldn't afford the price of the patent. So he asked Strauss to be his partner, and to pay for the patent. Strauss agreed. He applied for the patent, in both their names, in 1872.

On May 20, 1873, Levi Strauss and Jacob Davis received a U.S. patent for the process of making work pants with metal rivets. Davis moved to California to work for Strauss.

The riveted pants—they were called "overalls"— soon became a popular item. And over the years they evolved into what we know as Levi's blue jeans.

A pair of Levi's waist overalls, 1890.

The pants weren't called "jeans" until the mid-20th century. No one is sure where the name came from. Another legend suggests that "jeans" got their name from the Italian town of Genoa. Sailors there supposedly wore pants called "Genes."

The early jeans were made of blue denim and brown cotton duck cloth. Gradually, indigo-dyed denim became the most popular fabric used. The famous red Tab on the back pocket was added in 1936. The rivets were covered in 1937, because they scratched furniture and saddles. In 1966, they were replaced with stitching.

LEVI'S TODAY: Today, Levi Strauss & Co. is a billion-dollar industry. Levi's jeans are sold all over the world. The headquarters for the company is still in San Francisco. They also have offices all over the globe. When Strauss died in 1902, his nephews took over the company. Today, after 150 years, family members remain in charge of the business.

LEVI STRAUSS'S HOME AND FAMILY: Strauss never married or had children. But he was very close to his family. Levi Strauss was also an active member of the San Francisco community. He was involved in building the first Jewish synagogue. Over the years, he gave generously to charity. He also funded scholarships for needy students.

Levi Strauss died on September 26, 1902. He was 73 years old. Celebrated as an important businessman, he was also remembered for his charity. Strauss said this about life, work, and money: "I do not think large fortunes cause happiness to their owners. Those who possess them become slaves to their wealth." Instead, he thought it was important to give back to the community. The company continues his charitable work through The Levi Strauss Foundation.

HIS INVENTION: Levi Strauss's first name appears on millions of pairs blue jeans sold around the world. He never lived to see how his (and Davis's) invention would become such a popular clothing item. Many other manufacturers make jeans, but Levi's are acknowledged as the first. In 1964, the Smithsonian Institution marked his achievement by putting several pairs in the permanent collection.

WORLD WIDE WEB SITES:

http://www.levistrauss.com
http://www.pbs.org/weta/thewest/people/

Nikola Tesla
1856 - 1943
Croatian-Born American Inventor, Engineer, and Physicist
Inventor of the AC Electric Motor and the Tesla Coil

NIKOLA TESLA WAS BORN on either July 9 or 10, 1856, in Smiljan, Croatia. Croatia was then part of Austria-Hungary. It later became part of Yugoslavia, and is now Croatia. His parents were Milutin and Djuka Tesla. His father was a Serbian Orthodox minister. His mother was a homemaker. Nikola was one of five children.

SCHOOLING: Nikola moved with his family from Smiljan to Gospic, Croatia when he was seven. He attended the local schools. His family thought he would become a clergyman, like his father. But he did so well in math and science that it became clear he wanted a career in science. By the time Nikola was in his early teens, he spoke four languages fluently.

When Nikola was fifteen, he went to high school in Karlovac, Croatia. After four years there, he moved onto the Polytechnic Institute in Graz, Austria. While in Graz, he first came into contact with an electric motor. It was called a Gramme Dynamo. These were Direct Current (DC) motors and generators that sparked, popped, and arced a great deal. Tesla thought there had to be a better way.

After studying in Graz, Tesla attended the University of Prague in Czechoslovakia for two years. There, he studied engineering.

DISCOVERY AND JOBS: In January 1881, Tesla moved to Budapest, Hungary, where he worked in the government telegraph office. That spring, while walking in a park, the idea for the Rotating Magnetic Field came to him. This was "the better way" he had been seeking.

Tesla moved to Paris in 1882 and started working for the Continental Edison Company. His job was to repair Edison generating stations in Germany and France. Around this time, Tesla built his first crude AC (Alternating Current) motor.

Tesla decided to move to the United States in 1884. He arrived with four cents in his pocket. He found work right away at the Edison Research Laboratory in New York City. Tesla worked directly with **Thomas Edison**. He and Edison argued constantly about the relative values of AC versus DC. After a year, Tesla left to form his

Westinghouse AC dynamo, built by Tesla, 1893.

own company. A feud began between the two inventors that lasted years and left both men embittered.

The Tesla Electric Light Company was based in New Jersey. Tesla made arc lights for streets and factories. In arc lights, electricity jumps from one wire or electrode to another, like lightning arcing to earth, to make a very bright light. It was brighter than the Edison light that uses a hot wire to convert electricity into light.

In 1886, Tesla's company went out of business. He was broke, so for part of that year he worked as a ditch digger and street sweeper. By 1887 he'd found financial backing and opened the Tesla Electric Company. Here Tesla could put more time and effort into research, and by the end of the year he had invented the first efficient polyphase (AC) motor.

The benefit of Alternating Current motors and generators is their ability to send power over much greater distances than Direct Current. High Voltage Alternating Current can be sent hundreds of miles with only minimal loss, while Direct Current can only be sent about two miles.

In the late 1880s, Tesla met **George Westinghouse**, a wealthy manufacturer and inventor. Westinghouse purchased Tesla's patent rights to the AC motor, generator, and transformer. Tesla went to work for Westinghouse in an independent laboratory. Now the battle was on to determine whether Tesla's Alternating Current or Edison's Direct Current would electrify the world. Around 1890, Tesla became a United States citizen.

Tesla experimenting with electricity and photography.

In 1893, Westinghouse outbid Edison to provide electricity and lighting for the 1893 Columbian Exposition in Chicago. The exposition, or World's Fair, celebrated the 400th anniversary of Columbus's landing in the New World. It was also the first time electricity and electric light would be used at a World's Fair. And that electricity was Alternating Current.

The exhibit helped prove the benefits of Alternating Current. It also led to a contract for Westinghouse to build the world's first hydroelectric generating plant. In 1895, using the power of the Niagara River, the plant began providing Alternating Current electricity to cities as far as 25 miles away. This forced Thomas Edison to begin installing AC generators in all of his power stations.

From 1885 to 1898, Tesla was at his most inventive. He developed a working radio, high frequency generators, a remote control, and the Tesla Coil. The Tesla Coil could produce current of nearly any frequency or voltage. Whenever a car is turned on, a type of Tesla Coil provides the high voltage to the spark plug to get the engine started. During this same period Tesla experimented with particle beam technology, television, radar, and transmitting electricity without wires.

In the late 1890's, Tesla experimented on a larger scale. In Colorado Springs, Colorado, he discovered "terrestrial stationary waves." His experiments proved that the earth could be used as a conductor to send electricity anywhere in the world without wires. Using this theory, he lighted 200 lamps from a distance of 25 miles. He also created man-made lightning. Once, he was able to make a bolt of lightning over 130 feet long—a record that still stands today.

In 1900, Tesla, with backing from the wealthy financier J. P. Morgan, began building a wireless world broadcasting tower on Long Island. But Morgan withdrew his support, and the project ended. Tesla considered this his greatest defeat. After this, he began testing theories on rotorless turbines and other projects, but with little money, these ideas stayed in his notebooks. These valuable notebooks are still read by engineers today.

LATER YEARS: In 1915, it was rumored that Tesla was to share a Nobel Prize in physics with Thomas Edison. But it proved false. In 1917, Tesla grudgingly accepted the Edison Medal, the highest honor bestowed by the American Institute of Electrical Engineers.

The last 30 or so years of Tesla's life were spent alone, living in hotels. He never married or had children. On January 8, 1943, Tesla's body was found by a maid in his New York City hotel room. He was 86 years old. Hundreds of people attended his funeral. Dignitaries from around the world sent messages noting the loss of a great genius.

HIS LEGACY: Over the span of his life, Tesla received over 100 patents, for more than 700 inventions. He worked with Thomas Edison, who went on to fame as one of the greatest inventors and most celebrated Americans of the era. Tesla even bested Edison, in proving the superiority of the Alternating Current system for electricity generation and delivery. Yet this man, considered a great creative genius, died in obscurity.

HIS INVENTIONS: Tesla invented the induction motor, with rotating magnetic field. He also established AC power transmission as the superior method of electrical generation. While he is not remembered for his many inventions, they affect each of us, everyday through the "tesla," a unit of measure for the intensity of a magnetic field.

WORLD WIDE WEB SITES:

http://www.invent.org/hall_of_fame/143.html
http://www.tfcbooks.com/teslafaq/subjects.htm

Alessandro Volta
1745 - 1827
Italian Physicist
Inventor of the First Battery

ALESSANDRO VOLTA WAS BORN on February 18, 1745, in Como, Italy. His parents were from the Italian nobility. However, when Alessandro was born, they were quite poor. He had seven brothers and sisters.

ALESSANDRO VOLTA GREW UP with a keen interest in science, especially in the new area of electricity. His parents wanted him to be a priest, but he wanted to study science.

ALESSANDRO VOLTA WENT TO SCHOOL at the local Catholic schools. He was an excellent student. He studied the works of scientists of the day. When he was 14, he declared he wanted to be a physicist.

STUDYING AND TEACHING PHYSICS: In 1769, Volta published an important paper on electricity. He outlined how an electric charge is created, and transferred.

In 1774, Volta began to teach physics at a high school in Como. That same year, he created his first invention. He called it an "electrophorus." It was a device that provided a sustained source of static electricity. In 1777, Volta experimented with using the charge it produced to send a telegraphic signal. This was an early telegraph, developed in the 1830s by **Samuel Morse.**

INVENTING THE "VOLTAIC PILE"—THE FIRST BATTERY: Volta's most important invention was the "Voltaic Pile." It was the first battery. It is based on the idea that electric current can be created, and controlled, for use.

At that time, a scientist named Luigi Galvani was also doing experiments in electricity. While Galvani was dissecting a frog, the frog's leg twitched. What was the source of that motion? Galvani thought it came from the frog. He called it "animal electricity."

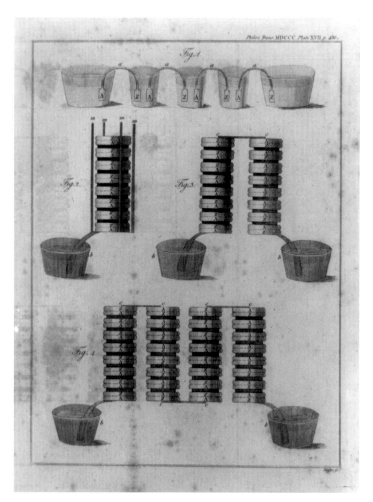

Diagram of Volta's battery, c. 1800.

Volta disagreed. He determined that it had nothing to do with the frog. Instead, it had to do with the nature of electricity. Specifically, it had to do with how materials conduct electricity.

Volta figured out that it was the *metal* that held the frog's legs, not the frog, that conducted the electrical impulse. Through this discovery, he developed his Voltaic Pile, in 1800.

Volta's Pile was made of discs of copper and zinc, stacked in a column. These discs were separated by discs of paper or cardboard soaked in salt water. At the top and bottom of the "pile" Volta ran copper wiring. Volta had done experiments to determine that metals, like copper and zinc, would create electric current when placed next to each other. The current was even stronger when the metals were in contact with salt water.

Volta's battery was the first device to produce a continuous flow of electric current. It was a major step forward in the history of electricity.

LATER LIFE: Volta became a very famous man. He was a member of several European scientific societies, and was honored by the heads of European nations. He spent his last years as a professor at the University of Padua in Italy. He retired to Como in 1819. Volta died in Como on March 5, 1827. He was 82 years old.

HIS INVENTION: By inventing the first battery, Volta created a device that, for the first time, allowed for the controlled use of electricity. For his great contribution, his name, "Volt," became the name for a unit of electricity.

WORLD WIDE WEB SITE:

http://www.energyquest.ca/gov/scientists/volta.html

James Watt
1736 - 1819
Scottish Inventor and Engineer
Inventor of an Improved Steam Engine

JAMES WATT WAS BORN on January 19, 1736, in Greenock, Scotland. His parents were James and Agnes Watt. James was a merchant and maker of instruments for ships. Agnes was a homemaker. James was one of five children. Three of the Watt children died in infancy. James's brother, John, died at sea as a young man.

JAMES WATT GREW UP a sickly child. His mother decided to teach him at home, rather than send him to school. Early on, he showed a great interest in math and science. He also liked to spend time in his father's workshop. His father had a business selling nautical supplies to the shipping industry. Watt learned how to make and repair instruments used on ships. He also liked to borrow his father's telescope and look at the stars.

JAMES WATT WENT TO SCHOOL at home during his early years. When he was a teenager, he went to a local commercial school. Watt lived at home until he was 18. In 1755, he went to London to learn to be an instrument maker.

INSTRUMENT MAKER: Watt studied instrument making in London with John Morgan. He returned to Scotland and began to work at the University of Glasgow. There, he used his skills to repair scientific instruments.

FASCINATED BY STEAM POWER: Around this time, Watt became fascinated by steam engines. It is important to note that Watt did not invent the steam engine. In fact, a steam engine had been **patented** in 1698.

STEAM ENGINES: All steam engines work on a basic principle: they convert heat energy into mechanical energy. All steam engines have a boiler. The boilers of Watt's time burned coal to boil water. When water is heated in a closed space and converted into steam, the pressure increases. When steam expands, it takes up many times the space of water. The force of the pressure of the steam forces a piston to move in a cylinder.

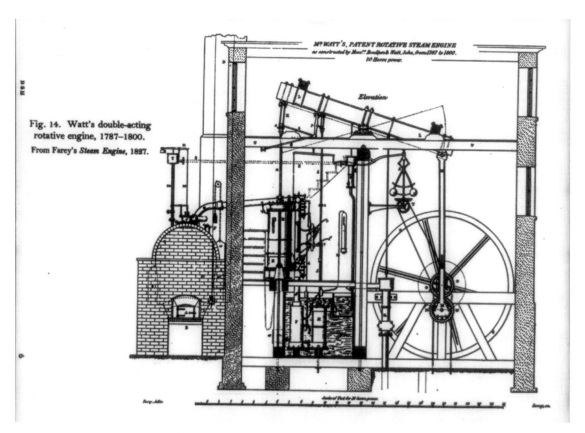

Fig. 14. Watt's double-acting rotative engine, 1787–1800. From Farey's *Steam Engine*, 1827.

Watt's steam engine, c. 1787 - 1800.

Throughout England, steam engines were used in mining. One of their main uses was to pump water out of coal mines. But there were flaws in these early devices. That's how Watt's name became linked to the steam engine.

INVENTING THE FIRST PRACTICAL STEAM ENGINE: When Watt became interested in steam engines, the most successful model was the Newcomen engine. It had been invented by Thomas Newcomen (1663 - 1729). Watt brought many innovations to this basic design.

While repairing a Newcomen engine in 1764, Watt saw the problem. Newcomen's engine used steam to create a vacuum beneath the piston in the cylinder. His engine used a water spray to cool the cylinder on every stroke of the piston. Then, it had to be heated again, using more steam. In that method, the Newcomen engine lost three-quarters of its steam—and power—as it heated the piston and cylinder.

Newcomen's engine used atmospheric pressure to drive the piston. His cylinder was open at the top. Watt began work on a new engine design that harnessed the power of the steam. His design included a sealed cylinder. This trapped the steam, and using the steam power, the pistons were pushed both back and forth in the cylinder. He diverted the steam out of the cylinder, into a separate compartment. He called the compartment a "condenser." The steam in the condenser cooled, while the piston remained hot. The increased pressure of the steam, and the use of the condenser, made for a more powerful, efficient engine. Watt **patented** his engine in 1769.

Now Watt needed money to build his engine. He went into business with a mine owner named John Roebuck. Roebuck wanted Watt's new engine to pump water out of his mines. Watt built his first engine at Roebuck's home. But their business failed. Out of money, Watt had to find work surveying. But he kept trying to find financing for his engine.

GOING INTO BUSINESS WITH BOULTON: In 1774, Watt went into business with a wealthy businessman named Matthew Boulton. Boulton had the money necessary to develop Watt's invention. Soon, their company, Boulton and Watt, became the most successful engineering firm in the country.

Orders for Watt's engine poured in from all over the country. Steam engines were once considered important only to mining.

Now other industries discovered that their machines, too, could benefit from Watt's efficient steam engine. Watt engines were used to power flour, paper, iron, and cotton mills.

Watt became a very wealthy man. He also continued to invent, and to make innovations for his engine. One of his greatest innovations was rotary motion. It converted the back-and-forth piston motion to a rotating motion. He incorporated a flywheel, an engine part that resists changes in speed by storing kinetic energy. He also used governors to control the speed. The result was a more constant, sustained power. His other innovations included the pressure gauge, which he invented in 1790.

THE INDUSTRIAL REVOLUTION: Watt's engines help to fuel the "Industrial Revolution." That's a term used for an era in the 1800s when factory production exploded throughout England, Europe, and the U.S. It was a time of great economic and social change. People moved from farms to urban centers, where they found work in factories. These factories mass-produced machinery used to build houses, factories, and more machines. The Industrial Revolution also brought about great changes in transportation.

Like **Henry Bessemer's** process of producing steel cheaply and efficiently, Watt's steam engine helped drive the Industrial Revolution. By 1800, 500 Watt engines were in use in the factories of England.

But Watt could be a stubborn man. He was very resistant to new ideas in engines. Because of his patents, he had the power to delay needed technological advances in steam engineering. Only after his patents expired in the early 1800s were high-pressure steam engines developed, by engineers like Richard Trevithick

(1771 - 1833). These led to such important inventions as the steam locomotive (see **George Stephenson**) and the steam boat (see **Robert Fulton)**.

LATER YEARS: Watt retired to his estate in Birmingham, England in 1800. He continued to be fascinated by new developments in engineering and science. He also belonged to several scientific societies.

JAMES WATT'S HOME AND FAMILY: Watt was married twice. He and his first wife, Margaret Miller, married in 1764. They had six children. Margaret died in 1773. In 1776, Watt married Ann MacGregor. They had two children. Watt died at his home in Birmingham on August 19, 1819.

HIS INVENTION: Watt's invention of an improved steam engine helped drive the Industrial Revolution. He harnessed steam in a cheap and efficient way that was used to power machinery that helped build the mining, clothing, food, and iron industries. As a measure of his importance, a unit of electricity, the "watt," is named after him. Watt also coined the term "horsepower," now used to describe the power of automobile engines.

WORLD WIDE WEB SITES:

http://www.bbc.co.uk/history/historic_figures/watt_james.shtml
http://www.cottontimes.co.uk/watto.htm
http://www.history.rochester.edu/steam/

George Westinghouse
1846 - 1914
American Industrialist and Inventor
Inventor of the Railroad Air Brake and Developer of an
Alternating Current System for Electrical Transmission

GEORGE WESTINGHOUSE WAS BORN on October 6, 1846, in Central Bridge, New York, near Schenectady. His parents were George and Emeline Westinghouse.

George's father ran a machine shop that manufactured farm equipment. He also had patented several inventions. When George was 10, the family moved to Schenectady, and his father established a new shop there.

GEORGE WESTINGHOUSE WENT TO SCHOOL at the local public schools. He also helped out at his father's shop, showing talent for working with machinery. Once George was asked to cut a pile of metal pipes into pieces of equal length. He devised a cutting tool to do the job in a few hours, when it was expected to take him days. At age 15 George invented a rotary steam engine—his first invention. He would **patent** 361 inventions in his lifetime.

THE CIVIL WAR: When the Civil War began in 1861, George, only 15, ran away from home to join the Union army. His parents forced him to return home, but in 1863 he enlisted and served in the New York cavalry. In 1864 he transferred to the Union navy, serving as an engineer aboard the steamer USS Muscoota.

FIRST PATENTS: After the war Westinghouse enrolled in Union College, but dropped out after a few months. He was more interested in practical matters, and went back to work for his father. In 1865 he patented his rotary steam engine.

Westinghouse was fascinated by the expanding railroad industry. He invented a device called a "car replacer." It could be carried on railroad cars and helped them slide back on track if they derailed. He also invented the "railroad frog." It was a piece of track that allowed cars changing tracks to "leap" from one track to another.

In the 1860s, western Pennsylvania was home to several budding American industries. Pittsburgh was at the center of it all. Coal, oil, steel, glass manufacture, food processing, and other industries were based there. Westinghouse's interest in railroads, which depended so much on steel and coal, led him to move to Pittsburgh in 1868.

REVOLUTIONIZING RAILROADS: Railroads were linking the country in the 1860s, but had major safety problems. Cars could only be stopped by hand-turned mechanical brakes on each car. Westinghouse developed and patented the first railroad air-braking system. This allowed a single engineer or brakeman to slow and stop a train.

Compressed air in a system of pipes and hoses applied the brakes to all cars on a train at once. He patented this system in July 1869, and formed the Westinghouse Air Brake Company. He went on to refine and perfect the railroad air brake. His system is employed worldwide to this day.

As railroad traffic increased, so did stoppages and accidents. Westinghouse realized the rail system needed better track switches, and signals to control them. With profits from his air-brake company, he purchased patents, improved them with his own designs, and developed an interlocking railroad switching system. In 1882 he established the Union Switch & Signal Company, based in Pittsburgh. Westinghouse's inventions would make rail travel faster and much safer.

NEW DIRECTIONS: Westinghouse took out more than 125 patents in the 1880s, many in new fields of interest. He applied principles he had learned from compressed air—the basis of the air brake—to improve the safety of natural gas pipelines.

Before electric lighting, natural gas was used widely for street lights. But controlling gas pressure in underground pipes was a problem. Fires from flare-ups and explosions were frequent. Westinghouse patented improvements for natural gas transmission and started a company to market his system.

WESTINGHOUSE ELECTRIC COMPANY: Westinghouse studied the work of electrical inventors in Europe. In 1885 he purchased the rights for an American system to supply electricity. Using a design by the French engineer Lucien Gaulard and his British colleague John Gibbs, Westinghouse hired engineers to develop his own electrical transformer.

A transformer takes electrical current and "steps up" or "steps down" the voltage in a circuit. Here, Westinghouse was applying ideas from his earlier work with natural gas transmission. He wanted an electrical delivery system that could control the intensity of voltage, just as his natural gas systems controlled pressure. He had a design ready for manufacture in December 1885. In January 1886, he formed the Westinghouse Electric Company.

"WAR OF THE CURRENTS": As Westinghouse entered the market, he had an imposing rival: **Thomas Edison**. Already world-famous for his invention of the phonograph and the light bulb, Edison had set up an electric power station in 1882 in New York City that illuminated 25 buildings.

Edison's system used Direct Current (DC). Westinghouse's system used Alternating Current (AC). Westinghouse had his first

Westinghouse AC dynamo, 1893.

major success with AC power with the lighting of the town of Great Barrington, Massachusetts, in 1886.

The two rivals competed openly in the marketplace and in print over which was the better way. At low voltages, Direct Current is safe and reliable, but cannot be cheaply transmitted over long distances. Edison's DC system required multiple "boosters" every few miles, and thick cables. Alternating Current, using transformers along the transmission lines, could travel many miles at high voltage, then be stepped down to lower voltage for home or industrial use.

TESLA ENTERS THE SCENE: In 1884 **Nikola Tesla** moved to the United States. He first worked for Edison, but the two disagreed about AC and DC power. Tesla left Edison's company. Tesla struggled in poverty, but worked to develop and patent the first electric motor that used AC power. His ideas came to Westinghouse's attention in 1888, and Westinghouse bought the rights to Tesla's AC motor, generator, and transformer. Tesla went to work for Westinghouse as a research scientist.

1893 COLUMBIAN EXPOSITION: With the "War of the Currents" still undecided, both Edison and Westinghouse entered bids to provide lighting for the World's Fair in Chicago. This was also known as the Columbian Exposition, in recognition of the 400th anniversary of Columbus's landing in the New World.

Westinghouse submitted the winning bid, since his AC system was able to use much thinner (and cheaper) copper cables than Edison's DC system required. With a dazzling 250,000 electric lights, the fair was a huge success. AC won the "war," proven both cheaper and safe.

FURTHER SUCCESSES: Westinghouse generators supplied hydro-electric power from the Niagara River to Buffalo, 22 miles away, in 1895. Electricity as a utility was on its way. In the next decade Westinghouse established companies in Canada, England, France, Germany, and Russia.

In 1905 his company introduced the steam turbine to America, and introduced the first AC locomotive the same year. Westinghouse systems were chosen for the new Manhattan and Chicago elevated railways, and for the New York City subway.

Westinghouse's companies employed 50,000 workers at the turn of the century, and were hugely successful. In addition, Westinghouse pioneered important advances for workers, including the Saturday half-holiday (1871), the first major step towards the five-day work week. He also instituted a pension fund for his workers (1908), and paid vacations (1913).

ECONOMIC COLLAPSE: In 1907 a financial crisis weakened the U.S. economy. This was before the establishment of the Federal Reserve Bank in 1913, and of federally insured bank deposits. The stock of a company called United Copper suddenly plummeted in value, affecting the entire stock market. Investors rushed to withdraw cash from banks. Short of cash, banks shut their doors, and credit rates soared. Many investors and bank depositors were ruined financially. Westinghouse found himself without sufficient cash or available credit to do business, and lost ownership after his company declared bankruptcy. He retired in 1910. He spent much of his retirement at his estate in Lenox, Massachusetts.

LATER YEARS: Westinghouse lost much of his wealth after the Panic of 1907. Despite having founded 60 companies during his life, he was out of business. By 1913 he showed signs of a heart condition, and his doctors advised him to rest. Finally, confined to a wheelchair, he died on March 12, 1914, at age 67.

GEORGE WESTINGHOUSE'S HOME AND FAMILY: Westinghouse married Marguerite Erskine Walker in August 1868. They were a devoted and happy couple, and were married for 46 years. Marguerite was an artist, and sculpted a bust of George for their home in Pittsburgh. They had one son, named George, who was born in 1883.

HIS INVENTIONS AND LEGACY: Few men in history can claim such wide-ranging achievements and influence as George Westinghouse, perhaps only his sometime rival Thomas Edison. Like Edison, Westinghouse applied imagination to practical problems, and found useful and profitable solutions. Westinghouse's air brake and signaling systems allowed rail travel to become much safer. Air brakes are also used today on most trucks and buses.

Westinghouse proved the advantages of AC power over DC, winning out over Edison's opposition. AC electricity today is the standard for utilities in America and the world. Other Westinghouse patents helped make natural gas safer to use and made subways and high-speed electric trains possible. Though his business career ended badly, his life's work is remarkable for creativity and success, both as an inventor and an employer. He was inducted into the Hall of Fame for Great Americans and the National Inventors Hall of Fame.

Emerging from bankruptcy, Westinghouse Electric Company survived its founder, and in decades to follow pioneered the tungsten-filament electric light, the electric range and iron, the first commercial radio broadcast, and the first factory-built radio receivers.

WORLD WIDE WEB SITES:

http://www.georgewestinghouse.com/
http://memory.loc.gov/ammem/papr/west/westhome.html
http://inventors.about.com/library/inventors/blwestinghouse.htm
http://www.invent.org/hall_of_fame/151.html
http://web.mit.edu/Invent/iow/westinghouse.html

Eli Whitney
1765 - 1825
American Inventor of the First Practical Cotton Gin

ELI WHITNEY WAS BORN on December 8, 1765, in Westboro, Mass-achusetts. His parents were Eli and Elizabeth Whitney. His father was a farmer, who also served as justice of the peace in Westboro. His mother was a homemaker.

ELI WHITNEY GREW UP in Westboro. At an early age, he showed mechanical ability. By the age of 15, Whitney was making nails to finance his college education. He also tutored children to make money.

ELI WHITNEY WENT TO SCHOOL in Westboro. He worked from the time he was in his teens until he was 23 to afford college. Finally, in 1788, he started at Yale University in New Haven, Connecticut.

Whitney graduated from Yale in 1792. Next, he decided to study law. To pay for his studies, Whitney moved South to take a job tutoring children.

STARTING OUT IN THE COTTON BUSINESS: Whitney traveled to Savannah, Georgia. He planned to teach while he studied law. In Savannah, Whitney met Phineas Miller. Miller managed a plantation owned by Catherine Littlefield Greene. She was the widow of American Revolutionary War General Nathaneal Greene.

Whitney was hired to work on the Greene plantation. His main job was to solve mechanical problems. The biggest problem by far was the slow and hard work of removing the seeds from cotton.

At that time, there were machines, called cotton gins, that had been in use for years. But they didn't really improve the major problem with processing cotton. Whitney defined the problem and came up with a solution. He created a gin that was faster, more efficient, and cheaper to build.

THE COTTON GIN: Whitney studied cotton processing on the plantation. The slaves who picked and cleaned the cotton used a comb-like device. He used that as the basis for a new cotton gin. By April 1793, he had a working model.

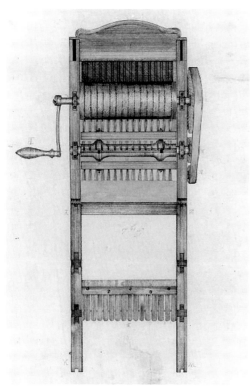

Whitney's cotton gin, c. 1793.

Whitney's cotton gin had four parts:

(1) A hopper that fed the cotton into the gin

(2) A revolving cylinder studded with hundreds of short wire hooks

(3) A strainer that took out the cotton seeds while allowing the cotton fiber to flow through

(4) Brushes that took the cotton off the hooks.

The gin required two workers. One turned the crank of the gin, while another fed cotton through the machine.

Whitney's cotton gin was an instant success. It changed the cotton industry. Whitney's gin could clean 50 pounds of cotton a day. Before that, it took one worker ten hours to clean just three pounds of cotton by hand. With Whitney's gin, a full day's work of many workers could be finished in one hour.

GOING INTO BUSINESS FOR HIMSELF: In 1793 Whitney returned to New England and went into business producing cotton gins with Phineas Miller. The two had ambitious plans. They wanted to control the complete process of cotton production. They planned to grow the cotton, process it using Whitney's cotton gin, and sell it on their own. By doing this, they hoped to monopolize the cotton market. But because of a wave of imitations, it was not to be.

PATENTS AND COURT BATTLES: Whitney got a **patent** for his invention in 1794. But word of his design had already spread across the country. What made Whitney's cotton gin so distinctive was its simple design and its ability to be made cheaply. It was a machine that could be copied easily. Imitations flooded the market.

Whitney took his imitators to court beginning in 1797. For 10 years, he fought against those who'd stolen his design. He lost most of the patent battles. It took him until 1807 to finally be recognized as the cotton gin's inventor. By then, the market was full of competitors. Because of his struggles, he once said that "an invention can be so valuable as to be worthless to the inventor."

IMPACT OF THE COTTON GIN: Despite Whitney's problems, the impact of the cotton gin was enormous. In 1790, the United States produced 4,000 bales of cotton per year. Just 30 years later, in 1820, production had risen to 73,000 bales per year. And by 1840 U.S. production was at 1,347,000 bales per year. By then, America was producing three-quarters of the world's supply of cotton. That fueled tremendous growth in the cloth industry. In New England especially, cloth and clothing factories sprung up to meet demand.

THE COTTON GIN AND SLAVERY: But the cotton gin turned out to have a negative effect as well. Whitney had hoped that with the invention of the gin, the manufacturing of cotton would become so inexpensive that slavery would disappear from the South.

It had the opposite effect. The gin made cotton production the largest industry in the American South. The rising production of cotton resulted in the growth and dependency of slavery across the South.

The expansion of slavery created the atmosphere that led to the Civil War. As the U.S. expanded, Northern and Southern states argued about the expansion of slavery into the new territories. The growing conflict reached a head in 1861, when the South seceded from the North, and the Civil War began.

OTHER INVENTIONS: Although Whitney's cotton gin was successful, he never profited from it. He was much more successful in the firearms manufacturing industry. He began building muskets in 1797, when the United States was on the brink of war with France.

The government told the nation's manufacturers that it needed 40,000 muskets. That seemed to be an impossible goal. The total production for the previous three years was only 1,000 muskets. But Whitney had an idea, and planned to supply the government with 10,000 muskets in a mere two years.

Musket-making at that time was a time-consuming process. Each musket was made by hand by a skilled worker. Each musket consisted of many parts, and all the parts were made individually, by hand. This made repairs of broken muskets next to impossible, as there were no common parts to every musket.

Whitney invented uniform and interchangeable parts for muskets, which allowed the guns to be mass-produced. He also designed machine tools to manufacture the parts.

Although it took Whitney 10 ½ years to produce his 10,000 muskets, he had invented a new way of manufacturing. He'd created a system of mass-production, which would later be perfected by **Henry Ford** in the American automotive industry. The invention was a success. But because of his earlier patent struggles, Whitney never patented his late inventions.

LATER YEARS: Whitney returned to New Haven in his later years. There, he built a factory surrounded with worker's residences. It became the town of Whitneyville.

ELI WHITNEY'S HOME AND FAMILY: Eli Whitney married Henrietta Edwards in 1817. They had four children. One of his sons, Eli Whitney Jr., took over the firearms factory in Connecticut. Eli Whitney died in New Haven in 1825 at the age of 60.

HIS INVENTION: Whitney's cotton gin changed the cotton industry in the U.S. It made cotton the major crop of the South. It also made the South more dependent on slavery. This was the opposite of Whitney's intent, but it was a result of his invention. Whitney also developed mass production and interchangeable parts. This brought changes to manufacturing, like the assembly line, still in use today.

WORLD WIDE WEB SITES:

http://www.pbs.org
http://www.classbrain.com

Frank Whittle
1907 - 1996
British Inventor of the Jet Engine

FRANK WHITTLE WAS BORN on June 1, 1907, in Coventry, a city in central England. His father, Moses Whittle, was foreman at a machine tool factory. His mother, Sara Alice Whittle, was a homemaker.

FRANK WHITTLE GREW UP loving aircraft and flying. His favorite toy was a tin model of an early airplane. When he was nine his family moved to nearby Leamington Spa. His father had bought a machine shop called Leamington Valve and Piston Ring Company. Frank helped out at his father's factory, becoming familiar with machinery and gasoline engines.

FRANK WHITTLE WENT TO SCHOOL at the local schools. When he was 11, he enrolled at Leamington College, a private secondary school. He didn't like school. But he spent many hours reading at the local library. He read popular science books on astronomy and aircraft engineering. He was also fascinated when he saw airplanes flying, something still rare in those years.

In January 1923 Whittle tried to enlist in the Royal Air Force (RAF). But he failed the medical exam because he was too short, only five feet tall. After a rigorous diet and exercise program, he gained three inches in height. He was able to join the RAF, and worked as an apprentice on the ground crew. But Whittle had bigger ambitions: he wanted to become a pilot.

FLYING CAREER: In 1926 Whittle passed the test to become a pilot. He was sent to learn to fly at the RAF College at Cranwell, near the east coast of England. At Cranwell, Whittle took courses in flying and aircraft design.

A NEW THEORY OF PROPULSION: In August 1928 Whittle was assigned to the RAF's 111 Fighter Squadron. He soon joined the RAF's Flying Training School as an instructor. He began to apply his engineering knowledge to aircraft design. He wrote a paper titled "Future Developments in Aircraft Design" in 1928. In it he discussed a new way to power airplanes.

At that time, airplanes got their power from piston-driven gasoline engines that turned propellers. The engines were much like those in today's cars. But as pilots tried to fly higher and faster, they found that the thinner air of the upper atmosphere made gasoline engines less effective.

At high altitudes, there is less available oxygen. Also, propellers have less air to push. Whittle theorized that compressing the air with a turbine—a special fan that turned at very high speed—might solve the problem. The turbine would be enclosed in a combustion chamber, and the spinning of the turbine blades would draw in air. Fuel introduced into the airstream of the engine would be ignited by air pressure. The result would be a high-speed exhaust of hot gas. The rush of the exhaust would propel the plane, much like an inflated balloon "flies" by the air expelled from it. This idea is the basis of jet propulsion.

PATENT APPLICATION: In January 1930 Whittle filed a **patent** for his jet engine design. In the meantime he was active in the RAF, testing floatplanes and performing test launches from the Ark Royal, an early British aircraft carrier. He did so well in his engineering studies that the RAF sent him for further study to the University of Cambridge. He earned a bachelor of science degree in 1936.

Whittle was now totally devoted to developing his jet engine. He left active pilot duty in the RAF in 1936. With two other former RAF pilots as partners and financial backing from a bank, he formed a private company called Power Jets. By April 1937 Whittle was testing his first experimental jet engine, dubbed the "WU," or "Whittle Unit." Still, Whittle struggled to find materials that could stand up

Whittle's first jet, the E28/39, 1941.

to the stress inside his engine. His early tests were not convincing, and the RAF became reluctant to support him.

ANOTHER JET ENGINE DESIGNER: At almost the same time, a German engineer named Hans von Ohain was developing a jet engine of his own. Neither Whittle nor von Ohain was aware of the other's work. Von Ohain developed a model jet engine as early as 1935, and successfully tested a working engine, running on hydrogen fuel, in February 1937. On August 27, 1939, the Heinkel He-178, powered by von Ohain's jet engine, made the first successful jet-powered flight. Von Ohain's independent work led to the development of Germany's jet aircraft of World War II.

WORLD WAR II: Whittle began to receive government support for his experimental work. With renewed funding and using newly developed metal alloys, he designed a reliable working engine. The engine was mounted on an all-new airframe built by Gloster Aircraft Company. The plane was called the E 28/39, or the Gloster Pioneer.

FIRST FLIGHTS: During trials the new airplane made a few short flights in April 1941, flying up to 200 yards. Then, on March 15, 1941, test pilot Gerry Sayer made a 17-minute flight in the E 28/39. In days to come the plane reached 370 miles per hour at 25,000 feet, faster than any conventional aircraft of the time.

BUSINESS BREAKUP: World War II had begun in 1939. The British government took over the development of jet engines from Whittle. Using Whittle's designs, other companies produced the Gloster Meteor I, Britain's first jet fighter, which entered service in 1944. Whittle made little or no money from his jet engine. He left the company in 1946. But his designs gave Britain a head start on jet-engine development. British Overseas Airways Corporation, now called British Airways, flew the first commercial jet aircraft, the De Haviland Comet, in 1949.

RECOGNITION: In 1948 the Royal Commission on Awards to Inventors finally gave Whittle recognition—and money—for his invention. He received a grant of £100,000. (That would be worth more than $500,000 today.) In 1991, he shared the Charles Draper Prize with Hans von Ohain. He also received numerous other awards and honorary degrees.

After the war, Whittle served as a consultant in the aerospace industry. He also designed a oil-drilling motor called the Whittle Turbodrill. In 1976 he moved to the United States and became a professor at the U.S. Naval Academy. He was also a consultant on jet propulsion for the U.S. Air Force, working at Wright-Patterson Air Force Base in Dayton, Ohio.

FRANK WHITTLE'S HOME AND FAMILY: Whittle married Dorothy Mary Lee in 1930. The couple had two sons, Francis and Ian. Ian went on to become a Boeing 747 pilot. The marriage ended in divorce in 1976. He died in Columbia, Maryland, on August 8, 1996, at age 89.

HIS INVENTION: Following his own ideas and applying keen engineering skill, Whittle realized that a turbine-driven jet engine would advance air travel to new speeds and altitudes. He made this realization a reality in 1937 with his first jet engine test. Although German engineer Hans von Ohain also developed a jet engine and aircraft, Whittle's designs were used by Britain and the U.S. during World War II and became the model for the industry.

Brian Rowe, retired chairman of GE Aircraft Engines, said of Whittle, "He came up with many of the innovations that we still use today." Jet air travel is now worldwide and commonplace, thanks in no small part to Whittle's jet engine. Today, the pioneering work of Frank Whittle continues at the University of Cambridge's Whittle Laboratory, devoted to research in turbomachinery.

WORLD WIDE WEB SITES:

http://www.raf.mod.uk/history/e281.html
http://www.invent.org/hall_of_fame/200.html
http://www.pbs.org/kcet/chasingthesun/innovators/fwhittle.html
http://www.bbc.co.uk/history/historic_figures/whittle_frank.shtml
http://www-g.eng.cam.ac.uk/125/achievements/whittle/telgraph.htm

Steve Wozniak
1950 -
American Computer Designer and Engineer
Co-Founder of Apple Computer and
Inventor of the Apple II

STEVE WOZNIAK WAS BORN on August 11, 1950, in San Jose, California. His last name is pronounced "WOZ-nee-ack." His parents were Jerry and Margaret Wozniak. Jerry was an engineer and Margaret was a homemaker. Steve has a sister, Leslie, and a brother, Mark.

STEVE WOZNIAK GREW UP in Sunnyvale, a city south of San Francisco. The area's now called "Silicon Valley" because it became the center of the computer industry. (Silicon is one of the main materials used to make computer chips.)

Steve loved sports, and played tennis and baseball as a kid. He was also fascinated by science and the way things worked. He started building computers when he was still in grade school. When he was in the sixth grade, he built a ham radio and got his radio license. He communicated with other radio operators all over the world.

Steve loved reading, too. He read electronics magazines, and even his father's engineering books. He also remembers loving the *Tom Swift* books. "They were about this young guy who was an engineer and who could design anything," he recalls. "He would entrap aliens, and build submarines, and have projects all over the world."

STEVE WOZNIAK WENT TO SCHOOL at the local public schools. He's a pretty humble guy, but admits that he was a math and science genius. He loved computers, and had actually built one by the fifth grade. "It played Tic-Tac-Toe," he recalled.

Soon, he was designing complete computers. They became "the love of my life," he remembers. "It was like solving puzzles. I tried to get better and better." He was always trying to make his computers smaller, which would later influence his ideas for Apple products.

Wozniak graduated from Homestead High School in 1968. He went on to college at the University of Colorado. He spent one year at Colorado, but didn't enjoy his classes. He spent most of that year on his own computer projects. He returned to California and worked for a while at a small computer company. He took some courses at a local community college, then went to the University of California at Berkeley. There, he majored in engineering.

Wozniak left college after his junior year. He moved back home and got a job at Hewlett-Packard. That's one of the first, and most successful, electronics companies in Southern California. In his spare time, he continued designing and building computers.

Wozniak was part of a group of early computer lovers called the Homebrew Computer Club. Through the group he met **Steve Jobs,** who would become his partner in Apple Computer.

FOUNDING APPLE WITH STEVE JOBS: Wozniak and Jobs decided to try their hand at building their own computer. Working in the Jobs's garage, they got started in 1975.

FIRST COMPUTERS: The first computers were huge machines. Just one computer could fill an entire room. And it didn't have the power or speed of just one of today's personal computers.

But like today's computers, the early versions worked on the same principle.

A BRIEF HISTORY OF COMPUTERS: The root word of "computer" tells the origin of the machine. Computers "compute"—that is, they perform math calculations. The earliest "computer" was actually an adding machine. It was created in 1642 by Frenchman Blaise Pascal. Pascal's machine was simple. He entered numbers into a machine using dials. Inside the machine were cogs and wheels connected to the dials. They moved according to the numbers entered. The machine could accurately add and subtract numbers.

The next major step forward happened in the 1800s. Charles Babbage, a British mathematician, designed a machine to process numbers. It had many of the features of a modern computer. It had an input mechanism (like a keyboard), storage (memory), a computing mechanism (CPU), and an output mechanism (a computer screen or printer). Babbage never built his machine. But his research was very influential.

The first modern computers were developed during World War II (1939 - 1945). Mathematician Howard Aiken developed the Mark 1, a computer that ran on electromechanical relays. It helped improve the accuracy of Navy artillery.

Another advance from the World War II era came about through the research of Alan Turing. Turing invented the "Colossus," a computer that broke the Nazi military code. It helped end the war in Europe. "Colossus" was important for another reason. It was the first computer to use vacuum tubes to store and process data.

The next major innovation in computers was the ENIAC. (That stands for the Electronic Numerical Integrator and Calculator). Previous computers were used for military purposes. The ENIAC was the first computer for general, commercial use. It was enormous: it weighed 30-tons, and used more than 17,000 vacuum tubes.

In 1948, John Bardeen, William Schockley, and Walter Brattain invented the transistor. It was another tremendous breakthrough. Transistors replaced vacuum tubes with smaller, cooler processors.

The integrated circuit, invented by Jack Kilby in 1958, introduced the true modern era in computing. Now one silicon microchip could hold millions of electronic components. It revolutionized the industry.

When Jobs and Wozniak started out, there were no computers for personal use. The large computers made by **Seymour Cray** or IBM were used by governments, corporations, and universities. Wozniak and Jobs had another idea. Why not build a computer for the average person to use?

Wozniak was designing calculators for Hewlett-Packard when he and Jobs started out. He discovered that the price of memory chips had finally gotten cheap enough for him to use in his computers. He began to visualize the Apple. "I had a TV set and a typewriter," he recalls. "That made me think a computer should be laid out like a typewriter with a video screen."

In high school, Wozniak had learned electronic circuitry. He knew "how to get a TV to draw—shapes and characters and things. So it's like all these influences came together and out came a product that I knew would be easy to use."

APPLE COMPUTER: Wozniak and Jobs founded Apple Computer in 1976. They built the first Apple, the Apple I, that year. It wasn't anything like the computer of today. It was just a circuit board. But it was a revolutionary start.

APPLE I: Wozniak remembers taking the Apple I to work. "I used it to solve some engineering and design problems I was working on," he recalls. "So I knew I had something good."

Wozniak (right), John Sculley (center), and Steve Jobs (left)
announce the new AppleIIc, 1984.

From a financial point of view, Wozniak and Jobs didn't really have a business plan. Wozniak recalls that it was "a $1,000 investment, and we'd have to sell 50 units to get our money back." He remembers not being sure they'd sell 50. Then, they received a $50,000 order from a local computer store. They were on their way.

APPLE II: In 1977, Wozniak and Jobs created a revolution in the computer industry. They released the Apple II. It was the first desktop personal computer, for the general user. It was small—it could fit on a desktop. It took up about the same space as a typewriter, with a screen, keyboard, speaker, and power supply.

The Apple II was a huge success. The company made $2 million the first year, and $500 million in its first five years. The two friends continued to work together, in the roles that best suited them. Wozniak was the engineer and designer of the computers. Jobs was the marketing genius. He was focused on the potential of the Apple. Like **Bill Gates**, who became his fierce rival, he could see that computers could be used in every home, and in every business. Jobs was able to convince investors, too. That way, they had the money to continue to develop and grow.

The phenomenal success made Wozniak and Jobs multimillionaires. But in 1981, Wozniak had a life-changing experience.

A PLANE CRASH: In February 1981, Wozniak was flying his small plane with his fiancee, Candy Clark, when the plane crashed on take off. Both Wozniak and Clark were seriously hurt. Wozniak suffered short-term memory loss. It was a very difficult time.

When he returned to Apple, he took a look at where the company was going. He missed "tinkering," he recalls. By that time, the company had hundreds of engineers. He felt he was "no longer important to the company," he says.

LEAVING APPLE: Wozniak took a leave of absence from Apple. He returned as a consultant over the years, but, in 1985, he resigned from the company. He decided to turn his talents to other things.

Wozniak went back to school and finished his college degree. He organized two big music festivals. He built a huge dream house, with rooms full of video games and computers. And, he decided he wanted to give back to the community.

KIDS AND COMPUTERS: Wozniak has spent most of the last 15 years, and many millions of dollars, to help improve education. He's

Wozniak working on his home computer.

"adopted" the Los Gatos School District in California. There, he devotes his time to get kids interested in science and computers. He works with the students on projects. And he works with the teachers on how to teach computer skills. He gives schools all over the country free equipment, and helps fund Internet access.

Wozniak has also funded children's museums, music and dance groups, and other community projects. He loves being part of kids and education. He says he wants to "spend as much time as I can doing what I like to do, which is work with computers and schools and kids."

Wozniak's many accomplishments have earned him many honors. He was awarded the National Medal of Technology in 1985. That's the highest award for inventors and innovators in the U.S. He entered the Inventors Hall of Fame in 2000. And he received the Heinz Award for Technology that same year. That honor cited his computer inventions, and his devotion to kids and education. It

Wozkiak with a group of his middle school students.

praised him for "lighting the fires of excitement for education in grade school students and their teachers."

STEVE WOZNIAK'S HOME AND FAMILY: Wozniak has been married three times. His first wife was named Alice Robertson. They married in 1980 and later divorced. In 1987, he married Candice Clark. They had three children, Jesse, Gary, and Sara. They divorced in 1990. He married again in 1990. His wife's name is Suzanne Mulkern.

HIS INVENTION: Wozniak's invention of the personal computer brought about major changes in modern life. His Apple computers were easy to use and affordable. That helped make personal computers a part of homes, schools, and businesses. As PCs caught on, they changed the way people learn, and do business.

WORLD WIDE WEB SITES:

http://www.invent.org/hall_of_fame/155.html

http://www.thetech.org/revolutionaries.wozniak/i_c.html

http://www.woz.org/

Wilbur Wright
1867 - 1912

Orville Wright
1871 - 1948

American Inventors of the First Aircraft Capable of Powered, Sustained, and Controlled Flight

WILBUR WRIGHT WAS BORN on April 16, 1867, in Millville, Indiana.

ORVILLE WRIGHT WAS BORN on August 19, 1871, in Dayton, Ohio.

Their parents were Milton and Susan Wright. Milton was a minister and Susan was a homemaker. Wilbur was the third and Orville was the sixth of seven children. Two of the Wright children died as infants. Five lived to be adults: Reuchlin, Lorin, Wilbur, Orville, and Katharine.

THE WRIGHT BROTHERS GREW UP in several places. Their father traveled often for his job, and sometimes the family moved with him. Over the years, the family lived in Cedar Rapids, Iowa; Richmond, Indiana; and Dayton, Ohio. The brothers lived in Dayton most of their lives

The Wright household was a happy, loving place. Milton and Susan Wright encouraged their children to be curious and independent. Wilbur recalled being inspired "to investigate whatever aroused curiosity."

Susan Wright was very mechanical. She fostered her children's interest in the way things work. Their father wasn't as mechanically inclined, but he did nurture his children's fascination with things. Once, he bought them a toy helicopter powered by a rubber band. They were fascinated. They took it apart, put it back together, and made sketches of the toy. It sparked a life-long interest in flying.

The brothers were incredibly close. From childhood to adulthood, they were each other's best friends. Wilbur once wrote: "From the time we were little children, my brother Orville and myself lived together, played together, worked together, and, in fact, thought together. We usually owned all of our toys in common, talked over our thoughts and aspirations so that nearly everything that was done in our lives has been the result of conversations, suggestions, and discussions between us." They even had nicknames for each other. Wilbur was "Ullam" and Orville was "Bubs."

WILBUR AND ORVILLE WRIGHT WENT TO SCHOOL at the public schools. Wilbur was a serious student. Orville was not as concerned about his studies. Once, Orville's teacher caught him playing with a toy aircraft during class. He told her that he and Wilbur were working on building a plane that would carry them.

Wilbur planned to go to college at Yale University, but a sporting accident changed that. During his senior year, he was seriously injured while playing hockey. At that same time, his mother was diagnosed with tuberculosis. He decided to stay in Dayton and devote himself to her care. Susan Wright died of tuberculosis in 1889.

STARTING TO WORK TOGETHER: The year their mother died, Orville dropped out of high school. He'd worked several summers as a printer's apprentice. A friend with a small press suggested they go into the printing business together. Orville agreed.

PRINTING BUSINESS: Within a year, Wilbur decided to join Orville in the printing business. They started a series of newspapers, with Wilbur as the editor. Their first paper was a weekly called *The West Side News*. Next, they published a daily paper called *The Evening Item*. They loved the creative side of running a paper, and the mechanical side, too. Their fascination and curiosity led them to build their own printing press.

The papers didn't make much money, but the brothers learned a lot. While continuing their printing business, they began to explore other things.

BICYCLE BUSINESS: In 1892, Wilbur and Orville turned their attention to bicycles. There were new developments in bikes that made them easier to ride. Earlier bicycles were made with one big wheel

Wilbur Wright working in bicycle shop, 1897.

in front. They were very difficult to balance. The new bikes had two wheels of equal size and were much easier to ride. Soon people all over the country became enthusiastic cyclists. The Wright Brothers opened a shop, where they sold and repaired bicycles.

In 1896, the Wright Brothers began building their own bicycles. The name of their shop was the Wright Cycle Company. They were always eager to learn. They constantly worked on improving their

545

bikes and the way they were produced. They built an internal combustion engine that powered the tools in the shop. Their work on bicycles led the ever-curious brothers to one of the most exciting areas of science and invention of the time: aviation.

AVIATION AT THE TURN OF THE 20th CENTURY: Throughout history, flight captured the imaginations of inventors. In the 1400s, **Leonardo Da Vinci** sketched early aircraft with wings that flapped, like birds'. In the 1700s, **Jacques and Joseph Montgolfier** successfully invented a hot air balloon. In the late 1700s, George Cayley developed a "fixed wing" aircraft. (That means the wings didn't move during flight). Cayley built the first glider to carry a human, in 1849.

By the time the Wrights got involved, people all over the world were working on flying machines. But the craft all lacked a way to *control* flight. Consequently, there were many failures, and deaths, in early flying attempts.

In 1896, Samuel P. Langley flew the first steam-powered model airplane in Washington, D.C. Another major figure in experimental flight was Octave Chanute. Chanute was an engineer and early champion of aviation. He sponsored inventors and innovators like the Wright brothers in developing gliders. One of those early gliders inspired the Wrights' own design.

Also in 1896, another leader in early aviation, Otto Lilienthal, died in a glider accident. Lilienthal was the best glider pilot of the era. He had flown more than 2,000 flights in aircraft he'd designed. What caused his deadly crash was his inability to control his glider.

The Wrights read of the efforts of Langley and Chanute and the tragic death of Lilienthal. They became committed to understanding the possibilities and problems of human flight. They read everything they could about current aircraft design and engineering. Through a systematic, thorough analysis of the problems of flight, they invented the first successful airplane.

LIFT, THRUST, AND CONTROL: The Wright brothers focused on three problems: lift, thrust, and control. "Lift" refers to the flow of air over and under the wings, which allows the plane to become airborne. "Thrust" is the movement of the plane forward, driven by the propeller and engine. "Control" was a more complex problem. They broke that down into "pitch," "yaw," and "roll." "Pitch" is the up and down movement of the plane. "Yaw" is the movement of the plane to the right or left. "Roll" refers to the motion that tips the wings up and down, allowing it to turn. Another insight into the control of an aircraft came from their knowledge of bicycles. Based on their experience, the Wrights also knew that a pilot could, like a cyclist, use his body to balance an aircraft in the air.

LEARNING FROM BIRDS: With all these ideas in mind, the brothers studied the flight of birds. Focusing on how the air flowed over a bird's wing in flight, the Wrights studied how air flow created "lift." They also noted how birds changed the shape of their wings in flight to allow turning or other maneuvers in the air.

"WARPED WINGS": From his observation of birds in flight, Wilbur made an important discovery. "The thought came to me that possibly a bird adjusted the tips of its wings so as to present one tip at a positive angle and the other at a negative angle," he wrote.

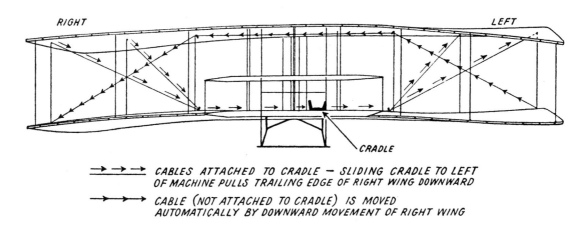

Wilbur Wright's drawing explaining the "Warped Wings."

Wilbur was eager to transfer his understanding of bird flight into solving the problems of human flight. In 1899, he made a biplane kite (a biplane has two sets of wings). The biplane was flexible enough to "warp," or twist. It mimicked the action of a bird's wings.

The idea came to him when he twisted a long cardboard box. The sides of the box were like the biplane's wings. As Wilbur twisted the box, one end of the wings turned up, increasing lift at that part. At the same time, the other end of the wings turned down, decreasing lift. This allowed the plane to "roll" right or left. Wilbur thought that he could control the twist, or warp, with metal cables attached to the wings on his biplane kite.

Wilbur's biplane kite was just 5 feet across. He and Orville tested it, and it worked. Next, they wanted to build and test gliders based on their design. They needed to find a place with consistent high winds and soft landing sites. They chose a small fishing village called Kitty Hawk, North Carolina, on the Atlantic shore.

Wilbur and Orville flying the 1900 glider as a kite.

KITTY HAWK: Beginning in 1900, the Wright brothers began a series of test flights with gliders at Kitty Hawk. The winds were strong, there were tall dunes from which to launch their gliders, and the sandy shore cushioned the fall of the gliders on landing.

In their first days at Kitty Hawk, the Wrights flew the glider as a kite. There were many crashes, requiring constant rebuilding of the craft. But one of the most remarkable things about the brothers was their ability to learn from their mistakes. They were never discouraged by the failure of a plane. They took down the data, rebuilt the aircraft, and tried again.

Soon, they began flying the glider with one of them on board. These early piloted attempts produced good and bad results. The "wing warping" worked, but the craft didn't get enough lift.

REFINING THE AIRPLANE: The Wrights returned to Dayton and continued to work on their aircraft. Over the next few years, they split their time between Dayton and Kitty Hawk. Back in Kitty Hawk in 1901, they tested their rebuilt craft. Once again they faced problems and crashes.

1900 glider, wrecked by wind, Oct. 10, 1900.

Wilbur gliding in level flight. Kitty Hawk, NC, October 10, 1902.

Returning to Dayton at the end of 1901, the brothers began to think there was something wrong with their data. They were using the calculations for predicting lift that had been accepted for years. They determined the data must be incorrect. So they decided to build their own experiment, from the ground up.

THE WIND TUNNEL: The remarkable Wright brothers, in attempting to create a better set of data, invented a device used to this day. Their wind tunnel measured the lift of an airplane wing. They tested almost 200 different wing designs in the wind tunnel. Using the data, they were able to build a better airplane wing.

When the Wright brothers returned to Kitty Hawk in 1902, they tested their new craft. The glider had enough lift. Now they concentrated on control: pitch, roll, and yaw. Both brothers took turns as pilot. In fact, they few some 1,000 flights in just three years. They became two of the best, most experienced pilots of their time.

551

Like Wilbur, Orville had his share of crashes. One, he recalled, ended in "a heap of flying machine, cloth, and sticks, with me in the center without a scratch or bruise." As always, they took the crashes in stride. They rebuilt the plane, learned from their mistakes, and moved on.

The test flight season in Kitty Hawk proved successful. Wilbur and Orville made glider flights of 622 and 615 feet each. They returned to Dayton. In the winter of 1902 - 03, they set their sights on a new challenge. They wanted their aircraft to be powered. So, they built a small gasoline engine, which they also designed. It was light—just 180 pounds—and produced 8 horsepower.

The Wright Brothers' Wind Tunnel, 1902.

They made another important innovation. Unable to find propellers that fit their needs, they created their own. In another exceptional insight, the Wrights saw that a propeller functions as a wing. "It was apparent that a propeller was simply a wing traveling in a spiral course," said Orville.

With a new plane, engine, and propellers, the Wright brothers left Dayton in the fall of 1903. They shipped the parts of the plane to Kitty Hawk, where they put it together. It was, according to Orville, "a whopper flying machine." Called simply "The Flyer 1," the plane was the largest they'd ever built, measuring 40 feet from wingtip to wingtip.

As always, the brothers faced failure. The propeller cracked and had to be replaced. There were other problems, too. But Wilbur and Orville persevered.

DECEMBER 17, 1903: On December 17, 1903, Wilbur and Orville Wright flew into history. First, it was Orville, who, at 10:35 A.M., flew the Flyer a total of 12 seconds, covering 120 feet. Next, with Wilbur at the controls, the Flyer covered 175 feet. Orville next flew 200 feet, and for the last time that day, Wilbur flew 852 feet.

The Wrights had accomplished what many thought was impossible. They had flown an aircraft capable of powered, sustained, controlled flight. But the Flyer was caught by a gust of wind that afternoon. It was destroyed and never flew again.

The Wright brothers sent their father a telegram with the news. Bishop Wright spread the news to the media.

Wilbur and Orville were eager to get back to work. They went back to Dayton, and back to work improving their aircraft. They

First Flight, December 17, 1903. Orville is flying the plane.
Wilbur is standing at the right.

decided they wanted to continue building and flying aircraft in Ohio. So they built a workshop and flew out of a site called Huffman Prairie, near Dayton. (It's now the site of Wright Patterson Air Force Base.)

1904 - 1905: Over the next few years the Wright brothers built several versions of their first Flyer. They improved all aspects of the plane, and by October 1905, they had a craft that flew 39 minutes, going 24 miles around Dayton. The plane could do figure eights in the air, and could even carry passengers.

PATENTS AND PROBLEMS: The brothers knew they had to protect their invention with a **patent**. A patent is a document granted by a government that protects the exclusive right of an inventor to make, use, or sell his or her invention for a specific number of years. The Wrights were granted Patent Number 821-393 on May 23, 1906, "For a Flying Machine."

Their first contract was with the U.S. Army. They agreed to develop an airplane that could fly for one hour at 40 miles per hour, and carry a pilot and a passenger.

Next, the Wrights signed an agreement with French investors to allow them to build planes in Europe according to the Wrights' design.

PROVING THEMSELVES TO THE WORLD: In 1908, Wilbur went to France. There were many people in Europe who didn't believe the Wrights' claims. So Wilbur showed them, in person. He gave a series of flights for the public, who were awed by what they saw.

Orville had stayed in the U.S. to work on the Army aircraft. During testing, the plane crashed. The crash killed his passenger, an army officer named Thomas Selfridge. Orville was also seriously injured. When he was better, he went to Europe. Soon, he and Wilbur returned to the U.S. They worked on the Army aircraft and trained pilots.

In 1909, Wilbur also made his first public flights in the U.S. In New York Harbor, he flew before one million amazed spectators. Soon, Wilbur and Orville Wright became two of the most famous people in the country.

Orville and Lt. Lahm making a world's record flight at Fort Meyer, Virginia, July 27, 1909. They flew 50 miles at 40 miles per hour.

Wilbur and Orville never liked the life of fame. Still, their old friend Octave Chanute said, it was their own doing. "I know that the reception of honors becomes oppressive to modest men. But in this case you have brought the trouble on yourselves by completing the solution to a world-old problem, accomplished with great ingenuity and patience at much risk of personal injury to yourselves."

THE WRIGHT COMPANY: In 1909, the brothers formed the Wright Company. They started a factory in Dayton to build planes. The planes were tested and flown at Huffman Prairie.

Wilbur flying over Governor's Island in New York Harbor, Sept. 29, 1909.

Wilbur also had to focus on patent problems faced by the company. Several American and European firms had stolen their technology and were making planes. This was patent infringement. They had not paid the Wright brothers for the right to make and sell airplanes that were clearly based on the Wrights' patented designs. So Wilbur sued these companies in court. This took up much of his time, and took him away from the planes and flying he loved. The company lost its edge over the competition.

A GLIMPSE OF THE WRIGHT BROTHERS IN THEIR TIMES: In 1910, Wilbur and Orville were interviewed by journalist Kate Carews. She described them this way: "Wilbur is the bald Wright brother, Orville the Wright brother with a mustache. Wilbur is all action, Orville looks as if he has affections as well. Wilbur is a family cut-up. Orville you'd go to with your troubles."

557

In that same interview, Carews asked the Wright brothers about the future of flight. She asked if planes would ever be used to transport people in large numbers, as trains did. "No," said Wilbur. "That would be too expensive." Asked if planes would ever carry freight, he again replied "No."

Asked about the airplane's use in war, Wilbur said they'd be used for scouting, but never for transporting troops.

Instead, the Wright brothers imagined airplanes becoming "automobiles of the air." Orville imagined "stations in every town for landing a launching of flying machines and the supply of gasoline."

WILBUR'S DEATH: Worn out from the effort to defend their patents, Wilbur became very ill. He came down with typhoid fever and died on May 30, 1912. He was just 45 years old. His father, Bishop Milton Wright remembered him this way: "A short life, full of consequences. An unfailing intellect, imperturbable temper, great self-reliance and as great modesty, seeing the right clearly, pursuing it steadily, he lived and died."

ORVILLE'S LATER LIFE: After Wilbur died, Orville stayed on at the Wright Company until 1915. That year, he sold his part of the company. But he stayed involved with aviation. He continued to work on improvements in aircraft. He was a member of the National Advisory Committee for Aeronautics. That group eventually became NASA (National Aeronautics and Space Administration).

Orville also served as a consultant during World War I for aircraft developed for military use. He became a famous, honored figure in America and throughout the world.

The Wright family house at 7 Hawthorne Street in Dayton, Ohio.
The family lived there from 1871 to 1878 and again from 1885 to 1914.

WILBUR AND ORVILLE WRIGHT'S HOME AND FAMILY: The Wright Brothers lived most of their lives in Dayton. Neither of them ever married or had children. They remained close to their siblings, especially their sister, Katharine. Orville Wright suffered a heart attack and died on January 30, 1948.

THEIR INVENTIONS: The Wright Brothers are two of the most important inventors in history. They invented the very first aircraft that was capable of powered, sustained, and controlled flight.

Their vision and accomplishment stand as one of the most important achievements in the history of invention. As Darrel Collins of the Kitty Hawk National Memorial stated, "Before the Wright Brothers, no one in aviation did anything fundamentally right. Since the Wright Brothers, no one has done anything fundamentally different."

The plaque next to a replica of the 1903 airplane in the Air and Space Museum outlines their contribution. "By original scientific research, the Wright Brothers discovered the principles of human flight. As inventors, builders, and flyers, they further developed the aeroplane, taught man to fly, and opened the era of aviation."

Wilbur and Orville Wright's invention changed the way we live. Air travel, made possible by their invention, has transformed our world. Every part of the Earth is now reachable by airplane. Their invention shrunk the boundaries that separated the people of the world. Space travel, which promises to shrink the boundaries of our solar system and beyond, is an advancement made possible by the remarkable Wright brothers.

WORLD WIDE WEB SITES:

http://wright.nasa.gov/wilbur.htm
http://www.first-to-fly.com/History/Wright
http://www.nasm.si.edu/wrightbrothers/
http://www.nps.gov/wrbr/

Zworykin with his kinescope, the receiver for his electronic television system, 1929.

Vladimir Zworykin
1889 - 1982
Russian-Born American Scientist and Inventor
Pioneer in the field of Electronic Television

VLADIMIR ZWORYKIN WAS BORN on July 30, 1889, in Murom, Russia. His parents were Vladimir and Elaine Zworykin. His father ran a commercial fleet of boats.

VLADIMIR ZWORYKIN GREW UP fascinated by electricity. He worked for his father during the summers, and he loved to help repair the boat's electrical equipment.

VLADIMIR ZWORYKIN WENT TO SCHOOL at the local schools. He went to college at the St. Petersburg Institute of Technology. He majored in electrical engineering. He studied with Boris Rosing, whose work was to make a great impression on him.

Rosing was fascinated by the idea of transmitting images—an early attempt at television. Rosing wanted to use wireless technology to send images. He and Zworykin worked on an early version of a cathode ray tube. Cathode ray tubes are vacuum tubes that transmit charged electron beams. Rosing's attempts weren't successful, but they sparked Zworykin's imagination.

After graduating from St. Petersburg in 1912, Zworykin moved to France. There, he studied x-ray technology at the College de France. He returned to Russia when World War I began, in 1914. During the war, he worked as a radio operator. After the war, as the Russian Revolution began, Zworykin decided to move with his family to the U.S.

FIRST JOBS: Once in the U.S., Zworykin started working for the Russian Embassy in Washington D.C. Soon, however, he'd found a job in his field.

WESTINGHOUSE: In 1920, Zworykin got a job with Westinghouse, a major electrical company founded by **George Westinghouse**. He worked with radio tubes and other electric storage devices. He continued studying, earning a PhD in physics from the University of Pittsburgh.

INNOVATIONS IN TELEVISION: Zworykin was still interested in television. He worked on a device called an "iconoscope." It was a scanning device that used an electron beam to scan an image one line at a time. It was very similar to an invention by **Philo Farnsworth**. And in fact, they've each been called "the father of television." Zworykin applied for a **patent** for his device in 1923. However, the patent didn't get approved until 1938.

Zworykin's next invented the "kinescope." It was a cathode ray tube that was basically a television receiver. It received the image sent by the scanning device, and displayed it. He applied for a patent in 1924. That same year, he became a U.S. citizen.

Zworykin presented his new innovations to his bosses at Westinghouse. They were not impressed. They told him he should spend his time on something "a little more useful." Zworykin stayed with the company for a few more years. But when David Sarnoff of RCA (Radio Corporation of America) showed interest in developing his television ideas, he left Westinghouse and joined RCA.

BATTLES BETWEEN RCA AND PHILO FARNSWORTH: Sarnoff was head of RCA at a time when the company owned all patents related to radio. Sarnoff saw the huge potential in television. He set out to own all the patents related to the new technology. To do that, he hired Zworykin and funded his research. Sarnoff claimed once that it had cost RCA $50 million to bring television to the public.

Sarnoff tried to buy Farnsworth's patents. When Farnsworth refused, Sarnoff set out on a decade-long legal battle. He tried to prove that Zworykin's, not Farnsworth's, inventions had been the first in electronic television technology. Farnsworth eventually won the many patent battles in court, but it was time-consuming and costly. And even though he'd won in court, Farnsworth never became known to the public as the inventor of electronic television.

In 1939, it was RCA that introduced the invention of television to the American public, at the New York World's Fair. The huge commercial success of TV was still years off, however. In 1941, the U.S. entered World War II. The government shut down all commercial television production. They wanted all television-based technology to help the war effort.

Throughout the 1930s, Zworykin continued to invent. He worked with infrared ray technology and helped develop night-seeing devices. He also worked on applying early television technology to develop the first electron microscope. During the war, Zworykin helped the U.S. army create weapons systems and night-vision glasses.

Zworykin also made innovations in the surveillance field. This led to the electric "eye" found in garage door openers and security cameras. He also worked on early systems for weather forecasting. Zworykin retired from RCA in 1954. But he continued to contribute electronic innovations, especially in the medical field. After his retirement from RCA, he became head of the Medical Electronics Center at Rockefeller University.

Zworykin received many honors and awards for his work in television. The most important of these include the Edison Medal and the National Academy of Sciences Medal. By the end of his long and productive career, he had more than 120 patents.

VLADIMIR ZWORYKIN'S HOME AND FAMILY: Zworykin was married twice. His first wife was named Tatiana. They had two children.

Several years after their divorce, Zworykin married again. His second wife's name was Katherine Poevitsky. Zworykin died on July 29, 1982. He was 92 years old.

HIS INVENTIONS: Today, Zworykin is known for his innovations in electronic television, an invention that has truly changed the world. It is a universal technology, available nearly everywhere on the planet.

For Zworykin, the value of the technology far outweighed the content of most television programs. He was once asked what he thought of American television. "Awful," he replied. "I would never let my own children watch it."

WORLD WIDE WEB SITES:

http://www.invent.org/hall_of_fame/158.html
http://www.museum.tv/archives/etv/A/htmlZ/zworykinvla/

Photo and Illustration Credits

Every effort has been made to trace copyright for the images used in this volume. Any omissions will be corrected in future editions.

Archimedes: Italian postage stamp honoring Archimedes, released May 2, 1983
Leo Hendrik Baekeland: Courtesy of Smithsonian Institution, Photo Numbers 86-44, 84-11359
Benjamin Banneker: Courtesy of the Maryland Historical Society, Baltimore, Maryland
Frederick Banting: Courtesy of Simcoe County Archives & New Tecumseth Public Library
Alexander Graham Bell: Courtesy of the Library of Congress
Karl Benz: Courtesy DaimlerChrysler AG
Tim Berners-Lee: Donna Covenev/MIT; Newscom.com
Henry Bessemer: Frontispiece to *An Autobiography* by Henry Bessemer, 1905.
Clarence Birdseye: Courtesy of Birds Eye Foods
Katherine Blodgett: AIP Emilio Segne Visual Archives, Physics Today Collection
Louis Braille: Courtesy of the Louis Braille School. Copyright © 1998 by Nancy Lucas Williams.
Rachel Fuller Brown: Courtesy of the Wadsworth Center, New York State Department of Health
William S. Burroughs: Courtesy of Unisys Corporation, Blue Bell, Pennsylvania
Wallace Carothers: Courtesy of DuPont
Willis Carrier: Courtesy of the Carrier Corporation
George Washington Carver: Courtesy of the Library of Congress; Courtesy Iowa State University Library/University Archives
Jacques Cousteau: Courtesy of the Library of Congress
Seymour Cray: Courtesy of City of Chippewa Falls Cray Supercomputer Collection
Gottlieb Daimler: Courtesy DaimlerChrysler AG
Raymond Damadian: Courtesy of FONAR Corporation
Leonardo Da Vinci: Courtesy of the Library of Congress
John Deere: Courtesy Deere & Company Archives
George De Mestral: Courtesy of VELCRO
Rudolf Diesel: Hulton Archive/Getty Images
Herbert Henry Dow: Courtesy Post Street Archives
Eastman George: Used with permission of Eastman Kodak Company
Thomas Edison: Courtesy of the Library of Congress
Gertrude Bell Elion: Courtesy GlaxoSmithKline
Philo Farnsworth: Copyright © Bettman/CORBIS
Alexander Fleming: Courtesy of the Library of Congress
Henry Ford: Courtesy of the Library of Congress; from the collections of The Henry Ford
Benjamin Franklin: Courtesy of the Library of Congress
Robert Fulton: Courtesy of the Library of Congress
Galileo Galilei: Courtesy of the Library of Congress
Bill Gates: Courtesy of Microsoft; Newscom.com. AP/Wide World Photos
King Gillette: Courtesy of the Library of Congress
Robert Goddard: Courtesy of the Library of Congress
Charles Goodyear: Courtesy of the Library of Congress

PHOTO AND ILLUSTRATION CREDITS

Gordon Gould: Copyright © CORBIS

Temple Grandin: Copyright Laura Wilson; Courtesy of Temple Grandin. Cover: THINKING IN PICTURES Copyright 1995 by Temple Grandin. Vintage/A division of Random House, Inc.; ANIMALS IN TRANSLATION Jacket photograph by Jason Fulford. Copyright 2005 Simon & Schuster Inc.

Wilson Greatbatch: Courtesy Greatbatch Research Institute.

Johannes Gutenberg: Courtesy of the Library of Congress; from the Gutenberg Digital Site, Goettingen State and University Library: Woodcuts of J. Amman, 1568.

Elizabeth Hazen: Courtesy the Wadsworth Center, New York State Department of Health

Elias Howe: Courtesy of the Library of Congress.

Edward Jenner: Courtesy of the Edward Jenner Museum.

Steven Jobs: Courtesy Apple; Newscom.com; AP Images

Dean Kamen: Adriana M. Groisman; AP Images; Newscom.com

W. K. Kellogg: Courtesy the Kellogg Foundation.

Willem Kolff: Courtesy of Northwest Kidney Centers

Stephanie Kwolek: Courtesy DuPont

Edwin Land: Courtesy the Polaroid Collections.

Jerome Lemelson: Lemelson Foundation; AP Images; U.S. Patent #4,258,387

Guglielmo Marconi: Courtesy of the Library of Congress

Cyrus McCormick: Courtesy of the Library of Congress

Elijah McCoy: University of Southern Indiana Dept. of Engineering

Joseph and Jacques Montgolfier: Courtesy of the Library of Congress

Garrett Morgan: The Western Reserve Historical Society, Cleveland, Ohio

Samuel F.B. Morse: Courtesy of the Library of Congress; Courtesy of Smithsonian Institution, Photo Number 74-2491

Isaac Newton: Courtesy of the Library of congress

Alfred Nobel: Copyright © The Nobel Foundation

Ellen Ochoa: Courtesy of NASA

Louis Pasteur: Courtesy of the Library of Congress; Used with permission of Pfizer Inc. All rights reserved.

Roy J. Plunkett: Courtesy of DuPont

Wilhelm Roentgen: Courtesy of the Library of Congress

Jonas Salk: AP Images; Courtesy of the Library of Congress

Patsy Sherman: Photo Courtesy of 3M Co.

C. L. Sholes: Photographs courtesy of the Milwaukee Public Museum

Igor Sikorsky: Courtesy of the Library of Congress; Photos of Sikorsky aircraft and vehicles were provided courtesy of the Igor I. Sikorsky Historical Archives

Percy Spencer: Courtesy of Raytheon Company

George Stephenson: Courtesy of the Library of Congress

Levi Straus: Courtesy Levi Straus & Co. Archives

Nikola Tesla: Courtesy of the Library of Congress

Alessandro Volta: Courtesy of the Library of Congress

James Watt: Courtesy of the Library of Congress

George Westinghouse: Courtesy of the Library of Congress

Eli Whitney: Courtesy of the Library of Congress

Frank Whittle: Courtesy of the San Diego Aerospace Museum

Steve Wozniak: Courtesy Steve Wozniak, Al Luckow Photographer; Acey Harper/Time Life Pictures/Getty Images; AP Images

Orville and Wilbur Wright: Courtesy of the Library of Congress

Vladimir Zworykin: Corbis Images

Timeline of Inventors and Inventions

c. 287 B.C.   Archimedes is born.

c. 212 B.C.   Archimedes dies.

c. 1400   Johannes Gutenberg is born.

27 B.C.   Caesar Augustus becomes the first Roman Emperor

c. 6 B.C.   Jesus is born in Bethlehem

c. 30 A.D.   Jesus dies in Jerusalem.

1452   Leonardo Da Vinci is born.

Johannes Gutenberg publishes the "Gutenberg Bible" the first mass-produced book using the movable-type method.

1492   Christopher Columbus sails across the Atlantic Ocean and becomes the first European to discover the New World.

1468   Johannes Gutenberg dies.

1519   Leonardo Da Vinci dies.

1564   Galileo Galilei is born.

1606   Galileo Galilei invents the first thermometer.

1609   Galileo Galilei develops his first telescope, much more powerful than Lippershay's.

1636   Galileo Galilei publishes his observations that the Earth revolves around the Sun.

1642	Isaac Newton is born.
	Galileo Galilei dies.
1665 - 1667	Isaac Newton develops his theories of gravity, optics, and calculus.
1667	Isaac Newton builds the first reflecting telescope.
1686	Daniel Fahrenheit is born.
1706	Benjamin Franklin is born.
1712	Thomas Newcomen builds the first steam engine.
1714	Daniel Fahrenheit invents the mercury thermometer.
1731	Benjamin Banneker is born.
1717	Daniel Fahrenheit develops the Fahrenheit temperature scale.
1727	Isaac Newton dies.
1736	Daniel Fahrenheit dies.
	James Watt is born.
1740	Joseph-Michael Montgolfier is born.
c. 1740	Benjamin Franklin invents the Franklin stove.
1745	Jacques-Etienne Montgolfier is born.
	Alessandro Volta is born.
1749	Edward Jenner is born.
1752	Benjamin Franklin flies a kite during a thunderstorm and determines that lightning is a form of electricity.
1753	Benjamin Banneker builds his wooden clock, considered the first in the New World.
	Benjamin Franklin produces the lightning rod.
1765	Robert Fulton is born.
	Eli Whitney is born.

1769   James Watt improves the steam engine by adding a condenser.

The American Revolutionary War begins.

1781   The American Revolutionary War ends.

Rene Laennec is born.

George Stephenson is born.

1782   The Montgolfier brothers invent the hot air balloon.

1783   First human flight, in a Montgolfier hot air balloon.

1790   Benjamin Franklin dies.

1791   Samuel F.B. Morse is born.

1793   Eli Whitney builds the first practical cotton gin.

1797   Eli Whitney starts a firearms company and creates the process of making interchangeable parts, the first application of mass production.

1798   Edward Jenner develops the smallpox vaccine.

1799   Jacques-Etienne Montgolfier dies.

1800   Alessandro Volta creates the first electric battery, called the "Voltaic Pile".

Charles Goodyear is born.

1804   John Deere is born.

1806   Benjamin Banneker dies.

1807   Robert Fulton launches the Clermont, the first successful commercial steamboat.

1809   Louis Braille is born.

Cyrus McCormick is born.

1810   Joseph-Michael Montgolfier dies.

1813   Henry Bessemer is born.

1814   George Stephenson builds the first practical steam locomotive.

1815	Robert Fulton dies.
1816	Rene Laennec invents the stethoscope.
1819	Elias Howe is born.
	Christopher Sholes is born.
	James Watt dies.
1822	Louis Pasteur is born.
1823	Edward Jenner dies.
1824	Louis Braille develops the Braille Alphabet, which made reading and writing possible for the blind.
1825	Eli Whitney dies.
1826	Rene Laennec dies.
1827	Joseph Lister is born.
	Alessandro Volta dies.
1829	Levi Strauss is born.
1831	Cyrus McCormick builds the first mechanical reaper.
1833	Alfred Nobel is born.
1834	Gottlieb Daimler is born.
1837	John Deere develops the steel plow.
	Samuel F.B. Morse and Leonard Gale build the first telegraph.
	Samuel F.B. Morse creates Morse Code, which makes it possible to send messages over the telegraph.
1839	Charles Goodyear develops the process for "vulcanized" rubber.
	Louis Daguerre invents the first practical photograph, the "Daguerreotype," fixing an image on a metal plate.
1844	Samuel F.B. Morse builds the first telegraph system, from Baltimore to Washington D.C.
	Karl Benz is born.

c. 1844   Elijah McCoy is born.

1845   Elias Howe invents the sewing machine.

Wilhem Roentgen is born.

1846   George Westinghouse is born.

1847   Alexander Graham Bell is born.

Thomas Edison is born.

1849   Levi Strauss opens a dry goods business in California.

George Stephenson dies.

Louis Pasteur begins experiments on fermentation.

1852   Louis Braille dies.

1854   George Eastman is born.

1855   William Seward Burroughs is born.

King Gillette is born.

1856   Henry Bessemer patents the "Bessemer Process" which makes the mass production of steel possible.

Nikola Tesla is born.

1858   Rudolf Diesel is born.

1860   W.K. Kellogg is born.

Charles Goodyear dies.

Louis Pasteur begins experiments with the use of heat to kill microbes, creating the process of Pasteurization.

1861 - 1865 The American Civil War.

1861   Telegraph communication is established across the United States.

1863   Leo Baekeland is born.

Henry Ford is born.

1864	Alfred Nobel invents dynamite.
c. 1864	George Washington Carver is born.
1865	Joseph Lister develops the antiseptic technique.
1866	Samuel F.B. Morse sells his telegraph company to Western Union.
	Herbert Henry Dow is born.
1867	Wilbur Wright is born.
	Elias Howe dies.
1868	Christopher Sholes invents the typewriter.
1869	George Westinghouse invents the airbrake.
1871	Thomas Edison builds the first research laboratory at Menlo Park, NJ.
	Orville Wright is born.
1872	Elijah McCoy invents the automatic lubricating cup.
	Levi Strauss and Jacob Davis patent their process for making blue jeans.
	Samuel F.B. Morse dies.
1874	Guglielmo Marconi is born.
1876	Alexander Graham Bell invent the telephone.
	Nikolaus Otto builds the first four-stroke gas engine.
	Willis Carrier is born.
1877	The Bell Telephone Company is founded.
	Thomas Edison invents the phonograph.
	Garrett Morgan is born.
1879	Thomas Edison develops the first practical light bulb.
1880	George Eastman develops the dry plate photographic process.
1881	Alexander Fleming is born.

1882   Thomas Edison builds the first electric power plant.

Robert Goddard is born.

1883   Gottlieb Daimler and Karl Maybach develop the first practical gasoline-powered internal combustion engine.

1884   Gottlieb Daimler builds the first motorcycle.

Cyrus McCormick dies.

1885   Karl Benz builds a three-wheeled vehicle powered by a gasoline engine. It is considered the first automobile.

William Seward Burroughs invents the adding machine.

George Eastman invents rolled film.

Elizabeth Lee Hazen is born.

Louis Pasteur develops a vaccine for rabies.

1886   Gottlieb Daimler builds the first four-wheeled automobile.

George Westinghouse forms the Westinghouse Electric Company.

Clarence Birdseye is born.

John Deere dies.

1887   Nikola Tesla invents the first successful AC electric motor.

1888   George Eastman introduces the Kodak, the first camera for general use.

1889   Herbert Henry Dow develops the process of extracting bromine from brine.

Several electric power companies founded by Thomas Edison merge to become General Electric.

Igor Sikorsky is born.

Vladimir Zworykin is born.

1890   Christopher Sholes dies.

1891   Frederick Banting is born.

1892	Rudolf Diesel develops the Diesel engine.
	Thomas Edison invents the motion picture camera and the "Kinetoscope."
1893	Leo Baekeland produces Velox, a new photographic paper that can be exposed by artificial light.
	Nikola Tesla and George Westinghouse demonstrate the superiority of Alternating Current (AC) for electrical power transmission.
1894	Karl Benz develops the Velo, the first production automobile.
	Percy Spencer is born.
1895	Louis Pasteur dies.
	Wilhelm Roentgen discovers x-rays.
1896	George Washington Carver begins teaching the principles of "crop rotation" at Tuskegee Institute.
	Henry Ford builds the Quadricycle, his first automobile.
	Guglielmo Marconi develops the wireless telegraph.
	Wallace Carothers is born.
	Alfred Nobel dies.
1897	Dow Chemical is founded by Herbert Henry Dow.
1898	Gottlieb Daimler begins to sell cars under the name "Mercedes".
	W.K. Kellogg invents corn flakes.
	Katharine Blodgett is born.
	Rachel Fuller Brown is born.
	Henry Bessemer dies.
	William Seward Burroughs dies.
1900	Gottlieb Daimler dies.

1901   Guglielmo Marconi sends the first wireless telegraphic message across the Atlantic Ocean.

Alfred Nobel's family establishes the Nobel Prize.

Wilhelm Roentgen is the first person to win the Nobel Prize in Physics.

1902   Willis Carrier develops the first air conditioner.

Wilbur and Orville Wright invent the wind tunnel.

Levi Strauss dies.

1903   Henry Ford starts the Ford Motor Company.

King Gillette and William Nickerson start producing disposable safety razors.

The Wright brothers fly the first aircraft capable of powered, sustained, and controlled flight.

1905   George Westinghouse builds the first electric trains in America.

1906   Philo Farnsworth is born.

1907   Leo Baekeland invents "Baekelite," the first plastic.

Georges de Mestral is born.

Frank Whittle is born.

1908   Henry Ford introduces the Model T Ford.

1909   Thomas Edison invents the alkaline battery.

Guglielmo Marconi is awarded the Nobel Prize in Physics.

Edwin Land is born.

1910   Henry Ford develops the moving assembly line, making mass production of automobiles possible.

Jacques Cousteau is born.

Roy Plunkett is born.

1911   Willem Kolff is born.

1912	Garrett Morgan invents the gas mask.
	Joseph Lister dies.
	Wilbur Wright dies.
1913	Igor Sikorsky designs the first multimotor airplane.
	Rudof Diesel dies.
1914	Henry Ford doubles his workers' pay to $5.00 a day, creating a new standard of employment for industrial workers.
	World War I begins.
	Jonas Salk is born.
	George Westinghouse dies.
1915	Elijah McCoy invents the "Locomotive Lubricator."
1917	Telephone service is available throughout most of the United States.
1918	World War I ends.
	Gertrude Elion is born.
1919	Wilson Greatbatch is born.
1920	Gordon Gould is born.
1922	Frederick Banting discovers insulin, and begins using it to treat people suffering from diabetes.
	Alexander Graham Bell dies.
1923	Frederick Banting and J.J.R. Macleod receive the Nobel Prize for the discovery of insulin.
	Clarence Birdseye develops the "quick-freeze" method of making frozen food.
	Garrett Morgan invents the traffic signal.
	Stephanie Kwolek is born.
	Jerome Lemelson is born.

Wilhelm Roentgen dies.

1924 Vladimir Zworykin invents the "kinescope."

1925 Seymour Cray is born.

1926 Benz & Co. merge with Daimler-Mercedes to form Mercedes-Benz.

Robert Goddard builds the first liquid fueled rocket.

1927 Philo Farnsworth invents the first electronic television.

1928 Alexander Fleming discovers penicillin, the first antibiotic.

Igor Sikorsky builds the first successful commercial seaplane.

1929 Edwin Land invents the polarized filter, used for sunglasses and camera lenses.

Karl Benz dies.

Elijah McCoy dies.

1930 Wallace Carothers develops Neoprene, the first synthetic rubber.

Frank Whittle develops the jet engine.

Patsy Sherman is born.

Herbert Henry Dow dies.

1931 Thomas Edison dies.

1932 George Eastman dies.

King Gillette dies.

1935 Wallace Carothers develops Nylon, the first synthetic fiber.

1936 Raymond Damadian is born.

Philo Farnsworth starts one of the first television stations.

1937 Edwin Land starts the Polaroid Corporation.

Wallace Carothers dies.

Guglielmo Marconi dies.

1938 Katharine Blodgett invents non-reflective glass.

Roy Plunkett invents Teflon.

1939 Igor Sikorsky builds the first helicopter.

The first successful flight of a jet-powered airplane, designed by Hans von Ohain in Germany.

World War II begins.

1941 The first successful flight of Frank Whittle's jet-powered Gloster Pioneer.

Frederick Banting dies.

1943 Jacques Cousteau invents SCUBA.

George Washington Carver dies.

Nikola Tesla dies.

1944 Leo Baekeland dies

1945 Alexander Fleming is awarded the Nobel Prize in Medicine.

Willem Kolff invents the kidney dialysis machine.

Percy Spencer creates the first microwave oven.

World War II ends.

Robert Goddard dies.

1947 Henry Ford dies.

Temple Grandin is born.

1948 Edwin Land releases the Polaroid Land camera, the first camera offering "instant photography."

Orville Wright dies.

1950 Steve Wozniak is born.

Willis Carrier dies.

1951 George de Mestral invents Velcro.

Gertrude Elion develops "6MP", the first successful drug treatment for leukemia.

Dean Kamen is born.

W.K. Kellogg dies.

1952   Jonas Salk develops the first successful polio vaccine.

1955   Tim Berners-Lee is born.

Bill Gates is born.

Steven Jobs is born.

Alexander Fleming dies.

1956   Patsy Sherman and Sam Smith invent Scotchgard.

Clarence Birdseye dies.

1957   Rachel Fuller Brown and Elizabeth Lee Hazen develop the first anti-fungal medicine.

Gordon Gould develops the theoretical foundation for the laser.

Willem Kolff builds the first artificial heart.

1958   Wilson Greatbatch develops the cardiac pacemaker.

Ellen Ochoa is born.

1963   Garrett Morgan dies.

1969   On July 20, Neil Armstrong becomes the first person to walk on the Moon.

1970   Percy Spencer dies.

1971   Stephanie Kwolek invents Kevlar.

Philo Farnsworth dies.

1972   Igor Sikorsky dies.

1975   Steven Jobs and Steve Wozniak start Apple Computer.

Bill Gates and Paul Allen found Microsoft.

Elizabeth Lee Hazen dies.

1976   Seymour Cray produces the Cray-1, the first supercomputer.

	Dean Kamen founds Autosyringe to manufacture his first invention.
1977	Raymond Damadian builds the first MRI scanner.
	Steven Jobs and Steve Wozniak build the Apple II, the first desktop personal computer for the general user.
1979	Katharine Blodgett dies.
1980	Rachel Fuller Brown dies.
1982	Vladimir Zworykin dies.
1984	Apple Computer introduces the Macintosh.
1985	Microsoft introduces the "Windows 1.0" operating system for personal computers.
1986	Steven Jobs acquires the Pixar animation studio.
1988	Gertrude Elion is awarded the Nobel Prize in Medicine.
1990	Tim Berners-Lee develops HTML, HTTP, and URL, and creates the World Wide Web.
	George de Mestral dies.
1991	Ellen Ochoa becomes the first Hispanic-American woman astronaut.
	Edwin Land dies.
1994	Roy Plunkett dies.
1995	Jonas Salk dies.
1996	Seymour Cray dies.
	Frank Whittle dies.
1997	Jacques Cousteau dies.
	Jerome Lemelson dies.
1999	Gertrude Elion dies.
2001	Dean Kamen invents the "Segway", a two-wheeled, self-balancing vehicle.
2005	Gordon Gould dies.

Subject Index

This index contains the inventors and inventions covered in this volume. It also includes major subject categories related to invention, including Cloth and Clothing, Communication, Computers, Electricity and Electronics, Food and Agriculture, Industrial Materials, Medicine and Medical Devices, Scientific Devices, and Transportation and Energy. Bold-faced type indicates the main entry on the inventor.

adding machine 78-81

air conditioning 88-93

aircraft 32,136,396-399,473-478, 526, 542-560

alternating current (AC).........174-176, 496-501, 512-519

antifungal antibiotic (Nystatin)........... 73-77, 297-301

Aqualung...110

Archimedes **1-5**, 238

Archimedes screw...........................1-5

artificial kidney machine.........336-340

automatic lubricating cup.......389-394

automobile

    see Benz 32-41

    Daimler...................................121-128

Diesel.....................................148-152

Ford 210-221

Baekeland, Leo **6-11**

Bakelite 10

Banneker, Benjamin.....................**12-15**

Banting, Frederick.......................**16-21**

battery 179, 502-505

Bell, Alexander Graham.............**22-33**, 172,197, 376

Benz, Karl.....................**34-41**, 125, 213

Berners-Lee, Tim..........................**42-48**

Bessemer, Henry.................**49-52**, 510

bifocals...229

Birdseye, Clarence.....................**53-60**

Blodgett, Katherine **61-65**

blue jeans 491-495

Braille, Louis.............................**66-72**

Braille system of writing

    for the blind............................66-72

bromine.....................................154-158

Brown, Rachel Fuller **73-77**, 299-301

Burroughs, William **78-81**

camera

    See Eastman 159-165

    Land....................................352-359

car

    see automobile

carburetor 121-128

cardiac pacemaker....................286-290

Carothers, W. H. **82-87**, 343

Carrier, Willis H. **88-93**

Carver, George Washington......**94-107**

cloth and clothing

    See Carothers...........................82-87

    De Mestral 145-147

    Howe.....................................302-305

    Strauss 491-494

    Whitney................................520-525

communication

    See Bell..................................22-33

    Berners-Lee 42-48

    Braille 66-72

    Eastman 159-165

    Edison 166-183

    Farnsworth 196-202

    Gutenberg 291-296

    Land.......................................352-359

    Marconi 371-380

    Morse 406-414

    Sholes....................................469-472

    Zworykin...............................561-565

computer

    see Berners-Lee.......................42-48

    Cray 113-120

    Gates......................................243-252

    Jobs 312-321

    Wozniak.................................532-541

corn flakes 328-335

cotton gin 520-525

Cousteau, Jacques...................**108-112**

Cray, Seymour..................**113-120**, 315

crop-rotation 101-107

Daimler, Gottlieb 37, 39, 40,

    121-128, 150, 213

Damadian, Raymond..............**129-132**

Da Vinci, Leonardo.........**133-138**, 474,

    546

Deere, John......................**139-144**, 382

De Mestral, George..........**145-147**, 362

Diesel, Rudolf **148-152**

diesel engine 148-152

Dow, Herbert Henry **153-158**

dynamite...................................421-426

Eastman, George.........9, **159-165**, 354,

    357, 413

Edison, Thomas Alva..........9, 30, 105,

    164, **166-183**, 197, 213, 219, 220,

    327, 379, 497-498, 515

electricity

    See Bell..................................22-33

Edison 166-183

Franklin 222-231

Gould 271-277

Morse 406-414

Spencer 479-484

Tesla 496-501

Volta....................................502-505

Westinghouse......................512-519

Elion, Gertrude Bell........**184-191**, 301

Fahrenheit, Daniel Gabriel.....**192-195**, 238

Farnsworth, Philo.....**196-202**, 563-564

Fleming, Alexander ...74, **203-209**, 298

food and agriculture

   See Birdseye.............................53-60

   Carver....................................94-107

   Deere 139-144

   Grandin 278-285

   Kellogg 328-335

   McCormick 381-388

Ford, Henry.........39, 41, 105, 127, 180, **210-221**, 524

Franklin, Benjamin 7, **222-231**, 407

Franklin stove 228-229

frozen foods process 55-60

Fulton, Robert.................**232-236**, 511

Galileo Galilei...136, 193, **237-242**, 416

gas mask 402

Gates, Bill.................**243-252**, 316, 538

Gillette, King............................**253-256**

Goddard, Robert....................**257-264**

Goodyear, Charles **265-270**

Gould, Gordon.........................**271-277**

Grandin, Temple **278-285**

Greatbatch, Wilson.................**286-290**

Gutenberg, Johannes **291-296**

Hazen, Elizabeth 74-77, **297-301**

helicopter 473-478

hot air balloon 395-399

Howe, Elias **302-305**

industrial materials

   See Baekeland 6-11

   Bessemer 49-52

   Blodgett...................................61-65

   Carrier 88-93

   Dow..153-158

   Goodyear 265-270

   Plunkett..................................445-448

insulin...16-21

Jenner, Edward 205, **306-311**, 441, 456

jet propulsion system..............526-531

Jobs, Steven **312-321**, 441, 456

Kamen, Dean **322-327**

Kellogg, W.K...........................**328-335**

Kevlar 341-346

Kolff, Willem **336-340**

Kwolek, Stephanie **341-346**

Laennec, Rene.........................**347-351**

Land, Edwin Herbert..............**352-359**

laser 271-277

Lemelson, Jerome....................**360-365**

light bulb 170-171, 174

lightning rod...........................227-228

liquid fuel rocketry 257-264

Lister, Joseph **366-370**, 441

Marconi, Guglielmo **371-380**

McCormick, Cyrus...................**381-388**

McCoy, Elijah...........................**389-394**

mechanical reaper....................381-388

medicine and medical devices

    See Banting.............................12-15

    Brown 73-77

    Damadian.............................129-132

    Elion....................................184-191

    Fleming................................203-209

    Greatbatch...........................286-290

    Hazen...................................297-301

    Jenner..................................306-311

    Kamen 322-340

    Kolff 336-340

    Laennec................................347-351

    Lister 366-370

    Pasteur 434-444

    Roentgen..............................449-453

    Salk 454-463

microwave oven 479-484

Montgolfier, Joseph and

    Jacques 230, **395-399**, 546

Morgan, Garrett **400-405**

Morse, Samuel F.B.....26, 114, 372-373,
    406-414, 503

Morse Code.............114, 372, 410-414,

motion pictures 178-179

motorcycle.................................125

movie projector 179

MRI (magnetic resonance imaging)

    scanner 129-132

Newton, Isaac 2, 136, 239, 260,
    415-420

Nobel, Alfred **421-426**

Nobel Prize

    see Banting 16-21

    Elion....................................184-191

    Fleming................................203-209

    Marconi................................371-380

    Nobel...................................421-426

    Roentgen..............................449-453

nonreflecting glass 61

nylon.......................................82-87

Nystatin 73-77, 297-301

Ochoa, Ellen **427-433**

optics 415-420, 427-433

Pasteur, Louis ..311, 367, **434-444**, 456

Pasteurization 434-444

peanut-based products............103-107

penicillin 203-209

phonograph 169, 172-174, 177-178

photography

    See Eastman 159-165

    Land....................................352-359

plastic......................................6,9,10, 11

Plunkett, Roy J..............342, **445-448**

polio vaccine............................454-463

printing press (movable type)............ 291-296

rabies vaccine........................... 440-444
radio 371-380
Roentgen, Wilhelm Konrad 130, **449-453**
rubber, synthetic (Neoprene)..... 82-87
rubber, vulcanized 265-270

safety razor 253-256
Salk, Jonas 311, **454-463**
scientific devices and instruments
    See Archimedes 1-5
    Banneker............................... 12-15
    Cousteau............................. 108-112
    Fahrenheit............................ 192-195
    Franklin 222-231
    Galileo 237-242
    Kwolek............................... 341-346
    Lemelson............................ 360-365
    Newton............................. 415-420
    Ochoa............................. 427-433
Scotchgard......................... 464-468
Segway 322-327
sewing machine................... 302-305
Sherman, Patsy **464-468**
Sholes, C.L. **469-472**
Sikorsky, Igor........... 136, 138, **473-478**
smallpox vaccine................ 306-311
Spencer, Percy L. **479-484**
steam engine............. 233-236, 485-490, 506-511
steam-powered locomotive 485-490

steamboat................................. 232-236
steel converter........................... 50-52
steel plow 139-144
Stephenson, George **485-490**, 511
stethoscope.............................. 347-351
Strauss, Levi **491-495**
supercomputer 113-120

Teflon...................................... 445-448
telegraph 26, 27, 114, 169-172, 372-373, 406-414
telephone................................. 26-33
telescope 239-242, 415-420
television 196-202, 561-565
temperature scale 193
thermometer.................... 192-195, 238
Tesla, Nikola........... 174, 379, **496-501**, 516-517
traffic signal............................ 400-405
transportation and energy
    See Benz 34-41
    Daimler............................ 121-128
    Da Vinci........................... 133-138
    Diesel............................. 148-152
    Ford 210-221
    Fulton 232-236
    Goddard 257-264
    Goodyear 265-270
    McCoy 389-394
    Montgolfier brothers............ 395-399
    Morgan 400-405
    Sikorsky........................... 473-478
    Stephenson........................ 485-490
    Watt 506-511

Westinghouse.........................512-519

Whittle.................................526-531

Wright brothers 542-560

typewriter.............................469-472

vaccine 306-311, 441-444, 454-463

VELCRO....................................145-147

Volta, Alessandro...............30, **502-505**

Watt, James.......35, 122, 149, 233, 486, **506-511**

Westinghouse, George...........176, 212, 498-499, **512-519**, 562

Whitney, Eli 218, **520-525**

Whittle, Frank...........................**526-531**

World Wide Web 44-48

Wozniak, Steve..........314-318, **532-541**

Wright, Orville and Wilbur......32, 136, 138, 379, 474, **542-560**

x-ray...449-453

Zworykin, Vladimir 199-201, **561-565**